The Tahiti Syndrome

Hawaiian Style

Andrew W. Gunson

Book two of the Naked Canadian cruising series.

Copyright © 2012 ANDREW W. GUNSON

All rights reserved.

ISBN:147933197X
ISBN-13:9781479331970

DEDICATION

I wish to dedicate this book to Janet, my life partner, shipmate, friend and compass rose. My love who dared to share a life and a dream with a dreamer.

I also wish to dedicate this volume to Damien and Savannah in as I hope that my two grandchildren will be inspired to chase their own dreams.

Other titles by this author.

Voyage of the *Maiatla* with the Naked Canadian: One Family's Mexican Odyssey

Second Edition

COPYRIGHT 2004, 2012 Andrew W. Gunson

Visit us on you tube for more about S.V. *Maiatla* & The Naked Canadian:
http://www.youtube.com/watch?v=SWzXNSGIKmw
http://www.youtube.com/watch?v=FATS_s_eTg0
http://www.youtube.com/watch?v=m-InE29LeAY

Please, check it out!

Globe & Sextant Publishing
a division of AJ'S Industries

Nanaimo B.C. Canada

The Tahiti Syndrome-Hawaiian Style.

First Edition

Copyright © 2012 Andrew W. Gunson
Published By Andrew W. Gunson
All rights reserved. No part of this publication may be reproduced or transmitted in any form or by any means or stored in a database or retrieval system without prior written permission of the publisher.
The author and the publisher make no representation, express or implied, with regard to the accuracy of the information contained in this book. The material is provided for entertainment purpose only. The author and the publisher are not responsible for any action taken on the information provided by this book.
This book is available in print from most online retailers.

All rights reserved.
ISBN-13:978-1479331970
ISBN-10: 147933197X

Printed in the USA by CreateSpace

Figure 1. *S.V. Maiatla* south bound off the coast of California.

Photo By

Susanne Tölzel & Joachim Probst
of the S.V. Pagena, Home Port, Wiesbaden, Germany.

Table of content

Prologue……………………………………………………………....1
Chapter 1 Inaugural Gale……………………………………….....8
Chapter 2 Fair Winds………………………………………….....18
Chapter 3 Memories…………………………………………….26
Chapter 4 Maui Time…………………………………………….....34
Chapter 5 The Tradewind Express……………………………....45
Chapter 6 The Poop……………………………………………….48
Chapter 7 Maui Landfall……………………………………….....59
Chapter 8 Loner in Paradise……………………………………...71
Chapter 9 Lahaina Lele-Relentless sun……………………….....80
Chapter 10 Flotsam and Jetsam………………………………….85
Chapter 11 Welcome to Lahaina State Harbour………………….91
Chapter 12 Explorers in Paradise……………………………….....98
Chapter 13 Lanai, the Pineapple Island……………………….....110
Chapter 14 A Run at Molokai……………………………………121
Chapter 15 Feeding Frenzy……………………………………….131
Chapter 16 Waikiki Bound……………………………………...136
Chapter 17 That is Gilligan's Island…… ……………………….....148
Chapter 18 Pearl Harbour……………………………………….162
Chapter 19 Tiger Shark Eat Sea Turtles don't Ya Know? ……........169
Chapter 20 The Dead Leap into the Western Sea………………..…...180
Chapter 21 The Little Pigs of Huleia River………………………..185
Chapter 22 Kauai, An Island unto Itself………………………….....195
Chapter 23 Painted Canyons and the End of the World……………….....205
Chapter 24 First Time around and SHARK!………………………..211
Chapter 25 The Wackiest Ship in the Army……………………….219
Chapter 26 Category Four Hurricanes Even Teach Whales to Pray…..229
Chapter 27 The Great Na Pali Coast……………………………….233
Chapter 28 The Forbidden Island of Niihau………………………. 243
Chapter 29 Wine, Stogies and a Fire- A Tribute to the Old Man……...253
Chapter 30 Kona Coffee and Wahiawa, the Bay that Bleeds…………258
Chapter 31 The Crew Arrives and Around We Go Again……….......268
Chapter 32 A Haunted Village and a Celestial Extravaganza………..273
Chapter 33 Homeward Bound………………………………….....285
Chapter 34 A Close Encounter…………………………………….294
Chapter 35 Twilight Visitors……………………………………….307
Chapter 36 Juan de Fuca Gales…………………………………….315
Chapter 37 Becalmed Again……………………………………….....322
Epilogue…………………………………………………………….327
About the Boat……………………………………………………..330
Glossary of Hawaiian terms……………………………………….333
About the Author…………………………………………………...334

Table of illustrations.

Figure 1 ------ *SV Maiatla* south bound off the coast of California.
Figure 2 ------ The islands of Hawaii are located almost in the middle of the Pacific
Figure 3 ------ *Maiatla's* route from Vancouver to Hawaii and back.
Figure 4 ------ Kara on her early morning watch after the gale had passed.
Figure 5 ------ Dolphins came to play on our bow wave.
Figure 6 ------ The crew takes a dip mid ocean, two miles deep
Figure 7 ------ Jim's birthday Dorado.
Figure 8 ------ The eight main islands of Hawaii
Figure 9 ------ Hawaii the "Big Island" where captain Cook was killed in 1779
Figure 10 ---- Maui, *Maiatla's* first landfall after 21 days at sea.
Figure 11 ---- A weary but happy crew to have finally made shore at Kahului, Maui -
Figure 12 ---- Kahoolawe ecological reserve just 7 miles from Maui, used as a bombing range.
Figure 13 ---- The Pineapple Island with *Maiatla's* course around and back.
Figure 14 ---- Melissa surfing at Lahaina Maui with instructor Brian looking on.
Figure 15 ---- The old leper colony of Molokai.
Figure 16 ---- Honolulu, Pearl Harbour and Gilligan's Island on the Oahu.
Figure 17 ---- Crossing the Kaiwi Channel with Diamond head. (also known as the Molokaʻi Channel)
Figure 18 ---- Samantha (on plank) and Melissa going ashore at Waikiki Beach
Figure 19 ---- Janet, Andrew, Melissa and Samantha standing at the same wall at Makapuu Point
Figure 20 ----- A happy Andy and Melissa moment at the Arizona memorial-Pearl Harbour.
Figure 21 ---- Kauai, *Maiatla* made two complete circumnavigation of the island
Figure 22 ---- The two meter White tip shark that swam directly below Jan at Secret Beach.
Figure 23 ---- Hanalei Bay pier surrounded by the mountains of Bali Hai.
Figure 24 ----- Hurricane Flossie developed into a category 4 hurricane on August 13 2007 with winds in excess of 130 miles per hour (113 knots) with her sights set on Hawaiian Islands and more importantly, *Maiatla*.
Figure 25 ---- The 1000 meter tall cliffs of the Napali Coast.
Figure 26 ---- A few days after their rescue they are happy that their Kayak is still afloat.
Figure 27 ---- The forbidden island of Niihau.
Figure 28 ---- The island bird sanctuary Lehua.

Table of illustrations cont.

Figure 29----Our friendly Monk Seal that came for a visit every morning.
Figure 30----The tuna caught after leaving Niihau breaking my run of bad luck with fishing.
Figure 31----My father's beach on Kauai.

Figure 32----Jan and *Maiatla* at the Bay that Bleeds
Figure 33---Kauuapea Beach (Secret Beach) with the little Island of Mokuaeae.
Figure 34----Mike and Kara repair the mizzen sail just before departure.
Figure 35----Lost At Sea-The Crew of Takaroa II departed from Hilo Hawaii behind *Maiatla*
Figure 36--Kara with her single surviving visitor preparing to let it fly away.
Figure 37---The broken Main Boom after *Maiatla's* near broaching.
Figure 38---Main Boom after repairs using rope, clamps and Jan's cutting board.
Figure 39---*SV Maiatla* line drawings.
Figure 40 About the Author.

The Coconut Palm

The Tahiti Syndrome

Hawaiian Style

There isn't any symbolism. The sea is the sea. The old man is an old man. The boy is a boy and the fish is a fish. The shark is all sharks no better and no worse. All the symbolism that people say is shit. What goes beyond is what you see beyond when you know.

Ernest Hemingway

Prologue

"The Tahiti Syndrome" is an expression used to describe a human longing for a peaceful, idyllic, natural setting when suffering from the stress of modern life. An observation once noted by (Star Trek's) Dr. McCoy in response to Kirk's reaction upon observing the American Indian lifestyle on the distant planet Amarind, commenting that Kirk's reaction is "A typical human reaction to an idyllic natural setting, back in the 20th century, we referred to it as the Tahiti syndrome. It's especially common to over pressured leader types like starship captains."

Captain Kirk went on to say that "It's like discovering Atlantis or Shangri-La….

Despite having been invented in the 20th century and repeated several centuries into our future, for Captain James T. Kirk of the USS Enterprise, the premise of the phrase has its origins in the very distant 16th century. In 1768, Captain Samuel Wallis and his crew of the HMS Dolphin, returning from an around the world voyage of discovery, told fantastic tales of a vast sea of islands whose inhabitants lived as Adam and Eve in the Garden of Eden; living and loving without inhibition, scantily clad if at all, and where chastity was not considered a virtue. Wanting for nothing, as all their subsistence needs were plucked either from the fruitful trees or pulled thrashing from the bountiful sea. The Dolphin's crew quickly spread the tale of the islands, and the mass exodus for Nirvana - the South Pacific - was poised to begin. In August of 1768, Captain James Cook aboard the HMS Endeavor was dispatched to the South Seas by the British Admiralty to observe the transit of the planet Venus, and it was upon his return and through Cook's detailed journals that Europeans learned of a magical, and wondrous Island called Otaheite. Western tongues had some difficulty wrapping around the numerous vowels of the Island's local name and Otaheite was quickly bastardized into what we better know today, Tahiti. Cook's reports and published journals of Polynesia, (many islands) which is encompassed in Oceania, fanned the flames that Wallis had set and before long, sailors from all over the western world were eagerly seeking out ships that were bound for the South Seas and the imagined paradise that it contained. The South Seas was no longer the barren wasteland as depicted upon contemporary charts, but a state of mind that fostered incredible and once unimaginable dreams. During the centuries following its discovery, the South Seas saw countless adventurers trek from the far reaches of the globe, in search of peace, fortune and the islands' legendary, promiscuous inhabitants, whose sexual favors, as the sailors soon learned, did not even have to be bargained for, but initially, were freely and eagerly thrust upon them by the jealousy-free and generous Islanders.

The islands' beguiling notoriety as a paradise not only grew, but the tale exploded as a new breed of explorer disseminated though the archipelagos and published written works that aided to entice noble and ordinary men alike from their dishevelled lives - to come, to seek their own paradise encompassed by an azure sea. Bold men such as, Jack London, Herman Melville, Robert Louis Stevenson, Mark Twain, and of course the audacious Captain Cook, to only name a few.

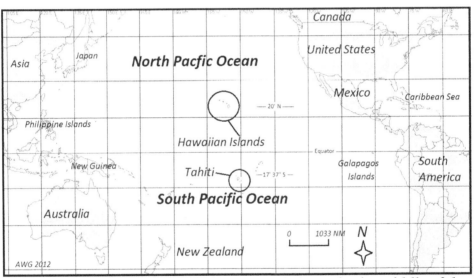

Figure 2. The islands of Hawaii are located almost in the middle of the Pacific Ocean.

Not all who ventured into the South Seas were swaddled in good intentions or seeking a means for personal redemption. The dark and less savory side of humanity saw the innocent and largely defenceless Islanders as ripe targets for exploitation; an easier means to further their own ends. Festering like an incipient wound, "Black Birding", the art of slave trading, rape, pillaging and out right piracy flourished in the early and middle years after discovery by the western world. They all came, men of influence, seekers of fame, fortune, religious zealots, and refugees alike, fleeing persecution or the oppressive morals of the puritanical western cultures of their days. All enticed by a perceived promise, they came, and they came in droves led by grasping hands and bared loins. All eager to conquer by deception, force, seduction and pelvic thrusts.

Sadly, as the word spread, Jesuit missionaries came to pronounce judgment on the heathens of the newly discovered pagan Sea, with western vices and commercial values, infecting the indigenous peoples like a virulent disease. The peaceful atolls and verdant volcanic isles of the South Seas rapidly morphed. Western civilization descended on the South Seas like a band of rabid head-hunters dismembering a corpse, dissecting with precision the still warm body that was the rich, "savage" culture, primordial humanity in the raw.

****

The *Maiatla's* very presence on this gale tossed north pacific, is in its self an act of sheer yet honorable defiance. Hostile by design to everything the mind of man can conceive, the open sea is, and always has been an alien environment that can easily, if it sets its mind to the task, parry the thrusts of man's feeble assaults.

Nautical literature, spawned from the heart of every great seafaring nation bordering the vast oceans of the world, at times characterized the sea equally as malevolent and benevolent. Temperamental seas capable of great compassion, or just as likely to mutate into a vile protagonist, filled with unforgiving rage, augmented with the full range of emotions normally attributed to land dwelling humans of the netherworld. The sea possesses a strange form of duality, lover and destroyer; with the voyager never knowing which face will greet him over the distant horizon.

Yet, how can the sea be both kind and giving, possessing mothering qualities as well as being capable of blind rage and vengeful destruction? Enacted countless times over the millennia; the scene of crude vessels as viewed from shore, surrounded by gentle vespers tickling a mirrored sea; fishermen hauling their hemp nets bursting with the ocean's seemingly limitless bounty. Yet poised on the distant horizon there is always an innocuous looking cloud concealing a divine moodiness, threatening to unleash the furies of an equatorial typhoon accented with gyrating waterspouts. The devil's own, spawning storms with the power to generate waves of such mountainous proportions that any beings not of its own world; life gestated within the eternally frigid womb of the black abyss, are doomed from the onset.

From far back in recorded time, man has sought to put a human face upon the Sea by attempting to identify human traits in, what has been wrongfully deemed, the willful actions of the sea. The personification of things that we have little understanding or control over, is man's way of putting a human face on the inhuman. It is our way of assigning blame when things go wrong.

The ancient Greeks were by far the most creative and successful in envisioning not one, but the many enduring figures of the world's great oceans. Frequently autocratic, these entities were believed to embody the very soul of the sea.

The Greek scholar Homer in 1000 B.C. told the tale of the shipwrecked sailor Odysseus, who after being allowed to escape his island prison by his lover, the goddess Calypso, a slutty sea nymph if there ever was one, attracted the wrath of Poseidon; the shaker of the earth:

He gathered the clouds and troubled the waters of the deep, grasping his trident in his hands; and he roused all storms of all manner of winds, and shrouded in clouds the land and the sea; and down sped night from the heavens. The East wind and the South wind clashed, and the stormy West and

North, that is born in the bright air, rolling onward a great wave. Then were the knees of Odysseus loosened and his heart melted, and heavily he spake to his great spirit:
Homer. The Odyssey. Book V.

Homer clearly speaks of the sea or Poseidon in this example, as possessing similar emotions and weaknesses as mortal man. Poseidon's jealousy is enraged by Odysseus's relationship with the goddess Calypso.

There is a long list of aquatic deities that the ancient Greeks claimed for their own. Oceanus, Triton, Pontus and Amphitrite, goddess of the sea, are just a few of the many gods that were said to possess the power to govern the world's navigable waters. The deity most familiar to contemporary mariners is classically represented as a merman, having the muscular upper body of a human and the scaly tail of a fish. He was often depicted as a bearded elder, clutching a trident, seated in a seashell chariot drawn by prancing seahorses. Poseidon, a newer god of a later generation, possessed the reputation for having a violent temper. Tempests and earthquakes are a reflection of his furious rage. It was said when Poseidon was angry, he would stir the waters with his trident, and taking the form of concentric foaming waves, his children traveled forth to torment sailors at sea and pound distant shores.

A fearful sailor is more likely to call upon a less temperamental deity, Triton. Triton is the son of Poseidon and like his father he also brandishes a trident, however Triton's special attribute aside from his milder temperament, is a twisted conch shell, on which he blows, like a trumpet, to calm the waters. When lesser gods or sea monsters are stirring the ocean into a tempest, Triton blows his conch, which sounds so terrible that all who hear it, imagine it to be the roar of a great beast and flee in terror, allowing the tortured seas to abate.

The Greeks were not the only early culture to invent, and then grovel at the feet of granite or marble edifices of such powerful deities. At about the same time Homer was ducking from Poseidon's wrath for putting the moves on his girl Calypso, the Polynesians were conjuring up powerful deities with their own unique idiosyncrasies.

Eons before the arrival of Captain Cook and the missionaries that introduced their concept of one heavenly God to Hawaii, the seafaring Polynesians had an intricate nature-oriented belief system which hosted a variety of deities called 'aumakua' (family guardians) that could be called upon for protection, comfort and spiritual support. The 'aumakua were thought to be the offspring of mortals who had mated with the akua (primary gods). The most important primary gods were Ku, Kane, Lono and Kanaloa, but it was the 'aumakua, the household deities, that commoners could call on in an easy, less ritualistic way.

'Aumakua were often deified ancestors whose bones had been specially stripped of flesh upon death, wrapped in kapa cloth and ceremonially prepared before the bones were placed in the custody of another descendant.

After his death, Cook, who the natives first believed was the embodiment of their god Lono, was prepared in such a grisly manor and his bones were squirreled away in secret caves about the islands.

When an individual died, it was thought that their spirit jumped from a rocky precipice, a leina, or soul's leap, designated on each island, to begin its journey to the ancestral homeland. In a shadowy place called Po, the ancestral spirits lived with the supreme gods and were transfigured into god-spirits, whose mana, or power, was almost as awesome as that of the akua. The spirit of a deceased ancestor first might serve as an 'unihipili', a spirit that normally took the form of an animal or sea creature who granted requests for mercy and gave warnings of pending disasters or destruction. The earthly individual who safeguarded the bones of the earthly remains of a 'unihipili' could summon him for guidance.

If the 'unihipili' was especially deserving, he became an 'aumakua, an ancestral god honored by his descendants and easily approachable in times of need.

An 'aumakua could manifest in varying forms such as a shark, sea turtle, hawk, lizard or any other animal, plant or mineral. Or the ancestral gods might appear in a dreams to furnish guidance or spiritual strength in difficult times. When a fisherman or craftsman was especially successful, credit was often given to his 'aumakua for intervening with the principal gods to impart the mana, or power, that enabled an earthly being to develop such skill. Many a canoe paddler has told of being lost at sea or in danger of being swept out to sea by the wicked currents that race between the islands, only to be saved by his 'aumakua in the form of a dolphin or shark.

As much as sailors and islanders alike would like to believe that the world's seas own a soul, and possess human-like qualities that can be bargained with, nothing can be further from the truth. The sea is neither benevolent nor malevolent, it is incapable of feelings of compassion or, more importantly to those who venture from the beach, contrived wrath. The inhuman cannot act human. The sea doesn't care if sailors cut a foaming wake across its trackless surface. Nor does the sea conspire to rid its domain of man's presence.

All the great oceans are unsentimental, mindless monsters that have less concern for man than a horse for the grain of sand it crushes under its hoof and this is why we must venture forth with the utmost in prudence and respect of the Sea's awesome power.

As Hemmingway noted, the sea is just the sea; it is what it is and nothing more. A fact that sailors from time immemorial have miserably failed to convincingly dispute. Yet sailors, and especially this sailor, receive a certain measure of comfort in the romantic notion that the seas, not unlike the vessels we so lovingly care for, not only possess a profound soul, but more importantly, they harbor a reasonable character that a covenant can be struck. Without this irrational coping mechanism - a strong belief that all can be tamed or bartered with, to temper man's indomitable baser instinct for survival; it would be virtually impossible to launch ourselves from the relative safety of the shore to venture over the horizon in such tiny and frail craft.

Yet despite man's belief in the benevolence of sea gods, or the ability of our technology to safe guard us, ships and theirs crews are continually lost in all the world's great seas. So the question begs to be asked, why would apparently sane men and women intentionally expose themselves to such peril on the high seas? Why do we do it? What is the rational? In truth all great voyagers must essentially been optimists or else they would never have gone to sea. But that still does not explain why? Why indeed would I go to sea? Likewise, I often questioned my motives for my travels. Are they searches? An effort to learn something evocatively profound that lays latent in me or are they an unconscious attempt to escape? And if so? Escape from what or whom?

These questions have been presented to me countless times over the years and each time I have struggled and horribly failed to formulate a convincing and coherent response. I usually counter by replying, "That's a good question, but I couldn't possibly explain it."

It is a coward's way out and I know it. Nevertheless, it is easier for me to confess to being deficient in my own language, than to admit that after spending nearly my entire life working or playing, on and under the sea, my mind stutters like a fuel-starved engine. I am at a loss.

Whether shifting sand dunes with a plastic bucket and spade as a child at my parents' beach front home, or as an adult tethered to a diving bell, deep beneath the frigid Beaufort Sea ice in search of oil, or sailing before the boisterous trades bound for distant shores, I cannot meaningfully explain the enigmatic force behind my desire to sail away.

The sea exerts a powerful force both physically and metaphysically, a mystical energy that is, on many levels, incomprehensible, pulling upon men and women as surely as the moon pulls the same seas into great tidal action.

For many, these dangerous voyages have concluded in either death or in a greater spiritual understanding. Perhaps this is why we venture back to sea time and time again, we are in search of an explanation, or a tangible mechanism that propels our passions.

****

It was in the first few days of the passage to Hawaii from Vancouver, British Columbia, that it dawned on me, I had an epiphany, a defining moment of significance that would alter my thought process and ultimately my life forever. In hindsight, or perhaps to an indifferent bystander, it was obvious, but at the time it was as obscure as the backside of the moon. I realised I was both searching, and escaping, searching for what and escaping from what, still elude me. Whatever my true needs , they were obscured from my view by the near impenetrable haze of rational thought and mind numbing indifference, a consequential symptom of contemporary living ashore, a near-incurable malady of the netherworld or modern society. I needed to abandon mainstream life, close my eyes and allow my senses to "feel" my life and permit my essence to emerge, to resurface where it could be seen and embraced. It was the 5th century BC, Greek philosopher Socrates (think toga!), who said:

The unexamined life is not worth living.

Socrates was suggesting that if we are unable to look inward and examine ourselves, to take stock of who we are and what we have contributed to humanity as a whole, we are nothing but mindless automatons or worse, mere animals reacting to baser instincts and environmental stimuli, impulsively humping the leg of mother earth in an effort to achieve some carnal release. We all need to take the time for personal examination, and soul searching. If you get one thing out of voyaging, it is a time to reflect and explore deep within the inner philosophic sea that is our soul.

****

We set sail for Oceania not only in search of the great, legendary, Hawaiian Island Archipelago, but seeking to discover a better understanding of myself, not only by analyzing my own motives and feelings, but by comparing my measure against those aforementioned adventures, explorers and artisans of times gone past, who have navigated the vast trackless seas before us.

This volume is not so much a contemporary biographical adventure travel log, but more of an attempt to tease the common threads out of the complex psyche of men and women who sail beyond the horizon, past and present- A phenomenon that has not diminished with the advancement of time. I will attempt to unwind the lash that binds Cruisers, Voyagers, and Adventurers alike, in an effort to achieve a better understanding of their unique kind - intrepid humans who throughout the centuries have risked life and liberty, tides and tempest in search of an elusive prize. Fame and riches may have been foremost in their minds; however, I suspect that they were, in truth, seeking a more metaphysical and profoundly personal prize. A reward or gift that can be neither bought nor sold, or bartered for at a distant trader's market or marked by an X on any ancient mariners' chart.

Chapter #1

Inaugural Gale

A strong nor'-wester's blowing, Bill!
Hark! Don't ye hear it roar now?
Lord help 'em, how I pities them,
Unhappy folks on shore now!
        -The Sailor's Consolation

elcome to my world!

The sailing vessel *Maiatla* stood hard on the wind under shortened sail driving headlong into a seemingly endless procession of greybeards, burying her bowsprit up to its socket. The boat plunged on, "brave" we called it. Breaking 3-meter waves driven by 40 knots of spume-laden wind beat the vessels port cheek with bone jarring authority. The seas here, some three hundred miles due west of the infamous Oregon coast were tormented, and riotous in nature. The evil spawn of the southerly gale seemed to take fiendish pleasure in tossing our tiny vessel about, creating havoc above and below decks. The thrashing seas transformed our refuge into a savage, nearly an uncontrollable version of herself-a topsy-turvy world where everything was in chaotically constant motion. With alarming regularity, once secured drawers and cupboards worked loose only to vomit their contents across the cabin with potentially lethal effect.

Despite the sea's best effort, *Maiatla* ploughed onward at over six knots powered by a single reefed main and a sharply cut staysail shuddering on the jib boom. Her clipper bow easily brushed aside each of the legions of waves, taking them in big gulps between breaths. *Maiatla*, our 52-foot center-cockpit ketch was powerfully determined because as directed by her crew of four, she was on a mission.

It was early May of 2007 and after six hard sailing days out of Mission, British Columbia, Canada, we were caught in the midst of a fierce North Pacific gale. (Beaufort Force 8 - 34 to 40 knots) The pelting rain mated with stinging spray shooting over the bow as *Maiatla* charged over each successive wave, sending torrents of sweeping water across her decks. Our destination, Lahaina on the Island of Maui, located in the center of the great chain that is the Hawaiian Islands, was still over two thousand long sea miles to the southwest. The dreary, monochrome grey skies grew blacker with the advancing night, with little enthusiasm I lurched my way out of my warm bunk in the aft cabin, struggling to don my sea boots, fleece and foulies in preparation for taking my trick, my turn at watch. The sole of my cabin, not unlike the rest of the boat, was littered with dozens of scurrying items that refused to stay put and the day before, I had deemed it safer and immensely easier to leave them where they lay.

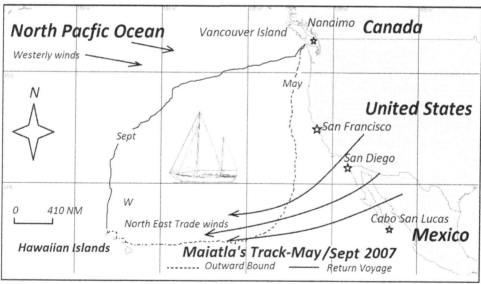

Figure 3. *Maiatla's* route from Vancouver to Hawaii and back.

Involuntarily, I cringed as I heard another cupboard unhinge itself to jettison its charges. The sound of breaking glass emanated from behind the closed door of the adjacent head. Reluctantly I went to see what the damage was this time. Upon entering the head, I discover that a small tub that once safely contained my daughter's nail polish collection had crashed to the marble countertop. A stinging odour bit into my nostrils as I watched a bleeding trail of florescent red polish ooze across the countertop and trickle down the cupboard doors, appearing like the scene of some grisly murder. With only time for a cursory clean up before the evening weather fax was due over the high frequency radio, I cursed the weather under my breath while quickly mopping up, being careful not to cut my hands on the shards.

With hands stained blood red, I held the weather fax that confirmed my nagging fears and our fate. Bold black letters spelling out the word "GALE" commanded the position on the chart that the GPS stated belonged to *Maiatla*. Although the gale would soon start to wane, we were still in for at least three more days of strong headwinds, incessant rain and the accompanying nasty seas.

Above the winds that whistled with urgency through the rigging, I heard the sound of concerned voices. Pulling back the companionway hatch that led into the canvas enclosed cockpit, I put on a smile as I greeted the three white-knuckled members of the crew.

"Evening all, how's things look up here?" Despite being cold, wet, and wedged into the cockpit in uncomfortable positions and perhaps a little scared, all answered positively while forcing nervous smiles.

My crew on this voyage consisted of my older sister Jackie, a feisty provincial corrections officer; her long time doting husband Jim, an associate for a national building supplier and an adventurous, sharp as shattered glass and precocious 18-year-old family friend by the name of Kara. We learned from a previous passage that Kara was prone to sea sickness; a malady that did nothing to deter her from signing on for this voyage. Fortunately, she had not yet succumbed to her gastrointestinal weakness.

For the third time in as many days, Jim asked with an uneasiness barely concealed in his voice, "Is this normal? I mean, being this rough and windy all the time?"

I wasn't surprised by the question; my trusting crew was green both in skin tint as well as voyaging experience. Aside from myself, none of the crew had ever been offshore before. I looked to seaward then to the three waiting faces that were glistening with either salt spray or beads of anxious perspiration, I couldn't tell which.

"As far as a gale at sea, yep this is pretty normal but as I told everyone before we left, we would probably run into this kind of weather for at least part of the trip, if we did, it would most likely be here off the Washington, Oregon Coast." I forced a chuckle, "But don't worry, this ain't bad. You should see it when it gets rough!" Receiving at least some small measure of reassurance from me, weak smiles crossed their tired faces.

Glancing around the bleak horizon brought little encouragement to anyone. But I wasn't lying; it could be a lot worse! And there was every possibility that it would be. I must confess, I do enjoy a challenge when sailing but I had limits and at this particular moment, I felt that I had reached mine. The reality is that a person would have to be immortal to enjoy the sea when it is at its worst.

The conditions were very ugly and the sea seemed to be unusually steep making for a turbulent ride. In 2002, on our return voyage from Mexico to Vancouver via the old clipper route, we spent a full 12 out of the 34 days at sea being pummelled by hurricane *Alma*. Perhaps it was my bleached memories, faded and diluted by distance, a deception of time and the successful completion of that voyage, but I don't remember the seas being this sadistic during *Alma*. I wasn't about to tell that to my once eager crew.

Despite the beating, we were still firmly in command of the vessel and she was making good headway and more importantly it was in the right direction, south, towards a warmer a climate! It was easy to be proud of *Maiatla*, because she was doing remarkably well but I couldn't help but worry a little, she was being worked hard and although much of her original rig and gear has been replaced over the years, she was still 25 years old and together, we had endured a lot of tough sea miles.

I was nearly twice her age but she seemed to match me ache for ache, scar for scar. An extension of myself, she talked to me in my sleep and I swear we groaned in unison when I heaved my weary bones from my berth or when she heeled heavily under her press of ashen canvas. I felt she were the quintessence of my soul. We shared a strange form of intimacy as our essences intertwined, sharing identical goals and fates, for out here, without my caressing hand upon her helm and her solidly beneath me like a willingly bedded lover, one cannot survive long without the other.

There was just enough daylight remaining for a quick tour of the deck and to perhaps throw in a second reef in the main. I thought I'd better to do it now, for in the pitch of night, the gyrating spreader lights tend to induce fits of vertigo and the wet deck conspires to launch inexperienced deck crews over the side. Jim and I secured our harness tethers to the windward jack lines that we had previously strung about the deck and made our way forward on bended knees while always clinging to something secure.

"One hand for you and one hand for the ship is the word," I declared above the wind and over my shoulder to Jim who was hard behind me. When I reached the main shrouds my stomach suddenly lurched as I spied the aft lower shroud on the windward side; it was coming apart at the Norsemen fitting which secured the shroud to the chain-plate and the deck. To lose this shroud in these winds could mean losing the entire rig, crippling the vessel and possibly crushing and carrying the deck crew over the side as the main mast came down. Vessels have been holed as broken spars still secured to the vessel by wire shrouds, are propelled by the wave's actions becoming lethal battering rams that can quickly puncture a ship below the water line.

This is the fate I'm convinced befell our 22-year-old cruising companion, Nick aboard *Wanderlust* as we beat our way out of the Sea of Cortez against the vanguard of hurricane *Alma* in 2002. Just before midnight and while trailing behind us by only a few miles, Nick reported over the radio that he lost his forestay but later confidently stated that he had it under control. When the grey dawn broke, *Wanderlust* and our friend were gone.

Fearing that our shroud would let go, I turned to give the order to bring *Maiatla* about when the strongest wind gust of the night assaulted us. Almost simultaneously an extreme wave struck *Maiatla's* port bow, causing the boat to roll heavily to starboard while shuddering violently. Our compromised rig was being tested even further. Taken by surprise, I was thrown backward, slamming into the mast while bashing the back of my head on an unforgiving halyard winch.

"That was stupid you butt head, hang on, damn it!" I said out loud to myself.

Jim was desperately clinging to a grab rail as the wave struck, exploding against the hull launching sheets of chilly water into the air, then rained down upon the deck, soaking both Jim and I to the bone despite our rain gear. Torrents of water were still sloshing through the scuppers as I fought to find a handhold, calling aft for the boat be tacked, in order to bring the wind onto the opposite side to relieve the stress on the damaged stays. Kara tended the sails as Jackie threw the helm hard to port. The seas seemed to abate a little as *Maiatla* bore off the wind to settle onto a more comfortable run. By the time I managed to inspect the entire rig, it was dark. I was relieved to find that the problem was limited to a single shroud but it was too dark and rough to attempt a repair that night. We prayed that the wind and seas would be better in the morning. We would have to nurse the rig through the night and trust that no further problems developed . We dropped the main and ran under staysail alone. The small sail produced sufficient headway to keep steerage but slowed our retreat back north, taking us in the wrong direction.

My first thought was to run to the east and Portland, Oregon. We could be there in two or three days, mend the rig and be back underway in less than a week, which by all accounts would be a prudent decision. The problem with this scheme was that my crew had plans for time on the beach in Maui, and planes to catch. Such a delay would ruin much of their hard won vacation time. Unlike them, I was not on vacation, living aboard full time with my wife and children, cruising where and when we pleased was our life, not a pastime; a lifestyle, not an event. Many a cruising vessel has been lost, dreams dashed upon the rocks because of the resolute demands of shore side timetables that compelled them to head to sea when it was best to stay secured to a quay in port.

It was decided it was best to wait until we had inspected the rig again in the morning before making the decision whether or not to scud for shore. I wasn't about to unnecessarily risk anyone's life by attempting to repair the rig in the dead of night in these conditions.

I believe the sea always looks worse in the mornings during a storm. The privacy of the open ocean closes in at night and in the cover of darkness your tormentor, your abuser, is hidden from view, cloaked in obscurity and wholly anonymous. From the cockpit the waves sounded striking like freight trains. The gale force wind, like a wolf in the night, its howl summons a latent primordial fear that raises the short hairs at the base of your neck, but at least you didn't have to stare the beast in the eyes. But when the grey dawn breaks, I usually first feel a sense of dread, then amazement for what we were enduring, then finally a swamping relief for having survived the long night. Daybreak confronts you with the shear vastness of the tumultuous seascape and your own insignificance measured against the towering seas becomes stunningly apparent. Aboard *Maiatla* we were all praying for dawn, however I believe I was the only one who was feeling the pangs of dread for what we might see in the sobering light of day.

I relieved my sister at the helm and flopped into the captain's chair, checking the GPS for course and speed, then the radar for vessel traffic. It only took a few seconds to discover that we were alone in this dark night on this broken sea. The force of the gale was strong and the rain incredibly heavy; the wind drove the rain and sea spray under the edges of the dodger to absolutely soak everyone and everything. Despite looking tired, drawn and utterly soaked, none of the crew left the cockpit. The cold of the night prickled our skin; nevertheless, as miserable looking as they were, everyone seemed to prefer to remain huddled together for reassurance rather than seek the warmth of their isolated bunks below.

I laughed to myself. It was a "milk run," I had been told by several sailors who had made the round trip voyage from Vancouver, Canada to the Hawaiian Islands. "Warm winds on your beam or stern all the way there and back home".
Although it was true that the pilot charts predicted decent conditions for this time of the year, June, I've learned from hard experience that any so called "easy passage" can bring on conditions that can cause any vessel to find itself in a fight for its very survival.

As I took stock of my little ship and exhausted crew, I had no doubt that we were in a fight for our own survival this very night. It was surprising that up 'til now no one had succumbed to seasickness, but that was all about to change. Someone has to be first, the novice sailor who in an effort to take their mind off the waves downs a dill pickle and a gassy soda without forethought, but with predictable and horrid consequences. But it would not be one of these novices that would yield first. I lurched for the leeward side of the boat and just managed to unzip the dodger and extricate my head before every meal I had consumed in the past 12 hours, accompanied by the usual disgusting guttural sounds, made a violent and messy exit.

Does the sight of your captain, your saviour upon the sea, up-chucking and moaning as if he had received a sharp kick to the groin, elicit sympathy or instill doubt about his ability to command the crew? Is the captain's potency as a commander ejected with his intestinal jetsam? Humility rarely comes with command but I had to chuckle along with the rest, that is, once I wiped the saliva streamers from my chin. It appeared that my sacrifice to the sea was not made in vain. The dismal spell that gripped the crew was now broken and all began to joke and tell tales of other encounters with the malady.

The daylight sea in the early morning looked so old and tired. The sea had settled some, and Jim and I prepared to go forward to attempt a repair to the rig. I thought it would be an easy procedure but I should have known better, nothing is ever easy at sea, least of all during the tail end of a gale.

I had spare rigging wire in the bilge but I wasn't about to attempt to scale the mast to the lower tangs and run a new stay in these seas. Instead, I opted to cut off the bad section of wire that was exposed just above the Norsemen fitting and move the Norsemen up until it bit once again into solid wire. I would only lose a couple of inches of shroud and that should leave me enough length to reattach the fitting to the deck chain plate and re-tension the rig.

We used the main halyard shackled to the toe rail as a temporary stay and quickly repaired the shroud. But when it came time to re-attach the shroud to the chain plate, to my frustration the shroud came up half an inch short. We hauled on the main halyard in an effort to bend the mast sufficiently to make the connection, the threads of the turnbuckle met the threaded stub of the Norsemen but I couldn't get them to mesh. In desperation, I slackened the starboard side shrouds, this was a very dangerous move and in hind sight a bit foolhardy. The seas were still running high and by doing this, the mast was allowed to wobble slightly from side to side, a jerky motion that threatened to tear the lower tangs from the mast with every roll of the vessel.

We only required a moment and I was thankful the stunt gave me the needed length to thread the turnbuckle and Norsemen together. While all this was going on, Kara, who was at the helm called out.

"There's a ship over there!" I looked where she was gazing and less than half a mile distant was a very large freighter. It had slowed and was paralleling us but heading in the opposite direction, he was obviously checking us out and I could imagine several people on that ship's bridge scrutinizing us through binoculars all the while commenting to each other, "Look at these nuts way out here in that little boat."

I didn't have time to get on the radio and have a chat, so I just stood to give a slow purposeful wave, and then went back to work. Satisfied that we weren't in any real distress, he altered course to the east and powered up and was quickly lost in the big seas.

Content again with the state of our little ship, we gybed her around to face the now small gale (Force 7 – 27 to 33 knots) and slowly added sail; with the sail's bellies swollen with wind we were once again making six knots while pounding through the incessant seas. We had lost 45 nautical miles during the night and it would take us the better part of the day to get back to the position we were at the previous evening. Ninety hard miles round trip and it would add almost a full day to our already long journey.

The next few days proved more or less uneventful, just gun-metal grey clouds and strong winds forward of the beam, but it kept us clipping along in the right direction- south. The only noteworthy entry that made the ship's log concerned Kara, who while sound asleep in her cabin, was violently awoken as a pair of drawers that cradled the ships files and a crafts' drawer containing paints and drawing material meant for the kids, simultaneously took flight, crossing the narrow corridor to crash into her berth. She would later tell of the harrowing assault that she endured as a six-pack of toothpaste tubes "missiled" across the room to viciously strike her in the head.

The crew settled into a routine of eating, sleeping and general socializing in convenient six-hour blocks. We paired up into two watches, Kara and I as one team, while Jackie and Jim comprised the other with Jackie taking on most of the cooking duties. Six hours is not too long to be on watch when you take turns on the helm and scanning the horizon. Kara and I formed an informal routine of standing watch and sleeping while on deck at night. When sleeping, we often had to secure our harness tethers to a winch to avoid being rolled off the cockpit bench.

In the evenings, on the high frequency radio, we reported to the Pacific Seafarer's Net, giving them our position, weather and state of the ship and crew. It was comforting to know that not only could our families follow our daily position on the Internet, it was also assuring that if we were to fall off the radar, so to speak, at least our last known position could be given to search and rescue. My crew took comfort in knowing that if all hell broke loose and they inadvertently found themselves treading water while vigorously kicking at darting fins and clutching tentacles, salvation was close at hand as we were being closely watched. Friends, Hams and computer geeks around the world would be stirred into action by a succinct S.O.A (Save Our Asses).

Yet in reality, despite the apparent close scrutiny of our families and sailing voyeurs alike that were living vicariously through our travels, our imminent deliverance was just an illusion. If a vessel is more than 150 nautical miles from shore, you can usually forget land based rescue, choppers won't go much beyond that offshore. So unless there just happens to be a coastguard cutter or naval frigate in the vicinity, you will have to hope that there is a commercial freighter nearby and (this is the key) willing to come look for you. And if they do find you, they will remove the crew from the vessel then steam away leaving your huge investment to its own fate. Like the Coast Guard they don't rescue property, only people.

Figure 4. A happy Kara on her early morning watch after the gale had passed and the seas had settled.

We were a full week and a half out from Mission, the seas had moderated a bit but the wind remained fresh, making for good sailing conditions. Kara and Jim were in the cockpit standing watch and enjoying the first real sunset we had since heading offshore. To the west, the sun's rays glorified the gilded ocean that spread before us. I was preparing to go onto the evening net while Jackie was rummaging around in the fridge looking for something to prepare for dinner when she suddenly exclaimed,

"Andy I don't think the refrigerator is working, the food is getting warm!"

I checked the cold plate, which confirmed Jackie's observation. It wasn't long before I discovered that there was nothing wrong with the refrigeration system but that the battery voltage was getting seriously low. Our 400 watt wind generator, located atop the mizzen mast was humming along fine, but the 350 watts of solar panels had been near useless with all the heavy overcast that dominated the skies for the past week. With an autopilot working overtime in the heavy seas, two refrigeration units working 24-7 (refrigerator and a deep freeze) and the busy ham radio schedule I was keeping, my 800-amp hour battery bank was taking a beating.

Not a problem, I would just fire up the genset and charge the bank. I went outside onto the aft deck where I keep our 1850 watt gas genset and gave the starter cord a sharp tug, once it was running I threw the switch. Nothing happened! After 3 hours of checking leads and connections I came to the conclusion that the wire running from the genset to my electrical panel and battery charger was shot.

No matter, I would just start the main engine and charge the bank the old fashion way using the ship's twin alternators. I switched on the starter battery, which was supposed to be totally isolated from the house bank and turned the key. Nothing! Three more hours of troubleshooting by flashlight and I finally discovered that the brand new and overpriced 8D battery that my mechanic in Mission had sold me had a dead cell. I flicked the battery selector switch and hoped that the house bank would start the engine, but it was even less enthusiastic than the starter battery. I was soon back to the gas generator from which I ran jumper cables through the aft cabin's hatch to the house bank and we waited two hours for sufficient charge to accumulate to fire up the engine.

It was now on the far side of midnight and I was exhausted, frustrated and tired of having to wedge and brace myself against the boat's relentless rolling while trying to work. Despite the cool temperatures I was soaked with sweat; but the engine was running and charging so I went to bed, but not for long.

I was in a sound sleep when with all the tact of Freddie Kruger wielding a chainsaw, something ripped into my dreams. Fortunately, I recognized the sound the instant I awoke. Shooting up into the cockpit, I ordered Jim to kill the engine. The engine overheat alarm was unmistakable and very irritating, having a similar effect on me as chewing tinfoil with a mouthful of fillings. As I opened the engine room doors, a rush of steam escaped into the corridor between the main salon and my aft cabin. In keeping with the trend of the day, I cursed out loud.

Thankfully, the engine did not seriously overheat or warp the head. The trouble was soon evident; I had no problem locating the loose hose clamp on a coolant line that was the principal culprit. A twist of a screwdriver and adding additional coolant put us back in business. Since the engine was down, I did a quick check of all the other hoses and fittings, and it was fortunate I had because many were similarly lose and leaking.

****

A full six months before departing for Hawaii I pulled the engine right out of *Maiatla* and commissioned my mechanic to do a total rebuild and he dutifully tore it down to the last nut and bolt, but accompanied by an inexhaustible supply of excuses he only managed to finish the job a full 5 days before we were due to head to sea, bound for Hawaii.

No problem, I would just run the engine at the dock under load for a few days, break the new engine in, and with my mechanic close by, we could fix any little problem that arose. Not so. Three days before our departure I was sickened to find an immense puddle of oil under the engine and with the low oil pressure alarm screaming. I only just managed to shut her down before she ran completely dry of oil. The main seal had blown, the brand new one my mechanic supposedly installed.

I was starting to have some serious doubts about the man to whom I just paid a small fortune.

The air was thick with blasphemous tirades as the engine came out of the boat for a second time to replace the seal. The engine was back in the boat and running within 36 hours, not some little feat. We departed for Hawaii on schedule and with less than 10 hours on the rebuilt engine. Optimistically, we decided to forgo a shakedown cruise and just head out.

****

Over the following week while cursing my former mechanic and dead battery, the engine, when it did start, bled oil or coolant from gaping wounds. No sooner had I had one gash sutured up than another drip would appear. It was disheartening; bolts rattled lose; water pumps mutinied; alternators fell off and belts shredded all with alarming regularity.

Late one night an alternator wire rattled lose, shorting out by contacting the engine block. *Maiatla's* interior lights flashed then went black. All of the vessels electrical systems were gone and the smell of burnt wiring permeated the boat with a smoky haze. We were 400 miles from the nearest shore and all of our electrical systems were dead, which meant no motor, no GPS and no radio for screaming help! My first instinct was to stumble in the dark to find my secret stash of Bacardi for a bracer to help me collect my thoughts, but the vivid memory of installing a watermaker in San Francisco some years back after having a power meeting with my old friend Captain Morgan and the ensuing problems that resulted, convinced me otherwise. Best to stick to a cup of Red Rose.

It took several tense hours of wire tracing through a burnt bundle and splicing aided by a small headlamp before I was able to locate the main short and complete the repairs, all the while hindered by anxious questions from a rightfully nervous crew.

Every captain loathes having stowaways aboard. Leaches and free loaders stealing a free ride is one thing but having these little saboteurs aboard could prove fatal for the ship and crew. At this point, I had no remaining doubt that *Maiatla's* dank bilges housed a covey of mischievous gremlins whose sole purpose was to frustrate me by messing with our boat's systems at every opportunity. If all of our difficulties were any indication, *Maiatla* was infested with the dirty little beggars. Legions of cockroaches would have been preferable.

Our lights once again blinked on and we were no longer blind and invisible in the night. I fought nearly daily with the gremlins to keep the engine up and running, a battle that lasted all the way to Hawaii. At times, I hate boats and more so, boastful mechanics.

Chapter #2

Fair Winds

A wet sheet and a flowing sea,
A wind that follows fast,
And fills the white and rustling sail,
And bends the gallant mast.
  - Allan Cunningham

The next few days brought clearer skies and flatter seas which allowed *Maiatla* to brazenly lift her skirt and scud onward between 7 and 8 knots and we would log our best day's run so far. One hundred and fifty-one nautical miles in 24 hours, a record I was hoping to improve on once we hit the northeast trades that were presently hovering off the coast of Mexico. Our best day's record was set in 2002 down in the trades headed in the direction of Hawaii when we logged one hundred and eighty-one nautical miles in 24 hours, but that was when we were riding the tail of hurricane *Alma* with hurricane *Boris* tearing up the seas behind us.

With that kind of motivation we were compelled to drive the boat hard. But for now we were making good headway and more importantly, the crew was happy after having a well-needed shower to wash off the grime and salt accumulations. The boat began to smell a lot better!

We had run our 200-gallon a day watermaker when the engine was employed so the water tanks were overflowing and we could well afford the extravagance. On a long passage, having the watermaker makes life much more civilized, fresh clean water for showers, brushing your teeth and just doing dishes in ample fresh water makes the expense and hassle worthwhile. Three full days later and the ugly memories of the gale were already quickly fading into the background. I laughed when I heard Kara talking to Jim.

"The storm was not that bad," Kara said.

Jim quickly agreed which surprised the hell out me. Jim, like the rest was still exhausted and had only made a minimal effort in tidying up his personal space; for the most part, we were all still sleeping amongst the debris that had been jettisoned from cupboards and drawers during the gale.

Jackie was cooking up some awesome meals, which also served to keep the crew happy. With our gimballed stove it was possible to still do some serious cooking even during the nastiest of weather, it just took a brave, determined cook with a strong stomach and no aversion to getting burnt.

On Monday, June the 4, we awoke to find a pod of pacific white sided dolphins riding our bow. They were beautiful and the pod numbed over twenty, playing in our bow wave for over half an hour. I never get tired of standing in the bow pulpit watching these mesmerizing and incredible animals play; the water was so clear we could easily see them over ten meters beneath the boat. With San Francisco now 450 miles off our port beam, the water transformed from its lustreless grey of the continental shelf to the cobalt, almost electric blue of the high seas. The color change was also a sign that the waters were warming up. With 5000 meters of water beneath our keel and with dolphins gleefully breaking water all around, we were truly riding on top of the deep blue sea.

Jim had been eager to deep-sea fish ever since we headed offshore so as soon as the weather permitted, out came the fishing rods, one on either side of the boat with an "army truck" green squid jig skipping merrily along the surface behind the boat. We hooked three nice tuna this day but disappointingly, in an explosion of frantic water all were lost when brought alongside; a story that repeated itself over the next few days, frustrating Jim in particular, to no end.

Figure 5.

Dolphins often came to play on our bow wave.

That night while enjoying a warm breeze and a goblet of red wine with Jimmy buffet serenading us over the speakers, we enjoyed our dinner meal all together in the cockpit. The quintessential picture of a blissful crew framed by the fiery western sunset. We squinted into the sun in an effort to see the elusive green flash: The emerald flicker that appears for a nanosecond just before the sun plunges into the sea for the night. Kara and I both called out at the same time.

"I just saw it!"

In all my time at sea I can only claim to have seen it three times. Jim and Jackie missed the show because before you can say, "there it is", it's long gone; they laughingly joked that we were just making it up.

Sailors have claimed for thousands of years to have witnessed the green flash, fostering many a lore and legend. But perhaps the green flash's literary beginnings first made appearance in 1882, when it appeared as a subject in the Jules Verne novel, *Le Rayon Vert*, the "The Green Ray", as the phenomenon is sometimes known. Verne waxes poetically about the color of the flash, describing it;

"a most wonderful green, a green which no artist could obtain on his palette, a green of which neither the varied tints of vegetation nor the shades of the most limpid sea could ever produce the like! If there is a green in Paradise, it cannot but be of this shade, which most surely is the true green of Hope."

One of Verne's characters also recalls a Scottish legend that claims that whoever has seen the green flash will never again err in matters of the heart. A fanciful thought but unfortunately, researchers have never found any trace of the legend in Scottish folklore. So it seems likely that the imaginative French author made it up himself.

After washing the dinner dishes and reporting to the Net, Kara and I readied ourselves for the start of our night watch. Kara made a slight heading correction to take advantage of a westerly shift of the 18 knot wind and watched as Auto settled down on our modified course. Since heading offshore, the wind had been predominantly from the south, but fortunately with enough of a westerly component to allow us to sail, more or less, in the direction we needed to travel. Kara set the radar up for the night, having it turn on every 10 minutes, sweeping the horizon; if nothing was detected and the alarms didn't sound, it shut itself down and waited for its next programmed sweep. A tireless watch keeper that I would have hated to do without.

I suggested to Kara that we move up onto the bow to get a better look at the stars. While nursing cups of hot chocolate and using the spinnaker like a bean bag chair, we looked up to watch a clear sky splashed with billions of stars, while calling out whenever one of the numerous shooting stars or satellites was spotted. The sea around us appeared almost friendly but I was surprised by the lack of bio-luminescence in the water. On our last voyage through these latitudes the excitable, glowing little creatures that were responsible for the watery lightshow were so thick that *Maiatla's* wake resembled a Roman candle streaking through the indigo sky. Back then, our glowing wake was visible for several minutes and extended hundreds of meters behind the boat. But not this time, hardly a twinkle was seen in the churning water.

The air bore the heat of the day and we were quite content sitting out on deck. Kara and I talked about everything that seemed important at the time and later, rambled on about nothing at all as the hours went quickly past. Finally, after feeling all talked out, we lay in comfortable silence, muted by the intensity of the moment, our senses lulled by the rush of the bow wave, succumbing to a state of mental tranquility. We gazed upward at the masthead light as it cut a circling swath through the heavens. *Maiatla* valiantly charged onward towards a horizon that appeared to advance before us, like an elusive ghost that forever drifted back beyond reach of an outstretched hand.

****

Up until then, I'd had little time to think about how I was missing Jan and the kids. This was the first voyage I had undertaken without them and I couldn't help but recall the web of circumstance that led to the decision to cruise to Hawaii, leaving them behind for the first part of the voyage. It was a strange feeling at night reaching across the bed in our great cabin and not feeling Jan's comforting form next to me, or inhaling her reassuring scent that was now fading from her pillow. I sorely missed her. Ironically, her absence just served to remind me just how blessed I was to have had this women at my side for the past twenty-five years. A women who loves me despite myself. She was the one who taught me that truly loving another means letting go of all expectations and accepting the other person for who they truly are. Lucky for me, but it was her misfortune to have succumbed to the charms of a dreamer who demanded she share him with his mistress, in this case, *Maiatla*. Yet, I think even *Maiatla* missed her as well. Melissa, our a beautiful sixteen year old daughter was still in school and since I only had a weather window of four months to cruise, to and from, the Hawaiian Islands, I decided to leave with the boat a full month before school let out for the summer. Jan would also stay behind to look after our precocious daughter.

Once we arrived in Maui and school was out, Jan and Melissa would fly over and join the boat, in order so we could spend the summer together as a family, island hopping in the sub tropics. It was a good plan but one that encountered some heavy weather which blew in from a surprising quadrant.

"What!? Four months in Hawaii!? I don't want to waste my entire summer stuck in Hawaii!" Melissa spouted when I first suggested the cruise. "I'm not leaving my friends, we have plans, big plans for the summer!"

"What kind of plans?" I demanded.

"You know! Plans! We are going to do stuff!"

Our lovely daughter had reached that age when suddenly friends were far more important than family and when all logic and reason are swamped by a pubescent hormonal tidal wave. Melissa dug in her heels.

"We are not going to Hawaii!" She categorically announced. Our Diva had spoken.

Being somewhat numbed by previous bouts of attitude displayed by our self-absorbed offspring, we just remained calm (relatively) and made a pronouncement of our own.

"Well, girl, it's not your decision, we are going and since we are taking the house with us, you better oil up because you are going to Maui!" I can dig in also. Melissa is stubborn. Takes after me!

In the months leading up to our departure, hardly a day passed when we weren't assaulted by a barrage of excuses why she couldn't go and as our departure approached, her pleas not to be exiled to an island prison, became ever more frantic until just two weeks before D day, I had had enough!

"OK, you win, I can't imagine what you think you will miss by not being here for a couple of months but if you find someplace safe to stay, you don't have to go. Call your aunts and uncles and see if you can room with them for the summer, but I can't tell you how big of a mistake this is; you will regret it," I added with little hope that reason would somehow now come into play.

Melissa beamed with all the pride of a conquering hero and she obviously relished the moment. I had called her bluff, I was just praying that I didn't have to follow through and leave her behind. I was so very much looking forward to having her all to myself for the summer so we could dive, surf and explore the world together as we have done as far back as she can remember. The thought of not having her with me was devastating; it tore at me.

I believe it was a few days later that the full consequences of her decision finally struck her. Melissa's bid to locate suitable accommodation that included a watchful relative, had failed. As I was sitting at the galley table reading Frommer's travel guide of the islands, Melissa quietly approached and informed me that she would be coming with us. But she had that defiant look of a child that laments, "OK, I will go, but you can't make me have fun!"

I was so relieved to hear that she changed her mind, but I was not so naive to think that her opposition to the voyage was over, far from it. I suspected that she thought that if she had to suffer through this, so would we.

****

As I sat silently on the foredeck with Kara, I realized that I missed my family terribly, more so at times like this, enjoying the fatherly type of conversation with Kara. Our son, Thomas would not be joining us at all this trip, which also saddened me. He was now twenty and he and his lovely girlfriend Kirstin were about to make Jan and I grandparents. A situation I was having a tough time coming to grips with, not because my young son was about to become a father, but because I did not feel old enough to have a twenty year old son never mind a grandchild. Despite wrestling with my own personal and selfish demons, we were extremely happy for them.

Our son had a life of his own and with Melissa spending more and more time away from home with friends, I found myself growing ever more despondent, bordering on depressed. It was a rainy, typically west coast winter's night some months earlier while suffering through a rather deep moment of melancholy that Janet suggested that I was mourning the loss of our children, that I was feeling a deep sense of grief since Thomas and Melissa were no longer kids. At first I balked at the idea, but over the following days the realization that it may be true finally took root. It was true! I was grieving as if a loved one had died and I was not sure how to handle these new and painful sensations. My two loving children were no longer there for me to play with. I found it upsetting that we were no longer the center of their world and I missed that more then I cared to admit.

I cursed the advance of time for causing my dear children to grow up and leave me. And here I was sailing away from them, it was my choice to go but it hurt nonetheless and the last thing I needed at this time in my life was to deal with another intense sensation because the previous few years had been plagued with powerfully negative emotions.

It had been almost three years since returning from our last voyage as told in my first book, *"Voyage of the Maiatla with the Naked Canadian"*, and we were desperate to get back underway and complete our planned circumnavigation that we started back in 2001. But dire circumstances were about to dictate otherwise.

It started quite innocently one day when Melissa then age 13, showed Jan some strange bruises on her legs, being a typical kid she was always doing something to injure herself so initially we were not overly concerned. However after Melissa's insistence that she hadn't injured herself, we went to the medical clinic for a check.

It was almost midnight when we received an urgent call from our doctor telling us to "get Melissa to the hospital emergency room and right now!"

The next few weeks found us making repeated trips to Children's Hospital for tests and blood treatments. What was first feared to be leukemia turned out to be another sort of rare and potentially fatal blood disorder with a name that commands most of the alphabet to spell out and whose pronunciation sounds almost apocalyptic.

With dying children in beds on either side of our lovely daughter we feared the worst. Our souls were hurting and our hearts were broken. As parents you would willingly swap places with your ill child but neither this nor coming emotionally apart yourself is an option. Fear is a deeply personal and a bitter emotion. I tasted true fear for the first time several years earlier when I had been told I had developed a vicious form of skin cancer, if the tumour had spread, the doctor calmly informed me, I had six months, maybe up to three years. I felt a primordial fear that day, a deep guttural, immobilizing, cold sweating, bowel loosening, pants wetting fear, but nothing like what I was now experiencing with my daughter. Timely surgery saved my life but what of Melissa? My emotional quakes quickly crumbled my atheistic facade and for the first time in many years I prayed, begged and bartered to a God that I had so casually forsaken.

I can recall only crying as an adult on three previous occasions. Twice when my children were born, I cried tears of joy first for Thomas then for Melissa. I cried again when one of my two best friends died, my father and now I cried again when my beloved Melissa took ill. Strange how two different types of human sensations, great happiness and enormous fear, two antipodal emotions that command completely opposite ends of the emotional spectrum, can elicit the exact same poignant response, tears.

If I ever needed to run away to sea, it was then, but my source of solace, the place that for my entire existence has offered me refuge, isolation from my worst fears, tormentors and unconditional absolution was now unavailable to me. But was heading back to sea truly an escape? An attempt to run away? Or an effort to regain some sense of control? We fantasized about taking Melissa away as if you could actually out run or sail away from a disease, fleeing like a pursued rumrunner into the night. But it was very clear that we could not take our daughter and cast off; we needed to stay and fight for Melissa's survival and our own emotions needed to be controlled and measured. Melissa needed our strength to cope and Jan and I needed each other more now than ever before.

Her attacks came in waves, a few times a week when even the most benign of activities could prove fatal to her by causing uncontrollable internal haemorrhaging. She was rushed countless time to the hospital for treatment but over the next two years her "Crashes" as we called them, became less frequent until after two years, her episodes came only every three weeks or so, a blessing and a sign of hope.

Finally, after a surgery and the removal of a no less than two spleens, her symptoms were all but gone but she was still faced with potentially a lifelong struggle. Now at sixteen, the doctors gave her cautious permission to travel. We would monitor her closely and for our first real cruise we would choose a relatively safe destination, where good medical care was available and if the need be, a quick flight home was close at hand.

The predominate emotion of the previous three years for both Jan and I, was an ever present demon, a gut wrenching, bone wearying fear. Moreover, if that wasn't enough, for me, guilt haunted me as well. I had been working out of town and caught a nasty bug. Upon returning home, Jan and both the kids succumbed to the illness. It did not hit Melissa any harder than the rest, but she took longer than the rest to recover. It would be some time later that her doctor suggested that some unknown recent virus had confused her immune system, turning it upon herself. The guilt I bore thinking that I might have brought it home to her turned my stomach.

Jan and I both felt like we had aged light-years and for me, the discovery of the first few grey chest hairs was the confirming sign that I was truly getting older and a sobering reminder that time, our time on this earth was limited and should not be squandered. To say we needed to get away at that moment would have been a gross understatement. There are times in everyone's life when they desperately need to find a way to rally their spirits and recharge by whatever means. *Maiatla* and the open sea was our means. Although thoughts of escape were the principal catalyst that initiated this Hawaiian voyage, it was by no means the only mitigating factor.

We came to accept our daughter's condition and how it had changed all of our lives. However, acceptance of things in one's life has nothing to do with resignation or apathy and it does not mean that you are running away from the struggle. Resignation and apathy fail to distinguish between what can and cannot be controlled and apathy paralyzes the will-to-action; acceptance frees it by accepting life as it comes and accepting it in its entirety.

****

Kara's presence that night on the deck was in part consoling to me, but at the same time, she served to remind me who was missing. I felt particularly distant from Melissa; I especially hated to be apart from her, for fear of being away if the unthinkable were to occur and she was to have a relapse… or worse. As I lay on deck I felt myself to begin to choke up and I was just about to excuse myself when Kara excitedly called out while pointing off to port.

"Look a light. What is that, a ship?"

I stared for a moment, as the prick of a light quickly grew brighter, growing in size and intensity.

"Probably a cruise ship," I offered.

"They are usually lit up like a small city and you can see them for over twenty miles." I rushed back to the cockpit to track the vessel on the radar and to make sure we were not on a collision course but the radar screen was clear as our night sky.

Puzzled, I turned back to the growing specter and watched. It only took a few moments to realize that the light was not a ship after all and in a display that can only be experience at sea; the moon peaked over the horizon while transforming into a gigantic orange ball before bleaching out to a stark ivory. Its welcoming light scattering like shattering glass across the broken wave tops. It was a beautiful and timely sight; my feelings of loneliness quickly fled. Feeling immensely better I fetched myself a glass of wine before returning to the foredeck to sit with Kara and silently watch as our grandest celestial neighbour wrenched command from the black of the night sky.

Chapter #3

Memories

*Like all great travelers, I have seen more than I remember,
and remember more than I have seen.*

Benjamin Disraeli

I have often been accused of having a good memory; although I must confess that its accuracy at times has been questioned. I have been asked how could I remember times and events with such vivid detail? The power of recollection! A sunset over a distant sea where the clouds took the shape of huddled animals or the question mark shaped scars on the dorsal fin of a dolphin that rode our bow wave months before. In giving it some thought, I'm not entirely convinced that I'm blessed with a particularly keen power of recollection, not any better than most. Perhaps it's just that many events in my life stand out in such sharp contrast to the everyday, mundane events, that they are stored in a special place in the forefront of my mind, a special repository reserved for just such things.

Could it be that the terrestrial lives of the inhabitants of the netherworld are often so fixated on the grinding domesticated routines of their everyday lives that little stands out from day to day as being all that significant or special? A life that is comfortably numb, full of trivial nondescript events, times, places and faces that don't deserve the honour of being stored in that special repository, to be recalled and relived when triggered or when the nostalgic need to be revisited is keenly felt?

Sir James Barrie, the renowned dramatist and novelist born in 1860 in Kirriemuir, Angus, Scotland, once told us that:

God gave us memory so that we might have roses in December.

The beauty of roses is that they may bloom from thistles or cabbage stalks, for man's chief distinction is that he is not a rational animal; that he is sometimes even an Artic explorer. Or perhaps even a cruiser?

Barrie never recovered from the shock he received at age six from his brother's death and its grievous effect on his mother, who dominated his childhood and retained that dominance thereafter. Throughout his life Barrie wished to recapture the happy years before his mother was stricken, and he retained a strong childlike quality in his adult personality. His happy childhood memories were the inspiration for his best known work, the timeless classic, Peter Pan. Barrie's assertion that roses were capable of blossoming from *thistles* or *cabbages* suggests that good things are capable of blooming from the cleaved stalks of awful memories. Roses are there to inhale only if we care to notice them.

Memories are powerful tools that can serve as a tonic to weary souls, for when you are down and depressed, recalling a happy or pleasant moment from the past may be all that is needed to fortify ones will to carry on. The proverbial "shot in the arm" or "kick in the ass".

Melissa was about six and Thomas ten when we sailed to the northern San Juan Islands in Washington State. The Pacific Northwest for Americans, the Southwest for Canucks, the Canadian "Banana Belt". We had spent the better part of the day hiking though the dense Arbutus forests in an attempt to visit all the island's secret little coves that slashed their way into the rocky folds. It was quite hilly and little Melissa's legs were giving out, so as any good Dad would do, I spent a great deal of time with her hoisted up, sitting atop my shoulders. Thomas, who had dashed ahead to make the next great discovery called back which prompted Melissa to squirm and demand to be put down. Back on her feet, she bolted off to share in her brother's excitement.

It was a warm day and we had hiked farther then we probably should have, it was a long way back to the boat and I was not sure my legs were up to the challenge. As Jan and I broke bush to exit onto another beautiful sand beach, I heard Melissa call to me.

"Dad come over here and let me climb on you!" We turned to see her atop a large boulder perched well above my head.

"Not now M, dad needs a rest," I called back. I was about to flop into the sand when Jan grabbed my arm.

"Go on and get her, make a memory." I huffed a little then headed over to the boulder where my little girl quickly climbed down just enough so she could leap onto my sagging shoulders. She squealed as I took off at a trot down the beach in howling pursuit of Thomas.

To this very day I have not asked my daughter if she remembers that day on that island or that moment when she climbed upon that particular rock to beckon me.

I'm more than curious, I need to know but I was deathly afraid to ask because if she failed to remember that instant in our time and store that memory in that special place up front as I had, then perhaps I failed her as a father in many other moments!

As a strangling man craves a breath, I needed to know! Did I fail to make our time together important or count? Or did she likewise file that moment away? Or discard it long ago and replace it with a more important memory? Whichever the case, that otherwise insignificant moment in our history is forever burned into *my* memory. But the question is: if Janet had not said, "go on make a memory", would I have? Even if I had gone to Melissa on my own accord and carried her off, would that day just have faded into obscurity with so many others, ignored like useless clutter in a dusty garage destined to be forgotten? Or was it Jan's very words that made that moment important? Important enough to keep it close, to store it up front in that special place? My special repository? To be used as a tonic, to be chugged two fisted by me whenever the insidious black clouds of depression cast a menacing shadow upon my mind?

As you get older the bulk of your memories lose their sharpness, others fade to black like an old movie, but the significant ones get reworked and become even more vivid with time, like a good story that gets better with each telling. Barrie's "roses from thistles stocks". It has been just recently that I've come to appreciate my memories, a gift of age I guess, or a curse depending on your point of view or the life you've led.

Memories have been described as being a snapshot of one's life and recalling and viewing them is equated to peering into a window from your past, as if a voyeur sneaking a peek at a scene frozen in time or flipping casually through the pages of a dusty photo album. Strange enough, that is not how I see it. In my mind's eye, my memories are more episodic in nature, a sporadic collage of short movies featuring my personal version of reality. Most of my memories are poignant and curt, some are absurd. Despite the few traumatic events I have previously mentioned, the bulk of my memories are very happy ones. I feel as though I have been blessed in many ways and I replay these movies repeatedly on calm days whenever I feel bored or unusually nostalgic. Many of these memories, I'm sure after repeated playing, scarcely resemble the original version or the actual events, but I'm not entirely sure that it really matters. It's the beneficial feeling that comes with the pleasant or exciting memory that is important. Scholars concerned with historical accuracy may beg to differ, but I'm more concerned with the psychological and physical benefits of good memories at the moment.

If memories possess a calming, pleasing or nerve soothing effect, could they then be stimulating the creation of endorphins within the brain? Endorphins are a strong analgesic, capable of inducing a pervasive sense of happiness and well-being. This class of compounds are similar in their action to opiates. Like a drug, can a person become addicted to the feelings of euphoria that certain memories create? If so, can we in turn become addicted to creating memories as well, in an effort to feed our junkie like endorphin addiction? Some scientists feel that endorphins released into the body may be another reason some people pursue dangerous activities such as bungee jumping. So-called thrill seekers and adrenaline junkies may not just be addicted to the rush of adrenaline.

Could creating memories be the stimuli or driving force that compels people like myself to seek exotic travel, swim with sharks or sail to forbidding places-to crave adventure? Could the desire to replenish our emotional drug supply cause us to venture off, to create new memories once we no longer receive the same rush that we had once received when the memory was first injected into our brains? Is that what I have been doing all these years?

Not searching or running at all, but creating? Creating new memories to keep my mind stimulated during times when health or financial obligations imprison me in the insipid netherworld?

I mentioned earlier that I have been accused of having a good memory, and yet I just confessed that in all likelihood many of my memories have been either filtered, consciously or unconsciously altered and may not resemble the actual events. In my defence, I recall when writing my first book, "*Voyage of the Maiatla with the Naked Canadian*", I had sent an excerpt to a friend who was the principal character within that chapter. I wanted her input and any more details that she thought were relevant to the story. It wasn't long before I received an urgent email from Emily saying that she liked what I had written but that I "had gotten a few things wrong". After explaining her views I had to question whether I was actually there at the time. Apparently *I* had it *all* wrong!

I had written the story based on the notes I had jotted down only hours after the event, so I was reasonably sure I had gotten it right. Emily however, was working from memories that were over a year old. Filtered and reworked and no doubt well played memories. I was amazed how different we both remembered that day. At the risk of upsetting a dear friend I stuck to my version and sent it off to my publisher. It is very apparent that when it comes to memory, nothing is absolute, the validity of the memory is strictly the domain of the proprietor, so in reality, there are three versions to every story: mine, yours and somewhere in all of it, is the truth. Someone by the name of anonymous once said:

"The truth should never get in the way of telling a good story".

That is not to suggest I don't make every effort to be accurate, but it becomes apparent that truth, not unlike a person's face, appears to change with one's perspective. So in reality, the truth is whatever we believe it to be and like truth, reality is whatever we perceive it to be. This all may sound a bit surreal but I believe this to be a gift that gives us some latitude in how we perceive ourselves and how we choose to shape our lives.

****

By our second week at sea the winds lulled, allowing the waters to lie down. The air temperature had been slowly but progressively increasing daily until we all found the noonday temperatures to be oppressive. Below deck was stuffy despite the open ports and hatches. The engine, which had been running for the past two days due to the light air, added its own heat and usual sweaty diesel engine aroma between decks. At night the encapsulating darkness only seemed to enhance the airless feeling of the cabin, as I lay naked beneath a single, light sheet. The latest weather faxes teased us as they showed the strong northeast trades cutting a wide swath, starting from Mexico and running unabated all the way past the Hawaiian Islands, the only problem was that we were two hundred and fifty miles too far north. After sailing for a full day, teetering between 1 and 3 knots, I decided to burn our precious fuel and run flat out, hell bent for the teasing wind belt to the south.

Late in the afternoon of June 9th, I lay in the aft cabin, sticking to the sheets of my berth as I thought how ironic it was that I had been so desperate to reach the tropics, but I was suddenly missing the cool breezes of the north. I rose up, to peer out the stern port, to view a sea as calm as a backyard pool with hardly a ripple upon its indigo surface; just a low ground swell to distinguish this great ocean from an inland pond. Off in the distance I watched a Fulmar swoop down to skim the water just as school of flying fish burst from the surface. The tireless engine droned on and I could hear the rhythmic slapping of the sails and ticking of the halyards against the spars. As the boat rolled, her mast monotonously pitched from side to side like a giant metronome that induced trance-like stares in all that sat on deck.

I couldn't stand it anymore; I broke from my cabin and bolted into the cockpit where Jim was standing watch, Jackie was on deck taking in the sun. I reached for the engine controls and threw the engine hard into reverse. *Maiatla* tore up the water's surface as she clawed herself to a stop. Rather stunned Jim demanded.

"What's the matter? Something fall off the engine again?"

"No, I just need a swim." I declared.

I climbed out of the dodger, grabbing the boarding ladder and quickly mounted it, then jumped. The water was blood warm, but still cool enough compared to the air to refresh me, and surprisingly the visibility below the boat was incredible. I could easily see down over 40 meters until the light faded into the uninhabitable abyss. It only took my sister a few seconds to follow and with all the commotion, Kara who was dozing in her bunk at the time, found the two of us frolicking in the water and she too quickly jumped ship.

Jim on the other hand muttered something about the boat sailing off without us and hungry great white sharks being in the area and he decided to stay aboard. Coincidentally, I found what looked like a dish soap detergent bottle floating by and it had what appeared to be a big bite taken out of it. I showed everyone who was treading water, which prompted all to start looking below for the obviously hungry culprit. As I scanned the depths for darting shadows I couldn't stop that thumping theme from "jaws" entering my head. We had a magnificent swim and just the refreshing break we all needed.

"I wager that we are the first people to ever swim in this part of the ocean and live to tell about it". I said with great satisfaction, while climbing back aboard.

A good bet, since we were over a thousand miles out to sea with a whole two miles to the bottom. After an hour of swimming with numerous breaks to peer nervously below, we were preparing to get back underway but I needed to perform one little chore first.

"Hey Jim, hand me a mask and dive knife from the port side hand hole, will you?"

"What's up?" he asked, as he stepped down the boarding ladder to pass me the gear.

"Oh, I just need to cut off all that fishing line wrapped around the prop."

It would appear that in my haste to stop the boat I neglected to retrieve the two sets of fishing gear that we were trailing behind the boat at the time!

It was a few years later while doing some reading that I came across some information that gave me reason to pause. Researchers studying the great white sharks of Guadalupe Island located off the coast of the Baja were baffled by the annual disappearance of the sharks. Early every summer the great whites would vanish and it was still a mystery until recently when a couple of tagged Guadalupe sharks were seen in Hawaiian waters. It has since been hypothesized that the sharks leave Mexico and head for Hawaii, possibly for breeding, and if this is the case, that day we were unknowingly swimming in the express lane of the "Great White Shark Super Highway". So, perhaps Jim's initial concerns about being eaten were not entirely unfounded.

After five full days of frustratingly light winds and listening to the ceaseless rattle and clamour of the tireless Perkins and the rigging flogging itself, we had all had about all we could stand of this seemingly never-ending calm. The weather fax continually insisted that the trades were still over fifty nautical miles due south, but we were once again heading due west, paralleling the winds we needed so desperately. For some reason I resisted altering course to the south. Illogical as it sounds, I hated motoring in any direction that didn't make miles towards Hawaii even if it meant reaching the trades.

Figure 6.
The crew takes a dip mid ocean, two miles deep.

I sat shirtless at the galley table, nursing a glass of red wine with sweat pooling beneath my forearms resting on the salon table. I carefully reviewed the faxes, weather synopsis, long-range forecasts and charts in an effort to come up with a navigational solution to our problem. I suspected that we didn't have enough fuel to motor the rest of the way to the islands so I felt I had little choice. I decided to risk losing two more days travel and alter from our westerly coarse which would take us directly to Maui and try motoring more to the south in an effort to engage the wind, after all, we were a sailing vessel.

But before ordering the course change I thought that a swim would be a welcomed and refreshing break before dinner. Again at mid ocean we hove-to and dove over the side. But this time, Jim, as tired of the oppressive heat as any, risked abandonment or becoming a road snack for a hungry white shark, and with the rest of us, made the plunge.

The feeling of the water was magical and we tossed *Maiatla's* life ring over the side and snapped, in hindsight, some chilling photos of three people clinging to the life ring, far out to sea with no land or ships in sight. Later, while viewing the pictures, I hoped that the camera did not possess any prophetic or fortune telling properties.

We played in the water for some time until Jackie noticed a distant cloud. Against the other white fluffy mats this cloud stood out from the rest, it was dark and it appeared to be full of energy, menacing and just what we needed. I could clearly see the rain shadow that was illuminated as the sun prepared to set for the evening. Even as we towelled off on deck, we could feel the wind, cool on our naked skin as it began to build with the squall's rapid approach.

The squall struck with winds gusting to 25 knots, rather anaemic as squalls go, but we were thankful for the burst of wind and we were able to kill the engine, at least for the moment. We scrambled to trim sail to make the most of our new wind which pushed *Maiatla* along at close to 7 knots. But our burst of speed and related jubilation was short lived, within thirty minutes we were back to motoring, the cloud was retreating to the east and leaving us worse off for having come. The humidity it left behind magnified the already unbearable heat, turning the ocean around us into a veritable sauna. We were in for another hot and sticky night between the sheets, both above and below deck. The feeble wind came and went in fits and spurts. Whenever the wind built to a point that the sails could move us at speeds exceeding 3 knots, we sailed. It was a lot of work setting and dropping sails at the whims of the wind, but we needed to stretch out our fuel and besides, the crew had little else to do other than sleep and tend the boat. A typical excerpt from the log:

June 8th, 2007.
Still flogging the sails and moving very slow 2.5 knots. Kara and I relived J&J and I did a sail trim, got back to 3.5-4 knots. But an hour later the wind shifted to the N and dropped to 4 knots, the swell was knocking the wind out of the sails----back to 1.5 knots of speed. Back to motoring.

0800hrs Engine overheating at higher rpms, suspect we have a bum fuel injector which I isolated and cleaned up but wind picked up before I reinstalled-back to sailing.

1000hrs
Wind is back. Tried hoisting the spinnaker, it helped for a while-3 knots speed but the wind died to 0 so down it came. I re-installed the suspect fuel injector and started the engine and it seems to be working ok, may be fixed. It's now noon and we have been motoring at 1500 rpms, giving us just over 5 knots. I will slowly creep up the rpms until we get back to our cruising speed.

Trying to get the noon fax to see where our wind is. Last fax last night said we should have 20 knots out of the NE. But no such luck. It lies a lot!

While checking our course this morning, I noticed that we just crossed our old return course to Vancouver when we sailed out of Mexico back in 2002.

Funny thing is our old logbook said that we had back then the exact same weather and were motoring also. Book also said that we had caught a 10 lb. dorado that morning. Jim hooked a tuna this morning but lost it beside the boat again.

Just motoring and waiting for the wind.

June 9, 2007

  Noon---- and still motoring have to watch our fuel a little more closely now. Still lots left but I need to transfer some to the now empty reserve tank so I will have enough to at least motor into the harbour if the main tanks are run dry. Still praying for wind, will download new fax in an hour or so. Hopefully it will have good news.

  Everyone needs to be in shorts now, it's hot and very humid in the cockpit. 25C. With broken clouds.

Wind slowly shifted into the NE at 8 knots, hope these are the building trades. Running wing and wing at 2.5-4 knots depending on the fickle nature of the wind. Hooked another big fish, but after half an hour it decided to run and broke the line .

Spent most of the night either sailing at 3 knots or motoring. Dark night, lots of stars and the occasional shooting star.

  .

Chapter #4

Maui Time

Ambition leads me not only farther than any other man has been before me, but as far as I think it possible for man to go.
From the log of Captain James Cook.

Being on watch, six hours on and six hours off, the days seemed to meld into each other, making it difficult to keep track of the time or day of the week. Each day had two mornings as we would rise after long sleeps twice each day which caused the day to feel long, especially with so little to do. The seemingly never-ending watches painfully dragged on. As I sat next to the ham radio scanning the airwaves looking to eavesdrop on someone's conversation, I remembered the last time I felt the days were longer than normal, but back then it felt totally different.

Some years ago while spending a week on the Island of Maui, I noticed that my perception of time had been mysteriously warped; the days elongated, time expanded. The days extended and inexplicably grew longer. The days were so pronounced and strung out that the events of the morning seemed unusually distant and remote when compared to the actions of the afternoon of the same day.

This phenomenon was not uniquely my own, Jan likewise experienced a similar feeling of being caught in a time warp, a retardation of the advancement of the day, not altogether an unpleasant experience at the time. Surprisingly, despite the long tiring days, the feeling of boredom never entered the picture. We discussed the day's longevity and this feeling was so distinct and tangible, that we invented a term to describe this phenomenon; we called it "Maui Time". At the time we did not consider where the source of power behind Maui Time originated, all we were concerned with was that it magically transformed our relatively short week in the islands into a seemingly incredible month long rejuvenating event. Astonishingly, the effects of Maui Time lasted long after arriving back home.

Later on a long winter's night at home, warding off the chill next to a roaring fire, we could not help but wonder if Maui Time was unique to Maui? A supernatural trick played on tourists by the Island's Mana, the divine power that haunts those ancient shores? Did our perceived time warp encompass just Maui or the entire archipelago? Or even perhaps the whole world.

Could a silent prayer under the equatorial moon to some primeval pagan idol, carved from a jawbone of a bristly boar, trigger Maui Time? Or possibly something more engaging like a traditional bloodletting, skull-crushing, human sacrifice to Pele, goddess of fire, lightning, wind and volcanoes; the lava spewing deity that inhabits a volcanic crater at the summit of Kilauea, on the neighbouring Island of Hawaii?

With the their blood lust satisfied, would the Island's Mana then give blessings and permit us to take this powerful new time warping tool on our journeys? Carry it with us in a satchel or discarded conch shell, and akin to a genie in a lamp, with a vigorous rub, call upon the diaphanous entity whenever we wished a pleasurable experience to last longer than normal time constraints would commonly allow? While traveling, visiting loved ones or even during a wild night of romping sex? A provocative or should I say, titillating thought? Are Maui Time memories just pleasant memories enhanced by an endorphin high which in turn creates an altered and a more perceptive and receptive consciousness?

Is Maui Time strictly a function of memory? Like the slow motion button on a CD player that when pushed gives you the time to scan the scene so your mind's eye is permitted to notice and drink in the most intricate of details. I believe for the most part, the art of having a good memory is not so much retention but attention, the power to focus on minute details and to organize and categorize them for efficient retrieval.

Perhaps that's what we were doing in Maui, enjoying and focusing on every moment of the day, scrutinizing and cataloguing each and every frame of every second with such detail and intensity that time actually slowed down, our minds testing the very concepts of space, time and relativity, a feat worthy of Einstein. Or perhaps Maui Time could have more secular and less mystical and anatomical origins attributed to the effects of the gallon jug of Hana Bay Rum I purchased upon arrival?

The rum notwithstanding, Maui Time may be an effect generated by viewing the world through the fresh, wide eyes of a child, when everything is new, fascinating, and engaging; with senses that are once again free to refresh themselves with the many new sights and sounds. Senses discovering for the first time the heady fung that clings to the ground of a tropical forest after the evening rain shower. The shrilling banter of songbirds in the rustling palms or the diamonds cast to the trade winds as a spinner dolphin bursts from the sea. On Maui Time, our senses seemed to have recovered the juvenile receptivity after years of abject apathy induced by city living, civilisation and the seemingly omnipresent effects of the netherworld hustle.

As a child, it seemed to take forever to grow up. Maui Time at work? But as we grew older the days contracted, the years began to fly by and our ability to fixate on the details of our daily adventures starts to abandon us. A de-evolution of our senses until as adults, we all but loose the capacity to see the wonders of the world through the eyes of a child.

It wasn't till some years later while doing the research for this book was I stunned to learn of an ancient Hawaiian legend concerning one of the Island's Divinities that shed some light of the origin of Maui Time.

MAUI SNARING THE SUN
Maui became restless and fought the sun
With a noose that he laid.
And winter won the sun,
And summer was won by Maui.
--Queen Liliuokalani's family chant.

Long before the days of written history when the ancient gods walked the earth and fished the seas, the demigod Maui was called before his mother, the goddess Hina. The goddess complained to her youngest son that the sun moved across the sky so fast every day that her tapa cloth would not dry. Wanting to please his mother, Maui, who was known for his tricks, devised a plan to solve his mother's problem. Maui descended into the deepest reaches of the underworld to confer with his ancestors. After a long time he returned to the surface with a stone axe and a mystical human jawbone. The upper jaw held all the knowledge of the heavens and the lower jaw contained knowledge of the earth. He then weaved a long rope out of his sister's pubic hair. (How he got this I can only speculate but would rather not!)

Under the cover of darkness, Maui scaled the great precipice that was the rim of the extinct volcano Haleakala (house of the sun) and concealed himself below the western most edge. Restlessly he waited for the sun that was asleep in the crater to rise and crest the ridge. When dawn finally broke, the first of the sun's fifteen golden legs straddled the rim. Maui quickly hurled the rope, the lasso missed its mark but landed and drew up tight, not around one of the many legs but around the suns genitals.

Stunned by the suddenness of the attack, the sun bolted for the western horizon and the safety of the sea. Upon seeing the sun flee, Maui secured the rope to a tree, bringing the sun to a screeching halt. Now that Maui had his prize fast, he slowly drew the sun back out of the sea to the mountain's crest. The sun begged Maui to let it go to proceed on its path across the sky. Maui agreed, but not before hacking off all of the suns legs, leaving only the weakest one. Maui then cut the rope and watched with great satisfaction as the sun ever so slowly crawled across the heavens to the west. Hence Maui Time was born.

****

On the morning of June 10th, I came on shift to find *Maiatla* sailing at 3 plus knots. After breakfast, I made Kara and myself a cheese, ham and onion omelette. I played with the sail plan, made a couple of tacks, but by noon the 2.5 knots we were making was killing me. In frustration, I started the engine in hopes of motoring into the 15-20 knots of wind, which according to the weather fax was still just south of us. Skies were 60 percent cloud covered but the sun was hot, and it was very humid. Although frustrating, the light wind conditions were not entirely unexpected; a couple of days before, we had dropped below the 35th north parallel into what is more commonly known as the horse latitudes.

Contrary to what some believe, it is not called the horse latitudes because sailors lose their voices from screaming over the high winds. The region between about 30° to 35° north and south of the equator is known as the horse latitudes or the subtropical high. This region of subsiding dry air and high pressure results in weak and fickle winds. Tradition states that sailors gave the region of the subtropical high the name "horse latitudes" because ships relying on wind power were often becalmed for days or even weeks; fearful of running out of water, sailors threw their horses and cattle overboard to save on water.

The region is also known as the "calms of Cancer" in the northern region and the "calms of Capricorn" in the southern hemisphere. I was hopeful that the winds would begin to fill in once we dropped below the Tropic of Cancer at 30° north latitude, the usual haunt of our elusive trade winds.

It was now our 13th full day at sea and we were fast approaching the 1000-miles left to go mark, more than half way there and everyone was starting to get excited. The thought that we were closer to Hawaii than home re-energized everyone, giving us a renewed sense of purpose. Still, the crew was slipping into a general state of lassitude and fatigue; the bone-mouldering humidity was taking its toll and it manifested itself in shortness of temperament and an irritability that kept conversations brief and to the point. I likewise felt the stress of being at sea for so long. My nerves were frayed from constantly fighting the mechanics of the boat not to mention the fluky winds. It forced me to make an effort to be patient and to control my responses, least I needlessly upset the crew.

The monotony of a long voyage is often broken up by a variety of means or events: Gales, gear failures or the sighting of ships and marine life is always an occasion that is welcomed and used to define a voyage by placing upon it tags for future reference for easier recollection.

Aside from the obvious need to know the date for navigation computations, dates or more so, the days of the week, which are so important ashore and the netherworld, are often meaningless to an offshore voyager. Sunday can just as easily pass for a Wednesday on the great expanse of the sea, and if a person did not possess a compass and could not ascertain east from west, then a sunrise can just as easily be confused for a sunset, the identity of the heavenly event only being betrayed by the passing of time and the inevitable raise or fall of the sun. It is singularly unique events, that can be as simple as discovering a precocious brown-footed booby perched precariously atop the pulpit or finding in the morning deck inspection, a flying fish, stiff in the scupper. These are the things that delineate the days of a sailor's voyage, not the named days of the week.

Still we have found that you don't have to be offshore to lose track of time. Jan and I were gunkholing along the west coast of Vancouver Island one summer, island hopping our way through the Broken Island group of Barclay Sound. One morning, I noticed that the ship's wind-up clock had stopped.

I inserted the key to wind it up, but I stopped myself. Later that day Jan asked me the time.

"9:45." I replied.

Looking a little puzzled, she glanced out of the head portlight at the late afternoon sun, then back to the stopped clock. She said nothing, only smiled. Several days passed before I felt the need to wind the clock, and only because I needed it for tidal information as we approached Victoria. Jan moaned in disapproval as she watched me give into my entrenched instincts and wind the timepiece.

****

Monday, June 11, was a remarkable day and one that will stand out for all of us, especially Jim. Kara and I were on watch, which started out as simply as any other. It was 11:00 a.m. and the winds had temporarily filled in, allowing us to sail fast on a broad reach under a full press of sail and a warm but cloudy sky. I was sitting at the helm quietly reading when the high-pitched buzz of one of the fishing rods startled me. I jumped to the rail and watched as an obviously big fish was ripping the line from the reel.

As I tensioned up the drag on the rod in an effort to slow the fish's flight, I called to Kara.

"Furl the headsail and dump the main, we need to slow the boat down!"

I was just about to remove the rod from its holder to play the fish when a great splash and a streak of incandescent blue burst from the water behind the boat. He was beautiful and full of enraged energy and not the least bit interested in surrendering without a fight. The large pelagic fish thrashed the air, leaping clear of the sea in an effort to throw the barb from its gullet.

"A Dorado! Ah, this is perfect!" I shouted, as I left the rod and shot past a perplexed-looking Kara, to disappear down below.

"Hey Jim! We got a big Dorado on the line and he's calling your name… pleading for you to help him commit suicide!"

Within seconds of my waking him, Jim was battling the fish of his dreams. After half an hour of playing the fish it was starting to look as though Jim's previous bad luck was about to change. Through laborious incremental gains, Jim managed to draw the now tiring fish close to the boat. Not wanting to risk losing the fish right alongside as we had with all the tuna so far, I suddenly had an Idea.

"Keep playing him Jim" I called out, " I need to get something!" I shouted as I bolted aft, through open the deck locker and began rummaging around.

"What are you doing Andy?" Jim called after me. "Grab the net! I don't want to lose this one!"

After tossing aside crab traps and coils of line, I found what I was looking for. Leaving the aft deck in a mess, I ran back forward.

"Ok Jim Bring him alongside "I said as I drew all the bands on my spear gun. There was an audible click as the trigger came to a full cock. Jim moved forward as I positioned myself between the mizzen shrouds for a killing shot. It was surprising how much fight the fish still had in him; the closer he came to the boat, the more violent his thrashing. A dorado (mahi-mahi or dolphin fish) is undoubtedly the most beautiful of the deep sea fish. They display colors and shades of yellow, blue and green that can only be described as electrifying, with all the intensity of charged neon.

However, once landed, the fish's vibrant colors quickly fade as the life drains from its slender body, turning silvery all over.

The fish was now alongside *Maiatla's* stern quarter and twisting so hard I was sure the line would break any moment. I quickly took aim and fired. The spear pierced the fish directly through the gills causing massive haemorrhaging. The fight was over. Jim beamed as he posed for the obligatory angler shots with a fish that stretched from his chest down to his feet.

"By the way Jim," I called over top of my camera. "Happy Birthday!"

Figure 7. Jim's birthday Dorado.

****

I made it a point that whenever the chart was up on the computer screen, to show everyone exactly where we were, we would all fixate on the little green boat that represented our diminutive home on the chart. Jim noted that it was such a little boat on a very big ocean. He was so right. The Pacific Ocean, this now quietly laying monster, is the largest single body of water covering a whole one third of the earth's surface, and containing one quarter of the world's water, a startling geographic reality especially when you are stuck, windless, in the middle of it.

The vast Pacific contains some of the loneliest regions on earth. An ocean capable of swallowing all the world's land masses and still possessing sufficient room and appetite to gobble up a couple of extra continents, if Mother Earth found the need to give birth to any. Consequentially, the Pacific Ocean contains the world's longest, unbroken sea passages, with thousands of miles between land falls; so challenging, this gargantuan ocean in a small boat should be done only after intense planning and by those who are capable of utter self-reliance, aboard a well-founded yacht. By contrast, the distance we were actually sailing, non-stop from Vancouver to Maui is about 2700 nautical miles, which is about the same as sailing from New York to England. In reality, our round-trip, Hawaiian voyage is comparable to making two Atlantic crossings in a four month time frame, not a small feat, I would think.

When you look at a chart of this vast ocean, carefully, as they are so tiny and hard to see, there is a chain of what could be fly droppings marching across the map. But those enigmatic specks represent some of the greatest islands in the world. The Hawaiian archipelago commences some 2,100 miles southwest of the North American mainland and is the southernmost state of the United States and the second westernmost state after Alaska. It is interesting to note that Hawaii is the only US state that does not share a border with anyone as it is totally surrounded by water. Most people are familiar with the eight main islands in the chain, which are, from east to west: Hawaii, Maui, Kahoolawe, Lanai, Molokai, Oahu, Kauai and Niihau, the forbidden island.

What most people don't realize is that these eight may be the biggest islands in the archipelago but they are not alone. Commencing 130 miles west of Kauai and Niihau, an additional 133 small islands and coral atolls arc across the Pacific for another fifteen hundred miles or so, terminating at 179 degrees west longitude at the tiny island of Kure, locate some fifty miles west of Midway Island, a mere two-thousand miles from Japan. Contrary to its name, Midway Island is not midway across the pacific but a full three-quarters of the way across.

The geology of all the Hawaiian Islands is the same, as they were all formed from volcanic activity initiated at an undersea magma source called a hotspot which is located today, south of the Big Island's coast. As the tectonic plate beneath the pacific Ocean moves to the northwest, the hotspot remains stationary, slowly creating new volcanoes and ultimately islands. Due to the hotspot's location, the only active volcanoes are located around the southern half of the Big Island.

The newest volcano, Lōʻihi Seamount, is located twenty-two miles off of the southeast coast of Hawaii. The new volcano is still one thousand meters below the surface and is not expected to make an appearance as an island for another ten thousand years. The last volcanic eruption outside the Big Island occurred at Haleakalā on Maui before the late 18th century, though it could have been hundreds of years earlier. In 1790, Kīlauea, on Hawaii, exploded with the deadliest eruption known to have occurred in what is now the United States As many as 5,405 warriors marching to battle on Kīlauea were killed by that eruption.

Due to their volcanic nature and subsequent erosion by the elements, all the islands display impressive geological features. Because the islands are so far from other land habitats, life before human activity is said to have arrived by the "3 W's": wind (carried through the air), waves (brought by ocean currents), and wings (birds, insects, and whatever they brought with them). This isolation and the wide range of environments (extreme altitude, tropical climate) produced a vast array of endemic flora and fauna no less impressive that what Charles Darwin had chronicled on the Galapagos Islands almost four thousand miles to the southeast. As a direct result of human interference, today Hawaii has more endangered species and has lost a higher percentage of its endemic species than any other U.S. state.

Hawaii's climate is typical for the tropics, although temperatures and humidity tend to be a bit less extreme due to near-constant trade winds from the northeast. Summer highs along the coasts are usually in the upper 30s °C, (80s °F) during the day and mid 20s °C (70s °F) at night. Winter temperatures are usually a few degrees cooler but not appreciably so. Snow is not an uncommon occurrence at the 4,205-

meter mark (13,796 feet) on Mauna Kea and Mauna Loa on the Big Island in the winter months. Mount Wai'ale'ale, on the island of Kauai is deemed to be the wettest place on the earth with an average annual rainfall of 11.7 m (460 inches).

Most of Hawaii has only two seasons: the dry season from May to October, and the wet season from October to April however local climates vary considerably on each island, grossly divisible into windward (Koolau) and leeward (Kona) areas based upon location relative to the higher mountains. Windward sides face cloud cover, so resorts are typically built of the leeward side of the islands. So if you don't like the weather where you are at, just drive up and around the island until the climate suits you.

The earliest habitation supported by archaeological evidence dates to as early as 300 AD, probably by Polynesian settlers from the Marquesas, followed by a second wave of migration from Raiatea and Bora Bora in the 11th century. Some archaeologists and historians believe that the later wave of immigrants from Tahiti, approximately 1000 AD, introduced a new line of high chiefs, the Kapu system, the practice of human sacrifice and the building of heiaus or alters. Regardless of the question of where the first peoples came from, historians agree that the history of the islands was marked by a slow but steady growth in population and the size of the chiefdoms, grew to encompass whole islands. Local chiefs, called ali'i, ruled their settlements and launched wars to extend their sway and defend their communities from predatory rivals, but that all was about to change with the arrival of the Europeans.

The 1778 arrival of British explorer, James Cook, was Hawaii's first documented contact with European explorers and the western world. However, Hawaiian oral tradition indicates that castaways, most likely Spanish were shipwrecked on the islands, sometime between 1521 and 1530, and intermarried with the indigenous peoples, but this cannot be confirmed. Cook named the islands the "Sandwich Islands" in honor of his sponsor John Montagu, 4th Earl of Sandwich. He published the islands' location and reported the native name as "Owyhee" which was later mutated to what we know the islands by today. After Cook's visit and the publication of several books relating his voyages and the discovery of a garden of Eden, Owyhee or the Hawaiian Islands was now wide open for exploitation by European visitors: explorers, traders, and eventually whalers and to some extent, contemporary cruisers. So, it was now *Maiatla* and her crew's turn to discover what was out there.

****

Encountering another vessel at sea, far from land is always a double-edged sword. The appearance of a ship above the barren horizon, or the flicker of a distant navigation light on a moonless night is usually a welcome affirmation that you are not alone in the world, that humanity still exists elsewhere and that you need only to broach the unchanging horizon to re-join the human race. Still, with every encounter, you are in danger of being ploughed under by thousands of tons of unfeeling steel, crushed beneath an unforgiving prow, puréed and churned out in a foaming wake, into a sea that will quickly hide the evidence of the crew's negligence, theirs and yours. The few erroneous pieces of flotsams and the resultant oil slick from ruptured fuel tanks will quickly be dispersed by wind and wave, removing all traces of the shattered hull and corpses that now lay thousands of fathoms below.

Once, back in February of 2002 aboard *Maiatla*, well beyond midnight and over a failing bottle of Old Monk Rum, I had a rather unsettling conversation with a fellow cruiser who was a retired British Merchant ship's officer. We were anchored in the busy La Paz Harbour in the lower reaches of the Sea of Cortez, nestled in behind the protective El Mogote and mangroves. The rest of our party guests had long since abandoned ship and returned home by way of their dinks to their respective boats that lay peacefully at anchor nearby.

After learning earlier that night of the merchantmen's forty-odd years at sea, I questioned him if their ship had ever run another vessel down? The cruiser's jovial expression suddenly creased with lines of anguish, he took a long slash of his dark drink as he searched though what were evidently, painful memories. I did not repeat my question, nor after feeling his discomfort, did I tactfully change the subject, as perhaps I should have, I just expectantly waited. I wanted a response and I felt I needed one. After repeated fortifying hits from his glass and as if an ashamed felon, he suddenly diverted his gaze, unable to meet my eyes as he began by clearing his throat.

"I don't think we ever ran down a yacht like ours, but I know of some other ships that have."

He paused as he shifted to the galley to refill his glass and collect his thoughts.

"We did our best to miss them; we kept a good watch…. The worst place was Southeast Asia, most small fishing boats would run feeble lights or none at all, I know we ploughed over some, straight through small fishing fleets offshore. I heard the crash and cries from the water but we couldn't stop, we didn't stop. The Old Man didn't want to know, so the crew on watch wouldn't make a report even if they saw it, it was never entered into the log."

He fell silent and I could see that he didn't want to say anymore, he received no cleansing from the telling, he was still haunted and his ghosts would not leave him, no pardons or absolution were forthcoming, just self-recrimination and loathing. He was obviously tormented so I didn't probe further. I now felt sorry then for asking, but at least I had my answer.

****

We were almost precisely halfway between Mexico and Hilo, Hawaii and it was surprising to note that up until now we had encountered so very few ships, only three since leaving Canadian waters and I think everyone was feeling a little complacent when it came to keeping a proper watch for shipping and of course, just when you least expect it….

It was 1:00 a.m. on mine and Kara's watch. *Maiatla* was making good headway on a fast, starboard reach, when Kara spotted a light on the horizon. She studied the pale light that she thought was a new raising star, but she wasn't sure.

Since celestial bodies normally rise in the east and set in a westerly direction, I had my doubts that it was extraterrestrial. So unless the earth suddenly began to rotate in the opposite direction, it had to be a vessel of some description.

I peered at Kara's "star" though the binoculars and for a moment I thought I detected a secondary light. I hit the button on the radar that woke it from its standby sleep and waited for it to make its first sweep of the ocean surrounding us. I was not surprised to see what Kara's sharp young eyes had noticed was actually a distant ship, but I was startled to see that there were two other ships in its company. The first vessel, Kara's "star", was approximately 10 miles off our starboard bow, a second ship was 12 miles out and directly ahead of us and a third vessel stood 12 miles off our port bow. I ran a VBL, (Variable Bearing Line) on all three ships and discovered that the two ships, the one off to our port and the one directly ahead of us were on a collision course with *Maiatla*. Our empty ocean suddenly got very crowded.

"Must be a fishing fleet," I said to Kara. "Keep your eyes peeled, there could be a bunch of small net tenders or drift net floats out there. I'll try and call them on the radio and let them know we are here."

Reaching for the VHF radio's handset I keyed the mike and put out a call, giving my vessel name, latitude and longitude. I repeated the call twice, but before I could hail the ships a third time, Kara excitedly exclaimed.

"I see another light over by the first one!" pointing off to our starboard at what she first thought to be a star. The attitude or course of the first vessel definitely had changed. Through the binoculars I could clearly distinguish the ships red and green navigation lights. I cursed and checked the radar's variable bearing line.

"That ship is headed straight for us as well and he is coming very fast!"

Roused by all the commotion, Jim and Jackie came topside to see what all the excitement was about.

"What's up, Andy?" Jackie asked, not sounding particularly concerned as she slumped into the seat next to me looking still half asleep.

"We are surrounded by ships, a fishing fleet I think and now all three are on a collision course with us. I tried the radio but there was no response."

"Could they be pirates?" Jackie asked. She was laughing but I think she was only half joking. Pausing for a moment to consider her suggestion, I realized what she was suggesting was quite possible. High seas pirates, not the sword wielding eye patch, peg leg, with a parrot type pirate, but the southeast Asian, deep-sea fisherman who strip pleasure boats for pocket change and send your corps to Davy Jones type of pirates. I considered trying to hide, to try and blend into the seascape but if they didn't know we were here before my radio call, it was obvious now that they knew as they were all steaming directly for us and whether or not we wanted to get to know them was no longer an option.

Everyone was peering outside the dodger at all the ships' lights that were now clearly visible and were heading straight for us. I had to make a decision, fight, flight, or just surrender. I didn't know who they were or what their intentions were, but getting run over in the dark looked like the greatest threat to me now.

"Jim, jump down below and turn the spreader lights on, it's a dark night and they should be able to see our sails all lit up!"

Without hesitation, Jim dropped back down the hatch and seconds later, *Maiatla's* deck and sails were ablaze in white light. No sooner were we all lit up than the closest vessel off to our starboard, which was now less than a mile away suddenly altered course to parallel us. Somewhat relieved that the first vessel appeared to see us, I turned my attention back to the two remaining vessels which were still on a collision course and they had already cut the distance between themselves and *Maiatla* by half and were still bearing down on us incredibly fast.

I returned to the radio and repeated my warning call, but the airwaves remained silent. Kara was watching the radar and she noticed that the obviously largest of the three vessels had altered course slightly to our starboard. I sat beside Kara and reworked the VBRs. I was relieved to see that the remaining two vessels had indeed altered course and would now miss *Maiatla*, but not by much.

Over the next several minutes, we watched nervously as the great glowing light grew closer and as the immense black shadow morphed into the shape of an Air Craft Carrier, I was sure glad I had not chosen to fight. It wouldn't have been fair as there were three of them and one of us! The massive vessel passed to our starboard at just over a miles distance and with the aid of the binoculars I could clearly see the fighter jets posed on a lower aft deck being tended by their crews.

"Hey Jim! I bet they have ice cream, do you think they will shoot over a tub if I ask them?" The tension was broken and a sense of relief filled our boat.

"To hell with ice cream, have them send rum!" Jim replied.

I joked that if we needed to board them, that we couldn't take any prisoners, as we didn't have the room.

"They won't be expecting terrorists way out here, being attached by a sailboat flying a Canadian flag, should be easy to take them." I said.

Jim suddenly turned serious.

"Be careful what you say, I bet they have night vision scopes and microphones trained on us right now and are watching our every move, and listening to every word we are saying."

A sobering thought, and probably not far from the truth.

Apparently, they deemed us little threat and it wasn't long before the floating airport and its twin destroyer escorts deserted us, presumably bound for San Diego. I was amazed that we were able to get so close to the war ships undetected. I believe if I had not turned on the lights and radar or sent a message over the radio, we would not have been seen, not until we were very close indeed. That aircraft carrier could have cut us in two, without notice. *Maiatla* and her crew would have been just another statistic; another vessel vanishes mysteriously at sea without a trace.

Perhaps their watch keepers were getting complacent as well, being so far out to sea on this otherwise deserted stretch of ocean.

Chapter #5

The Trade Wind Express

When you spend so much time pushing, caring for, cajoling and maintaining a beautiful racing machine like this, you get very close. She's looked after me well, and I look after her. I haven't been lonely at all.
- Ellen MacArthur

We were into our 15th day at sea and our target latitude was 20 degrees north, our rhumb line that we planned to follow all the way into Maui. Earlier, *Maiatla* had reached 28 degrees, north latitude and had been, over the past few days, slowly working her way southward, into the fringes of the northeast trades, whose authoritative character began to dominate the local weather patterns. Named from their ability to quickly propel trading ships across the ocean, the "trade winds" normally lay between 30 degrees latitude and the equator and are typically steady blowing about 11 to 13 miles per hour. However, the weather reports and my faxes showed the main body of the unusually narrow trades were located farther south than normal for this time of the year and reports indicated that they were blowing much stronger than customary, a condition forecasters predicted would last the better part of the week.

If the weather forecast wasn't disconcerting enough, we also had the ITCZ to worry about. The Inter-tropical Convergence Zone or ITCZ for short, was located just south of the narrow band of trades and it appeared to be threatening to migrate further north. The ITCZ could bully the trades, driving them north, leaving us to wallow in stagnant air. When approaching the equator, sailors usually notice the stiffness of the raising air... rising, not blowing. This depressing (to sailors) phenomena, was dubbed the doldrums. The doldrums are usually located between 5 degrees north and south of the equator. The tradewinds converge in this region, producing convectional storms that produce some of the world's heaviest precipitation. Typically the ITCZ moves north and south of the equator, depending on the season. The location of the ITCZ can vary as much as 40 degrees to 45 degrees of latitude north or south of the equator based on the pattern of land and ocean.

But for now, tradewinds in excess of 40 knots could be expected along our route, accompanied by frequent rainsqualls. It was an El Nino year, which usually has a dampening effect on the trade winds, but obviously not where we were now. It appeared that just beyond the horizon the Devil was stirring fire and ice. The strong winds blowing across the north-setting current, set up an uncomfortable chop but for the moment we were happy to have the wind to sail instead of motoring. But we were now facing the possibility that we could find ourselves windless if the ITCZ chased the trades northward, it would seem that the sea was determined to make us earn our passage to the islands of our dreams.

Maui was still 845 miles to the west of us; we were enjoying a great sail under a single-reefed main, a full mizzen and a poled-out jib. The comfortable sail plan thrust us along at a very respectable 7 knots with frequent bursts into the 8 and 9 knot range as *Maiatla* snatched the crown off the odd four-meter wave. In a great rush of white foam and spray she would lift her stern, then suddenly like a toboggan on a snow-capped slope, she would relent to the demands of gravity and quickly accelerate down the face of the wave with a hiss in a short-lived, mad sprint.

Surfing twenty tons of wood and fiberglass is always exhilarating, sometimes, especially while gripped by the night, the ride is often downright blood curdling as the autopilot or white-knuckled crew steers, fighting the stern's tendency to overtake the bow as the boat is catapulted downward into the developing trough while steep watery walls threaten to collapse atop your small vessel, swallowing her whole. As the stern rises, the bow digs in, and the force of the wave pushes the bow, wanting to slew the boat sideways, potentially exposing the vessel's beam to the full force of the waves, easily causing her to broach, rolling over onto her side allowing water to flood into the cockpit or pitch the deck crew over the side, or worse, capsize the vessel completely as the ballast in the keel is overpowered in a thunderous rush.

In extreme wave conditions a small vessel can actually be "pitch-poled" or somersaulted end over end as a steep wave catapults the stern overtop of the bow. Such a rollover or cartwheel would prove devastating if not fatal. The rig is usually lost as masts are ripped from the deck and water floods in if a companionway hatch or ports are carelessly left open and in a matter of minutes the vessel can quickly founder. Such is the risk of off the wind sailing in big seas.

One of the most harrowing accounts of a sailing vessel being pitch-poled was documented by Miles Smeeton in his book "Once is Enough," a chilling read for any voyager. The author and his wife Beryl tell of their two separate attempts to round Cape Horn aboard Tzu Hang, their 46 foot wooden ketch that was pitch-poled by highs seas on each of the two attempts, and their subsequent month long survival ordeals after each incident.

****

The high morning cloud began to flee when the sun broached the horizon. As the orange orb permitted us our first glimpse of what the new day was about to bring, it became very apparent that we were in for a hard and exhausting day. Directly off the port bow, a set of ominous low black clouds with a dense skirt of rain stippled a sea that was being whipped white from the volatile wind gusts that came with this particular tropical thunder squall.

It had been an unusually rolley night and I suspected that sleep was fleeting for most of the crew. Kara looked rather haggard this particular morning but oddly content as she nursed her morning cup of hot chocolate while wedged into the corner of the cockpit. With her harness's lanyard securely wrapped around a jib winch to prevent her from sliding off the seat with each of *Maiatla's* deep rhythmic rolls, she appeared to be, for the most part, eager to embrace her morning watch.

"Hate to disturb you Kara, but I think we need to take in some of the headsail. You pull the furling line as I ease the sheet." I pointed out the approaching squall and our need to reduce sail in preparation for the wind gusts I was sure were coming.

Shortly after taking in a third of the headsail the winds hit with authority, veering sharply while gusting up from 25 to 35 knots causing the sails to luff and whip with such ferocity that a batten in the mizzen tore out of its pocket as the entire rig shook violently. Kara disengaged Auto and hand steered to follow the change of wind as I clambered onto to the aft deck to quickly douse the mizzen before she tore herself completely apart. Moments later, the deluge started and before I could finish securing the sail to the mizzen boom, I was soaked to the skin by the cold stinging rain.

Thirty minutes after her unceremonious arrival, the squall departed as abruptly as she had come, leaving behind a confused sea and a thick, "stick to your clothes" humidity. The sun once again made an appearance by shining in "spokes" through the broken cloud cover.

With the mizzen out of action and Auto again maintaining our course, Kara and I shook out the second reef of the main, then allowing the headsail to unfurl to her full breadth. The excitement of the morning squall was repeated often this day as a steady procession of squalls paraded over the horizon, striking us on an average of every two hours or so. The repeated handling of sails soon had everyone aboard fit to be tied as the boat worked us like rented mules.

Despite the challenging conditions, we still managed to log 155 nautical miles in 24 hours. There was still a lot of open ocean that separated us from our destination but at least we had finally reached what we had been seeking, the northeast tradewinds which were now poised to help us on our pilgrimage.

Chapter #6

The Poop

On life's vast ocean diversely we sail,
Reason the card, but passion is the gale.
- Alexander Pope

Seventeen days out and we were now firmly locked into the trades as we logged a solid 165 miles in the previous 24 hours. However, both the boat and crew were looking the worse for wear from all the hard work and withering heat. The sea's temper was inflamed and she was running high and full of barn-door breakers, 3-4 meters most of the time and the odd 5-meter wave just to keep us awake by knocking us about. Jackie and Kara commenced being seasick and it was obvious from their shrunken postures and sallow complexions that they both wanted this trip to end. They had that, *"Stop the boat I want to get off!"* look on their faces.

The blustery rain squalls continued as if programmed to do so and around noon the gut wrenching sound of tearing cloth summoned us to action as our old mainsail finally gave up the ghost as it split horizontally, the full-length of the boom, along the first set of reef points. Threads and bits of sailcloth fluttered downwind like the entrails of a slaughtered beast caught in a whirlwind of cataclysms. Kara and I quickly reefed the sail down to the second set of reef points and re-trimmed the shortened sail. I had suspected that the old mainsail would fail somewhere along this voyage so in anticipation, I had ordered a new main from Lee Sails in Hong Kong just prior to departing home. I was now hoping the old, reefed-down main would carry us the rest of the way to Hawaii, I was not looking forward to fitting the new, untried sail in these conditions.

As the log below indicates, our last few days at sea were trying ones. Log excerpt:

June 15, 2007 0800hr
Took a large wave on the leeward deck this morning, it startled Kara as she was sitting on the low side of the cockpit at the time and would have gotten soaked if the dodger had not been closed.

Closed all portholes to keep out the spray, which is now more regular so the heat and humidity below is pretty ugly.

Still overcast but hot and humid. A few sea birds swooping down but otherwise an empty sea.
Sump pump for shower is also on the fritz but didn't realize it until everyone had a shower. Shower water dumped into the bilge, Will try and fix today as well.
Sailing well under half a headsail and a single reef in the main, doing 7-8 knots. Sea is very confused.

1800hrs
While waiting to report to the net we took a wave up the port side, striking the galley window with a great thud. A large amount of water poured down the open hatch and soaked me while sitting at the galley table waiting to do the net, computer just missed a direct hit.

June 16 2007
It was a rough and windy day. Big seas 3 and 4 meters with a nasty cross chop. Still cloudy with lots of little rainsqualls. Most uncomfortable day. Wind 20 to 30 knots odd gust to 40.
Spotted a ship on radar but couldn't pick him out of the waves. At least I knew he was out there somewhere. Spent the whole day sailing under headsail alone. But after the 8 pm net wind and seas dropped a bit so we hoist the mizzen, less one batten, sailing good at 6-7 knots.

June 17, 2007
Lots of wind to day and big seas. Gust up to 30 knots and waves pushing 3 meters. Very rough on the boat today but the crews spirits are still up but they are looking forward to our landfall in a couple of days. We are only 325 miles out of Maui and at the rate we are traveling we should be hitting harbor around noon on Monday.

I checked on the water situation today and found that we were pretty low. An investigation of the shower revealed that it was running at a good trickle. I could only presume whoever had the last shower a couple of days ago didn't turn it off all the way. So I'm running the engine and making water. Wind seems to be dropping a little and the seas are lying down so I hope we will have a more comfortable night tonight. I dropped the mizzen this morning and found that another batten had ripped out of the sail. I found the batten on the deck so I will just have to sew it back in later.

June 18, 2007. The tropical squalls made for a remarkably filthy night last night with zero visibility, perhaps the blackest night that I have ever known. Maiatla heroically yet blindly charged on while smothered in a quilt of absolute darkness. It was comforting to know that the sea around us, save for a few fishing boats, the odd freighter and perhaps a sleeping whale or two, was largely empty which was confirmed by the enigmatic sweeps of the radar.

It would have been more than nerve-wracking to be sailing blindly through an area strewn with uncharted reefs and unlit coral atolls as the early explorers had done. Aside from the Hawaiian chain in the central Pacific, the vast portion of the North Pacific encompasses an emptiness that is cosmic in nature and almost defies the imagination's ability to conceive its vastness. The North Pacific is virtually an endless sea of wind driven, undulating dunes, mindlessly charging from horizon to horizon. An unbroken expanse stretching for over five thousand nautical miles from the misty shores of the Pacific Northwest to Russia's rugosa rose scented shores of the Island of Shikotan.

In total contrast, the South Pacific contains in excess of thirty thousand islands and countless reefs and to study the chart, it would appear as if you could day-hop, beach to beach, from the Marquises all the way to Australia, almost six thousand nautical miles. If you were to take a chart of the Pacific and put a pin prick at every island and reef, the chart, when held up to the sun, would appear strikingly like a map of heavenly constellations.

In a remarkable example of purely bad luck, Ferdinand Magellan, after circumnavigating Cape Horn by the Straights of Magellan in 1520, managed to navigate almost the entire breadth of the South Pacific without sighting a single island or wrecking upon any reef. His crew were suffering from scurvy, starvation and thirst, after sailing almost ten thousand miles in over ninety days; Magellan finally sited the island of their salvation, Guam in the Marianas. Magellan would record in his log that the Pacific was a vast empty wasteland and he was determined never to challenge its expanse again. The western world would have to wait over two hundred years before discovering what eluded Magellan, the volcanic isles and coral atolls; the jewels of the South Pacific.

****

The rain and wind squalls refused to give us a break and we spent the night hoisting and dropping sails while listening to the big waves slap up our stern with a great thud, then hiss as the sea retreated. The ripped main still seemed to be holding up but the mizzen sail suffered another grave insult as the last of her three battens poked a hole through the sail, and like a single particle of confetti in a hurricane, fluttered downwind to be lost forever. Likewise, the clew on our big headsail split so we had to take it down and put up our smaller, No. 3 (storm) headsail. More damaged gear to have repaired once we raised landfall.

By midnight I was more than ready for my bunk when Jackie and Jim reported topside to relieve Kara and myself. I was exhausted so I just stripped off my wet clothes and didn't bother to towel off the salt water before I crawled into my damp and funky smelling bunk that hadn't seen a clean sheet since our departure. I was "baching" it.

The left-over adrenalin from having to unfurl and wrestle the big headsail off the headstay foil and bag it, was still pumping through my veins, the vibrating rush making sleep near impossible despite my fatigue.

As I lay in the dark listening to the boat, I was amazed by the variety of sounds that penetrated the hull and deck, the moans and rattlings of *Maiatla's* cloistered ghosts. I could hear the wind build then die in puffs and pants like the breath of some great sea beast. If you focused on the whining wind you would swear that you could hear faint rhythmic feminine voices calling out, beckoning. It was easy to imagine the voices were the sirens of ancient sea lore. The legendary sea nymphs that lured lonely and desperately horny sailors to their doom.

I snuggled deeper into my sheets all the while listening to the reverberation of the rain pelting the deck and reaching sails, the constant rush of water as it streamed over *Maiatla's* guiding rudder and the elevated pitch of muddled and anxious voices from the darkened cockpit. Each quarter of the boat possessed its own collage of distinct sounds, grunts, squeaks and laments that resonated throughout. The rattle of the dishes in the galley cupboards, the whining chatter of the engine rooms' autopilot as it fought to maintain its programmed course, the creak of the straining mainsheet block as a gust pressed the canvas, or the sloshing of boarding seas as they escaped through the leeward deck scuppers. A mélange of sounds all overshadowed by the rapid tapping of a slack halyard against the foremast, a rapid rhythmic beating like the heart of a frightened bird. They were all sounds that long ago had become so familiar that it was impossible not to take comfort in them despite their apparent aggravating nature.

    I was almost asleep when a particularly large wave climbed up the stern then dropped onto our deck with a thud and a crash sending shivers through the boat and corresponding chills through me. For a moment I lay listening for any indication of panic from the watch crew or sounds that may indicate that the boat was in trouble. Seconds passed into minutes and I had just decided that *Maiatla* had taken and survived the wave unscathed when a new and ominous sound began creeping into my consciousness, a thumping that was neither rhythmic nor comforting and it was coming from the stern.

    Quickly I dressed and bolted topside, flicking on the spreader lights as I went. My appearance surprised Jackie and Jim who were also straining to see what had happened. Foolishly not taking time to put on a harness, I slipped outside the dodger and crawled my way aft to peer over the stern where I was shocked to find the dinghy davits empty. Apparently the large wave had come aboard and claimed our venerable old dink.

    I braced myself and leaned over the transom where I found our dinghy being dragged behind *Maiatla* by its one remaining set of falls, she was safe and afloat for the moment but with every wave that caught us, our dinghy surfed down the face only to slam hard against the hull with a great bang.

    "Jim…. Jackie furl the headsail" I yelled," drop the main and mizzen while I try and keep the dink from torpedoing us!"

    While the sails were coming down, I attempted to keep the dink from pounding herself to pieces and retrieved the dinghy's bow line by leaning precariously out over the side with my head just centimeters from the rushing water. All the while straining to see beyond the flood of light in search of the next wave that would board us, or take me away. About the time the boat came to a stop, I had the dinghy's painter in my hand. I called to Jim to bring me a knife to cut the remaining falls. Once done, I managed to pull the little boat along the leeward side.

    Now that *Maiatla* was effectively hove to, the apparent wind gusted to new heights and armed with stinging rain, was now ripping through the rigging at a steady 40 knots; with the 4 meter waves on our beam just trying to stay on the wet deck demanded real footwork. I had Jim and Jackie hold the dink alongside while I retrieved the spinnaker halyard. By lying on the deck and leaning precariously over the side, I managed to secure the snap shackle on the halyard, to the dinghy painter's eyebolt; she was now ready to haul aboard.

Jim and I manned the halyard winch and began to crank. Just when it looked like we were going to succeed in salvaging our little boat, another monster wave, the brethren to the one that first attempted to claim the dink struck us a hard blow amidships, the force of which propelled *Maiatla* sideways, causing her to roll heavily to starboard. Jackie and I, who had a better grip, grabbed Jim as he was being thrown in the direction of the open sea. We saved Jim from diving into the waves but the halyard was in turn released and raced out in the process.

By the time we all recovered our balance, I discovered that the slide sideways had driven *Maiatla* overtop of the dinghy which was now totally flooded and completely under the boat.

"Quick, Jim! Crank on the winch again!" I called, as I madly tailed the winch.

Jim began to frantically work the winch and just when the bow of our dinghy was again visible, a great "Snap!" rang out above the wind and the dink fell back into the sea. The spinnaker halyard block had burst under the great strain, allowing the dinghy to sink away while taking ten meters of halyard with it. Jim and I both grabbed the line as it raced over the side and quickly tied it off to the nearest stanchion.

After finding new hand holds we all paused to catch our breath. The dinghy was now completely under the boat and there was a sickening sound emanating from beneath our feet as our tender started to pound the hull directly in front of the rudder. Fearing it would damage us and not wanting to risk losing anyone over the side in these black conditions, I decided it was best to cut the dinghy loose. Retrieving the knife from my pocket I slashed at the taut line.

I listened to the heavy fiberglass dink clunk the rest of the way under the boat and harmlessly pass the vulnerable rudder and propeller shaft. I was relieved to finally see the dink resurface just beyond our stern. She had turned turtle and was barely afloat. But it was free of us and would cause no further harm. We didn't have time to mourn the dink's loss; we were laying broadside to the waves and very susceptible to boarding seas, we needed to get *Maiatla* back underway before another wave decided to climb aboard and punch in a galley window.

I spun the wheel as Jackie and Jim went about unfurling and setting the headsail. Once back underway with a reefed main and the jibe poled back out, I suddenly realized that Kara, was nowhere to be seen.

With all the commotion it would have been near impossible to sleep. I suddenly felt sick to my stomach and my bowels loosened. It suddenly occurred to me that she may have come on deck to help and had fallen overboard unnoticed. I gazed back at our churning wake and the towering seas as illuminated by the spreader lights. The odds of recovering a person that had gone overboard on this bleak night was close to nil. I engaged Auto and bolted down below, bursting into Kara's cabin fearing the worst, but I was relieved to find her tightly cocooned in her berth with the lee-cloth in place to prevent her from being hurled out. Startled, Kara glared at me with wide questioning eyes.

"Is everything alright?" She asked.

I was relieved to find her aboard and safe but curious as to why she had not come topside to lend a hand.

"Yes, everything is fine, but didn't you here all the shit going on topside?"

"Ya, I did, but I thought if you needed me you would have called."

I just laughed and told her good night.

The loss of our hard shell dinghy had me upset but since it wasn't the first tender that we have donated to the sea, it didn't hit me too hard and fortunately, we always carry a spare in the form of a rollup inflatable for just such an emergency. At least we would still be able to row ashore when we arrived in Hawaii.

After hearing this story, several other sailors asked me why had I left the dinghy swinging in the davits when I went offshore? Would it not have been safer strapped to the deck in an inverted position? It was a question I had asked myself and in hindsight....

On our first offshore foray in *Maiatla* I had the dink on deck while sailing from Vancouver to San Francisco and at that time, we didn't encounter any seas that even remotely came close to endangering the dink, and likewise while getting pummeled by hurricane Alma off the coast of Mexico a year later, the dink stayed put in the davits, so I felt confident leaving her to swing on this voyage. That said, we also had seas climb aboard that could have ripped the dinghy off the deck as well, so which ever method was better would be dictated by the type and condition of the seas and perhaps just dumb luck.

****

Paradoxical is the only way I can describe the powerful feelings I experience after a long sea passage and when landfall is imminent. When the realization strikes that I have actually completed the voyage successfully and survived (not meaning to sound melodramatic but voyaging is nothing if not an exercise in survival against the elements), I'm always bursting with conflicting and extremely contrary emotions with meteoric mood swings resembling that of a manic-depressive.

The sight of land first conveys a sense of triumph, unabashed jubilation, and a narcosis similar in effect to that experienced by divers breathing nitrogen-rich air at great depths, which causes a state of blissful euphoria and general sense of wellbeing. This manic state, in turn spawns the dire need to celebrate which usually entails, on my part anyway, the consumption of copious quantities of rum and making a fool of myself.

Nevertheless, the party is usually short lived and as sure as each coin boasts two sides, likewise there is a flip side to my euphoria. Despite the ordeal of the passage, there is always a part of me that hates to see the conclusion of the voyage, the conclusion of our routine and camaraderie. To be faced once again with the prospect of having to deal with the netherworld automatons that typically infest the shore, not unlike the mindless maggots that swarm a bloated corpse, our arrivals habitually spawn depressing thoughts within me.

However, these shores where supposed to be the gateway to the islands of paradise as promised by Melville and Twain; I was hoping to find individuals that possessed a freer, friendlier and more adventurous spirit amongst the natives. I would be disappointed and at times I wonder why I freely do this? Do I truly do it of my own free will or is there some malevolent beast that compels me to set sail, just to test my character? Do any of us actually possess free will? I have my doubts. I recall a quote by the American author and inventor Isaac Bashevis Singer who said: "We have to believe in free will, we have no choice".

Figure 8.   The eight main islands of Hawaii

I have recently become aware of the concept; the idea of free will, and what part it plays in our lives. We make decisions every day. What time do I get up? What show do I watch on TV? Should I sell the house, buy a boat and sail away? The fact that we deliberate and think of ourselves as deciding what to do demonstrates that we think of ourselves as having free will, the freedom to decide for ourselves while believing that we have real options, real choices to make, and why not? We _are_ truly free human beings, aren't we?

If we believe in free will, we must also support the concept of morality. When you praise or condemn people on their actions, you assume that they had a choice in the matter and choose to be good or bad. However, praise and blame make no sense unless people had real choices in the first place. So ergo, without freedom, there can't be any morality. This argument can be applied to the soldiers working the Nazi death camps. Were they morally culpable for their actions or were they devoid of any real choice?

We all naturally believe that we are free. We naturally believe that the future is wide open to us and we can be whatever we want it to be. I would suggest that this is a universal view held by most (excuse the pun) free thinkers. Yet, when you look in depth into the concept of free will, you may see that it is all just an illusion; that we are not truly free after all, not in a meaningful way that would truly count. No doubt, our belief in free will is important, but do we actually control it? Deep down, we all want to believe that we can shape our world and make a difference in our lives and the lives of others.

It's remarkable that we think of ourselves as being free considering that for a large portion of our lives, the most formative of our years we have absolutely no control over our lives whatsoever. We have no say when where we were born, or who or what race our parents were. We have no say in our parents parenting style, finances, beliefs, or prejudices. We have no say in what sex we are, or what religious affiliation we are raised in. Our friends and classmates are chosen by geography and more importantly we have no choice as to whether we would ultimately die.

When you take in account all the things that we didn't have any control over in the first part of our lives, nature, nurture, and environment, it's amazing that we consider ourselves free at all. But that all changes when we are an adult right? Wrong! Long before you even think about leaving your daddy's house, the netherworld has already been boring deep into your psyche, programming your mind to conform - preparing you to be integrated into the Borg society, the collective netherworld mindset.

Our concept of free will is challenged on a daily basis and most of us don't even realize it; not by Nazi despots or religious cults but by mainstream beliefs and our own spiritual leaders and teachings. People swear and live by biblical prophecy. There are tens of millions who also believe in clairvoyants, people who can see into the future, people who see our lives, not as they are but as what they will be in the future. If you are one of the above then you will have a hard time arguing that you have free will.

If God has a plan for the human race, if we have a destiny to fulfill, if biblical prophecies foretell the coming of the anti-Christ and the ultimate destruction of the world, if a clairvoyant says that on April 3rd, 2057, I will be shot dead in bed by a jealous husband (I should be so lucky- sorry honey), then no matter what decision I make, I'm doomed. If no matter what road I choose, it leads me back to face a shot gun in a strange women's bed, then, no matter what moral decision I make, I **will be** splattered all over the head board and humanity will ultimately be trampled by the four horses of the apocalypse as prophesised. An ordained fate or prearranged destiny is the stake driven through the very heart of free will. If you believe your life is already laid before you, then you cannot possibly claim to possess free will! How can your choices have real meaning? If no matter how you choose to toss a coin and it always comes up heads, then being free to choose how to flip the coin is worthless, meaningless.

I was sitting in the cockpit late one night, on my watch, precisely where were we were at the time, I cannot say, except that we were closer to Maui than Vancouver. I had been wading my way through an abridged version of Plato's Republic when I began to think of the choices that I had made in my life and about the concept of free will. I would later try to explain my views on the subject to Kara one night but I believe I miserably failed. I latter contrived an analogy which I hoped would demonstrate my point. If you think of life and society as being a box, with the four walls, a floor and ceiling representing all the things which determine who we are, i.e. genetics, upbringing, geography and the like, then you place a cat into the box to represent us as free thinking people. That cat can freely choose where it walks, where it sleeps, it can choose whether it stands or stretches and where it defecates. It exerts its free will to do whatever it wants, but can you really say it has free will within the constraints of the four-sided box? Granted the netherworld is much more complicated, multifaceted but it is our box nonetheless.

Do I believe in God? Do I believe he has a plan for man? A destiny for me? I'm going to wimp out here, mostly. Do I believe in free will? The ability to make meaningful choices that bring real meaning to my life? Again, mostly.

All the great philosophers throughout the ages have contemplated this question and still with all that deep thinking gray matter, there is no general consensus on this subject. So, I guess I fall into prodigious company when I claim not to have the answer to this question either. But it's an interesting exercise in reasoning. So you may ask, what does all this have to do with sailing to Hawaii? As I said in an earlier chapter, if you get anything out of cruising it's time to reflect and ask questions. It gives you an opportunity to philosophize about your own life. But to what end you may ask? Does philosophizing have any real purpose? Is it practical? See, this is a philosophical question! And yes, it can be practical if it helps you to realize your goals, if it helps you to know who you are and what life in this world is all about.

****

By midnight the trade winds gave their final gasps as the seas began to abate and it was now a pleasant sail. Although I'm sure he pulled his punches, it was as if Poseidon finally conceded that we were actually going to succeed and decided to calm the waters in tribute to a fight well fought.. It was Pierrie Corneille (1806-1864) the French tragic dramatist that said, *"Triumph without peril brings no glory";* and with our destination finally in reach we all were certainly feeling glorious with a sense of achievement.

I know no other place to encounter a sense of satisfaction and self-worth then on a small vessel at sea. I am not talking about the kind of achievement that comes with winning a ball game, trophies or gaining that big promotion or any other kind of achievement that must come with world applause to have any meaning. I'm talking of the type of achievement that is deep and personal and only has value to you, an intrinsic value. It comes with no applause or accolades, but when viewed in retrospect, fills your heart with warmth and pride forcing a smile to cross your face so pronounced that onlookers might think you simple minded. Successfully birthing your children is the kind of achievement I am talking about. I often think of one particular achievement, and it fills me full of pride whenever I pull it from my special repository.

****

We were beating against the ass end of hurricane Alma off the coast of Mexico as hurricane Boris threatened us from behind, as we fought to gain southern ground in an effort to get out of harm's way. For twelve days, my family and I battled the elements until we were beyond exhausted. On which particular day during this ordeal I'm referring too, I do not recall, as they all seem to meld together into one great set of blurry recollections, but it was well into it when it occurred.

I had gone down below for something to eat, and it was my turn for sleep, as I clung to a grab rail to keep from being hurled about the galley, I happened to look out the companionway to see my watch relief at the helm of *Maiatla*. Melissa who was eleven at the time was dressed in all her foulies and girthed with a life harness clipped to the ship, she sat in the captain's chair with her hands firmly on the wheel. She could not hear the wind that screamed like banshees ripping at the canvass dodger as she had headphones on and as she sat there, her head bobbing to tunes that only she could hear. Next to her was my fourteen year old son, Thomas, likewise battened down and tethered in, as he feverishly thumbed his Gameboy, all the while the storm ripped sheets of water from the waves. Our two children were then responsible for *Maiatla* and all the lives aboard her, a responsibility that they routinely and readily accepted as a netherworld child would accept a paper route or mowing the lawn.

I swelled with great achievement that day, not because my seamanship had saved us from the storm, but because I was able to see my two children, sitting blissfully in the cockpit and confidently in command of their whole world. I went to my bunk and slept.

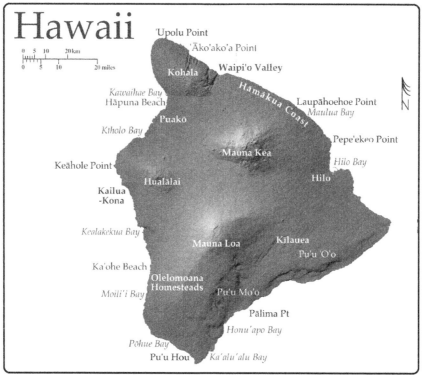

Figure 9.   Hawaii the "Big Island" where captain Cook was killed in 1779

As we approached the Hawaiian Islands, I realized that Jackie, Jim and Kara had accomplished what remarkably few have done and lived to tell the tale. Sailing across the expanse of the Pacific was a grand achievement for them, and me as well.

By midnight on our 21st night at sea, the lights of the Big Island of Hawaii were clearly visible off our port beam. I was now regretting my decision to bypass Hilo in favor of a Maui landing. We would miss seeing the active flow of the volcano Mauna Loa and the Kona Coast where Captain Cook was killed and dismembered in 1779 by the local inhabitants at Kealakekua Bay. I had been uncertain of our arrival date in the islands, and flight arrangements for my crew flying out and my family flying in to join the boat was easier made through Maui.

The Island of Hawaii, called the Big Island, is volcanic and the southeastern-most in the Hawaiian Islands chain in the North Pacific Ocean. It is larger than all of the other main Hawaiian Islands combined, making it the grandest island in all the United States. The Island's greatest dimension is 150 km (93 miles) across and has a land area of 4,028 square miles, comprising 62% of the Hawaiian Islands' total land area. The Island of Hawaii is built from five separate shield volcanoes that erupted somewhat sequentially, one overlapping the other, forming an island roughly the shape of an arrowhead.

Under a full press of sail, *Maiatla* chased the sliver of a moon to the west and our destination that lay just beyond the horizon, still sixty-odd miles to the west.

Chapter #7

Maui Landfall

"I have visited, a great many years ago, the Sandwich Islands-that peaceful land, that beautiful land, that far-off home of profound repose, and soft indolence, and dreamy solitude, where life is one long slumbrous Sabbath, the climate one long delicious summer day, and the good that die experience no change, for they but fall asleep in one heaven and wake up in another." Mark Twain.

It first appeared as a pencil thin line on the horizon, the towering volcanic summit of Haleakala grew until the verdant landscape filled the western horizon. The crew was thrilled and spent the early morning hours watching the burgundy sunrise over our shoulders as the golden light illuminated the rugged north shore of Maui. The Island was crowned with puffy tumbling clouds that appeared positively primeval, a palace fit for the Island's gods.

The ragged extreme top of the extinct volcano, Haleakala, (House of the Sun) was shrouded in a gauze of mist, a fluid translucent veil, it's naked black shoulders, streaked with cascading waterfalls, tumbled downward until the delicate verdant lace of the tropical rainforest, sparsely at first, claimed the lower and gentler plains of the ancient mountain.

As the landscape reached the sea, the dense yet intermittently broken jungle canopy permited sporadic peeks at the underlying black rock and antediluvian lava flows. An avalanche of leafy-green tapestry abruptly came to a halt high above the sea-foam and spray of the ocean. An isolated fortress protected by jagged and crumbling precipices, eons old, the citadel walls cut and slashed by the torrential rains of countless wet seasons, pounding waves and the occasional tectonically generated tsunami. Maui bares the knurly and weathered features of a gristly old man, living in the balmiest place on earth.

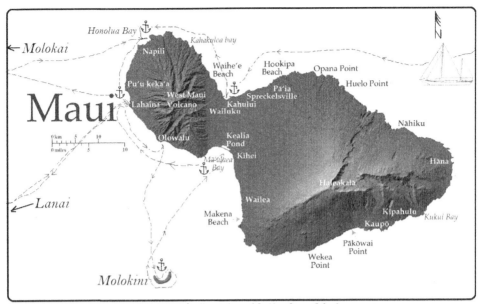

Figure 10. Maui, *Maiatla's* first landfall after 21 days at sea

Aside from the goat trail that has the audacity to be called the "Hana Highway"; a narrow road that concedes to the will of every crack and crevice of the terrain as it twists and winds along the cliff face, or the plantation style homes that scar the hillsides, the scene has changed little in the few hundred years since Captain Cook's time, or for even the past thousand for that matter.

Hawaiian oral tradition seems to indicate that Spanish castaways, most likely, shipwrecked sailors, landed on the island of Maui sometime between 1521 and 1530. Versions of this story are told throughout the chain, from Hawaii itself all the way to Kauai, giving some credence to Spain's claim to have discovered the islands some two hundred years before England. In the Maui version, several white men and a woman were shipwrecked during the reign of King Kakaalaneo at Kiwi near Waihee. The men married, and had families, becoming ancestors of some of the islands great chiefs.

These claims although unproven, are likely, as Spanish ships regularly sailed between Asia and Mexico or South America; their westerly route passing to the south of the islands, and north of the chain on their return voyage. However, officially, the first European to see Maui was Captain James Cook, when on November 26, 1778, he raised the Island, but Cook never set foot on the shore because as recorded in the ship's log that he was unable to find a suitable landing. Cook must have had more pressing matters elsewhere because Maui boasts many beaches and is by far the most accessible Island from a landing stand point. The first European to visit Maui was the French admiral Jean-François de La Pérouse, who landed on the southeast shore of what is now known as La Perouse Bay on May 29, 1786.

The island of Maui is 40 miles long from east to west and 25 miles wide from north to south, making Maui the second largest of the Hawaiian Islands and the 17th largest island in the United States at 727.2 square miles. Maui is also the second youngest island in the Hawaiian chain and it is interesting to note that the Island has hundreds of streams, a few which are navigable by small boat or canoe but none that are considered to be rivers. When I discovered this little fact, I went on to try and learn the difference between a stream and a river which I thought would be an easy task, but I was wrong. Even Webster's Dictionary is vague in its descriptions. The only consensus seems to be is that both rivers and streams are natural flowing bodies of water with the only difference being the volume of water they transport, but again, no hard numbers are offered as a guide so it would appear that this question is subjective.

The 2010 census sets Maui's permanent population at 144,444, with only Oahu and Hawaii boasting more bodies per square mile. Maui's diverse landscape is the result of a unique combination of geology, topography, and climate. Each volcanic cone in the chain of the Hawaiian Islands is comprised of dark, iron-rich/quartz-poor rocks, which poured out of thousands of volcanic vents over a period of millions of years.

The Island of Maui was formed when two volcanoes were close enough to each other that lava flows on their flanks overlapped one another, merging into a single island with a broad plain forming between. The older, western volcano has been eroded considerably and is cut by numerous streams, forming the peaks of the West Maui Mountains with its highest peaks rising to 1,764 m (5,788 feet). The larger, younger and more noted volcano to the east, Haleakalā, significantly dwarfs its neighbor, climbing to more than 3,000 m (10,000 feet) above sea level, but if measured from its base at the seafloor, the volcano is more than 8km (5 miles) tall, making it one of the world's highest "mountains". Haleakalā's last eruption occurred around 1790 which resulted in hundreds of deaths. Although considered dormant by volcanologists, the Island's volcanoes are capable of further eruptions.

****

It has been almost ten years since I last viewed these calling shores. It was shortly after a malignant melanoma; a particularly nasty and typically, life-ending tumor, had been excised from my ear, and after the doctor's pronouncement that the cancer would "probably not" take my life; that I last ventured here. Emotionally relieved at the doc's assertion, while simultaneously feeling naked, mortal, and utterly vulnerable from the attack, not to mention extremely paranoid; Janet and I had fled to these peaceful shores to rethink our life's plan. It was on this island's pink and black sand beaches that the decision to change our lives was formulated then a short time later, acted upon.

****

The cancer and more so, Maui had inexplicably changed us, changed me, all those years ago and returning now was like re-visiting an old friend and mentor. We ultimately set sail and became "cruisers", a life that suits our style and a course, until this very day, that our hearts still steer. I was happy to be back!

There is an inexplicable thrill in setting off across great oceans bound for distant shores, leaving the vulgarity and pettiness of the netherworld far behind with nothing but the barest of essentials necessary for sustaining yourself and your family for what could be months at a stretch. Entering a world that does not bear the obvious scars that are all so often left by the heavy hand of man. Reveling in the abundance of raw, and at times, violent nature.

The shear vastness of the oceanic seascape and isolated tropical isles has a way of putting all human effort, wants, needs and challenges into perspective, creating the kind of lucidity of mind that can only be found on wind swept mountain tops, cloistered monasteries or in near death experiences.

****

I must have still been ripping through the manic stage of my arrival ritual because something compelled me to root around below for something to wear that looked "Hawaiian". Frantically, I searched until I found an outfit that seemed to fit the bill. Quickly donning a green and black flower print dress that Janet had tucked away (I would later feel her wrath for stretching the dress out!), I then garnished it with a couple of leis that Melissa had brought home from a Hawaiian theme pool party held at our local recreation center, back in Mission. I topped off my costume with my wide brimmed "Tilley", I must have made quite a sight but the indignity I suffered through while wearing such garb was well worth it. Climbing back into the cockpit, everyone laughed which was the effect I was shooting for. Kara had trouble containing herself as she reluctantly posed for a picture with me up on the bow with the Island of Maui as the backdrop. My stunt aided in the emotional release; many of the hardships of the voyage were already starting to fade into the back recesses of our memories.

The north shore of Maui is very abrupt, rugged with only a single harbor that can provide a safe haven for weary sailors and the only official port of entry on this side of the Island. Maui is a figure-eight shaped island with its head about one third the size of its base and it is in the dimple between head and base that the busy harbor of Kahului is located. The northeast shore is on the wetter, windward side of the Island and greenery dominates the landscape all the way up the steep slopes to an elevation where the duo of extinct volcanoes, that *are* the Island of Maui, decide the vegetation has encroached far enough.

We cruised close to the beach as *Maiatla* ran westward down the north shore in an effort to get a better look, while being careful to swing wide around Pauwela and Papaula Points, as reefs extend quite far offshore. The white teeth of the breakers appeared, grinning, just to port. To run aground on a lee shore, at this stage, would not only be embarrassing but judging from the size of the crashing waves, could and most likely would prove to be fatal for both boat and crew.

Kahului is the largest community on the Island and it sprawls along the north shore of central Maui. The community hosts Maui's main airport-Kahului Airport, along with a deep-draft harbor, light industrial areas, and commercial shopping centers. There is a resident population of over 22,000 with a racial makeup approximately thirty percent white, or persons having origins in any of the original peoples of Europe, the Middle East, or North Africa which includes immigrant souls with Irish, German, Italian, Near Easterner, Arab, or Polish ancestry. A further thirty percent are of Asian decent, primarily Fillipino who make up the largest Asian group on Maui, followed not too closely by the Japanese. Surprisingly, only eleven percent of residents can claim Pacific Islander heritage, with Tongan Islanders being the most prevalent, the remainder consists of African Blacks, Native Americans and Hispanics of mainly Mexican decent. Maui, is reported to be one of the most racially diverse places in the world. Twenty-four percent are of multi-ethnic background, more than any other in the US. Today there are less than 8,000 "pure" Hawaiians, and that number could be as low as 5,000. There are, however, as many as 275,000 "native" Hawaiians spread thought the chain. Officially, a native Hawaiian is someone who has at least 50% Hawaiian blood.

Kahului is the retail center for Maui residents and there are several malls and major stores (including department stores in the Queen Kaahumanu Center); retailing changed greatly here with the recent arrival of big-box retailers from the U.S. mainland, including Wal-Mart and Home Depot, making it an ideal place for cruisers to re-provision after a long ocean passage.

I called the harbour master on the radio and identified ourselves, and requested permission to enter the harbor. Needless to say, I was shocked when the otherwise polite gentlemen refused us entry and informed me that this harbor facility was for commercial vessels only and that I would have to sail around the Island and check in at Lahaina on the south shore. For us, that meant another 30 miles and a night arrival in an unfamiliar anchorage, not to mention, an up-wind beat, into stiff tradewinds as we rounded the western end of the Island. I was not happy, and I wasn't about to give up so easily, thinking quickly, I keyed the mike.

"Kahului harbor master, this is the sailing vessel *Maiatla* again. We have been at sea for 21 days, we are extremely low on water and fuel, we are having engine troubles and have sustained some rig damage. We need to land to affix repairs and to take on water. Is there anywhere else nearby we can land?" All that I had asserted was true; however, the direness of our situation was grossly exaggerated. I knew there wasn't another place for us to land; I was wagering on him taking pity on us.

I was again politely told to stand by and for several minutes we circled just outside the breakwater waiting for a response.

"Damn it!" I said to no one in particular while making sure the mike was keyed off. "I want to get to shore for a steak and then I need to sink my ass into the soft sand of some beach while clutching four Vulcan fingers of Captain Morgan!"

Finally, the harbor hailed us.

"OK, skipper. How long do you think you need to stay to do your repairs?" I thought for a moment before responding.

"Should be able to get back underway in three days or so, so long as I can get the parts I need for the engine."

Three days I thought would be reasonable, they can't possibly refuse me that much time… in reality, I would have been grateful for just a single night in port, secured to an immovable dock where I didn't have to worry over the boat breaking down or running into something hard. The stiff trades taught us the beauty of a sheltered harbour.

"We should be able to accommodate you for that long, but we have a cruise ship coming in and you will have to wait until it's secured to the passenger terminal before you can enter, and you must stand off her by at least 100 yards, is that understood?" His voice suddenly turning stern, almost menacing.

"Cruise ship? What cruise ship?" I said aloud, as I turned back to the open sea.

It was immense and only half a mile behind us, and closing fast! The *Pride of America* was impressive in size but what assaulted my eyes was the gaudy, Hawaiian floral scene depicting idyllic Island life that sprawled along its entire length. Palms, flowers, and parrots all in vivid tropical colors. I couldn't help thinking that it looked like Walt Disney had thrown up in Technicolor all along the ship's side.

I wheeled *Maiatla* around and bore away to give the ship the clearance the harbor master demanded and just to make sure that we complied, a red, US Coastguard inflatable motored out to take station between us and the cruise ship. The little high speed boat boasted a very menacing tri-pod mounted machine gun with a pimple-faced guardsmen attached who stood rigidly in the bow while keeping the business end of his weapon pointed in our general direction. I believe his sole task was to prevent us from assaulting the ship and we all hoped that the youth was not too eager to unleash a hail of bullets. I could only guess we looked menacing or that they were fearful that we would somehow interfere in the scabrous business of the port.

We were eventually given clearance to enter and we were instructed to proceed to the head of the dock and tie alongside directly in front of the harbor office that looked remarkably like an airport control tower.

Figure 11. A weary but happy crew to have finally made shore at Kahului, Maui - Jim, Jackie, Kara.

As we entered, the Coast Guard inflatable, with its intense looking crew sporting flack vests and automatic side-arms accompanied by multiple high capacity magazines, once again took up station between us and the now docked cruise ship.

The presence of the little, but extremely lethal gunship was direct fallout from 9/11, and the inflatable suicide attack on the *USS Cole* in the Gulf of Aden that killed seventeen US sailors, just eleven short months before the Twin Towers fell. Despite flying the friendly colors of an ally and the apparent lack of offensive assault capabilities, (spear guns and a slingshot with a full bag of marbles don't count) we would be menaced by these fast attack craft frequently throughout our travels in the islands.

As we ran bumpers and dock lines, I searched for our designated spot alongside pier number two. It was obvious where we had to go but I was not happy with the wharf's set-up. The minimal tide was out and the low water exposed the entire 8-foot diameter of the giant truck tires that the harbor was using for bumpers. I was now having second thoughts about stopping here. The well-worn tires were big, black and covered in gel-coat gouging marine growth and I was sure the decaying rubber would leave great black streaks down *Maiatla's* generally white hull, leaving her looking like a Davie Street hooker who attempted to apply mascara on a carnival's Hellevator. But, we were committed so I throttled down and prepared to go along side.

Womb-like, naturally safe, warm and welcoming like the spread wings of a long-time lover is the best way to describe a harbor, any harbor after an arduous sea journey. (Masculine interpretation-female version might include a box of chocolates and Fabio) We had truly arrived in the islands and it felt wonderful to walk ashore and stand on a surface that didn't conspire to up-end us. The tropical air was warm but instead of being laced with the delicate aromatic scent of hibiscus and coconut oil, it was the biting, acrid bouquet of diesel and harbor sludge at low tide, that assaulted our senses. Absent were the bare breasted Hula girls of the past in grass skirts placing leis about our necks, but their contemporaries were all busy performing on the adjacent dock for the well-healed guests of the *Pride of America*, with breasts piously concealed of course. Apparently, we had slunk into harbor relatively unnoticed by the local nymphs. We were not greeted by thousands of swimming mermaids eager for copulation with the white skinned demi-gods as Cook and his crew were, in fact we were greeted buy no one at all.

****

I found it interesting to note that when Captain George Vancouver and his crew visited the islands in May 1792, he found the Island ladies were much different than the ones we would encounter today, both physically and morally, or at least by European standards. Apparently, one of Vancouver's officers was a rather randy young knob by the name of Thomas Mamby, whose journal reveals that his main interest in the islands was not to trade in household chattels; no, the form of trade he had in mind was more amorous in nature. Thomas wrote, *"The girls were by no means equal in beauty to the Otahitieans (Tahitians), they are darker complexion and not so pretty featured. Instead of graceful ringlets to gratify the eye, the hair is cropped close to the head except in the fore part, where it is plastered up with lime, which gives it a dirty red colour."*

Mamby was referring here to his preference for blonds as the Tahitians had many an old Polynesian beauty secret which included bleaching of the hair, head, as well as pubic, with citrus juice. The Marquisesian women adorned themselves similar to the Tahitians but they often lathered coconut oil over their bodies to keep the skin soft and supple, it also made for a fine insect repellant. When freshly applied, the enticing coconut aroma of the women coupled with their natural beauty and insatiable sexual appetites, was hard for the seamen to resist. However, when the oil went rancid, it would have a similar effect on sailors as the insects, which may entail the holding ones breath during love making. Perhaps this is the origin of the term "Quickie". Thomas also noticed in Hawaii that all of the sexually available women were missing their front teeth, which he assumed to be some sort of fashion statement. He recorded,

"Some abominable custom has deprived every women of her fore teeth. The deuce take the inventor of such fashion.".

At this time, Thomas Mamby was unaware that a Hawaiian sign of mourning was to knock out a few teeth, even gouge out an eye if the loss was of an extreme nature. A beloved chief or member of the royal family may qualify for an ocular sacrifice. Since few people lived to adulthood without losing a loved one or family member, the entire nation sported toothless grins. In Thomas's writings he never mentioned bedding any, one-eyed toothless women, so perhaps he had drawn a line in the sand concerning the level of depravity in which he would engage. Nevertheless, if the young, randy lad was put off by the ladies' smiles, he gave no indication of it as he proudly recorded in his journal that after receiving a canoe load of "good-natured brunettes," he spent the night ashore with two beauteous nymphs. Thomas Mamby must have been quite a stud, because in the morning, each of the two young women presented him with a package containing six pearls.

****

Aside from a few prominent and strategically placed, manicured coconut palms, Kahului; with its fuel tank farm, decaying warehouses, grimy workshops and noisy delivery trucks kicking up the black and red volcanic dust, could have been any small industrial port virtually anywhere in the free world. It was scarcely the place I had left home for, but it was a welcoming site nonetheless. We had safely made landfall in Oceania and we were all eager to explore and mingle with the natives who disappointingly looked remarkably like us. Except they had better tans.

It was late afternoon and our first order of business was to meet the harbour master, who proved to be very friendly and accommodating. After paying an astonishingly reasonable fee for the privileges, he warned us that we would have to be gone by noon, three days from now because there was a fuel barge due and we were in his berth. As we discussed the terms of our stay, I noticed three women performing what looked to be clerical work behind the counter, two white the other caramel in color with beefy hips. For a moment, I thought I had found a descendant of one of Mamby's girls as she was missing one of her eye teeth. Although from her size, I had trouble imaging her swimming a mile offshore to clamber up the side of a ship only to repeat the process after performing aerobically with half the ships company. Was she a casualty of the islands mourning tradition or the victim of poor dental hygiene? Whichever the case I had trouble not staring at her great, gappy smile. We then cleared in with a surprisingly indifferent US customs officer who took one look at the oily tires and refused to climb aboard *Maiatla*. He just quickly took our details, issued *Maiatla* an Island cruising permit then departed, apparently unconcerned for the reams of contraband and endangered species or the kilos of B.C. pot still stored aboard. (I'm being sarcastic here, -----there was no pot!). Officialdom now satisfied, we were free to wander in search of a bar and restaurant where we could celebrate; apparently all were eager to find someone, anyone who would listen to our harrowing voyage to paradise.

After our first full day in port, we got most of *Maiatla's* necessary chores completed, the most important of which was the purchase of a new starter motor and battery for the engine, and drinking water. Diesel was not to be had, because all fuel was delivered by trucks, and a special "environmental permit" was required before fuel could be delivered to any boat. Apparently, a permit took the better part of a week to obtain, so we had to make do with what was remaining in our tanks. On day two, we made a few trips to Costco and Wal-Mart, which solved most of our provisioning problems, both food and liquor and a new Hawaiian sling for spearing fish. Kara even made a quick trip up the mast to reattach the radar reflector that had been ripped from its mounts by the halyard that parted when our dink decided to drop back into the ocean. That done, and a new halyard run; it was time to relax.

Just outside the north gate of the harbor compound, we were delighted to find our first tropical beach. It wasn't spectacular but the coarse sand was pink and the surf, driven by the constant trades pounded in. As we clambered over pillow lava rock to get to the beach, we passed by several locals that were fishing the surf with long poles. They were well tanned, rotund, and generally weather-beaten looking, Polynesian teens clad only in board shorts and sandals. Apparently, concern for our welfare prompted them to speak to us. The leader's slow, muddled diction was a little hard to follow at first, not unlike a Louisiana redneck with a mouth full of grits.

"Hey Haole, you'd can't swim here! Many big mano here, you go find better beach at Kihei with all the rest of the haoles!"

The big youth reeked of condescension and insincerity but lacked any truly intimidating nature. It was like being menaced by a brown Pillsbury doughboy. Even out here, in the middle of the ocean, there were schoolyard bullies posturing for his crew. But, I wasn't particularly threatened, I was confident that a swift kick to the pineapples would have him on the ground, spewing poi. He again asserted that there were many "mano"-tourist eating sharks here and that we best stick to the haole-tourist side of the island. I'm not sure what is was that gave us away as tourists, since we were all dressed in our best Hawaiian garb. It must have been our shipboard swagger and our relatively pasty-white complexions that betrayed us as new boat arrivals.

Fortunately, the rest of my crew were ahead of me and did not hear the teen's warnings. I glanced along the beach that seemed to stretch forever, and down by Papaula Point, a couple of miles distance, I could see dozens of wind surfers skipping across the surface. I pointed them out to my concerned locals.

"Why aren't the sharks attacking them"? I queried, as I pointed out the boarders.

The teen just smiled as he looked at his friends, then with a big grin he offered.

"Dem dudes wear rubber suits, manos don't like rubber, it sticks in der teef, brah!"

As I moved on, the youth flashed me the traditional shaka sign. Anyone who has visited the islands has no doubt seen the famous hand gesture coupled with the greeting "shaka, brah!" A shaka sign – the unmistakable pinky and thumb salute – is perhaps ultimate symbol of aloha and local culture in Hawaii. Interpreted to mean "hang loose" or "right on," the shaka is a constant reminder that in Hawaii, it is not the norm to worry or rush. The shaka sign represents the embodiment of "island style." It signals that everything is alright.

I flashed the shaka back, but somehow I doubted his shaka was sincere. I decided it best to keep his bit of shark dietary information to myself and secretly hoped that I wouldn't have to apologize to anyone later. Especially, Kara's mom. We placed blankets in the sand just above the high-water mark, next to an Acacia koaia. The particularly knurly windblown scrub of a tree is native to the islands and it provided limited shade against the hot sun between dips in a foaming sea.

Undaunted by the possible presence of hungry manos, I, along with the rest, ventured into the surf, all the while keeping a wary eye open for fins cutting the surface but I had heard that it was always the shark that you don't see that gets you! I've seen Jaws!

****

On one of the many bus rides to the malls, for provisions, Kara and I found ourselves talking to an elderly women from Michigan who had just arrived aboard the same cruise ship that we followed into the harbor. The women possessed the creased face of someone who was once beautiful. She appeared to be enthralled as Kara excitedly explained how we had spent three hard weeks sailing here. The women recalled seeing our boat along the quayside; suitably impressed, she asked many questions of our voyage. After some time, the old lady paused for a moment and gave both Kara and I a gauging, inquisitive glance. She then asked, with some measure of reluctance, if Kara was my wife.

After a nervous laugh, I quickly explained that Kara was simply a family friend and that our relationship was more of a father–daughter one. Kara at first appeared to taken aback by the question, I likewise wasn't sure if I should have been flattered that I could possibly look young enough to be this beautiful, 18-year-old's husband, or insulted that she could possibly believe me to be a dirty old man from some nefarious polygamist cult who had just taken a new young bride. Kara, I felt may have been a little hurt perhaps thinking that she appeared much more aged than her actual tender years.

Yet in hindsight, I believe this woman saw in Kara's shining brown eyes what Jan and I had seen when we first met her back home just a couple short years ago. Despite her petite, youthful appearance and bubbling child-like enthusiasm, Kara's eyes betrayed her "Old Soul." At the tender age of 18, she was intuitive, a young women cloaked in an aura of maturity that radiated a level of confidence that can only be gained by living a long and adventurous life. Mark Twain possessed an "Old Soul" which was evident in his many great works of literature, and likewise, when speaking to Kara, you could sense an ancient and profound presence that compelled you to consider the possibility of reincarnation, her youthful body, a vessel for the re-embodiment of not just one past life, but possibly many. It was as if long ago

Kara had found her personal center and it was a little unnerving at first, while in her presence, I couldn't help but sense that this girl had lived and loved before.

Or could it be, as she was a devout Christian, it was the omni-presence of God that was staring back at you? And it was *his* wisdom of the ages that emanated from her, and touched you. Whatever it was, it was nonetheless, pleasant to have her around. In keeping with her adventurous soul, I was sure that this voyage had aged her present life metaphysically, adding buckets of water to an already deep well. Yet, despite her hunger for adventure and her personal strength, after considering the rough passage we had just completed, I felt sure, for her, voyaging across great oceans in small boats was over, but I have been proven wrong before and would be again and very soon.

With clouds of darting bugs buzzing the dock's tall light stands, the sun quickly dropped behind Maui's western mountain range as the cooler night air, draped in advancing shadows quickly swept down off the mountain's phallic-like spires to embrace the harbor. It was our second peaceful night in port, we barbequed fresh steaks aboard, sipped on my home-brew Shiraz while making merry well into the night. My intent was to sleep in the next morning and lounge about lazily for most of the day, but a frantic banging on the cabin roof just after daybreak summoned me topside.

Still very groggy and suffering from some mild pains of excess, I had a little trouble focusing on the obviously agitated and concerned looking Hawaiian security guard who suddenly appeared to be relieved at seeing me poke my head out of the hatch.

"Hey man, you guys have to go right now they are coming in!" he shouted, as he began to untie our mooring lines and toss them aboard.

I was about to order him to quit, but the blast from an air horn cut me off in mid-sentence while raising the short hairs on the back of my neck. As I shot a glance to seaward, I suddenly realized what all the fuss was about. Just a mere 100 meters to seaward, was a very large and obviously heavily laden fuel barge; it was being pushed sideways by an equally large, ocean-going tug and from the way the skipper was laying on the horn, it was obvious that they intended to land right where *Maiatla* was and use us as a bumper if we didn't get out of the way, and fast!

It only took a few seconds to fire the engine up and thankfully, the new starter actually worked. Quickly I engaged the throttle just as the guard tossed our last line aboard. The engine belched a cloud of blue smoke as I waved a thanks to the guard while putting *Maiatla* on a course that would take us between the moving barge and the concrete jetty. We managed to slip past the dock and barge with a mere couple of meters on either side to spare. Those aboard the tug where obviously a very friendly sort, (I'm being sarcastic here!) because as we passed by, they all waved the two finger shaka sign as they broke out in grand smiles. They all appeared quite amused at seeing the haoles scramble. A rather rotund and dark-skinned Tongan-looking fellow in board shorts and white mesh Tee-shirt, positioned on the bow of the tug cupped his hands and called out the proverbial Hawaiian greeting with great exaggeration.

"A-lo-ha!" He then cut loose with a great belly laugh. Aloha is an idiom that can mean either hello or goodbye and in this case, I believe the emphasis was on the latter. I felt obligated to wave back, but as I did, I couldn't help uttering to myself.

"What Assholes!" (Uncharacteristically, I resisted presenting my own single finger salute in reply) Unceremoniously, we were given the "bum's rush" out of town and *Maiatla* was back underway. Welcome to Hawaii!

Chapter #8

Loners in Paradise

"I went to Maui to stay a week and remained five. I never spent so pleasant a month before, or bade any place goodbye so regretfully. I have not once thought of business, or care or human toil or trouble or sorrow or weariness, and the memory of it will remain with me always."
Mark Twain.

The coast between Kahului and the extreme western point of Maui is beautifully rugged, windswept and for the most part surprisingly deserted. The tradewinds were still boisterous but no one seemed to mind the stiff air, the abrupt wakeup call or our narrow escape from the harbor. All were eager to be back underway after our brief but rejuvenating shore leave. It's a short but pleasant 15-mile, downwind sail along the coast to Honolua Bay located just beyond the whitewashed Nakalele Point lighthouse that lords over the burnt looking landscape. Just inshore, and spouting like a surfacing whale, a blowhole erupted as the groundswell pounded against the broken rock face. A fleeting veil of mist, slashed with a rainbow swept up, over a hundred meters, ascending the cliff before evaporating in the early morning sun.

It was a beautiful morning out on the water and we were surprised that aside from a pair of large sports fishing boats outward bound for a day of Marlin fishing, we had the entire north coast to ourselves. After all, this was an island nation, encircled by millions of square kilometers of unbroken ocean; surely, these islanders must take to boats, as birds take wing or fish to the sea. Hawaii is the initial stepping stone for all who desire to venture into the atoll-studded south seas and likewise these volcanic peaks are the last port of call for all bound for the Americas that lay over two thousand windward miles in the direction the day is born. I thought Hawaii would be a mecca for boaters, especially cruisers, both local and transients alike, so where were all the boats?

Where were all the cruisers and the shellback(1) beach potlucks that were typically the social centerpieces of the cruising lifestyle elsewhere? Since the windward sides of all the Hawaiian Islands still presented transoceanic sailing conditions, I suspected that everyone else was basking in the sun and skipping to the more tempered winds in the lee of the island. Or at least that was what I was hoping. But as time would eventually reveal, *Maiatla* and her crew of inter-island explorers were an oddity and would become an object of intense curiosity.

After enduring the dirt and grime of the busy commercial port, we were now in search of a tranquil anchorage, coral reefs and a more private place to decompress and to perhaps meet some fellow cruisers and associate with like-minded people with whom we could compare salty tales over tankards of Hana Bay rum. We were in desperate need of a royal Gam.(2)

> *(1) The ceremony of "Crossing the Line" is an initiation rite in the Royal Navy and other navies that commemorates a sailor's first crossing of the Equator. Originally, the tradition was created as a test for seasoned sailors to ensure their new shipmates were capable of handling long rough times at sea. Sailors who have already crossed the Equator are nicknamed (Trusty) Shellbacks, often referred to as Sons of Neptune; those who have not are nicknamed (Slimy) Pollywogs.*
>
> *(2) In the 19th century a Gam was the meeting of two (or more) whaling ships at sea. The ships each send out a boat to the other, and the two captains meet on one ship, while the two chief mates meet on the other. The contemporary version is the social gathering of cruising vessels at anchor combined with furious dinghy activity between vessels with the exchange of ceremonial boat drinks.*

The four of us had been alone long enough, it was time to end our monastic isolation, but seeking out fellow cruisers would not hurt our coveted "loner" status that seemed to be a badge of honor to be worn upon the chest by many offshore voyagers. In fact, cruisers love being loners together, forming almost a symbiotic relationship, a pact forged between boats and their crews, out of the need for self-preservation and protection from the netherworld, not to mention the dire need for a good party once in a while.

****

In all truth, at this stage of my life, rapidly encroaching on the half-century mark, (middle age, I think it's called) I am happy to be labeled a loner. Aside from the inevitable maturing folds about my waist, (buoyancy compensators) I feel quite comfortable in my own skin, I grew up a solitary, introspective child and for the most part, quite content to do so. It is generally believed that loners, for a variety of reasons, choose to be loners; a conscious decision on their part. I do not recall making the decision to become a loner, however in hindsight, the decision, if indeed I did make one, was made at an exceptionally early age.

I recall being six or seven, playing alone in the sand dunes behind my parent's beachfront home on Lake Ontario. There were many neighborhood children to choose from for friends; still I remember being quite content being alone, building sand bunkers for my collection of plastic soldiers. Likewise, some years later as a Cub Scout, much to my Scoutmaster's annoyance, I would leave the pack, to wander off into the wilderness in search of whatever beasts prowled or dwelled in the nearby caves. The Scout's team games and activities held little interest for me, which also infuriated my Scout leader to no end. Despite the bribe of a new stone fireplace that my father had constructed for the Scout's brand new lodge, I was eventually, unceremoniously ejected from that organization for my "lack of cooperation and team spirit." If I was traumatized by being rejected by such a prodigious organization, I was not aware of it, in fact I was probably relieved at being exempt from all the social obligations that membership demanded.

By my early teens (aside from feverishly trying to get laid for the first time), I had become a sailor in earnest and spent countless hours in small boats, racing my brains out with a single partner, competing at the National level; or just cruising Hamilton Bay, alone in my little boat and quite content to spend the entire day searching for breezes as I darted between passing lake freighters.

By high school, I actually enjoyed my reputation as being a quiet loner. I dare say a "Fonzie-type" character, (less all the chicks). But I knew what I liked and wanted, and I had decided that it was alright to be different, to be alone, to be a loner. I knew my parents were concerned that I didn't seem to have many friends, and I felt for them, but I didn't care about what others, outside the family thought. Nevertheless, the netherworld harboured many erroneous opinions concerning loners, a sentiment that goes back to the very beginnings of civilization as we know it.

Man is by nature a social animal; an individual who is unsocial naturally and not accidentally is either beneath our notice or more than human. ... Anyone who ... does not partake of society is either a beast or a god.
~Aristotle's Politics

****

"Loner" is often society's label for a person who avoids, or is isolated from human interaction. There are many reasons for solitude, intentional or otherwise. However, generally most believe that various mental illnesses and social difficulties can be linked to the desire for reclusiveness. The term loner is usually used with a negative connotation in the belief that humans are innately social creatures and those that do not participate are different. The loner label has often been applied pejoratively by the media to individuals they deemed strange or pathetic.

Insecure loners find it excruciating to be in the physical presence of others because they worry they will be judged negatively. Anxiety is a common feature of their social interactions. Self-hatred is sometimes the underlying motivation for why a person may isolate him or herself. Introversion is often associated with the loner personality and it is thought it goes right along with a raft of other problems: arrogance, selfishness, mental instability, inhumanity, or just plain evil. They're the weird ones, or the suspicious ones, or the untrustworthy ones. A loner can also become a freak through his isolation. Humans learn how to be human through social interaction.

When you are raised by wolves (or cruisers?) you behave differently, and are thus a little freaky. It is commonly believed that many psychological disorders originate from a deficit in human interaction. The child that was never taken to the breast or left for hours to their own devices without the influences of doting parents. Then that person will be shunned. Thus, sociopathic mass murderers are fashioned and spectacularly disturbing headlines, involving cannibalism and power tools, are most often associated with asocial loners and introverts, which in turn reinforces the belief that being a loner is not a natural thing, they are the "boogiemen" of the night and a problem for the netherworld, a problem that needs to be eliminated.

Well, if thinking of all of the above doesn't make a person want to shed their loner status like the putrid skin of a leper, then they probably are in fact, a sociopath, uncaring and unmoved by what others feel or think. But I don't believe it's that simple, it's not to be one or the other. To be an antisocial loner, a freak with mental problems or as noted by the great philosopher Aristotle, either a Beast or a God, or a loner by choice.

It is my conviction that a loner can be driven by less ominous forces. After all, whether it be aboard a great warship with thousands of souls to govern or a tiny sloop with a crew of two aboard, an effective captain must be separate, a loner by design or how else can he lead? If mental illness is truly associated with being a loner, then why is it that society grants ship's masters so much power? A Ship's captain holds the power of life and death over their ship and crew! The same can be asserted for commercial aircraft pilots, military officers, and corporate CEOs.

Introverts, loners, or cruisers aren't just less sociable than their extroverted brothers, but they may actually engage and interact with the world in a fundamentally different way. It may be that non-loners or extraverts relish the nuances of social interaction with others. Loners tend to focus more on their own ideas and on stimuli that may not register in the minds of others. Social interaction can actually drain them, while "quiet time" invigorates.

It is a generally accepted as fact that many perceived loners are overly self-conscious and believed to be people who are constantly sizing up their own? attributes. But contrary to common netherworld beliefs, not all loners have a pathological fear of social contact. Perhaps they or we, just simply have a lower need for affiliation and there is a great difference between the loner-by-preference and the enforced or shunned loner-the social freak. Those who choose the solitude of the open ocean over the butt cheek-to-jowl commune of typical urbanites may be simply aligning themselves with their own personal temperaments and they merely prefer traveling through their own personal wormhole to their private, interior universe.

Psychologists have gone so far as to suggest that socially withdrawn people have an increased sensitivity to all kinds of emotional interactions and sensory cues, which may mean that they find pleasure where others, non-loners do not. While a few studies have shown a correlation between creativity, originality, and introversion, perhaps more striking is the greater enjoyment introverts seem to reap from creative endeavors. As an offer of proof, MRI studies have shown that during social situations, specific areas in the brains of loners experience especially lively blood flow, indicating a sort of over stimulation, which may explain why loners find crowds so wearying.

The same research likewise suggests that introverts may be more attuned to all sorts of positive experiences as well. This added sensitivity, psychologist speculate, could mean that people who are reserved have an ability to respond more quickly to panic situations or show unusual empathy to a friend in need, due to their stronger emotional antennae. Further research has bourn this assumption out by demonstrating that withdrawn people typically have an extremely high sensory acuity. Because loners are good at noticing subtleties that other people miss, loners are well suited for careers that require close observation, like writing and scientific research. Now that this is understood, it comes as no surprise that Emily Dickinson, Stanley Kubrick, and Isaac Newton were all loners and prone to introspection.

****

In light of all that is now understood about the significant differences between the pair of loners, the social freak and the loner by choice, the Yin and Yang of the twin faces of the same side of the coin, a better understanding of loners can be achieved. Yin, the dark shaded personality which is the enforced or shunned loner- the mass murdering, skin eating, head collecting social freak as opposed to Yang, the luminous and the more sensitive, more introspective loner-by-preference type. I can honestly claim (or hope anyway) to be more associated with Yang, the later personality type opposed to the former and darker Yin.

****

After a blissful day of coastal sailing, *Maiatla* glided into the calmer waters created by the mountain's wind shadow. We cautiously picked our way through the coral reefs, to find a barren sandy patch deep within the bay, close to shore in which to set our hook. Finally, at anchor, we were at last in an idyllic, tropical cove. The excitement was rampant and there was a race to see who would be the first to don their snorkeling gear and make the plunge on the coral reef. The bay, we were about to learn, was home to over a dozen green sea turtles, now snoozing on the bottom, as well as a gregarious pod of spinner dolphins that rested during the day after a night of feeding offshore. Neither species seemed to mind sharing their aquatic turf with the crew of *Maiatla*.

With the entire crew frolicking in the sea, I took advantage of being abandoned for the moment. I chose to stay aboard and relax. At peace with a cold Corona in a coozy, naked in the cockpit, basking in the building heat of the morning, I was content to be beautifully protected from the winds and constant ocean swell, not to mention relieved of the stress of being continually underway.

The beach was not the most ideal for sun worshipping as it was strewn with softball to bowling ball sized rocks, with tangled jungle crowding the shoreline. However, the panorama offered by Honolua Bay is nonetheless inspiring. To the west across the constantly windswept Pailolo Channel, the former leper colony of Molokai humped out of the sea. Likewise the Isles of Lanai and its distant neighbor, Kahoolawe shimmered through the heat induced sea haze to complete the mystical image. A beautiful place but I felt a little disappointed by what I saw just up the coast.

The jungle first gave way to the hillside sugarcane fields, then like a scab, the sprawl of endemic tourist condos and hotels dominated the remainder of the coastline. Honolua Bay is the last of the wild places on this side of the Island. From the number of high-level cranes that threatened the sky, there was every indication that civilization was poised to swamp what little wilderness remained. Fortunately, the bay its self is a designated marine conservation area.

As the morning wore on, from the hill top road, tourists braved the steep jungle path to reach the shore, to swim and harass the turtles. By 10:00 a.m. four large catamarans had tacked into the bay, retrieved submerged mooring buoys and disgorged a couple hundred loud and about to be sunburned bathers to likewise poke, prod and chase the local wildlife.

From the deck of *Maiatla* it suddenly became obvious that our little bit of paradise had been discovered by a herd of netherworld escapees in flowered apparel, many of whom were obviously Canadian because as soon as they motored by, they cheered and shouted accolades and questions upon seeing the red and white Maple Leaf fluttering from *Maiatla's* backstay.

A couple of the charter captains pulled their boats alongside so their guests could converse with us. I was a bit concerned at first having such large boats drifting just meters away but it soon became obvious that they were being handled by experienced crews. Instead of relaxing peacefully in the warm morning sun I suddenly found myself answering a barrage of questions, some of which were asked by people who had started their Happy hour a little early. The question most asked was, did we actually sail all the way here from Canada and how long did it take? Reasonable questions, but no matter where we go there is always someone who asks,

"Where do you anchor at night while crossing the ocean?"

Despite the nautical ignorance it was still fun to tell them of our voyage and most are suitably stunned to learn how long it took us to get here. The time we spent travelling here was longer than most vacations. All the admiration was equally thrilling and annoying.

By noon the crew returned to the boat all excited and full of stories of what they had seen. After some lunch Kara, Jackie and Jim decided to have a nap and retreated below which seemed like a good idea to me but Kara was still full of youthful energy and demanded that I set up the swing. As *Maiatla* had been our home for over seven years at this point, I had devised numerous ways to entertain our two, boisterous children and one was our version of a tire swing over the creek. I would take our spinnaker pole and attach one end to the mast approximately two meters above the deck, then I attach our bosom's chair to the spinnaker halyard which I passed through a block snapped onto the other end of the long pole.

The victim would slide into the seat and I would hoist them skyward while dangling from the end of the pole. Once aloft I would swing them out over the water. The kids loved it and would squeal as I swung them on a great arch out from *Maitala's* side, often dipping them into the cold water in the process. Kara likewise took great delight in being suspended and I had to resist dunking her but since the water here was warm as a bathtub as compared to the icy pacific northwest little pleasure could be derived in dumping her.

Later, while the rest of the crew was still napping, Kara and I took our roll-away dink ashore for a short excursion for a little exploring. On the beach, we found an local, female environmentalist, who by her 70's retro attire could have been a

Grateful Dead groupie. She had set up a table with literature about all of the area's rich history and natural attributes. She informed me that there was a push to save the adjacent wooded hillside from developers, but she spoke as if they were fighting a lost cause.

I asked her about the submarine mooring buoys that I heard the local charter boats had installed around many of the islands. The lady first gave me a strange gauging look before answering me as if I was a little child or perhaps just a plain simpleton.

"No sir, there are no submarines in this bay, but there is lots of sea turtles." I imagined her wanting to conclude our talk by patting me on the head before sending me off.

"Not submarines with periscopes!" I said rather defensively. "Submerged mooring buoys to tie a boat to. You know, underwater, so you can't see them."

From the expression on her face I could see that she still didn't have a clue as to what I was talking about.

"I'm sorry, she finally said after a long thoughtful pause, I don't know anything about that!"

With that comment she handed me another pamphlet on the local plant life then directed her attention to another pink couple who had sauntered up to the table and we were quickly dismissed.

Hawaiians don't like to clutter up their spectacular scenery with unsightly mooring buoys. To avoid the floating eyesores, the charter boat people install the mooring floats with enough line so the buoy is two meters or so below the surface. Securing the boat to these moorings requires making a dive with an anchor line in hand and of course knowing where they are helps. Most of the charter fleet here in Hawaii have numerous secret mooring buoys around the islands for their own exclusive use.

Many countries have employed submerged mooring buoys in an effort to protect the delicate undersea environment. In the early 1980s, I worked for the Underwater Archeology Society of British Columbia, installing mooring buoys overtop of historical shipwreck sites along the BC coast in the effort to protect the old wrecks. The programme proved very successful in preserving the delicate historical sites. A technique often used by divers was to drag and anchor over the bottom in the area of a suspected wreck site, hoping to snag the wreck. An effective method but the anchor would often cause severe damage to the ships soft and decaying timbers. One wreck I worked on was a old paddle steamer that sank in 1887, it's corroding iron and riveted boiler was laid wide open by an 100Lbs anchor of a local dive charter boat.

By evening, the magic returned as the charter boats fished the last of their swimmers aboard and the beach goers retreated back into the jungle to their parked rental cars. The tourists returning to the safety offered behind resort walls, to drink and gorge themselves by tiki-torch light and to get royally soused to the beat of native drums at the expertly choreographed luaus.

As the shadows grew long and after the spinner dolphins put to sea for the night, Kara and I ventured back ashore to broach the jungle that concealed the raucous birds whose twittering calls wafted out to the boat on the warm breeze. There was no doubt that the jungle that greeted us bore little resemblance to the one the ancient Hawaiians had known. A great deal of the primordial forests here, as in much of Hawaii, had been overrun by transplanted species from other parts of the world, brought to this normally isolated archipelago by sailors and settlers without knowing the devastating effect it would ultimately have on the indigenous vegetation and vulnerable wildlife. The coconut palm, breadfruit, banana trees and even the noble pineapple were all transplanted from other regions.

Still, the new jungle bore the enticing scents of blooming flowers combined with the tang of raw earth, a thick and fleshy, musty vegetable fung, that seemed to stick to our clothes. The jungle canopy was dense but where it was broken, the light streamed through, and usually, a lone coconut palm, thick with great nuts thrust up into the sky. Waist high grasses carpeted the ground, obscuring the sprawling roots and knurly bases of the massive trees that sprouted from the red volcanic soils, causing us to walk carefully or risk tripping. Massive limbs groped in every conceivable direction sporting complex webs of dangling vines, thick as a man's wrist, creating a natural "jungle-gym" for climbing. Many of the heavy branches were draped in a thick tapestry of delicate grey-green moss that hung like woven fishing nets set out to dry in the tropical air. As we made our way down the muddy trail, our eyes captured little more than fleeting streaks of red and yellow. We saw Java Sparrows and Chestnut Mannikins, exotic little birds darting though the underbrush as they fled before us. A tan devil-eyed mongoose bolted across a little creek as we made our way up the trail that led to the meandering road that caped the hill top.

When engulfed by the cooler shade of the jungle, it was almost impossible to not to feel the jungle's brooding personality. A surreal, haunting quality that, when you stopped and waited quietly, wormed its way into your pores, slithering under your skin, raising the short hairs on the nape of your neck.

****

With a history dating back to 450 AD, Honolua Bay once contained a village, where for generations, people struggled, bore children and lived out lives that often ended violently. There is no written record of a village on this site but its existence is still quite evident; rubble walls that once encircled the village houses and gardens can still be seen in the underbrush. Old world shadows hung heavy in the air here along with the stone relics from the past, a microcosm of the human story, waiting for slow dissolution by wind and rain.

It is said that all of Hawaii is a magical and supernatural place, not in the sense that the tourist board hyperbole suggests. But in the sense of spiritual power or *Mana;* supernatural, as in: being overrun by malignant ghosts, spirits and menacing gods. When talking with locals, most will confess to having encountered "the others", the earth bound spirits with whom they share the islands, most notably and feared are the "Night Marchers" or "Spirit Ranks".

In Hawaiian legend, Nightmarchers are the ghosts of ancient Hawaiian warriors. On certain nights, encouraged by a full moon they are said to come forth from their burial sites to march out to past battles or to other sacred places or heiaus(temples). Anyone living near their path may hear chanting and marching, and must go inside to avoid notice. They might appear during the day if coming to escort a dying relative to the spirit world. Anyone looking upon or being seen by the marchers will die unless a relative is within the marcher's ranks. Some maintain that if you lie face down on the ground they will not see you. Others say that this only works if you are naked. Still others believe that you should be naked, lie face up and feign sleep. (Halloween night could provide endless opportunities for Hawaiian nymphomaniacs!). Placing leaves of the ti (plant) around one's home is said to keep away all evil spirits, and will cause the huaka'i pō to avoid the area.

The belief in Nightmarchers is so strong that many of the islanders will refuse to build a home on known ancient trails for fear marchers will parade through their houses and take them with them.

****

Kara, who has never seen such jungle before, climbed up into the giant limbs of a sprawling Acacia and demanded I take her picture. Giddy with excitement she called down to me.

"This tree here!" she said, as she stamped her foot on the tree limb. "I'm going to move to Hawaii and build a tree house in this one! A house like in the movie the Swiss Family Robinson and I'm going to raise a bunch of kids in it. Do you think the people who own this land would mind?"

Kara loved to climb and even gave a try at swinging, Tarzan-like on a vine. We continued up the hill until reaching the cliff top where we took pictures of *Maiatla* gently swinging on her hook, surrounded by crystal water, sprawling coral and reaching palms. I could even see the spinnaker pole attached to the mast and protruding over the water, with the bosun's chair dangling from the end. Not until the sun set over Molokai and the full moon floated from behind Maui's mountains did we begin to make our way back through the jungle to the beach, all the while being extra wary of Nightmarchers.

None of us wanted to leave Honolua Bay, but Janet, Melissa and my niece Samantha were soon due to arrive. After three relaxing days, we were forced to leave and make our way up the resort infected coast to Lahaina, the cruisers hub and the welcoming hosts of the Vic-Maui yacht race, the Lahaina yacht club.

Chapter #9

Lahaina, Lele-The Relentless Sun

Live in the sunshine, swim the sea, drink the wild air.

Ralph Waldo Emerson.

As in many of the islands, the arrival of foreigners paved the way for new forms of commerce on Maui, three primary sources of the islands' wealth were established in the 1800s: sandalwood exports, whaling and sugar processing. The brickwork and chimney remains of an old sugar refinery is still a prominent fixture in the center of town.

Under King Kamehameha the Great, Hawaii established foreign trade and began selling sandalwood to China. In 1821, some two million pounds of this fragrant wood was exported to Asia. Three years later, demand was so high that the royal family required their subjects to pay their taxes in the form of sandalwood. At around the same time, the first whaling ship arrived at Maui from New Bedford, Massachusetts. Though whales were not plentiful in Hawaiian waters at that time, Lahaina; located in a local wind shadow formed by the volcanic slopes, served as a safe harbor from which ships would set off to hunt whales in the North Pacific.

The old town of Lahaina provided a place to anchor, restock food supplies, ship parts and a place to acquire medical attention. In 1846, some 400 whaling ships from all over the globe visited Lahaina, sometimes as many as a hundred at a time and by the 1900s, Lahaina was the center of the global whaling industry. Ships often lay anchored for months with their idle crews languishing ashore engaging in various forms of debauchery with the easily corruptible natives. Whaling boosted the island's economy, but it also increased such social problems as drinking and prostitution, much to the angst of the island's missionaries. However, by mid-century, whaling began to decline rapidly as whales became scarcer and the petroleum industry in Pennsylvania grew more successful. Lahaina's fortunes began to diminish with the dwindling whaling fleet and continued until the early 1970s when tourism began to revitalize the old sea port.

Tense relations between Maui's whalers and missionaries erupted in 1825 when the whalers blamed the missionaries for preventing women from visiting the ships. Verbal threats and a show of knives and guns escalated to cannon shots fired from a whaling ship at a missionary's home on Lahaina's Front Street. (Which was located next to the Baldwin Mission House and across from where the public library now stands.) The shots missed, reportedly on purpose, and the offending ship left Lahaina, but tensions continued.

Mark Twain visited Maui in 1887 with the intent of exploring some of the many ancient ruins and temples that abounded about the island and while doing so, he made an observation concerning the effects of missionary works on the native population. Twain wrote:

Nearby is an interesting ruin--the meager remains of an ancient temple--a place where human sacrifices were offered up in those old bygone days...long, long before the missionaries braved a thousand privations to come and make [the natives] permanently miserable by telling them how beautiful and how blissful a place heaven is, and how nearly impossible it is to get there; and showed the poor native how dreary a place perdition is and what unnecessarily liberal facilities there are for going to it; showed him how, in his ignorance, he had gone and fooled away all his kinsfolk to no purpose; showed him what rapture it is to work all day long for fifty cents to buy food for next day with, as compared with fishing for a pastime and lolling in the shade through eternal summer, and eating of the bounty that nobody labored to provide but Nature. How sad it is to think of the multitudes who have gone to their graves in this beautiful island and never knew there was a hell.

Mark Twain -- Roughing It.

Twain states that: "*he (the native) had gone and fooled away all his kinsfolk to no purpose;*" which refers to the Hawaiian version of absolution which the missionaries told them had no meaning. The Hawaiians believed that if they offered up a relative for sacrifice to the gods for breaking some Kapu, (Hawaiian code of conduct) they would be absolved and forgiven for any transgression that they may have committed. If you were a big Kapu breaker, it might have been tough appeasing the gods if you came from a small family but if you had some in-laws you didn't care for...

As in whaling times, Lahaina today is still overflowing with travelers from all nations. Aside from the odd cruise ship, most are flown in, but no matter how they arrive, the numbers are staggering. Over 8 million a year, so it's surprising that the islands don't settle beneath the waves from the shear combined weight.

****

Under clear skies with little wind, we motored past the town's seashore with its two story wood structures crowding the waterfront, many of which are supported by piles over the water. The majority of the restaurants, clubs and shops sport balconies so customers can peer into the water to watch the many tiny reef fish dart between the rocks with the occasional sea turtle closing on the shore to graze on the green algae growing in the rocky shallows. From early photos of the town, it's obvious that it has changed little from the time of the whalers, just more spread out and a few hundred more Hawaiian Tee-shirt boutiques, surfboard shops and jeep rental agencies.

A shallow lava and coral reef guards the shore from intrusion and if the breaking waves didn't convince you that getting closer was a grave mistake, then the 15 meter tall mast protruding from the water atop the wreck of a Rhodes 38 sloop, should. Seeing a wrecked vessel at the mouth of a harbor should give any prudent skipper cause for a pause. I would later learn that the wreck had occurred a couple of years earlier; the vessel had broken free from its moorings and was driven upon the reef. At first, some concerned locals initiated a rescue operation but they were quickly shut down by warnings from the Lahaina Harbor Master. He promptly informed them that if they touched the vessel, they would all become liable for any damage done to the reef and that the State had stiff fines ready for anyone involved. Since the owner was absent, as he was in the military stationed on Oahu, the now abandoned yacht, in full sight of town, and the Lahaina Yacht Club and its sympathetic members, was permitted to grind its self to pieces until after a couple of tortuous days the once lovely vessel finally settled to the bottom for good.

A couple of cruisers who were living aboard their own boats on neighboring moorings secretly dove the wreck at night to salvage what they could for the owner. I was appalled and found this whole affair troubling as it went against everything that we as seaman know is right. However, as I was going to learn, this apparently illogical stance of the State of Hawaii, concerning the custom of the sea, was just the tip of the proverbial iceberg-ah, volcano.

Although we found the individual people of the islands extremely friendly and helpful, not to mention being suitably impressed that we could sail such a small boat so far, the state and local governments were outright hostile towards boaters in general, regardless of whether they were foreign or had domestic status. Staying out of the harbor brought little relief from the state's obvious campaign of discrimination against the water folk, the little gunboats of the US Coast Guard were always out and about and apparently eager to hassle boaters whether they were at anchor or underway. We would only be in Lahaina a few days before *Maiatla* would herself have a rather ugly brush with officialdom and by our departure from the islands three months later, I would be aghast at just how boater unfriendly the state of Hawaii truly was, both politically and geographically.

The small boat anchorage off Lahaina is an open roadstead that is constantly harassed by the energetic, gale induced swell that originates somewhere near Japan. The 1 to 2 meter swell is usually running at oblique angles to the current or whatever little wind that may be blowing, so all of the vessels moored or anchored here, rolled from gunnel to gunnel with great enthusiasm. Without a second hook(anchor) set off the stern to keep the bow into the swells, it was nearly impossible to sleep there. We made numerous attempts to set *Maiatla's* hook but with little success. We moved several times, but it wasn't until we ventured further out, just beyond the red nun marker, off the narrow harbor entrance that we finally found decent holding, but it was in water deeper then I preferred, 20 fathoms(120 feet). We were holding fast, but it didn't take long for the large wakes from all the boat traffic entering or leaving the harbor to convince us that we needed to move as soon as possible. I later made several dives in Lahaina anchorage and discovered why the holding was so poor. A great deal of the bottom was covered with a heavy carpet of low-lying coral, which offers no holding at all. Likewise, the few sandy patches, were not much better as the coarse, white sand layer was thin, barely covering the lava rock.

I pumped up the inflatable and we all motored ashore, through the dreadfully narrow harbor entrance. It was a little unsettling. The cut, or passage through the reef is scarcely over 40 meters wide and the shoaling water encourages swells to build in excess of 3 meters in height on either side of the channel. Just a few meters away from our dinghy, the roaring surf came complete with gangs of surfing teens showing off while shooting the curls. If all the aforementioned wasn't distracting enough, having to share the channel with a steady stream of large fishing and day tour boats heading in and out kept us precariously close to the edge of the channel, with its coral tops and white water. (Soft bottom inflatables do not like coral!)

Lahaina State Harbor was, to say the least, disappointing. The small and exceedingly narrow boat basin was hidden behind a rubble wall with a perimeter dock and tar soaked piles that permitted bow and stern ties only. I couldn't imagine that the tiny port could hold more than a hundred boats at one time, even with then stacked like cords of wood with their bows pointing into the docks with their sterns tied to wobble pilings. The harbor appeared to be packed to over capacity, mostly with vessels engaged in the charter business, the balance consisting of privately owned and apparently worn out sail and sports fishing boats of all descriptions. Not to mention an 8-meter fishing boat with its decks awash and only held off the bottom by its four mooring points.

The docks and boardwalks in the harbor, some with missing planks and tetanus inducing punji sticks masquerading as protruding nail heads, were in various stages of disrepair and it was obvious from the condition of walkways and handrails that paint was a scarce commodity in the islands. To make matters worse, the groundswell pounded straight though/over the reef, rebounding off the concrete walls lining the basin, creating a violent serge that swept through the harbor, causing all the boats to spastically dance about, rising up and down, straining and sporadically jerking at their numerous and extremely oversized mooring lines, all the while grinding their fenders against adjacent boats or decaying piles. It was my intention to talk to the harbourmaster about a temporary berth so I could affix some repairs, but after seeing the conditions within the harbor and how congested it was, I wasn't sure I even wanted *Maiatla* in there.

The Lahaina Yacht club is just a short walk from the harbor, down the waterfront; the old, inconspicuous clapboard two-story building is stuffed, in between a trendy Hawaiian bistro and a T-shirt souvenir shop. This is the club that bi-annually sponsors the Victoria to Maui yacht race and when the manager learned that we had sailed from Vancouver we were instantly made honorary members and given free rein of the tiny club which boasts a bar and restaurant (cheapest booze and food(good) on the strip!) and showers for the unwashed seafarer. Typically, the interior walls of the club were covered with photos of past race winners and visiting yachts from around the world as well as a variety of nautical antiques, some of which appeared to be permanent fixtures perched atop well-worn barstools. The club's outdoor patio hovered over the sea, which concealed a tiny dock below, so anyone wanting to make a clandestine entrance could land by dink and materialize through a trap door in the floor located conveniently adjacent to the bar. Drunks may likewise make a nippy exit by simply dropping through the floor and if the drunk just happened to be on the floor away, it just took a quick jerk on the latch and they were gone like the Phantom of the Opera. As it wasn't a race year, the club had several free moorings located just offshore which they kindly offered to us while we were in town. Only after a single night on the hook, I was happy to accept a mooring as it removed my worry of *Maiatla* dragging anchor and possibly joining the lonely Rhodes upon the reef.

As a tourist destination in the Hawaiian Islands, Maui boasts most of the best beaches, whales and porpoise, along with great diving just offshore and of course the seemingly limitless sun for anyone who is not heliophobic or prone to skin cancer. Aside from lacking an active volcano, (not sure that this would be a plus!) Maui had everything we could ask for.

But we didn't have time to dally and take in the sights, Jan and the kids were due to arrive in a couple of days; while the rest of the crew played tourist, I used the time to clean up the boat and to make a few repairs in preparation for their arrival.

Chapter #10

Flotsam and Jetsam

I must go down to the seas again, to the lonely sea and the sky,
And all I ask is a tall ship and a star to steer her by.
John Masefield – Sea Fever

In maritime law, the term flotsam applies to wreckage or cargo left floating on the sea after a shipwreck or accident. Anything with buoyant qualities usually pops to the surface. Flotsam can include anything from galley trash to barrels of waste oil, fishing nets and floats or the crew's personal effects. Likewise, more valuable items, such as empty lifeboats or trucking containers full of Rolex watches and fine china. It is estimated that as many as 10,000 (not a typo!) shipping containers fall off container ships and are lost at sea annually. Storms are often to blame. Lloyd's Register of shipping, London, England, estimates that as many as 1000 large (over 100 tonnes or up to 75 meters long) vessels are lost annually worldwide, including the loss of two vessels over 200 meters long (15000 tonnes or more) each and every week. Considering that most wreckage sinks to the bottom, it is depressing to think about how much trash is scattered across the world's seabed.

Still, just because this loot is floating around, like ocean going perches for weary blue-footed boobies, it doesn't mean it's free for the taking. International maritime law generally dictates that flotsam, whether found afloat or on the seabed or beach is still the property of the original owners if they choose to claim it, and under the law. There is no time limit.

Jetsam on the other hand applies to cargo, equipment or garbage voluntarily thrown overboard, jettisoned, from a ship in distress, that either sinks or washes ashore. And since it was voluntarily cast off, it's up for grabs but the original owners can still petition the courts to order the return of the items. Contemporarily, the phrase flotsam and jetsam is often used loosely to describe any object found floating or washed ashore. Bottles, steel drums, plastics of all sorts and more recently in my home waters of British Columbia, perhaps the most unusual form of flotsam has been washing ashore. Since 2007 as many as eleven severed feet still in their shoes have washed up on beaches in and around Vancouver. The police don't suspect foul play but the source of the feet still remains a mystery.

We have seen our share of debris floating thousands of miles from the nearest land. After ramming mussel encrusted oil drums and skirting lost or abandoned drift nets in mid Pacific, we have no doubt that all the world's oceans are filled with such odious jetsam and that due to oceanic wind driven currents, both flotsam and jetsam, like an invading armada, continually assault distant shores, littering otherwise pristine beaches with netherworld debris. I'm sorry to say that despite their remoteness, the Hawaiian Islands are not immune to the deleterious and unsightly invasions. While passing between the various islands we would see many examples of such pollution, floating and cast upon paradise's beaches.

The 2011 tsunami that swamped Japan, added tens of thousands of tons of debris to the east flowing, Pacific current. The North Pacific's guts now churn with flotsam consisting of everything from refrigerators to store manikins, lawn chairs and rubber gardening gloves. It's as though one hundred Wal-Mart's vomited, regurgitated their entire inventory of netherworld chattels into the sea. Oceanographers estimate the debris field caused by the tsunami is approximately 3,700 kilometers long and 1,800 kilometers wide and is due to start arriving in Hawaii in the spring of 2012 and will continue to circle the Pacific for decades.

****

Shortly after the discovery of Oceania, the human version of flotsam and jetsam began washing up on the islands' beaches by the boatload. The first, were deserters or castaways from Spanish trading vessels that started to ply the northern Pacific over four hundred years ago. Then came the deserters from the European naval exploration vessels that later re-discovered the great South Seas, followed by the traders and New World whalers who left behind more than their share of dubious humanity.

By the 19th century, a new wave of missionaries and other religious zealots washed amongst the island. Most would succeed in their quest to subjugate the natives, others retreated in abject failure to return home or wander about the islands surviving by beachcombing and trading with the very people they had come to convert, often turning "native" themselves. As world travel became easier, the outcasts from society and the netherworld began searching the remote islands for a place where they felt they belonged.

It is interesting to note that the first appearance of the word "beach-comber" in print was in Herman Melville's *Omoo*, in 1847. Melville described a population of Europeans who lived in South Pacific islands, as "combing" the beach and nearby water for flotsam, jetsam, or anything else they could use or trade. However, the vast majority of beachcombers were simply unemployed sailors like Herman Melville, as he himself deserted his whaling ship on June 23, 1842 in the Marquises. Melville's life as a beachcomber was characterized in his first book, Typee.

Whether lured into staying in the islands by the simplistic living or the local flora and fauna (randy, pubescent nymphs with flowers in their hair), or inspired to jump ship by tyrannical captains, beachcombers in all their various forms were destined to become permanent fixtures in the South Seas. Although less obvious today, these individuals, who are quite adapt at blending in with the true locals and half-soused sun burnt tourists, continue to arrive. All the flotsam and jetsam and wild spirits from the madly complicated, modern netherworld, whether they are nefarious or bring positive cultural change to the shores which they assault, the beachcomber still exists and it was not surprising to find them thriving in Hawaii as well as much of the South Pacific.

****

It was our second day in Lahaina and after spending a miserable night rolling on the mooring, (I was too lazy to set a stern hook the first night) I took the dink ashore to drop the crew off so they could do a little sightseeing. On the way, I noticed a little black ketch tugging on a private mooring. The Mariner 31 was looking rather sorry, as she appeared to be undergoing a refit. Her decks were cluttered with raw wood, tools and other implements often used to rebuild a boat. It wasn't the vessel's general state of disorder that caught my eye: this little boat looked oddly familiar as she wallowed between the swells. Not giving it much more thought, I motored on, to the harbor's fuel dock to drop off the crew before moving to the dinghy dock where we were permitted to leave the inflatable for the day.

As I pulled up to the dinghy dock, I noticed a lean young man squatting Neanderthal-like on the rough, concrete quay. He was shirtless, clad only in sandals and faded board shorts with washed out blue stripes on the hips., hanging off his hips. His dark hair was cropped short, Marine Corps short and his muscular form was encased in a leather skin that was beyond tanned and quickly approaching black, from years of exposure to the tropical sun. His body structure, facial features, and presence were obviously Caucasian, not Polynesian and, as the ladies would later inform me, not at all unattractive. (Being a rampant heterosexual I myself, could not support their observations). What did catch my eye was not his general casual appearance, but the fact that he was intently watching me… staring even. No sooner had I tied my dink to the dock, the young man approached.

"Hey! You off that big Canadian ketch out there? Sail her from Canada?" he said rather forcefully but with all friendliness.

His name was Mike and despite owning the muddied accent of a person well-traveled, his suburban, Midwestern dialect with its overemphasis on the vowels leached through as he spoke about the "wooter" in the harbor. I could have guessed that he was from Philadelphia, and in a matter of minutes, (apparently he liked to talk, usually in convoluted run on sentences) I had most of his life story, which he freely offered between technical questions concerning *Maiatla*. Without any feigning interest on my part, I quickly learned that he was a 28 year old fishing boat captain for a local charter company and that he lived aboard his own sailboat out in the harbor and had been doing so for the past 8 years. No small feat considering the night we had just experienced on the hook. I didn't mind talking to him at first but after a short while I began to find his questions and all the personal information that he was volunteering a little bothersome, bordering on annoying. Besides, I was anxious to get my chores done and perhaps find a place for a cold beer as the blistering Maui sun was already becoming uncomfortable despite my big brimmed Tilley.

I asked Mike about a good local diesel mechanic and he was quick to make a recommendation as well as where to get boat parts, then he effortlessly picked up right where he had left off, expounding on all the apparent deficiencies of his home anchorage.

After about twenty minutes of patiently listening, I had had about enough and was now looking for an opportunity to politely end our talk and walk away; after all, I had errands to run and beer to drink. I thought I had found my opportunity when he finally finished telling me about how he had trained as a chef, when all of a sudden he switched gears and started to talk about his boat, Isabella, a black hull 31 foot Mariner Ketch.

His change of subject was so abrupt that I missed my opportunity to exit courteously. I was suddenly listening to his very extensive list of intended repairs and his monologue lasted several more minutes when right in mid-sentence he abruptly fell silent. Again, I was caught short and from the inquisitive look upon his face, I could see that he was expecting me to say something. Not sure what to say and fearful that I might inadvertently launch him into another dissertation, I offered something that I thought was safe.

" You know, your boat looks a bit like a boat I knew in the Baja, it was called *JeSeaCa* and it belonged to a fella also named Mike, we sailed out of the Baja together back in 02".

Without so much as a hint of surprise, Maui Mike promptly informed me that he had indeed purchased the boat from Baja Mike a few years before, renamed her Isabella and had been working very hard to repair all the deficiencies that Baja Mike had built into her. Suddenly, I felt a sinking feeling as I realized that I had unwittingly set him up for another monologue. As Mike excitedly rambled on, I mentally regressed, thinking about the circumstance in which I came to know his boat and the previous owner.

*****

It was the end of May, in 2002 and *Maiatla,* along with dozens of other boats, was trapped in the Sea of Cortez by the early arrival of the first storm of the season. Hurricane Alma would show herself to be a complete bitch. *Maiatla* was hunkered down with four other cruisers in a little bay just outside of La Paz, waiting for the storm to exhaust itself. However, our plan to wait Alma out was foiled by a second storm developing down in the Gulf of Panama; this depression would eventually be dubbed Hurricane Boris and he was not waiting for his big sister Alma to die before heading up county to play havoc with us.

We had a meeting of skippers and all agreed that it was time to break out of the Sea and take our chances with the weather. The 32 foot, *Fleur de Mer,* with a young couple aboard; a single handler, Nick on the 22 foot sloop *Wanderlust;* and Baja Mike's *JeSeaCa* were all bound for Hawaii; *Gypsy,* a Shannon 37, likewise with a young couple aboard was headed for San Francisco and of course *Maiatla* bound the farthest north with her sights set on Vancouver. Our plan, was to sail between the two storm fronts by dropping down south, out of their way, then bear west, avoiding the typical paths of these tropical storms. But, as always, the best laid plans…

It took *Maiatla* 12 days to clear both storms, nevertheless, we emerged on the far side relatively unscathed. (Just some shattered nerves and sleep deprivation!) Baja Mike proved himself a competent seaman, landing on Lanai as planned with *JeSeaCa* intact. The rest of our tiny fleet was not so fortunate: *Gypsy* diverted to San Diego to make repairs to storm damaged gear; likewise *Fleur de Mer* limped back into La Paz, so heavily damaged that it would be a full year before they were ready to sail again. It was apparent that fate had set itself against the tiny boat. Once again, they were caught by a early storm; Hurricane Oscar trapped *Fleur de Mer* in La Paz harbor and sank her before she could clear the anchorage.

And as for *Wanderlust*, our young friend Nick and his dog Ally, who departed with us, , neither he nor his boat was ever seen again. The shipwreck of *Wanderlust* and the loss of her crew had become another ghostly parable of human history. Another boat and crew tragically lost at sea without a trace, no gravestone on a sea that instantly obliterated all signs of *Wanderlust's* passing.

****

As Mike rambled on about the financial arrangements concerning *Isabella*, a thought suddenly occurred to me. With no small effort, I interrupted him.

"Hey Mike, my wife, daughter and niece are flying in and I wonder if you would do me a favor?"

Mike's puzzled expression betrayed his apprehension to making any kind of commitment to my unknown proposition, but after hesitating for several moments and perhaps out of sheer politeness, he finally relented.

"I guess, what is it? Do it if I can."

"When my niece arrives would you mind letting me take a photo of the two of you, together, on *Isabella*?"

Again he hesitated, he probably suspected that I was trying to set him up on a blind date with my "tank" of a niece. I could sense that he was searching for a way out, but lacking a feasible retreat he reluctantly submitted.

"Ya, sure, I guess, but why?"

I broke out in a huge grin at the thought that I had brewing, which I'm sure unnerved him all the more.

"Well, I would like to send the picture to my brother and tell him that my niece, Samantha, met some guy and was sailing off to the South Pacific with him. I'll say I tried to stop her, but couldn't. He will just shit himself, but don't worry, she's 22, and a very hot looking Babe!"

If Mike had any hesitation in fulfilling my request, it was instantly vaporized by the words, very hot babe.

Mike quickly accepted my invitation to row out to *Maiatla* when he had a chance, for a beer and to meet the rest of the crew. He seemed particularly interested after learning that another 18 year old female, Kara, was aboard. While Mike stumbled through an un-characteristic pause, perhaps while pondering the possibilities with the ladies. I leapt at the opening to scuttle our talk and made my escape.

As I strolled down the palm lined dock, I mulled over my strange encounter with

Maui Mike whose behavior and excitement, I imagined, was not unlike that of a shipwrecked sailor who after many months of isolation, would blather on at the first man to step ashore. Aside from Mike's obvious eccentricities and gifted ability to quickly expose raw nerves with just a few (I think) unintentional sentences, he was intelligent, well spoken, polite and perhaps in small doses, tolerable. I had already decided that I liked him.

For better or worse, we were destined to become friends and ultimately, together we would traverse thousands of miles of open ocean, cross the equator and flee hurricanes while visiting places that few even know exist. But it would be some time before I would become better acquainted with this beachcomber that is Maui Mike and learn just how much he would impact all of our lives.

Chapter #11

Welcome to Lahaina State Harbour.

For whatever we lose (like a you or a me)
it's always ourselves we find in the sea.
    E.E. Cummings

My wife Janet, daughter Melissa and my niece Samantha all arrived without a hitch. I greeted them at the airport with kisses, hugs and flowery leis. It had been over a month since I had seen my family and I think I was as happy to see them, as they were to be here. Even Melissa appeared to be excited by what lay ahead. I was hopeful that her initial protests had been hollow ones and that she would allow herself to have fun while she was here. I desperately wanted to have time with her, to share and experience this magical place that is Hawaii. I loaded everyone into the rental jeep, which I had acquired for a couple of days. With the top down, we sped off into the tropical night.

"Wow! I forgot how the air smells here," Samantha said, rather giddily as she stretched her arms above her head to in an effort to catch all the passing fragrances of the island. "And the air is so warm I don't need this jacket that I was wearing on the plane!"

"Yep, the weather has been good ever since we arrived and the water is beautifully warm, I'll stop at the coast when we get to the other side of the island, so you can paddle your feet in the sea." I said, as I looked into the open back seat to see both girls struggling to contain their long hair as the air rushed by.

It was a dark night with stars flooding the heavens, so many stars in fact, that the feeble lights of the Kahului City did little to diminish them. We hung a sharp left, off the city bypass, onto the Honoapiilani Highway that cut through the sugar cane fields of central Maui. A short time later, we pulled off at Maalaea Bay; the road only stopping the jeep when my tires began to sink into the soft sand.

"I know you can't see much now, but this is a big bay and the beach stretches for miles in that direction." I said, as I pointed at the lights of Kihei, across the water. The jeep's headlights illuminated the gentle shore as the waves rolled in.

"Take your shoes off and feel the water, you'll want to go for a swim!" I said.

As both girls did as I instructed and ran for the water, Jan and I held back to embrace each other and drink in the moment.

"Well you did it, Captain. You got us all here, now what are we going to do? Do you think you can handle all of us on board for two months? Keep us entertained?" Jan asked rather playfully.

"No problem Babe. It will be great! There is so much to do and see and I think I met a guy that may help to keep the girls busy while I entertain you!"

"Well you can forget that, the boat is way too crowded for any of that stuff!" Jan said, as she pulled me in closer.

"Hey! I have been at sea for weeks! And besides, I'm the Captain and you have to do what I say. It's the law of the sea!"

"Well we will see about that later, Captain, but it's getting late and we should be getting back to the boat. Is it far?"

The remainder of the drive down the coast road to Lahaina went quickly as there was little reason to stop; it was too dark to see anything anyway. As I drove, Jan and I held hands; neither of us wanted to let go. I steered and shifted gears with my left hand; while holding the wheel straight with my knees.

From the parking lot next to the Lahaina boat harbour, we could see *Maiatla's* cabin lights as she swung on her hook within the anchorage.

"She looks to be rolling a quite a bit; is it always so rough here?" Jan asked with concern in her voice as she squinted in the direction of our home.

"Yes, it's a little rolley, but I want to move and when we do, I will set the stern hook to keep her bow into the swell."

"Well, I hope no one gets sick out there tonight, you may have to row out the stern anchor tonight! I think I'll sleep. I'm exhausted, but I'm not sure about Sam, she's not used to any of this, you know."

Jan was concerned, but for the moment, all I wanted to do was get everyone safely out to the boat and settled in for the night. I snatched the handheld radio that I had clipped to my belt and placed a call.

"*Maiatla, Maiatla, Maiatla,* this is *Fish Killer, Fish Killer, Fish Killer.* Over!" I said.

"Go ahead, *Fish Killer,* this is Maui Jim!" Jim answered.

Fish Killer is the name our children had giving the dinghy many years ago and the nickname had stuck, but "Maui Jim" was a new one for us, apparently Jim decided that he need his own special radio persona.

"OK, Maui Jim, we are all at the dock. Can you bring the dink ashore so we can start ferrying everyone out to the boat?" I asked.

"Aye, aye, Captain! Be right there!"

With three new bodies aboard, *Maiatla* had to accommodate a total of seven for a full week before my sister, her husband and Kara had to fly back home to their old lives. For now we would have to make do with the tight accommodations, which meant two people would have to sleep outside in the cockpit. Not a particular hardship as the bench-seat cushions are quite comfortable and with the fully enclosed cockpit, it was like sleeping in a tent with big windows. The only drawback could have been the early morning sun would burn the retinas out of your eyes if you happened to be facing the wrong way when the sun peaked over the mountains.

The family's first evening aboard was grand! We barbecued steaks and drank wine while watching the sun set over the distant islands. I was particularly happy to have Jan and Melissa back with me as I was eager to show them all the things that I had already discovered. But, everyone was exhausted from their travels so it was off to bed early, but it would not be a pleasant night for me as discontent slid between the sheets with me.

"This damn boat is rolling too much, I'm going to get seasick in my sleep! When are you going to set a stern hook?" Jan demanded, as she jammed a pillow in behind her back to keep from rolling with the swells. (she had me on the other side).

We had been securely riding on the yacht club mooring for a couple of days now, but lacking Jan's encouragement, I had not found the energy or time to set the stern tackle. In my defence, I had talked to the local harbour master about getting a dock for a few days, so I didn't want to waste my strength humping an anchor and chain about if we were headed into the harbour anytime soon. I had a few boat chores to do that would be easier done at the dock, not to mention that with all the people aboard, getting ashore was a real problem as it took three full trips in the dinghy. We would have one more night out here before we could head into the harbour, I may have been the Captain, but there would be no arguing with the Admiral.

After breakfast and ferrying the kids to the beach, I readied the stern gear by lowering the Danforth anchor and chain into the dink. While Jan paid out the anchor rode from *Maiatla's* stern, I motored inshore for a hundred meters or so and dropped the hook. Back onboard, I wrapped the rode about the genoa primary winch and cranked in the slack until *Maiatla* showed her backside to the shore, in turn putting the incessant swell on her nose and the wind on her beam. Over the next few hours, we had to repeat the process four more times as our anchor dragged, causing *Maiatla* to swing, broadside to the groundswell. Finally, in frustration, I donned my snorkeling gear and jumped overboard to have a look. The water was amazingly clear as I could easily see the bottom over fifteen meters below. It instantly became obvious to me why the anchor was constantly dragging. The bottom was carpeted with a thin layer of white coral over top of black volcanic rock. The carpet of coral resembled a shag rug and was easily broken: I could see where our chain and anchor had dragged across the delicate sea floor. Fortunately, this was a designated anchorage and the big fines for damaging the coral were not applicable here. But I nonetheless, felt horrible for destroying such beautiful formations. On the bottom, there were tiny, intermittent patches of sand a scant few meters in diameter and unless the anchor happened to land on one of these isolated pockets of sandy real-estate, there was no way any hook would hold.

For what I hoped to be the last time, I motored the dinghy out, and with my face in the water aided by my mask, I carefully aimed the anchor at a convenient white sandy patch as if I were dropping a bomb from a plane. Several red and black Damselfish scattered as the anchor scored a direct hit on my first try. The flukes of the anchor had no trouble digging-in, and again, as I tightened the anchor line, our boat's nose rose to the western swell. The Admiral was once again happy!

Aside from the bouncy conditions and the constant stream of mainly charter vessels during the day, it was a beautiful anchorage. The warm breezes were usually light, paralleling the beach or coming from offshore. At night, the sky was always clear and when the moon was full, the view of the distant islands of Lanai and Molokai appeared surreal, almost magical as they hovered over a black rippling sea. Music would float out from shore from the various waterfront nightclubs and bars but unlike Mexico, the volume was tolerable and for the most part, the music was pleasant and died down shortly after midnight.

The following morning we pulled the stern tackle, untied our bow from the mooring and headed for the harbour mouth. The day was beautiful, sky clear and the water was as calm as the proverbial millpond despite the ten-knot offshore breeze. Thankfully, there wasn't a charter boat in sight; they all had headed out to sea either before or just after the crack of dawn. There was every indication that it was going to be a glorious day in paradise as the sun was already warm on the naked skin. With the Maple Leaf flying stiffly off our backstay, I swung wide of the starboard channel marker and at full throttle we bore down the center of the channel into the tiny harbor as if we owned it, only slowing as we approached the right-turn dogleg that would lead us behind the rubble breakwater. The fuel dock and harbour office, which was closed, as it was not yet 8:00 a.m. was located at the crotch of the dogleg and I would quickly learn that all who enter, do so under the steely gaze of the harbour master and his evil minion.

When I had met the harbour master at his office the previous day, he was standoffish, rather aloof, but dryly polite. When I offered a smile and my hand, he responded in kind but he was curt and I definitely had the feeling that my arrival was a big imposition for him and his harbour. He was obviously not impressed by where we had come from, and even less impressed by our desire for dock space within his harbour. His minion, was a former island cop with a nasty disposition and the word arrogant wouldn't even begin to describe the man.

As I was informed by the harbour master, there was only one berth reserved for transients; not one dock; one, single slip! And it was only big enough to accommodate a solitary boat of *Maiatla's* size! This berth was also available for locals who visited from other islands, so we were fortunate to get the dock at all as it was usually booked up most days. We could have it but for three days only. This was our first real indication of the state's hostility to boaters. Our second would arrive in the form of a red-faced man, yelling and screaming at us.

Our assigned slip was first-in-line on the seaward side of the harbour; bow in, we pointed towards the breakwater and the open ocean beyond. I had no trouble coming alongside and the crew quickly secured *Maiatla* to the decaying wooden dock. It only took a few moments to realize the deficiencies of this location. Despite being fully behind the rubble wall, there was little protection from the heavy groundswell, which was amplified as it surged up through the narrow channel, and into the harbor. Every fifteen seconds or so *Maiatla* was thrust against the dock with such force I was scared that all of our fenders would burst under the pressure.

Just as physics dictates that everything that goes up must come down, the retreating serge violently jerked us away from the dock with such abruptness that anyone standing casually on deck would have their feet pulled from beneath them. To combat this we ran a bridal which was attached to the bow and stern on the outboard side of the boat with the end of the line run forty meters or so along the breakwater to better secure the boat and dampen the motion. As I watched *Maiatla* get violently jerked from side to side even with her restraints, I started to think it would be better back in the rolley anchorage, where there was less likelihood of hull damage or careening into an adjacent boat if one of our dock lines were to part.

Remembering the harbor master's warning of the day before: to check into the office as soon as we arrived, I decided to hoof it around instead of taking the time to launch the dinghy and mount the outboard. From our slip, the harbor office was only fifty meters away, directly across the channel and off our stern. A very short dinghy ride, but going on foot meant a half-mile detour, around the perimeter of the harbour.

"Hey Jan, get the kids to run the water on the dock for a few minutes before filling the water tanks and then give the boat a good rinse to get the salt off of her, I'm heading over to check-in. OK?"

There were plenty of eager hands to tidy up the boat, so Jan just waved me on my way. I took off along the boardwalk. It was just after 8 am, but the sun, rapidly rising over Kihei, was already hot on my cheeks, forcing me to retreat under the brim of my Tilley. When I reached the office, I was surprised to find it still closed, I peered in the window but saw no indication of life so I thought I would just hang about for a bit to see if someone showed up. As I began to wander around the building to have a look, Melissa saw me and called over to me from the deck of *Maiatla*..

"Hey Dad! A man was just here and he yelled at us, saying that we were not allowed to be here and that we had to leave right now! Mom told him we couldn't as you were not here right now, he got madder, then swore before he left!"

I was a rather shocked to hear this.

"Who was he? Where did he go?" I called back though cupped hands.

"Don't know! Think he went that way!" She said, as she pointed back down the dock.

"What did he look like?"

"Brown shirt and long pants, I think?"

Now I was mad! Determined to find out who this guy was, I ran back around the harbour in search of the prick in brown, but I reached *Maiatla* before finding him. Jan was now on deck and she looked visibly shaken.

"Jan, did you talk to this guy? Who was he?" I asked.

"Just for a minute. I think he was with the harbour, he tore into Melissa first, then he told me we had to go. He was very nasty and abusive. I told him you'd just gone down the dock to the office. And that we wouldn't be leaving without you!"

"OK. Don't worry about it. I'm going back to the harbour office and if he shows up again call me on the handheld radio. I'm going to find out what's going on."

I snatched the radio from the cockpit and leapt back onto the dock. Royally pissed off, I jogged, back around the harbour, back to the office. All the while, looking for this man in brown along the way, half thinking I could use the handheld to bash the asshole up alongside the head if I were to find him.

By the time I arrived at the office, the Open sign was prominent and I pushed through the door into the air-conditioned office where I found three middle-aged ladies sitting at desks with a tall man in brown searching through a filing cabinet.

"Excuse me!" I said, rather loudly as I bellied up to the counter. All turned to look at me, and a single women approached.

"May I help you?" She asked, while giving me a perplexed look partially hidden behind a practiced smile.

"Yes, you may. I own that boat out there on the visitors' dock and I would like to know if someone from this office was just over there, ordering me and my family off the dock?"

The woman I was speaking to, first looked a bit stunned but then suddenly turned to the man behind her. The man, upon hearing my question, jumped to his side of the counter, across from me. "That was me!" he said while sounding not just a bit angry. He raises a large hand to point his stubby finger at me. "And what do you think you are doing coming in here and tying up without permission and taking water?! These docks are all reserved! Now you get back aboard and get out of here! Right now!"

If I was upset before, I was now livid. I squeezed the handheld radio so tight in my fist I thought it would burst.

"First off, who the hell are you to be talking to me in this way? You have no business yelling at my wife and kids no matter who the hell you are!" I shot back.

He raised his voice by several more decibels. "I'm the assistant harbour master and unless you get your ass out of here, I will be calling the police and having your boat impounded! He said as he leaned further over the counter in an effort to intimidate me." But I wasn't buying into his posturing nor backing down which I think pissed him off all the more, judging by his scrunched up face and the amount of spittle he was ejecting.

"Oh, really?" I said. "Well, I talked to the harbour master yesterday. He told me to come in this morning and that I had the dock for the next three days!"

The man was as arrogant as ever and was showing no signs of softening.

"I have no record of anyone coming in this morning, so get off my dock!" he ordered, again raising his voice to new heights. All the woman appeared to be upset with what was transpiring and the women who was at his side had now retreated back out of the strike zone with the rest. They could see that I was brandishing a fully charged radio and wasn't afraid to use it.

"No record? Well, why is my boat name scribbled on your board, next to the transient dock?" I pointed over his shoulder to the white board hanging on the wall. It showed a diagram of all the slips and corresponding boats assigned to them.

"There!" I pointed past his head. "*Maiatla* is written right there, and if you cared to look at the name on my stern, you asshole, you would see that I did have the slip booked and that I'm supposed to be here!" *Maiatla* was plainly visible from the office and why he had not looked at the name of the boat before now just escaped me.

For the first time since the beginning of our confrontation the man retreated, but just a little. He looked hard at my boat, then again at the white board all the while saying nothing.

For a moment the office was quiet, a pregnant pause is what I think you call it. Finally after several seconds he turned to the woman I first spoke to.

"Fill out the papers and sign him in," he said.

Without so much as an apology, he went back to his filing cabinet. He may have been through but I wasn't. I perhaps should have lowered my voice but I couldn't.

"Is this how you people greet foreign travelers? Tourists? I have never been treated this badly anywhere before! And, don't you ever dare to raise your voice to my family again you asshole!" I said, as I glared at him over my pointing finger.

I half expected him to charge me like a bull, but I was ready to clip him with my radio if he did! But, he said and did nothing more. He was done.

All three women appeared to shrink further as if wanting to hide.

"I'm very sorry for the misunderstanding," the woman who first approached said.

I could tell from the look in her eyes that her apology was sincere. I suddenly felt my anger waning as fast as a harpooned inflatable. I probably sounded a bit like one as well as I finally took a deep breath and exhaled in an effort to calm myself down.

"Do you have your vessel's registration and custom's clearance papers with you?" she asked.

It was my turn to retreat as I realized that these ladies were not the enemy. I lowered my voice.

"Thank you." I said, as I handed her my paperwork. "But, I would like to know who this man's superior is. And I want the number of the State Harbour Authority, I will be filing a complaint over this!"

The lady quickly completed my paperwork, handed me two gate keys and then without so much as a sideways glace at the assistant manager who appeared to be busy with paperwork, handed me an official looking paper.

"You will find all the contact information you requested on here. If you have any questions or concerns we are here from eight to five, week days." She wished me a good day and smiled. I got the distinct feeling that this was not a new occurrence and she has had to make apologies for this moron before.

I thanked her, and made a move towards the exit while casting a backwards glance at the now quietly sitting prick; he didn't even look at me as I kicked the door open and left the building.

So ended my welcome to the Lahaina State Harbour!

Chapter #12

Explorers in Paradise.

I find the great thing in this world is not so much where we stand, as in what direction we are moving: To reach the port of heaven, we must sail sometimes with the wind and sometimes against it - but we must sail, and not drift, nor lie at anchor.
        Oliver Wendell Holmes.

Once settled at the dock, the crew went about playing tourist while I attended to the boat chores. Our little gremlins were not going to give me a break just because we were in Hawaii! First on my list, was a mechanical service for our refrigeration system. It cost a few hundred dollars to learn it was just fine; the trouble originated with having low battery voltage and it was resolved by being more diligent at aiming the solar panels at the sun. Our starter motor was also acting up. The culprit was the same as the refrigeration system; low battery voltage meant the starter needed high current to turn it over; the high current created excess heat, which finally toasted the starter motor. Out came the starter for a rebuild. Fortunately, Mike was spot on with his recommendation for a mechanic shop; they went out of their way to help us. After Inquiring about locating a new fuel injector, I found a shop that had a full set in stock that they were clearing out. I bought all four for the price of one. What a deal!

The intermittent climb in engine temperature at my normal rpm's was eventually blamed on a loose hose clamp in the engine water intake system. When the vacuum increased with the engine's speed, a small amount of air would be sucked through the raw water pump, reducing the flow and causing the heat exchanger to heat up. I went through a long, tedious process of elimination to discover the root cause, but it was an easy fix as the cure was administered with the single twist of a screwdriver followed by a celebratory reunion with my old friend Captain Morgan.

Our three days at the dock flew by and fortunately, we had no further contact with the harbour office. Mike had vanished on a charter the day of the girls' arrival but he was kind enough to leave me the keys to his old Mazda truck which Jan took advantage of. We hit the local markets to stock up on fresh foods. Jan had prepared the larder well before we left home so aside from fresh fruits and vegetables we were well provisioned. I needed to take on fuel but we had a problem because we still did not have the proper environmental permit and it didn't look good for getting one anytime soon. Humping one hundred and fifty gallons of fuel, five gallons at a time in jerry cans from shore did not appeal to me and the mere suggestion of it made my young crew groan. Mike's mechanic friend told me to check with the yacht club as they had a permit and a fuel card that would unlock the self-serve pumps at the fuel dock. Sure enough, as an honorary member of the Lahaina yacht club, all I had to do was leave a credit card with the club office and return with the printed receipt from the fuel dock and we were all done.

Jackie and Jim found sleeping in the cockpit at the dock a little unsettling, as early morning dock walkers would peer in on them while asleep. One morning they were rudely awakened with a cold shower as the a crew member of the neighbouring charter boat decided to hose down his decks while not realizing, or caring, not sure which, soaked *Maiatla's* cockpit tenants as they had left the dodger windows open. Feeling like they were specimens on display in an aquarium, Jackie and Jim finally opted to move to a local hotel for their last few nights on Maui, which in turn alleviated the boats overcrowding.

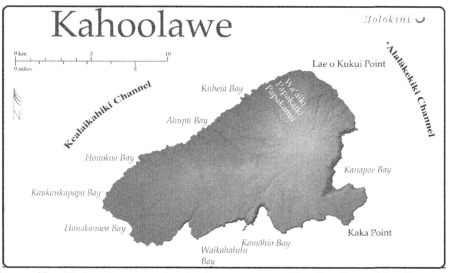

Figure 12. Kahoolawe ecological reserve just 7 miles from Maui, used as a bombing range by the U.S military up until 1990.

With our boat duties completed, it was time to move back out to the anchorage. We gladly departed from the harbour early in the morning, brandishing a few new scars on our hull from constantly buffeting the dock. We powered out of the hideous harbour with its ogre of an assistant manager and nosed into the swells; glad to be headed back to our mooring ball in the less congested roadstead.

With the boats mechanical needs attended to, it was time to start exploring in earnest, so with that in mind, I rented a jeep. With the ragtop down, we hit the road. We spent the following week touring the island, driving down beaches and up volcanoes; doing all the things normal, land-based tourists do. We drove up the volcano Haleakalā, and photographed the rare and endangered Silversword plant. We visited the deep, lush 'Iao Valley, which features the 'Iao Needle, a natural rock pinnacle, surrounded by cascading falls where local youth dive from cliffs and bridges for pocket change tossed into the water by tourists. The often rotund lads were a bit pushy and I thought of them as being the islands' version of squeegee people. And, of course, on Jackie and Jim's last night in town, we all attended the mandatory luau and pig roast, complete with Polynesian dancers with more than ample breasts and gyrating hips, at one of the countless resorts. The outdoor banquet was catered by young men and women with taught, bronzed bodies and engaging smiles. Rain gear was passed out for protection against the torrential, yet fleeting, evening downpours.

Jan and I even managed to steal a day away and find a secluded spot on Mekena Beach to soak up some sun. If you scale the old lava flow that separates Big beach and Little beach, you will stumble into the clothing optional crowd with (soon to be red), white bits that would hurt the eyes if not for dark sunglasses. There are many recognized nude or topless beaches in the islands, most are in discrete hidden away places, but to find one, all you have to do is ask a local.

Generally, nude sunbathing or swimming is illegal in Hawaii and some State beaches have security guards that enforce the rules, with Kauai being the more prudish and conservative of the main eight islands. Despite all the government's effort to ban the bare buns, lounging about bare ass, is quite popular and practiced to varying degrees on all the islands. The government's frustration with determined nudists is nothing new in Hawaii; Mark Twain noted in 1887, when the pious missionaries attempted to cloth the natives for church services:

The natives soon manifested a strong proclivity for clothing, but it was shortly apparent that they only wanted it for grandeur. The missionaries imported a quantity of hats, bonnets, and other male and female wearing apparel, instituted a general distribution, and begged the people not to come to church naked, next Sunday, as usual. And they did not; but the national spirit of unselfishness led them to divide up with neighbors who were not at the distribution, and next Sabbath the poor preachers could hardly keep countenance before their vast congregations. In the midst of the reading of a hymn a brown, stately dame would sweep up the aisle with a world of airs, with nothing in the world on but a "stovepipe" hat and a pair of cheap gloves; another dame would follow, tricked out in a man's shirt, and nothing else; another one would enter with a flourish, with simply the sleeves of a bright calico dress tied around her waist and the rest of the garment dragging behind like a peacock's tail off duty; a stately "buck" Kanaka would stalk in with a woman's bonnet on, wrong side before—only this, and nothing more; after him would stride his fellow, with the legs of a pair of pantaloons tied around his neck, the rest of his person untrammeled; in his rear would come another gentleman simply gotten up in a fiery neck-tie and a striped vest.

****

Later, on one afternoon, after a shopping spree ashore, I loaded Samantha and Melissa into the dink at the dinghy dock and pushed off to motor back to the boat. There was a steady stream of incoming charter boats, so I had to drift about, mid-harbour, waiting for an opening to make our exist out of the channel. A knot of obvious tourists stood at the end of the breakwater, admiring the ocean view and snapping pictures of one another. Their attention suddenly fixated on us, as they spied our tiny dink dodging several incoming boats, turning into their large wakes to prevent getting swamped. Our manoeuvres were similar to a Chihuahua, dancing around the feet of a room full of excited partygoers. The tourists were also perhaps wondering why three people in a miniature rubber boat were trying to head out to sea. Little did they or we suspect that things were about to get more exciting! For some of us anyway!

We crested a large wake without getting soaked and turned sharply, back towards the channel that would lead us clear of all the traffic. Sam excitedly snapped pictures of the shore and boats, all the while jabbering incoherently from behind her camera about something which totally escaped me. This was not an uncommon occurrence; Sam would often prattle on, or change the subject quickly, charging off on a tangent; leaving me wondering if I had momentarily blacked out, ignorant and behind in the conversation. Melissa just sat quietly in the bow, showing little interest in anything other than keeping her butt dry as water splashed over the bow as I powered up. Melissa had been fine for most of the day, and I had had high hopes for her earlier in the day, but like most pubescent teens, her mood had switched in an instant and she now appeared to be in an emotional tailspin as water splashed up her back. She now owned the look that said, she wished she were anywhere else but here. I knew it would be futile to try and talk to her at this moment so I did the smart thing and kept my mouth shut. This was easy as Sam was still doing all the talking, leaving little opportunity for anyone else anyway.

A lull in the traffic gave me an opportunity to gun the little mercury and shoot out the harbour entrance. Once clear of the breakwater we nosed into the rising swell as I aimed the dink for the outer reef marker.

"Hey! Look, surfers!" Sam called out as she pointed beyond the reef.

There, in a tight cluster just inshore of the anchorage, was a group of bronzed teens, milling about on surfboards, sizing up the incoming waves.

Perfect! I thought. Surfer boys! Just what I needed to distract Melissa and perhaps get her out of her funky mood. Without hesitation and regrettably, without forethought, I diverted the dink with the intent of trolling for teenage boys. After all, how hard could it be as I had the perfect bait? A pair of beautiful girls and with Sam's gregarious nature, I was sure all I had to do was get her within eyeshot and she would draw them in like ravenous gulls to a fish ball.

"What are you doing, Dad?" Melissa broke her silence, as she suddenly acknowledged life beyond her own proximity.

"I just want to talk to the boys about the surfing here. Perhaps we can take some lessons," I lied, as part of my ruse.

I recalled being a seven year old boy with a six foot surfboard tackling a fifteen foot wave on Waikiki beach, an event that nearly drowned my father as he swam out into the surf in an effort to prevent me from killing myself. At nearly fifty, I had no real desire to let history repeat itself by learning how to hang ten now. But, I was getting desperate to find a diversion, anything that would bring my daughter out of her shell. Melissa turned to look at the boys.

" Hello-o-o-o!" Sam waved and called.

Moments later, we were surrounded by inquisitive boys, bobbing on surfboards. Sam began to work her charms by bombarding the youths with questions. Melissa seemed to perk up as she watched her outgoing cousin do all the work which seemed to come natural to her. I was feeling rather pleased with myself and believed that I had just pulled off a major coup. I did my best to blend into the background, not wanting to interfere with the chemistry that was going on as we drifted about. I was intent on watching the interaction between the girls and the surfers, which was a big mistake.

In my excitement, I had failed to fully comprehend the correlation between the presence of surfboards and the close proximity to breaking waves. In the few minutes it took to initiate contact with the surfers, we had inadvertently drifted towards shore, the shallow reef, and the sunken Rhodes. The mast protruding from the water should have been the first clue that perhaps we were not where we should have been. I was so distracted by what Sam was saying to a boy that had come alongside, that I had failed to watch my surroundings. Melissa turned to stare over my shoulder, then wide-eyed, she frantically pointed.

"Ah, thanks, Dad!" was all she said.

I shot a glance over my shoulder just in time to see it charging in like a speeding torpedo! The two-meter breaking wave struck with such force that the three of us were momentarily airborne. I flew over top of both girls, and all three of us were unceremoniously dumped into the sea. When I broke the surface, I saw the girls treading water and I watched as the dink, still upright, surf away on the remnants of the wave.

"Quick girls, swim for the dinghy before the next wave hits!" I yelled.

We recovered the dink and were fortunate that it had not capsized, but it was full of water.

Quickly, I pushed the girls up, into the dinghy and pulled myself in. I took a few seconds to take stock of our situation. Everything that was in the dinghy before the wave, was either soaked or gone; life jackets, oars and gas can all were flotsam now, drifting over the nearby reef. Thankfully all of the girls' purchases were floating in the bottom of the dinghy. Sam was stilling clinging to the Ziploc bag that contained her new digital camera but the baggie was full of water. But, I could not concern myself with that stuff now, I had to get us back beyond the surf line. I jerked the starter cord and mercifully, the mercury started on the first pull. I gunned the motor and wheeled the sluggish, water filled dink around, aiming her back out to sea. It was a godsend that the following sets of waves failed to break, but their steepness nearly flipped us. I drove, as the girls franticly bailed with their hands; we powered up and over the threating swells without further incident. Once I was sure we were again in safe water, I stopped the dink to take a breath and to help with the bailing. The look of the sodden girls in their street clothes struck me as being a little funny and I gave a nervous chuckle.

"Boy, the water is sure warm, hey?" I offered.

Needless to say, the girls were pissed off. It only took a few seconds for them to recover from their shock before tearing into me. Fortunately for me, they were interrupted when several of the surfers paddled up alongside and handed us the lost chattels that they had recovered from the surf or the bottom. I thanked them and we quickly slunk away in the direction of *Maiatla*. I had no doubt that our little mishap had been fully observed by the hawk-eyed tourists on the breakwater not to mention the thousand-odd souls meandering along Lahaina's waterfront. It must have been quite a spectacle from shore. Aside from my ego and captainship taking a direct hit and Sam's digital camera getting a dunking, there were no other casualties. Well, at least my plan worked! The girls did meet some surfer dudes!

It was time to get off the mooring and find a secluded anchorage down the coast for a little snorkeling and sun worshiping. Hekili Point, located just five nautical miles south and down the coast from Lahaina, was even less protected than the open roadstead at the yacht club, and more exposed to the late morning winds that would build and funnel between the mountains of north and south Maui. Nevertheless, the coral reef was reported to be nice, expansive and sported many friendly sea turtles. We spent our last night in Lahaina at the yacht club where we had gone for dinner. On the way home, we bumped into Mike and a fellow beach bum friend of his. Mike had just returned from a job and was eager to get acquainted with the girls. Likewise, Samantha and Kara liked what they saw and both were anxious to mix with these obviously virile locals, but the sexes would have to wait to get together as our departure from Lahaina was imminent.

Our early morning motor along the coast was scenic but utterly windless, and finding a good anchoring spot close to shore and not in the delicate coral proved to be quite a problem. The white patches of sand were clearly visible though the ten meters of transparent water, but most were not large enough to lay sufficient ground tackle to ensure solid holding when the inevitable winds arrived later in the morning, as they always did. The winds in central Maui were as predictable as the passing of the sun. As the morning aged, the land heated up and by eleven am, the strong winds blew. In the evening, the opposite happened; as the sun set, so did the winds. It was a cycle as old as the islands themselves.

Along with another vessel, we scoured the reef, looking for a suitable place to drop the hook. To facilitate this, Jackie donned her snorkeling gear and jumped ship to direct our numerous and unsuccessful attempts at anchoring in amongst the great branches of reaching coral. Finally, after an hour of dropping and recovering the ground tackle and I hate to say, snagging some delicate branches in the process, we were secure enough for now. But I was worried about dragging: our anchor acting like a bulldozer, tearing through the delicate ecosystem, when the winds built to their fullest. I would just have to watch closely for a while to make sure we didn't drag out of our tiny sand patch.

Jan decided to stay back and watch the boat as everyone else hit the water. No one was disappointed; the reef was as promised, and we swam for hours and miles in pursuit of colourful fish and lazy turtles that did little more that lie about on the bottom and casually swim out of arms reach if we happened to venture too close.

I found it interesting to note that some of the turtles we saw were covered with numerous wart-like tumors, which seemed to leave no soft tissue unaffected. The turtles necks appeared to be the first target of the bulges, but they soon spread to the eyes and mouth regions of the animals. The lumps were often as big as golf balls, or larger. I was sick to see one animal, that appeared to be wearing a grisly mask; the poor creature was blind in one eye, as a tumor had taken over the entire right side of its face. I would later inquire about the sea turtles affliction, and what I learned was rather shocking.

****

The fibropapillomatosis virus affecting the turtles was very similar to the herpes or papilloma virus commonly found in humans. The tumors are a benign growth spread by an unknown pathogen. Although not clearly supported by scientific evidence, the close proximity of people may well be the culprit in the turtle's case.

Green sea turtles have developed these tumors or wart like lumps, that appear as lobe-shaped tumors and these tumors can infect all soft portions of a turtle's body. The tumors grow primarily on the skin, but they can also appear between scales, in the mouth, on the eyes, and on internal organs and can grow from a blanch spot (white) on the skin to a full blown tumor within a year. Apparently, most of the turtles that get infected with the disease steadily become sick and most will die from the condition. The disease seems to run rampant in the juvenile turtles and most perish within two years; in adults, the disease is less predictable and the older animals have a better chance of survival. Although some turtles have shown signs of remission and have survived much longer than normal, this is not typical.

The sad truth is that scientists aren't yet certain what causes the tumors or how they are spread but stress from human contact and or pollution are prime suspects. This condition is not just isolated to the Hawaiian Islands as turtles in other locations where humans congregate such as Florida and Barbados have likewise succumbed to the disease.

****

Our group slowly split up and I found myself swimming and holding hands with Melissa. I had purchased a digital underwater camera with an external flash in hopes of getting some spectacular shots of the abundant marine life. Melissa suddenly had aspirations of becoming a great underwater photographer but soon learned how tough it was to even get close enough to the spooky fish to get a shot, never mind a good one. Together we gently pursued the turtles, but only managed to get several shots of the animals backsides as they retreated. Within a couple of hours, Melissa had given up wanting to be another Jacques Cousteau and passed the camera back to me. We continued to explore the reef together and had a blast. I was warmed by the big smile my daughter sported whenever she spied a new fish or creature. She dove to collect shells and peer into holes like a little kid on an Easter egg hunt, manifesting a trait she must have inherited from me because I'm still much the same way. This day reminded me of the countless hours Melissa, Thomas and I had spent snorkeling in Mexico just five years previous, a time that was arguably one of the happiest in my life. I was content to swim with my daughter again and all the cost and hardship that I had endured just to get here was worth it for just these few precious hours with her.

We would only spend a single night here, as trying to keep the boat from spinning in the wind and our anchor chain out of the coral beds proved to be a challenge. We planned to move on at first light.

****

I don't recall precisely when I had first seen her, but I do recall that it was many years ago, perhaps as long as twenty. Her picture was on a creased and worn, colour post card that I had discovered, again in a place I do not recall. What I do remember was how striking she was. She was curvaceous, well-formed, and almost naked with only a delicate verdant lace to conceal her hunched back and a single dropping shoulder. The mere site of her, enticed images of the exotic to dance in my head and I would often hold the card and imagine myself being there, right there next to her. I would point at the exact spot where I wanted to be. It would even be safe to say that in some ways I lusted after her, even fantasized about lying next to her in her embrace. I knew, even back then, that one day when I sailed to the South Pacific I would seek her out, find her and revel in her timeless beauty. The post card was long gone but simple and mute image stayed with me all these many years and served to fuel my deep desire to travel to the exotic and often erotic South Seas, and here, in Maui, my time had finally come. Molokini lay less than eighteen miles to the east of Lahaina and she was beckoning me to come visit. How could I refuse her?

Molokini is a partially sunken volcanic crater just 2.5 miles off the coast of Maui; an uninhabited island that has a landmass of just 23 acres. The tiny island is nestled between the islands of Maui and Kahoolawe, almost in the center of Alalakeiki Channel. Molokini is a beautiful underwater sanctuary for marine life and is truly one of Maui's most breathtaking snorkeling and diving locations and arguably the best in the entire Hawaiian chain.

Part of Maui County, Molokini is now a popular destination for scuba diving and snorkeling with many tourist boats coming each day from the south coast of Maui. The crescent shape provides protection from waves and ocean currents, making this area one of the top ten dive sites in the world. Molokini's back wall, on its rugged south coast, drops off to depths of 300 feet where it is reported that valuable black coral, used in fine jewelry grows in the deep water. Inside the island crescent, is a reef with clear views up to 150 feet. These waters are home to about 250 species of fish and colourful coral and with the nearby drop off, deep water, pelagic fish and Humpback whales are often seen here.

In Hawaiian legend, Molokini was a beautiful woman. She and Pele, the fire goddess, were in love with the same man. The jealous Pele cut her rival in two and transformed her into stone. The woman's head is supposedly Puu Olai, the cinder cone located by Makena Beach. Her body is the crescent shaped Molokini.

The beheading notwithstanding, Molokini wasn't always peaceful. During and after the Second World War, the US Navy used the island for target practice. Naval gun crews fired tens of thousands of rounds; everything from machinegun fire to the big guns of the battleships trained upon the tiny island. Even the Air Force took their turn and unleashed ordnance from fighters and heavy bombers alike. In 1975 and again in 1984, the US Navy detonated in-place unexploded munitions found within the crater and large tracks of seabed and coral gardens were destroyed The resultant public outcry prompted a thorough search and risky manual removal of unexploded munitions which were recovered and disposed of in deep water by volunteer divers. A 2006 survey confirmed the effectiveness of the clean up as it reported finding no evidence of unexploded munitions on Molokini itself , which is a now a designated bird sanctuary and landing is strictly prohibited

*****

We arrived at Molokini before most of the dive charter boats, which improved our chance of locating an unoccupied submerged mooring buoy as anchoring was also prohibited in the bay. Jan motored *Maiatla* about, as I donned my gear and jumped ship in search of a mooring. The moorings were nearly impossible to see from the surface unless you were directly over one. But once in the water, the white buoys were easy to find and I soon had *Maiatla* firmly secured.

Again, as fast as I could deploy the boarding ladder, the crew jumped overboard and were all exploring the marine park. Jan opted to stay aboard, so Melissa and I hit the water and worked our way along the shore while being dazzled by the throngs of colourful fish that darted about. Being away from the shore and any rain runoff, the visibility was near limitless. With fish dancing around the rising bubbles, we swam over top of scuba divers that looked so close you would think that you could easily dive and touch them, despite being over thirty meters below. We had covered about half a mile following the shore and only stopped once we reached the outer most tip of the island. We began to swim around the corner, but suddenly stopped as the bottom dropped away into the black abyss. The growing current attempted to pull us the rest of the way out of the bay, into the open sea beyond.

I grabbed Melissa by the hand and told her to swim hard. For several minutes, we finned, but made little headway. I pulled her closer to the rocks in hopes of getting out of the tidal flow - it worked. Back around the point, we rested for a few moments on some submerged rocks before taking our time heading back to the boat. Despite nearly being sucked away, Melissa and I thoroughly enjoyed the snorkel. It was another great father-daughter moment for me.

Back on board, an excited Kara told of all the colorful fish they had seen but when a reef shark passed below them, they decided it was time to seek the safety of the boat and beat a hasty retreat. If the sharks had been hungry, they had lots to choose from as there were at least eight dive charter boats bobbing nearby on moorings and all had vomited scores of swimmers into the water. It could have been a scene from any shipwreck disaster movie that left hundreds treading water, just waiting to be eaten. The bay was now rather congested and being somewhat intrigued by my glimpse of what was just around the corner, I made a suggestion.

"Hey guys, how about we take the boat around the back of the island, next to the cliff and the deep water drop off and do a drift snorkel? We can get Jan to drop us in, and we can let the current take us and the boat can follow. I bet we will see some big fish on the other side, what do ya think?"

Being the consummate explorer, I knew Jackie would throw in with me as she would rarely question my sanity in these matters, but the rest might find the deep water and pull of the current unsettling, not to mention seeing the boat powering away after dumping them off in the ocean. Kara, lacking better judgment and perhaps already forgetting her narrow escape from the reef shark was the first to announce that she was in. Sam and Melissa after a few minutes of contemplation likewise agreed that it would be fun. Jim on the other hand opted out of our expedition and volunteered to stay with Jan and help her keep an eye on us as she drifted nearby while keep our home away from the cliffs and off the rocks.

Within minutes of dropping the mooring buoy, *Maiatla* was firmly in the grip of the strong current that swept down the length of the island. Jan maneuvered the boat to within forty meters of the rocks and one by one we all jumped. The current was strong, impossible to swim against, but we had no trouble moving across the current to the rocky shore. The cliff arose straight up out of the water with no possible place for a landing, not even a small boulder to climb upon. The underwater scene was no less dramatic as the sheer cliff face continued on, straight down for perhaps twenty meters before sloping steeply outward to finally disappear in the black depths.

A heavy swell was coming from the south and as the current took us around the island, the waves built to two meters or so in height. The waves pounded the rocky face then bounced back, creating a washing machine affect immediately adjacent to the rocks, forcing us to stay at least ten meters away. The swirling bubbles in the water left behind by the swells beating the rocks hindered our visibility, and to make matters worse, the sun was already well into the west so we were in the deep shadow cast by the island. All this combined to make the water look dark and menacing.

Once we had formed a tight group, I led everyone along the wall, while we all peered down, through the water, wide-eyed at the drop-off below us. Surprisingly, the rocks bore little coral and the normally ubiquitous reef fish were scarce. I dove down to see if there was more to see deeper down but I found it was much the same. All in all, I was rather disappointed, but everyone seemed to be enjoying themselves so we carried on. I peered over top of the waves to see *Maiatla* doing lazy circles a few hundred meters away and gave Jan a casual wave to signal that all was well.

I continued to lead the tour with the hope that the marine life would improve further around the island, I also kept an eye trained on the open depths in hopes of seeing some of the big, pelagic, open ocean fish that should be out here. It could be possible to see marlin, swordfish, tuna, barracuda, or giant manta rays and if we were really lucky, a Humpback whale would swim by. After covering a mile or so, little of interest showed itself and I could see that Samantha, who was not the strongest of swimmers, was getting tired of fighting the surging waves. We had been in the water for almost an hour and I felt it was time to signal for a pickup. I peered back down below for one final look and in some ways, I was sorry that I had.

It glided silently out of the deep gloom, perhaps fifty meters away and twenty or thirty meters below us. He turned sharply and slipped back into the darkness. I hovered on the surface and watched for a few minutes before he reappeared in the same spot only to vanish again just as fast. I was not sure of the species of shark but it was at least two to three meters long and if I had to guess it was probably a

Galapagos shark, or it could have been a tiger shark, but with my fleeting glimpse and the light flickering through the water, I could not tell if it had the telltale stripes of a tiger or not. At this point, it really didn't matter, as both these species of sharks can be aggressive to humans and it would be a good idea to get out of the water. I peered around the surface and fortunately, everyone was right next to me and closer to the shore, putting me between the shark and my group (this may not have been a good thing from a self-preservation view point). The shore still offered no place to land so we would have to tread water until our taxi arrived.

"Hey guys, I think it's time to get back, stay together until Jan gets here with the boat, OK?" I said.

I waved my hands above my head to signal that we were ready to be picked up, and I began to feel a little sense of relief to see *Maiatla* coming our way. Although I have been in the water with big sharks before and doubted that we were in any real danger of being attacked, I still felt uneasy and just a little vulnerable. I was reasonably sure no one else had seen the shark, and I didn't see the need to enlighten them. Jackie would be fine if she knew and Melissa had swum with giant rays and with aggressive elephants seals weighing in at several tons, so I was confident that she would keep her cool, but I was not sure of Kara and Samantha. Having someone panic at this point could prove more dangerous than having the shark somewhere below. So, I kept my mouth shut.

"Hey Andy! It's too rough up that close, and I don't feel comfortable bringing the boat in there, can you guys swim out to me?" Jan called to us. She had brought the boat in as close to shore as she dared, but she was still a good sixty meters away and not surprisingly, just about on top of where I had last seen the shark.

"OK everybody, let's all swim to the boat, and stay together!" I called over my shoulder. I grabbed Melissa's hand and with my face down in the water watching the depths, we quickly swam for the boat. *Maiatla* was rolling heavily from side to side, as she stalled broadside to the swells, making it difficult for everyone to get their fins off and board the boat. I must say that I was relieved that the shark had not made another appearance, or if he had I never saw him. Being the last to board, I took one final, hard look below the boat before climbing the ladder to make sure I wasn't going to get bitten in the ass!

With everyone safely aboard, we hoisted sail and beat our way clear of Molokini and laid a course for Maalaea Bay located next to the community of Kehei, just a few short miles away. Maalaea Bay is smack dab in the middle of the Maui wind tunnel, but the western swell would not enter the bay, and the bottom was fine sand, which offered good holding. We planned to spend the night before heading back to Lahaina during the morning calm.

Maiatla was hard on the wind; she pounded her head into the great swells. Every third wave broke over the bow, sending water sluicing down the deck.

"Now Dad, this is what I'm talking about!" Melissa said while sporting a big grin, as she clung to the bow pulpit waiting for the next boarding wave to soak her. Our sail to Maalaea Bay was wet and wild. The wind pick up the farther into the bay we went, until final I had to reduce sail just to keep under control.

"Hey Dad! Look at the dinghy!" Melissa said, as she returned to the cockpit, finally having enough of her foredeck shower.

I turned to look behind the boat and cursed as I spied our dinghy. The wind was gusting; whipping around the little boat so hard, that it had flipped the soft bottom inflatable and we were merrily dragging her along. The recovery process took half an hour and we lost a set of oars and a gas can in the process. Fortunately, I had removed the outboard motor, which saved it from a dunking, if not a ride to the bottom. As the sun set, the wind quickly vanished and with the sound of distant waves crashing on a beach, we settled down at anchor to a very peaceful night.

In the still of the early morning, I loaded a sad Kara into the dinghy to begin her long journey home. She had taken a job at a Christian kids' camp for the summer and it was time for her to return to her version of the netherworld. We motored ashore to land on a beautiful sandy beach. With bags in hand, we cut through the dunes up to the main road where we caught the bus to the airport. Kara gave me a final big hug and as she did, she vowed that she would return in August to crew *Maiatla* on her long voyage home.

As I waved her off and caught the bus back to the beach, I was overcome with sadness. Kara, in a very short time had become part of my family, I was proud of her for the moxie, courage, and determination that she displayed while at sea and I would be pleased to have her sail with me again.

Kara would likewise have to wait to see Maui Mike again, but see him she would as Mike had expressed an interest in sailing back to Canada with us as well, a proposition which I was giving serious consideration.

Chapter #13

Lanai, The Pineapple Island

Every time we walk along a beach some ancient urge disturbs us so that we find ourselves shedding shoes and garments or scavenging among seaweed and whitened timbers like the homesick refugees of a long war.
  Loren Eiseley,

We spent one more night anchored at Maalaea Bay then in the morning beat our way back to Lahaina to drop Jackie and Jim off at the dock so they could return to their hotel for their last night before flying back to the netherworld. They were as unhappy to leave, as we were sad to see them go; unlike Kara they would not be back. The only upside to having three people leave was that the boat suddenly got forty percent bigger. It was now just Jan and me, Melissa and Samantha left aboard.

I was pleased to see our familiar mooring ball and we no sooner had the stern hook out, when Maui Mike rowed up in his dinghy. Mike promptly appeared, acting as if he had just been passing by and decided to drop in for a neighbourly visit. Aside from the brief encounter over a week ago on the street in front of the yacht club, this was the first time Jan and the girls had a chance to get to know Mike. Again introductions were made all around and with beers in hand, Mike entertained everyone with stories of how he found himself living in the islands and his plans to sail south once his boat was shipshape and more importantly, paid off.

I couldn't help notice that Mike had strategically placed himself between Samantha and Melissa while paying particular attention to the girls' reactions to him. I was impressed with his apparent smoothness and tact, which he was now displaying, unlike my first encounter with him. I wouldn't go so far as to say he was suave, but he had definably polished up his act for the ladies. It didn't take long before he had everyone's full attention. I was ecstatic that he and Sam seemed to be hitting it off, and even more ecstatic that he appeared to have taken my warning seriously to stay clear of my sixteen-year-old daughter! Under the threat of death, he was polite to Melissa and wisely reserved all his sexual energy and charisma for Melissa's older cousin Samantha who had his undivided attention.

Melissa on the other hand, true to her sixteen year old nature, declined to participate in any of the normally obligatory pleasantries, and refused to hide the fact that she really didn't want to be here. The fact that *Maiatla* was rolling heavily did little to sooth her rather prickly nature. Jan and I could tell from our daughter's demeanor that she wasn't being taken in by Maui Mike's charm despite his platonic attempts to win her over.

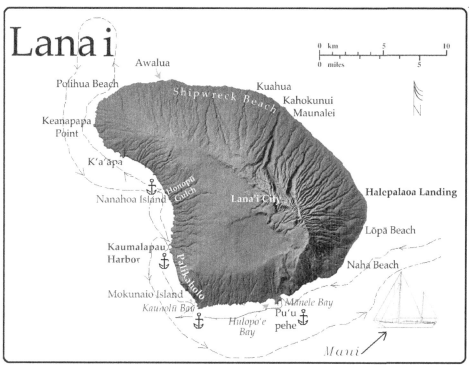

Figure 13. The Pineapple Island with *Maiatla's* course around and back.

In a break between stories about island life (breaks were few with Mike), Samantha complained about the amount of sun she had been exposed to that day. She slipped her shirt straps off, exposing the red, raw skin of her shoulders. Always quick to help, Mike rooted around in his bag, retrieved a tube of surfer's salve and without hesitation or invitation began to squirt it liberally upon Samantha's burnt shoulders, gently messaging the lotion into her shoulders. At first, Sam was obviously surprised by Mike's forwardness. They had really just met and here he was rubbing her down as if they were long-time friends, but her initial apprehension was melted away by the soothing effects of the cream and Mike's gentle touch.

Aside from my warning to Mike to refrain from any physical contact with the captain's daughter, I had similarly informed him that the girls came as a package. We had invited Samantha along as company for Melissa and more importantly, as a buffer for her parents. Any invitation was to include both, neither was to be left out, which Mike didn't seem to have a problem with, in fact he had already formulated a plan. Melissa, for the moment, seemed to be tolerating Mike and although not buying into his roguish charm, she quickly perked up when he suggested that they could all go deep sea fishing or surfing and mentioned that he had a sixteen year old deck hand that Melissa might like to meet.

The kids, as Jan and I now called them, made plans for the following day and times were agreed upon. As I sat to one side with a beer, watching the latest pirouette of this social dance, I was inwardly pleased with myself for scooping up Mike. I now possessed real hope that our distraught daughter's outlook would take a turn for the better. Additionally to Melissa's delight, she discovered that she could pirate internet service from nearby motels if we were close enough. It didn't take long before she was again on Facebook and Nexopia with all of her friends back home, who surprisingly seemed to take pleasure in tormenting her, making sure she was very aware of all the things that she was now missing; Melissa's best girlfriend seemed to be the worst at upsetting her. In reality, I believed that her friends were just envious of her for being in Hawaii for the summer and they somehow found comfort in belittling what she was now doing. It was sad and selfish of them not wanting Melissa to enjoy herself. Instead of being happy she was in a beautiful place like Hawaii, our daughter felt like she was being punished, banished to the far reaches of the world; condemned to an isolated existence with her elderly parents. But, such are the workings of the teenage mind.

Even though Mike had not yet spent any time with Kara, he mourned her early departure. But he kept his mind occupied by focusing all his attention entirely on Samantha, for the next three weeks anyway until Sam would retreat north as well. Kara was scheduled to fly back and rejoin the boat in August, which would give Mike a second shot at getting close to Kara without having Samantha about. Apparently, Mike had been scheming to "work the two girls" this summer, but I also discovered that he wasn't the only one making plans. The girls had formulated a scheme of their own. It wouldn't be until long after arriving back home would the girls confide in me that they had agreed to "share" Mike for the summer. What that involved I did not know, but I think I was afraid to ask.

Over the next few days, Mike would come around after work, collect the two girls and head ashore in the evenings, saving them from the old farts, who were recuperating from their busy day ashore. Mike had also brought his sixteen-year-old deck hand, Anthony around to meet Melissa. Our daughter seemed to take a shine to the young man, and for the first time, I had real hope that she could have fun with someone her own age. After an evening ashore with Mike, Sam and Anthony, she was smiling! For the first time since arriving in Hawaii, Melissa truly seemed to be enjoying herself, and more surprisingly, she seemed to be looking forward to more adventure. Life was again good on our boat!

The girls mildly protested as I announced that we would be sailing for a nearby island for some snorkeling and wouldn't be coming back to Lahaina for about a week. I would have invited the two boys, Mike and Anthony, but they had to work so we left them behind for now. We temporarily left Lahaina, sailing across the channel to Maui's nearest inhabited neighbor.

****

Lanai is the sixth largest, and fourth youngest of the Hawaiian Islands and is known as the Pineapple Island because of its past as an island-wide pineapple plantation. Lanai was formed by a single shield volcano creating a volcanic landmass of rolling tablelands and steep, eroded gorges. Red lava cliffs and thorny mesquite bushes give way to giant stands of towering Cook pines. The island is somewhat comma-shaped, with a length of fifteen miles running north to south and ten miles west to east. The land area is approximately 140 square miles, making it the 42nd largest island in the United States. Lanai is separated from the Island of Molokai by the seven-mile wide Kalohi Channel to the north and from Maui by the eight mile wide Auau(to take a bath) Channel to the east.

The only town on the island is Lanai City, a small settlement with a long history and frontier atmosphere. In 2010, the Island's total permanent population was just 3193, down ninety residents from ten years previous. There is only the Lanai Hotel downtown, for visitors. There are no traffic lights, no shopping malls, or public transportation on the entire island and only a few paved roads. Much of the island is only accessible by four-wheel drive vehicle, and not even that, after a good downpour. However, the island does boast having all the modern amenities of most cities today including one school: Lanai High and Elementary School, serving the entire island from kindergarten through senior high school.

Throughout and before recorded history, Lanai was under the control of nearby chiefs from Maui. Its first inhabitants may well have arrived as late as the 15th century. The name Lanai is of uncertain origin, but the first people to migrate here were most likely from Maui and Molokai, probably establishing fishing villages along the coast initially, but later branching out into the interior where they raised taro in the fertile volcanic soil. Life on Lanai remained relatively tranquil until King Kamehameha I, who brutally rose to power, commencing around 1780 to ultimately rule the entire Hawaiian chain by 1810. King Kamehameha seized control of Lanai by indiscriminately slaughtering people on every part of the island. It was reported that so many were killed that when Captain George Vancouver sailed past the island in 1792, he didn't bother to land because of Lanai's apparent lack of villages and population.

European eyes first saw Lanai on February 25, 1779, when Captain Charles Clerke sighted the island from aboard James Cook's *HMS Resolution*. Clerke had inherited the command of the ship after Cook was killed at Kealakekua Bay in February of that year. After making notes in the log about the discovery of Lanai, the *Resolution* would continue north on Cook's quest to seek out the entrance of the fabled Northwest Passage. An Arctic route which they hoped would take over top of the Americas back to England.

By the 1870s, a Mr. Walter M. Gibson, an American had acquired most of the land on the island. Thought to be born in 1822 in the southern United States, Gibson was generally believed to be a bit of an unsavory character. An American sea captain who spent most of his life running afoul of the law as most of his schemes seem to upset local governments or leave his business partners holding the proverbial short end of the stick. After failing to make a go at running guns through the Caribbean, he fled to the East Indies where he was promptly accused and jailed on charges of attempting to form a rebellion. After escaping his jailers on the island of Java, Gibson apparently saw the light and turned to religion.

In 1859 he went to Utah Territory where he joined The Church of Jesus Christ of Latter-day Saints and managed to persuade the church president Brigham Young to allow him to establish a Mormon colony in the Pacific. Gibson arrived in the

Hawaiian Islands in 1861, and founded a colony among Mormons already in the islands. He purchased land on the island of Lanai with funds from the colony in his own name. After charges of embezzlement of church funds arose, Gibson was then accused of preaching false doctrine and was promptly excommunicated from the church. With his church gone Gibson tuned his hand to cattle ranching. In 1873 Gibson moved on to Oahu where he started his own newspaper called the Nuhou and immediately ran for public office. He successfully ran for the House of Representatives in 1878 as a candidate of the King's Party, portraying himself as the "voice of Hawaiians". In 1882 he was appointed Minister of Foreign Affairs, and then in 1886 he was appointed prime minister of the Kingdom of Hawaii. He would eventually serve as Attorney General, Minister of Interior, as well as the Secretary of War. It appeared that Gibson spent most of his time in politics stirring up trouble as opposed to playing diplomat. By 1887 the people of Hawaii had had enough of Mr. Gibson and he was ousted from his latest parliament post. Fearing for his life he fled to San Francisco where he would die a short year later, a popper and a broken man.

In 1899, Gibson's daughter and son-in-law formed the Maunalei Sugar Company on Lanai, headquartered in Keomuku on the windward coast downstream from Maunalei Valley where they raised sugarcane. However, Gibson's daughter's business only survived until 1901. Nevertheless, many native Hawaiians continued to live along the windward coast, supporting themselves by ranching and fishing until pineapples displaced ranching when in 1922, James Dole, of the Hawaiian Pineapple Company, bought the entire island of Lanai, developing it into world's largest pineapple plantation.

Pineapple and sugarcane are still prominent on the island today but these industries are waning and tourism is now taking root in the form of a couple of beachfront resorts on the south side of the island, offering seclusion under the five star, Four Seasons umbrella.

****

Once clear of Maui's wind shadow and to Melissa's horror, internet service, it was a quick reach across the channel, in the boisterous tradewinds, to one of the only two "real" harbours on the island: Manele Bay on the most southern tip and much larger Kaumalapau Harbor around the corner on the western shore. When we first approached the island it was hard to imagine that it was even possible to land anywhere amongst the towering cliffs, but as we got closer, tiny sand beaches started to appear at the head of the many deep grottoes. The water was deep right up to the shore, which permitted us to closely skirt the shore, in relative safety, for a better look. Lanai is a Mecca for cave divers, because many of the cliffs are honeycombed with old lava tubes, creating an intricate labyrinth of submarine caverns and tunnels. We would pass directly by one of the most famous caves, and I was hoping that the weather would permit me to make a dive here, over the next few days.

The cavernous Lanai Cathedral, which is an ancient submerged lava tube is laced with a maze of intersecting tubes, sporting numerous holes in the ceiling that appear as if they were stained glass windows. Flickering beams of washed-out sunlight filter down through irregular shaped holes, illuminating the cathedral floor and alter-like structure in its center. One of the many tubes has been dubbed "the shotgun" because if a diver times the serge correctly, he will be taken on a thrilling ride as he is shot through the five-meter-long tunnel from one cavern to the next. The shadows and seclusion of the cathedral are also home and offer shelter to a numerous variety of colorful tropical fish, all hiding from the larger predators marauding just outside.

The caverns around the island and the locally infamous shipwreck beach, located on the north shore and sparse population, intrigued me most about this island. However, her shear ruggedness and wicked offshore currents would tax our resolve to dive, snorkel and explore here.

We rounded the blunt headland that marked the eastern most point of Manele Bay, dropped and furled the sails and then motored into the tiny inlet, seeking a place to drop our hook. At the very head of the inlet, tucked away in an even smaller cove was a shallow, tiny, boat basin which could in no way accommodate us; it was, at best, suited for small runabouts and fishing boats small enough to be mounted on trailers. But more of interest to us, was the large ferry dock, used by the inter-island passenger ferry which ran to Maui twice a day. The brightly painted yellow ferry was busy loading foot passengers before its final run of the day. Adjacent to the ferry dock, a large catamaran was allowing her twenty-odd passengers to roam ashore to regain their sea legs after a rollicking sail from Maui. I recognized the twenty meter long catamaran as being part of the *Trilogy* charter fleet. This big cat was in fact our old finger mate at the dock in Maui harbour… the one that showered my sister early one morning.

Good holding for our ground tackle was hard to find, but after several tries under the watchful gaze of the *Trilogy's* captain, I was finally satisfied and shut down *Maiatla's* engine for the night. The tiny bay was rather open and *Maiatla* took on a decidedly nasty roll. I knew it wouldn't be long before the Admiral had me deploying the stern tackle. But first, I thought, since the late afternoon sun had already had the decks too hot to walk on without shoes, a refreshing snorkel along the rocks might be in order, but it would seem that I was the only one who thought so. Sam, Melissa, and Jan all retired to the shade of the cockpit or comfort of their berths to spend the afternoon leisurely reading. Not being deterred, I hit the water alone and quickly left the harbour to seek seclusion around the point.

The shore outside the harbour bore a striking resemblance to the rougher side of Molokini with only sparse coral and few fish of interest. Perhaps it was the constant hammering of the swells that kept it that way, but I found myself moving quickly along the shore in hopes of finding something worth looking at. After a couple of hours, having covering a good couple of miles of shoreline, finding little of interest I began to get tired. When I started back I noticed that I now had a stiff head current. Not looking forward to a hard swim back, I headed for a cut in the rocks, looking for a way up out of the water and a path along the shore. It didn't take me long and I easily found both, with my snorkeling gear in hand and only wool socks to protect my feet I followed what looked like a goat trail that I believed cut across the headland and would hopefully lead me back in the direction of the harbour.

The ground was dry, rocky and covered in a red dust that drifted up to stain my wet legs. It was the type of landscape one would expect to find on Mars except this terrain came with little thorny scrubs that like to lash out and slash unprotected legs.

After only a few hundred meters, small trickles of blood snaked down the calves of my legs only to be sopped up by my red dirt stained socks. The thorns were from a species of mesquite tree that has recently spread to inhabit the arid regions of most of the Hawaiian Islands. The thorny bushes are not indigenous but are actually native to the parched coast of north western South America. Apparently, in 1828 the bush was introduced to the Hawaiian Islands by Father Alexis Bachelot, the head of the first catholic mission to Hawaii. On the grounds of the Catholic Mission on Fort Street in Honolulu, the good father planted a tree that he had raised from the seed of a Peruvian tree growing in the royal gardens of Paris.

By 1840, the progeny of that single tree became the principal shade trees of Honolulu, and were already spreading to the dry leeward plains on all of the neighboring islands. One story is that the missionaries intentionally introduced it so the thorns would make the locals wear shoes. Mesquite is known here as "Kiawe," pronounced "kee-ah-vey" which perhaps, not coincidentally, is the sound you make when you step on thorns that are long enough to puncture to soles of your shoes. Father Bachelot's legacy continues to torment tourists today, as there is hardly a beach in the islands that isn't defended by the barbed wire-like plant, another example how the missionaries changed the face of Polynesia.

The intense sun forced me to squint, while burning my scalp through my thinning hairline and to top it all off, my throat was parched and I was sure my tongue was starting to swell. I found the whole scene a little ironic as I suddenly realized that I was marching through a scorched desert surround by all the waters of the world.

After a good hour of scaling hill after dale without seeing any signs of civilization, I was starting to think I probably should have stayed in the water. And despite the inherent danger that goes with leaving a bloody scent in my wake, I was actually considering returning to the ocean to leap back into the sea, but, as I crested another hill, I spied a large teen for an instant, just before he vanished over a nearby rise.

Within a few minutes and to my relief, I was surrounded by a group of teenaged Hawaiian boys who were taking turns leaping off a cliff, into the sea. I was not only glad to see the apparently friendly boys, but *Maiatla* as well, as she drifted peacefully on her hook below me. I talked to the progeny of the hotel's housekeeping staff for a few minutes and watched as they screamed and jumped off the cliff, to disappear in an eruption of water and bubbles a full fifteen meters below. After re-surfacing, they spent several minutes precariously scrabbling up the cliff to regain our ledge. My route home would have been clear if not for the fact that jumping would mean landing closer to the rocks than I felt comfortable and that I had in hand my snorkeling gear, which made for a tidy excuse for not following the kid's example. I again peered cautiously over the edge. While emitting a wailing cry and flailing his arms and legs, a boy, whose head barely reached my navel, jumped. Discretion and common sense won out and despite the playful goading I received from the boys, I took the coward's way out in the form of the winding path back to the harbor's waterfront.

I arrived at the dock to find that the passenger ferry had long since departed and the now fully loaded catamaran was preparing to do the same. As I stood at the concrete edge, admiring the enormous rig of the boat, I heard a voice from behind me. As I turned, I recognized the young captain of the catamaran, *Trilogy*. He was tall, well-tanned and perhaps in his late twenties or early thirties. He was neatly dressed in a plain tan, long sleeved shirt, knee length shorts, ball cap and white sneakers.

"You're off that Canadian ketch out there aren't you? I saw you come in.," he said, first pointing over my shoulder at *Maiatla* then presenting his hand for a shake.

I must have looked quite a sight standing there with my wounded legs, my now off-white t-shirt, tan shorts and tattered blood stained socks, all covered with streaks of red dust. In addition, my face and head were well on their way to becoming sunburnt. It had been a grand afternoon! I wiped the grime from my palm and presented my hand in return as I introduced myself.

I found the man quite pleasant. He was very interested in our voyage and I was surprised to hear that he and his fellow charter boat captains had been monitoring our travels around Maui, and had been doing so, ever since we first arrived! Apparently, a cruising boat actually taking the time to explore the islands was an anomaly, not to mention that my big Maple Leaf, flying off our stern was hard to miss. He spent the next several minutes bombarding me with questions and when he found out that we were from Vancouver he became even more excited.

"So you know Victoria on Vancouver Island, do you? My wife is from there! I'm from California but we will be moving to Canada later this year," he offered.

"Why would you want to do that? I asked. Looks like you got a dream job here in paradise. You do know that it rains a lot on the west coast of Canada, don't you? And it can get cold, I mean icicles hanging from the eves and shoveling snow kinda cold."

"Yea. I know. But the weather is why we are going. I like to ski, so don't mind the snow but I have spent too much time out in the sun, I've been having little skin cancers show up on my arms, not the real nasty kind but I need to get out of the tropics for a while." He rolled up one of his sleeves to show me a scar where a small tumor had been removed.

I could relate fully, as I had a run in with that demon as well. We talked about skin cancer for a few more minutes until we were interrupted by a call from his boat by his mate who declared that all was ready to depart.

"Look, I got to go but it was nice meeting you," he said, as he began to slowly walk back to his boat with me in tow.

"So are you planning on staying on Lanai for a while?" he asked.

"For a few days at least to do a bit of snorkeling around the island," I said.

"That's great! Hey, but if you find it a bit rough out in the bay, you can have our dock, it's Friday and we won't be needing it for the weekend, but you would have to be gone by early Monday morning or my boss would get pissed at me."

"That would be awesome, thanks and don't worry, Monday we will be out of here."

"Hey, if you want a ride back to your boat jump on, I'll cut right past ya!" he offered.

I didn't hesitate to grab the ride. I climbed the boarding stairs and took up station next to the helm with my new found friend who quickly had the boat fired up. He gave a sharp wave to his mate who was already on the dock removing the last of the mooring lines. With the rather sedate looking passengers milling about the forward deck looking for a place to sit, we departed. I found it a little odd that none of the passengers seemed to acknowledge my sudden appearance or even appeared the least bit curious as to why I was there. I obviously didn't look like a tourist and I certainly wasn't one of the spit and polish crew! I didn't have any more time to consider what the passengers might be thinking as moments later we were up to ten knots and bearing down on *Maiatla* at warp speed.

As I mulled over my conversation with the captain, his last few words naggingly replayed in my head. "I'll cut right past ya." he had said.

Suddenly, I realized exactly what he had meant! Any delusions that I might have entertained of the cat gently pulling alongside *Maiatla*, quickly vanished as the captain turned to me with a smile.

"You better get ready to jump or you will be coming back to Lahaina with us!" he yelled over the roar of the engines.

It took a few seconds for my sun scorched brain to accept that not only was he **not** going to pull alongside, he wasn't even going to slow down! I quickly made my way to the end of the starboard pontoon and jumped as we shot past *Maiatla*, at less than twenty meters distance. The instant I hit the water, I tumbled in the boats churning wake, swallowing water only to have it burn as it shot back out my nostrils. By the time I broke the surface, gagging and spitting, *Trilogy* was speeding away and my obligatory thank you wave was wasted as neither the captain, crew nor passengers cast a backwards glance at me. Perhaps wrongly, it left me feeling not just a bit rebuffed. You would think they would want to see if I was going to drown!

It all happened so fast, that I didn't even have time to don my flippers before my leap. I clutched my gear to my chest and using my legs only, I swam like a frog back to the boat. I climbed aboard a relatively peaceful *Maiatla* that was still wobbling from my taxi's wake. Not much had happened since my departure; all were sleeping or reading down below just as I had left them. I wasted no time in getting cleaned up and moving the boat to the dock.

As a fiery sun set to the west and a splinter of a moon peeked above the Isle of Kahoolawe, the crew reveled in the opulence of actually having the boat motionless at a nice, new concrete dock with a hose that spewed seemingly limitless fresh water. We barbecued chicken, broached the liquor locker and later, under a tall dock light buzzing with bugs, we bathed the boat, did our laundry and then bathed ourselves. To the ladies' delight, I hauled the dinghy onto the dock and filled it with water, added some bubble bath and stirred vigorously with an oar. Jan and Samantha were positively giddy with pleasure as they soaked and splashing about in the makeshift tub with cooler and wine in hand. Under an indescribable sky the festivities lasted well into the night and while Sam and Jan played rub-a-dub-dub in the tub, Melissa and I sat on a dock locker and just laughed and talked.

Our weekend was spent exploring the red rock cliffs about the harbor, snapping photos of the local flora and fauna and wandering through the grounds of the luxurious five star resorts, like we owned the place. I would have ordered a drink and nestled down next to the pool amongst all the hot babes in bikinis if I could have figured out whose room to charge the cocktail to!

During the day, hotel guests waiting for the ferry would mill about, gawking at *Maiatla* and the bolder ones after seeing us lounging in the cockpit, would ask all sorts of questions: How did we get the boat here? Is this boat capable of crossing oceans? How long did it take to sail here? and my favorites; when crossing the ocean, where did we anchor at night and get gas?

Talking to the tourists and educating them on the realities of offshore voyaging was all part of the fun of the adventure. We had a great weekend ashore but true to my word, by Monday morning we had departed and ventured around the corner in search of another anchorage and a place to snorkel.

The west coast of Lanai while offering protection from the tradewinds, proved to be rather inhospitable for cruisers as it was wide open to the ever present westerly swell, necessitating the setting of the stern hook every night as per the Admirals' command. As we first noted on the other side of the island, the water was deep right up to the shore, forcing us to anchor directly next to the rocky beaches or beneath towering cliffs, so close that a man tossing a rock from the top could easily hit us. Not that a bombardment from above was likely, as all the islanders and guests we had encountered appeared to be friendly; I only mention this to illustrate the close proximity of every boats' nemesis: hard bits!

The most comfortable anchorage with good holding proved to be within Kaumalapau Harbor. The obviously commercial port received large barges that serviced the town, hotels and small airfield, however we only witnessed one such tug and barge arrive in the four days we were there. Once the tug and her crew had left, aside from a few dock workers moving crates on a distant pier, we saw no one else. The harbour also protected a few rough looking fishing boats bobbing on growth encrusted mooring balls in water that was anything but inviting; with its muddy hue, there was no telling what creatures lurked below. However, Kaumalapau would prove to be a good base to venture from during the day on snorkeling forays.

After a bit of trial and error, the best snorkeling spot we discovered was just a half mile northwest, up the coast in a deep bight, where the swell was refused entry. The water was shallow, less than four meters and the lava rock on the bottom opened up in numerous round holes, two to three meters in diameter where great schools of small fish loved to congregate. This is the first place and time since arriving in Hawaii that I managed to coax Janet into the water with her snorkeling gear.

I had been up to now, rather frustrated with Jan's lack of interest in seeing what was below. She was a good swimmer and had been seen me dive and snorkel for almost thirty years, so I did not understand her apparent lack of interest. Much of Hawaii's magic lay beneath the water and I desperately wanted her to experience it with me, so I was relentless in prodding her. Why she relented this day I do not know, but after spending the day in the water with me, she could not get enough and donned her gear anytime I would. I was elated and excited to show her all the subsea wonders that I could.

I recalled a basic and well know physics law that states, "for every action there is an equal and opposite reaction", a perfect example of this law materialized in a strange way this day: I now had Jan in the water, but for some unknown reason,

Melissa's mood had done a one-eighty and she had decided that snorkeling wasn't fun anymore and after a quick pass over the reef she returned to the boat, declining to swim again all the rest of our time on Lanai.

With Jan and Samantha in hand, we explored the coral-encrusted lave tubes and poked our heads in partially flooded sea caves full of big-eyed squirrelfish, or yellow and black striped damselfish. Jan suddenly found herself dazzled by the color and variety of all the fish, being most intrigued by the tiny, ruby cardinal fish. The tiny fish liked to cling to the edges of the rocks and Jan found that she could watch just by hovering on the surface. Often when we turned to look behind us, we would spy a serpent-like trumpetfish that liked to follow us about. Every now and then as we peeked around the rocks, we would spook a giant green parrot fish as it grazed upon the coral; and as if to cast us an insult, it would void its bowels, shooting sandy poop at us before fleeing!

The weather remained fine, so after a few days of splashing about on the west side, I thought we would try working our way around the corner and sail up to shipwreck beach. The northern stretch of deserted beach received its name from the numerous rusting hulks that dot the shoreline. There is a strong westerly current that wants to drive vessels ashore as they sail down the Kalohi Channel between Molokai and Lanai. This current, combined with the strong tradewinds funneling between the islands, smacked us right on the nose; no sooner had we cleared the lee of the island, than we had to close all ports and hatches, as green water began breaking over the bow.

"Why are we doing this? We don't have anything properly secured down below, Andy!" The words were no sooner out of Jan's mouth when a great crash was heard from down below as the dish rack full of pots and plates decide to relocate to the galley floor.

"I just wanted to see if we can get close enough to one of the shipwrecks to do some snorkeling but it does look a bit rough for that doesn't it?"

From the answering look on Jan's face, I knew what I had to do. Before anything else hit the floor, we gybed the boat and ran with the wind like scalded cats, back into the lee of Lanai.

We spent one final night in the commercial harbour before heading around the southern end of Lanai. I planned on diving the Cathedral lava tubes before leaving Lanai but as we approached Kamaiki Point, the strong tradewinds were driving three meter waves which rebounded off the cliffs, creating an ugly slop, rough over the dive site. On the bottom, underwater, it did not matter, but Jan and the girls would have to endure being tossed about for an hour while I explored below; it would have been punishing. Regretfully, I pointed *Maiatla* offshore to clear the slop. We set sail for Lahaina and to Maui Mike and Anthony who were impatiently waiting for the girls' return.

Chapter #14

A Run at Molokai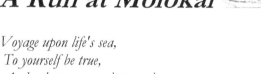

Voyage upon life's sea,
To yourself be true,
And, whatever your lot may be,
Paddle your own canoe.
Sarah Bolton, Paddle your own Canoe, 1854.

Back on the club's mooring ball for a few days, we replenished our perishable supplies while giving the girls a chance to hook back up with their shore-side fellas. We also took advantage of surfing lessons that were offered by a nearby surf shop.

"Ah, come on, Dad! Don't be a chicken! Come and take lessons with Sam and me!"

Melissa was pushy to say the least and all my protests and stories of how I nearly drowned her Granddad the last time I tried to learn how to surf, did nothing to deter her. I was hoping to find something else that we could do together to create another father daughter moment, like bungee jumping, mountain climbing or shark wrestling; anything but surfing! But, as usual, I gave in to her, and I soon found myself squeezing into an undersized rental shorty wetsuit that made me look like a pregnant seal. To protect my legs from chafe, I pulled on some tattered board shorts and as I gazed into the mirror in the store to model my new attire, I wasn't sure if I should grab a board and head for the beach or a squeegee and paper cup and perch myself on the nearest street corner. I glanced this way, then that, in the mirror; my image as a homeless surf bum was complete!

Our surfing instructor was in his late thirties; lean, with dark hair and similarly dark complexion. He reminded me of the Hispanic Officer Francis "Ponch" Poncherello, from the 70s TV series, CHiPs. Brian, our Eric Estrada look-alike quickly informed our group of ten surfer wannabes, that he was a direct descendent of Hawaiian royalty and had more Hawaiian blood coursing through his veins than Caucasian, which was obviously the more undesirable side of his gene pool as far as he was concerned. Despite making his living teaching the predominantly Haole (White, pronounced how-lee) tourists how to ride the waves, Brian made it quite clear that all the Haoles in Hawaii should return the islands to the indigenous peoples, and leave on the first jet out of town, making sure to empty their pockets and leave the condo keys in the conch shell by the door! Divorce Hawaiian style; complete with the obligatory alimony payments, courtesy of the American Taxpayer.

Brian even made comments about his support of the islands' eco-terrorists that were torching new condo developments on Maui and some of the other islands. One such attack occurred while we were tied to the dock in Lahaina, when a fire set at a nearby construction site spreading to the surrounding hills. The fire stopped the flow of traffic along the coast while threatening numerous inhabited subdivisions and business. Lahaina was effectively cut off for several days as a thick choking smoke drifted over the town. The distant chattering in the air wasn't that of the Coqui tree frogs, but the buzzing of fixed-wing and helicopter water bombers, fighting to save property and to gain the upper hand on the blaze.

If you look at the underhanded way the authority of the Hawaiian Monarchy was undermined, while paving the way for the annexation of the Islands by the United States, there is little room for doubt as to why the natives are still pissed off and threatening to rise up and take back what they believe is rightly theirs. After all, the Kingdom of Hawaii was a sovereign nation from 1810 until 1893.

In 1891, Queen Liliuokalani, the last Hawaiian monarch, came to power and her mandate was to transfer power back to the royal families by changing the constitution. This of course, did not sit well with the Haole businessmen, so with the help of the armed cruiser, USS Boston, resident Americans and some European businessmen staged a violent coup in order to overthrow the Queen. Stripped of her powers, Queen Liliuokalani remained as a figurehead for the state, mainly to appease the Hawaiian people. The islands were now an independent republic, which lasted from 1894 to 1898, when Hawaii was finally annexed by the United States as a territory, becoming a state in 1959. It's interesting to note that in 1993, the U.S. Congress passed the Apology Resolution, admitting wrongdoing and issuing an apology to the people and State of Hawaii, but there has been no mention of returning the Island Kingdom to the indigenous peoples.

But Brian and his cohorts keep asking.

When you look at the remaining watered-down, native population wandering around Wal-Mart and Costco, with shopping carts full of Spam, Hostess Ho Hos, and Ding Dongs, they appear to be a people who have lost most of their collective memory and oral traditions; they have lost their cultural identity. If you stare into their beautiful brown eyes, you can see that there is little of their identity remaining, as they appear to have lost their very souls; their essence, their zeal for life. Nevertheless, many Hawaiians are struggling to recapture a sense of who they once were by re-importing from Tonga, Tahiti and the Marquesas Islands memories and traditions in an effort to replace what white America had bred out of them. They are searching for who they once were, and who they are now, and any South Pacific tradition or culture was better than what was forced upon them by western society, or so it seemed.

Brian and his kind had every right to be angry, but if he showed his anger to me, he could forget receiving a tip.

As it was the 4th of July, I highly suspected that with all the Independence Day celebrations planned around the Island, Brian was particularly disturbed on this day, and in turn, his anarchistic tendencies were flaming especially brightly - just a theory!

Brian led us, with longboards cradled under our arms, from the surf shop, down the street, between a series of tee-shirt and coffee shops, bound for the nearby beach. After a brief lecture and instruction on the sand, we hit the water. The surf, next to the harbour was breaking huge; thundering in like an express train through a pipeline. I stood in waist deep water wondering what I had gotten myself into this time, as a steady procession of snarling, bone-crushing breakers, a full one meter tall, crashed before me in a frothy spume. I turned to see Janet atop of the harbor wall, peering through the video camera viewfinder.

"Great!" I said aloud. "It's going to be recorded!."

Brian led the parade beyond the surf break, lined us up, and one by one he give us a reminder of his instructions. He then waited for an appropriate wave, before giving the student a stiff push as the swell surged by. Surprisingly, most of the students managed to find their feet and enjoyed an exhilarating, albeit short, ride to the beach.

Melissa seemed to be a natural and after a few attempts, she was soon riding the waves all the way in and would have to jump from her board before hitting the beach. Samantha didn't do as well as her cousin, but still managed to get up on the board for a few respectable rides, but her dismounts were always painful and she would rise to the surface, sputtering saltwater. While sitting on my board, I noticed that the younger the rider, the better they did. After watching a few of the twenty-something-year-olds do face plants into the bottom, after being hurled from their boards, I figured I was doomed.

When Brian came to me, he had a strange look on his face that could only be described as a cross between revulsion and disdain, the kind of look perhaps one would make if compelled to change a stranger's dirty diaper. I could only surmise that I represented everything that he hated about the islands: I was General Custer to his Sitting Bull. This seemed to me, an appropriate analogy as at the moment. I certainly felt like he was setting me up to be slaughtered!

I watched Brian select a wave for me and I definitely didn't have a good feeling about it. The wave came, and he pushed. As instructed, I brought my feet under me and stood up. That's all I have to say about that! As I lay in my berth later that night, I hurt. My arms ached, my legs ached, and my coral-cut calves and shins throbbed. Still, it was kind of fun… the girls had a blast and Jan nearly split her sides open watching me get dumped time and time again.

Later that night, friends of Mike's, Allen and Pat, were throwing a BBQ on their sailboat, moored in Lahaina harbour, with the intent of watching the city's Independence Day fireworks along the waterfront. After hearing about us from Mike, Allen and Pat invited us all aboard for burgers and drinks, which we readily accepted. Our hosts were typical cruisers; gracious and very welcoming, so we felt right at home. I was particularly pleased to learn that Allen was a mechanic and local diesel guru, so I spent most of the evening picking his brains about concerns I was having aboard *Maiatla*.

The harbour had a festive air. The docks were abuzz with people, drunk and sober alike and the fireworks, although not grand, were fun all the same. As Jan and I mingled, I noticed that Samantha and Mike had slipped away to a quiet spot on the other side of the breakwater and from where I was, it looked like they were kissing. I started to feel a bit worried that things, for these two, were going just a bit too fast, but I knew that we would be leaving very soon and whatever the two of them started here, would, most likely, end here. But don't you just hate it when your gut tells you that you may be wrong?

Figure 14.
Melissa surfing at Lahaina Maui with instructor Brian looking on.

What with the surfing, BBQ and fireworks, it was a great day here in paradise.

I was very pleased to see that the girls were enjoying themselves. I was particularly relieved that Melissa had finally given herself permission to have some fun, so much fun in fact that I was starting to fear that her and Sam would put up a great fuss when I suggested that it was time to move on to our next island. Samantha had a little better than a week left in her vacation, and she was due to fly out of the Honolulu Airport on the island of Oahu. Ala Wai Boat Harbor, located just meters from the famous Waikiki, was over seventy-five miles from Lahaina. But, I still wanted to visit Maui's other neighbor, which just happened to be on the way.

The Island of Molokai is relatively young, geologically speaking. It was a little over one and a half million years ago (give or take a week), when two volcanoes pushed through the surface of the Pacific Ocean and created the island of Molokai; with Kamakou in the east, Mauna Loa in the west and the much later and smaller Kauhako which formed the Makanalua peninsula on the north side. The volcanoes were not born with these Hawaiian titles; these names were given to them later, much later by the locals!

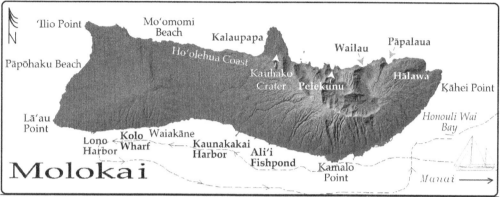

Figure 15.   The old leper colony of Molokai with its population of contemporary netherworld refugees and human flotsam, are isolated, distrusting and possibly suffering from terminal xenophobia.

Over eons, the north side of the island eroded and fell into the sea, leaving behind the vertical sea cliffs, which today make up most of Molokai's spectacular and inhospitable north shore. Next to the Napali Coast of the island of Kauai, Molokai boasts the most dramatic shorelines in the islands. It is the fifth largest island in the Hawaiian archipelago, with some 260 square miles in area, thirty-eight miles long, and ten miles wide at its widest point. Molokai is anchored in the center of the 8 major Hawaiian Islands, lying 25 miles southeast of Oahu, and just over an hour sail or eight miles from the eastern end of the Maui, across the Pailolo Channel, and just a little farther to our mooring buoy at the Lahaina yacht club.

The population of Molokai is estimated at 8,000 residents, half of whom live in or near the principal town of Kaunakakai. Nearly forty percent are of Hawaiian descent so the islanders claim themselves to be, "The Most Hawaiian Island." Hawaiians first came to live on Molokai about 650 A.D. as people island-hopped through the chain, seeking fertile soil and productive fishing grounds for their ever expanding population. As the Hawaiians had no written language, most of their pre-contact history has come from chants, passed down from generation to generation, which have kept fairly accurate chronology of events, battles and genealogy.

The islanders flourished for generations un-hindered by the outside world until November 1778, when Captain James Cook sighted Molokai on his first visit to the Sandwich Islands, as he named them. But, first contact wasn't made until 1786, when Captain George Dixon anchored off Molokai's coast. He and his crew were the first Europeans to set foot ashore, making contact with a peaceful people.

In 1832, a Protestant mission was established at Kalua'aha on the east end by Reverend Harvey Hitchcock, to serve an estimated population of 5,000. His church has not been maintained, but the walls and part of the roof still stand today. A white marble headstone marks his grave on the hill east of what remains of his church.

The oldest known Hawaiian settlement on Molokai is in Halawa Valley, at the eastern end of the main highway that crosses the length of the island. There are many places in the islands called Halawa as in Hawaiian it means "curved" which physically describes much of this place with its scalloped ridges. The eastern side of the island was heavily populated in pre-contact Hawaii, a result of ample water from the mountains, fertile, level land for farming, and a rich and abundant ocean. That all changed in 1948 when an earthquake in Alaska sent a tsunami charging across the Pacific, reaching a unprepared Molokai in under ten hours.

The Halawa Valley was flooded for a full two miles inland, engulfing the taro fields under thirty meters of water and drowning most people caught before it. The silt and salt left behind, poisoned the fields and farming hasn't been the same since. Most of the people who survived, moved away to more fertile grounds. Over time the population of the valley has grown, but still has not recovered to the time before the great wave.

A drive along the south shore of the island bears testimony to the reliance on the ocean by early Hawaiians. Ancient Hawaiians practiced advanced fish husbandry and aquaculture; more than 60 fishponds were built along the south shore of Molokai. Most have nearly disappeared, but a few have been reconstructed and are used daily by residents for aquaculture. Legend also tells us that Laka, goddess of the hula, gave birth to the dance on Molokai, at a very sacred place in Ka'ana. This is recognized on Molokai every May, at a celebration of the birth of hula, called Ka Hula Piko. I found it surprising that the island of Kauai likewise claim that the Goddess Laka invented hula in the shadowy hills adjacent to the Na Pali Coast. But unfortunately neither the Hawaiian elders or scholars can agree on the birth place of the Hula dance, except that it is originally Hawaiian in origin.

Molokai is probably best known to the world as being a former leper colony with its rather famous and selfless Father Damien de Veuster who arrived from Belgium to tend to the afflicted. Father Damien developed the Leprosarium in the Kalaupapa Valley where he did what he could to alleviate the suffering. Sixteen years after coming to the island, Father Damien died on April 15, 1889, at age 49, as a patient in his own Leprosarium. The Kalaupapa Valley is still home to a small group of lepers that reside there, in solitude, to this day.

In doing my research of Molokai before the commencement of my voyage, I learned many more remarkable things about the island and its people, some of which the Chamber of Commerce failed to mention. The first is that most Hawaiians think of Molokai and its people as being their poorer relations: perhaps best forgotten and never worthy of your current address. Little has changed on the island in the past thirty years, the population is much the same and a few new buildings have gone up but others have fallen in decay.

There is little or no work in the agricultural field as the pineapple plantations are gone and most of the residents are on welfare. It's reported that feuding is common amongst the haves and the have-nots, between the island's cliques and clans. Molokai has a tourist trade, but it is only a fraction of that of its more popular neighbor, Maui. Tourist developments on Molokai reside in an atmosphere of local resentment and entitlement. Molokai's population of Hawaiian "Brians", augmented by a tidy cull of nineteen sixties' draft dodgers, other contemporary netherworld refugees and human flotsam, are isolated, distrusting and possibly suffering from terminal xenophobia. As in most places that are remote, isolation breeds suspicion and possibly paranoia amongst a more inbred population, creating tight extended family units that are easily united against what they perceive as a common enemy.

With all of the above to recommend it, Molokai was a must see on this voyage, so late one evening I brought the charts up on the computer, plotted a course for a spot approximately one third of the way down the island at Kamano Harbour on Molokai's south coast and braced myself with three fingers of Captain Morgan. The drink was to fortify myself against the onslaught of protests I anticipated from the girls after announcing that in the morning we would be casting off!

"Dad! We can't leave now! We have plans with Mike and Anthony! Sam and I don't want to leave now, we need to go shopping!" Melissa protested.

"I know dear, but I told you both the other day that we have to get moving. Sam's got a flight to catch and she wants to spend time at Waikiki, there is lots of shopping there and we can go to Pearl Harbor as well. Won't that be great?" I offered, as a lame substitute for what she thought she had going here.

I stood fast! Well, mostly I did! After some intense pleading from my daughter, I announced that we would still be sailing in the morning, but that we will return after spending a day or so on Molokai. OK! I wimped out! But I like to think of it as being compromising.

We departed from Lahaina at first light and set a course across the channel. The Island's eastern ramparts caught the sunrise which formed a halo-like crown that quickly descended the fortress-like precipices until dissolving into the sea.

"Who wants bacon with their pancakes?" Jan polled the groggy set of girls sitting at the galley table.

We were still within Maui's deep wind shadow and the morning winds farther out had not yet been fortified by the rising thermals created as the surrounding land heated up. It was a fabulous morning to be on the water and by the time breakfast was finished, the winds filled in and we were quickly under full sail, bounding over the waves, with twenty knots of wind on our starboard quarter. After clearing away the breakfast dishes, Jan flopped onto the cockpit bench next to me.

"I see you decided not to tow the dinghy and put in on the foredeck. That's smart, I think," she said.

"Yep. It looks rough over on the far side, so I thought it best to bring it aboard." I said, as if I had a choice in the matter. I have lost our dinghy far too many times over the years to risk hearing another, "I told you so," from Jan.

"Did you secure everything on the aft deck? The solar panel and grocery cart?"

"Yes Babe, the panel and the shopping cart are bungeed down. Don't worry, they won't go anywhere!" I said, with as much conviction as I could muster.

The great island rose out of the sea to great us. She was tall, green and knurly with a shoreline white with humping and pounding waves.

"Where is this harbour supposed to be? All I see is breaking waves and the tops of a few houses back in the bush. Are there any harbour markers out here?" Jan queried, as she scanned the distant shoreline through the binoculars.

"Jan, according to the chart, that big crescent-shaped bowl in the hill is where the town is, the east point of the bay should line up with the east point of the bowl," I said, pointing to the corresponding location on the island.

"Don't see it Andy, are you sure we are in the right place?" Jan asked, with more than a little concern in her voice.

I peered again at the laptop computer at my side, zooming in on the harbour detail.

"According to the GPS and the chart, we are right there. I said, pointing to the chart.

"The harbour mouth should be right in front of us."

We were both looking from the electronic chart to the shore and back again, trying to figure out what we were seeing.

"Wait a minute! I think I see a few boat masts on the other side of the waves!" Jan said, "But I can't see how they got in there! We must be at the wrong place. Are you using the best chart we have?"

I was starting to get a little flustered, what with Jan second guessing me and my own uncertainty, so I took the binoculars from Jan to have a look for myself.

I scanned the shore, then the chart beside me, then the shore again. *Maiatla* was still on a fast reach and the shore was rapidly approaching; if we didn't find the channel markers within the next few minutes, we would have to turn back out to sea.

"Wait a minute! I see a red channel marker! Oh yea! There's the green! I see them now, but holy shit, they must be kidding!" I said, incredulously.

The channel… a narrow cut through the reef was marked as on my chart, but the surrounding reef made for a real obstacle course. Making matters worse, incoming waves broke on either side of the harbour entrance, with the ensuing backwash of white foam from either side meeting in the center of the channel. The overall effect gave the appearance of breaking waves across the entire entrance. No wonder Jan could not see a way in! The closer we got, the less I liked what I saw. By this time, everyone was in the cockpit peering through the dodger at one of the most inhospitable looking harbours I have ever come across.

"Sorry guys, but I'm not going to risk the boat trying to get into there; it's too rough right now." But there is Lono Harbour a little ways down the coast, we can try and get in there," I offered to the crew, as consolation. We were all disappointed but it couldn't be helped.

We gybed the boat and headed back out to deep water then turned to run parallel to the shore. The land was heating up, causing the winds to build with gusts over thirty knots, raising steep wind waves, which were overpowering the three-meter groundswell. Quickly passing relatively flat land, bordered by mangroves, it was a fast roller coaster ride as we covered the twelve miles in just under an hour and a half. Our arrival at Lono was a further disappointment as the channel through the reef was even more poorly marked. After heaving-to to have a crew conference, we all agreed that we couldn't land here, but what to do now?

"Look, we are well on our way to Oahu and it would be a real bash to head back, upwind to Maui, so I think we should just carry on." I said.

"No way, Dad! You had promised that we would go back, Mike is going to take us out tomorrow night, Sam and I have plans!"

Against my better judgment, we reefed *Maiatla* down and began the long slog back to Lahaina. It would take us a full eight hours to cover the thirty-odd miles back.

All were disappointed to be leaving without landing on Molokai, but we had just been introduced to the realities of cruising the Hawaiian Islands. I felt bad for letting Molokai beat me but I was focusing on the better part of valor. Discretion. I had a lot to lose and navigating through shallow reefs that are constantly under bombardment by surf and ocean swells was new and scary to me!

As we continued to cruise the islands over the next two months, we would become more experienced and would soon be negotiating harbour channels and passages with less than a fraction of a meter beneath our keel, complete with breaking waves on either side of the boat. By doing so, we would gain access to the tranquil inner lagoons and inshore sanctuaries of these great islands.

I gazed longingly back at Molokai, and I couldn't help but have the utmost respect for mariners, both past and present, who have successfully sailed these waters as they are not for the faint hearted.

As we worked our way back up the coast, we again passed Kamano Harbour. Surprisingly, I had not heard the last of this place, as in just six months' time, our Maui Mike and one of the girls who flew back to spend Christmas with him, would put *Isabella* upon this very reef while attempting to enter the harbour. Fortunately for Mike, it was a calm day and the local Molokai fire department would rescue all while saving *Isabella* from ending up like the lonely Rhodes of Lahaina. After witnessing the conditions surrounding these islands, and in particular Molokai, I could not think less of him as a captain for going up onto the reef.

A particular quote came to mind. It has long been thought that it was a fourteenth century evangelical preacher and martyr, John Bradford that said, when seeing criminals being led to the gallows at the tower of London, "There but for the grace of God, goes John Bradford." Of course John Bradford's name would later be dropped from the saying and the words, "go I," were substituted. Whether or not Bradford coined this phrase matters little, but it seemed appropriate here. If these were Bradford's words, they were indeed prophetic, as he would later be sentenced and burned at the stake by Mary Tudor, Queen of England for his Protestant faith.

As we worked our way up the Pailolo Channel, we were slowly carried to the south by the currents, until I suddenly realized that I could see the rusting hulks that dotted shipwreck beach. The distance to the beach was hard to estimate but it was getting too close for my liking, Mike had warned us that the currents right alongshore were strong, and would drive you ashore if you were careless. I was at the helm, with Jan and Melissa on either side of the cockpit ready to do the sheet work.

"Hey guys, we are getting a little close to Lanai, we need to tack. Ready about?" I said.

The sails went limp, then fluttered madly in the strong wind as *Maiatla* changed direction, nosing through the big waves as Melissa cranked on the genoa winch to bring the sail in on the new tack. We had just regained our headway, when the boat took a decidedly heavy roll to starboard, then there was a great crash that emanated from the aft deck.

"What was that noise?" Jan demanded to know. "Andy, something's come lose!"

The words were hardly out of her mouth and I was out of the cockpit, and clinging to the grab rails, preparing myself for the next hard roll that I knew was coming. As the boat dipped her rail, I saw the object that was causing all the commotion and ruckus. The very expensive, fold-up shopping cart that we had just recently purchased at the Kahului Costco had broken free and was now on its two wheels, rolling back and forth along the deck, in unison with *Maiatla*, apparently the two bungee cords I used to secure it, had broken.

Before I could even work my way aft, the boat took another deep plunge and the shopping cart skidded across the deck, bashed into the cap rail, committing suicide by leaping over the side! I could hear the, "I told you so," in my head even before Jan knew she owed me one! I slunk back into the cockpit.

"Did you find what was banging around?" She asked.

"Yep! It was the shopping cart."

"Did you secure it better this time?"

"Nope!"

"Why not?"

"Ain't there anymore, I didn't like it anyway, one wheel pulled to the left!" I offered with a grin.

The winds and waves were beating us up, so we altered course and sometime later we managed to drop anchor at Honolua Bay at the west end of Maui. This was the first bay that we had discovered after getting run out of Kahului by the fuel barge. We were just in time to see the sun set over our belligerent Molokai and the friendly spinner dolphins head to sea for the night. As we sat in the cockpit with wine in hand recovering from our failed assault of Molokai, I could not help but admire the now distant island, that had shunned us much like the rest of the world had once shunned the island's leprous inhabitants. Out of fear for our very lives and the survival of *Maiatla*, we had surrendered to the apparent will of this island fortress with its turbulent moat. She would not let us get to know her, not today anyway. Perhaps that is how she held tight to her mystique, held tight her virtue with her legs snapped shut! She was selective as to how many would get to know her, who she would let in and embrace. However, this was a common trait of the wild and remote places of the world that are buffeted by wind, weather, and the sea. Isolated places where ghosts and gods, beasts and monsters roam free. Places that are as dangerous as they are beautiful, impossible places like the island of Molokai.

Chapter #15

Feeding Frenzy

There is nothing so desperately monotonous as the sea, and I no longer wonder at the cruelty of pirates.

James Russell Lowell, Fireside Travels, 1864

Our arrival back at Honolua Bay was unexpected, but that is what often happens when you go cruising; the wind and currents fail to co-operate, and you find yourself either backtracking or discovering something new and wonderful. It was another predictably beautiful day, so as not to waste it, Jan and I hit the water after breakfast for a swim next to the boat. Floating on our backs, it was like taking a luxuriously warm bath, only with palm trees in the background and real floaty fish darting about! Jan had worn one of her bathing suits. I, true to form was suit-less, preferring the added buoyancy that comes with swimming without heavy clothing to drag you under. That's my story and sticking to it!

It was still early, so we had the tranquil bay all to ourselves, but that wouldn't last long as I could already see the first of the snorkelling charter boats powering around the distant point and they were headed straight for us.

"Where are you going?" Jan asked as I began to breast stroke my way back to the boarding ladder.

"I'm going to get some shorts, don't want to scare the tourists. You know how hung up some of these Americans are about see a naked ass!"

"Ok, grab me some bread while you're down below. There are a few fish under the boat and I want to feed them."

I quickly returned properly attired with a few slices of stale bread, which I tossed to Jan who was still treading water next to the boat. Jan began to break up the slices and immediately there was a small school of fish around her, gobbling up the tiny pieces of bread. I was sitting on the side of the cockpit when the first charter boat, a twenty meter catamaran, slowed then stopped next to us, not more than five meters from Jan treading water. The boat was overloaded with jubilant tourists lathering on sunscreen and preparing their snorkelling gear.

"Hey, aren't you the Canadians that were at Lanai last week? Saw your boat over there!" the skipper called over.

Before I knew it, we were answering all the usual questions about our voyage. Apparently, a good portion of the passengers were Canadian as well, some called out the names of their home towns and were pleased that I knew of them or had been there at one time. I guess it somehow made them feel connected to us and our voyage. A vicarious link.

It didn't take long for someone to notice the growing school of fish darting about Janet in the water..

"What are you doing? Why are all those fish around you?" A lady called to her.

"I have bread and I was just feeding them," Jan said, still chumming the water around her, which continued to attract more and more fish. She showed the crowd her last slice of bread and began to break it up, tossing it onto the water. It was hard for Jan to see all the fish about her; if she had, she may have thought twice about throwing more food. From the deck of *Maiatla*, I could see the seething mass of darting fish that extended well beyond ten meters all around her. When she threw out the last of the bread, the giant fish ball exploded into a furious feeding frenzy, there were obviously too many fish and not enough food.

Several cameras came out and a woman who was dazzled by the sight began asking questions. While Jan was trying to answer, she suddenly squealed as she was abruptly bitten by something from down below. Jan spun around in the water and squealed again and again as she was repeatedly nipped.

"What's the matter?" the now concerned looking woman demanded to know.

"The fish are biting me! Jan yelled back, half laughing between squeals, yelps and nips. Go away!" she repeatedly shouted, while pounding the surface of the water with her hands. Apparently, Jan's old suit had split at her hip allowing a quarter-size patch of white skin to show through, which the fish were mistaking for something eatable. The crowd began to chuckle at her predicament and to make matters worse, the captain seeing an opportunity, decided to add fuel to the already out of control blaze by retrieving from down below several more handfuls of bread and casting them into the water, next to a frantically splashing Jan.

Realizing that any discrimination between the bread and her had long since vanished, the fish ball was now attempting to eat her alive. Having enough, Jan made a mad dash for the boarding ladder with the ravenous fish in hot pursuit as she became the focus of the feeding frenzy. By the time Jan managed to get back aboard, the crowd was laughing and cheering and once she regained her composure, Jan had to laugh right along with them. Aside from the tiny red patch on her hip, and a couple of tattered nerves, she was unharmed. With the in-water entertainment over, the people wished us luck and moved on. After a nerve-settling cup of tea, we did the same; we hauled anchor and made a quick run back to our yacht club mooring.

We spent the day tidying up the boat and sending emails, as we once again had internet service courtesy of a local restaurant. After work, Mike and Anthony drifted by to collect the girls and they were all off to wander about town. Later that evening, Melissa returned alone, as Samantha had stayed aboard Mike's boat to continue her evening. Melissa said that she'd had a good time after spending the evening with Mike's young deckhand and it was very obvious she was excited. We questioned her about her night but true to her nature, she offered few details. We would just have to be content with her being happy for a change. She seemed to have taken a shine to the fellow and was looking forward to immersing herself in island life, of course with his eager help. She was so excited in fact that she asked if she could use the cell phone to call her girlfriend back home, snatching up the phone she disappeared into her cabin.

Moments later, she popped her head back out the door.

"Hey Mom! Nicole says, "Hi," to everyone!"

Jan was standing in the galley making tea and I was reading at the galley table. We both yelled back a "hello", as Melissa held the phone out, so Nicole could hear us. Not being satisfied with that, Jan cupped her hands around her mouth and yelled, "Did Melissa tell you she met a cute boy that's going to teach her how to surf?"

Uncharacteristically Melissa looked embarrassed, almost appearing to blush.

"Oh Mom!" She retorted through a big grin before quickly retreating into her inner sanctum, slamming the door behind her.

Early the next morning, I was in the galley making tea for Jan and me when I heard the bump of a dinghy alongside. I peered out the hatch, and saw Samantha climbing aboard. Maui Mike bid me a, "Good morning," before rowing away in his dink back to his boat.

I was a little taken aback as I had not realized that Sam was not in her cabin last night or this morning, but since she was wearing the same clothes that she departed with yesterday, it wasn't hard to draw a conclusion.

"Morning Sam, did you have a good night?" I asked.

"Hi, Uncle Andy. Yes, it was fun. Mike cooked dinner for me when we got back to his boat last night. He's a really good cook you know. It was late by the time we were done, so I just spent the night."

"I'm glad you enjoyed yourself Sam, but there are a couple of things that have me concerned. I know that you are an adult but you should have let me know where you were and that you would not be coming home. If we had to leave all of a sudden due to weather or whatever reason, I need to know where to find you, OK?"

"Oh. OK, Uncle Andy." If Sam resented my interference into her social life, she gave no indication of it.

"You must remember Sam, that we are in a foreign country and I'm responsible for you and I would never forgive myself if you were to go missing, I need to know where you are and who you are with, OK?"

"Sure, no problem," Sam said, as she started to make her way to the companion stairs.

"And the other thing I wanted to discuss with you is your spending the night aboard Mike's boat," I said, with more than that a little discomfort evident in my voice.

"Again, I know you are an adult and what you did last night is none of my business, but I invited you along on this voyage principally as a companion for Melissa and I don't think that spending the night with Mike sets a good example for her, do you understand what I mean?"

Sam had stopped at the top of the stairs to listen to my second objection and if she felt any discomfort with my broaching this subject, again she gave no indication of it.

"Oh. OK, Uncle Andy. I understand, it won't happen again." With that, she vanished down below to her cabin.

By the time I got back down below Jan, who had been wondering where her morning cup of tea had gotten to, entered the galley.

"Hey! Where is my tea and breakfast? You going to do pancakes and bacon?" she asked.

Asking if I was going to "do pancakes" was Jan's way of placing an order. Which was fair enough, I usually cooked breakfast when aboard, especially on the weekends. In hindsight this may have not been a good thing, because every day aboard was like a weekend.

"If you want. But you will have to mix the batter, I seem to screw it up all the time," I said, hoping to get some sympathy and help with the pancake making.

"You are just lazy and won't learn!" Jan said, with a grin as she elbowed her way past me to find the mixings.

"You got me, but you will still have to do the mixing. I'll cook!" I said.

Jan pulled the sliding pantry open and retrieved the pancake mix.

"Here! I'll teach you. Jan said, promptly placing the mix in front of me on the counter . "I'm sure even you could learn to mix batter! Wish we had some blueberries to go with it!"

As my still foggy brain fought to find a smart-ass reply in an effort to get out of taking on this new chore, another dinghy bumped alongside.

"Hey, Babe! Do you want to see who that is? I'm still making tea."

Jan stuck her head out of the hatch and began talking to someone. Seconds later she dropped back down, and headed for forward to Melissa's cabin and knocked gently on the door.

"Melissa, are you awake? That boy is here to see you."

Melissa's reply through the door was instant and forceful.

"Tell him, I don't want to go ashore, send him away!" she said, in a tone that was dripping in bitterness. Then, her door then shot open. "OK! I've been to Hawaii; can I go home now while I still have some of the summer left?!" She yelled.

I was still stirring the tea but froze at hearing Melissa's sudden outburst. I was stunned!

Without waiting for a reply from either of us, Melissa disappeared, back behind her closed door just as quickly as she appeared.

"What the hell happened between last night and this morning?" Jan asked, as she looked at me, first with shocked surprise then growing despair on her face.

"I'm not sure! But I bet Nicole said something to her last night that got her all pissed off and moody again."

"But what could she have said? Melissa was on cloud nine last night?"

I thought for a moment.

"I wonder if it had something to do with your comment about her meeting a cute boy? Isn't Melissa kind of dating someone back home?"

"I don't know, maybe, but that shouldn't stop her from meeting new people, she's just hanging out with him!" Jan was as dumbfounded as I was.

I could not be sure, but I suspected that her jealous friend(s) had continued to tease her about everything she was missing at home, and I believed that it was more than Melissa could stand. She felt as though she was the one missing out, that her life was passing her by. She could not see that being here, in Hawaii, was a once in a lifetime opportunity for her and that, yes, she would miss some things back home but what she was doing here was very precious. We tried to tell her that her friends would all be there when she got back and they would be doing all the same things as they had always done. In reality, she was missing very little and most certainly nothing of consequence. However, our loving daughter would hear none of it. You can't see what you can't see!

Over the next couple of days, Melissa refused to leave her cabin other than to use the head and to eat. She declined further invitations to go ashore with the now very confused young man, and she continued to demand daily for a flight home.

If our daughter's sudden change of temperament did anything, it made it easy to up anchor and sail for the island of Oahu. Early one morning with much regret, frustration and bewilderment, we quietly dropped the mooring lines and retrieved the stern hook for the last time and departed Maui, swinging *Maiatla's* nose to the west.

Chapter #16

Waikiki bound

The sea has never been friendly to man. At most it has been the accomplice of human restlessness.   Joseph Conrad

Our single day's run down the Kalohi Channel between Lanai and Molokai was mostly uneventful with the strong tradewinds and two-meter seas on the stern. I intentionally gave Lanai's Shipwreck Beach, with its wicked onshore current, a wide berth, as it wouldn't take much in the form of poor judgment to add *Maiatla* to the sadly decomposing relics that dotted this coast. Every half mile or so, is an unadulterated reminder of man's inability to tame the sea. My sense of apprehension deserted me as I cast a departing glance over my shoulder, at the last of the rusting tombstones. I was expecting the winds to back more to the northeast as we cleared the bottom end of Molokai, but the conditions we had, held. With the headsail poled out and the main set to fly wing-and-wing, we had an exhilarating sail over great, humping seas while being eyed by a flock of circling frigate birds.

It was nice to see the weather cooperating and we should be able to cover the seventy-odd miles to Oahu and arrive before dark, perhaps we would even catch a mahi-mahi along the way as I had set the meat hook in hopes of snaring dinner. On a sleigh ride with the famous Diamond Head as our mark, it was a fast sail across Kaiwi Channel to the next stop on our whirlwind tour. The sun was shining, the air warm and the crew were happy to be back underway ready for new discoveries, at least for the most part.

Melissa was perched in the shade, in the corner of the cockpit, reading, and thankfully, she had not mentioned anything more about what had transpired in the previous days, but she was obviously still brooding. Jan and I were both a little quiet

THE TAHITI SYNDROME-HAWAIIAN STYLE

this morning, tending the helm and sheets with our heads still reeling from Melissa's sudden return to the dark side. Samantha, in her bikini, lounging, perched on the cabin top in the hot morning sun, was working on her tan, lathering on oil between bouts of picture-taking of the approaching island. Sam had spent our last night in Maui aboard; she had already said her good byes to Maui Mike and had little heart left to go ashore for anymore sightseeing. Mike had taken a yacht delivery job, he had already flown to Oahu to pick up the boat and along with a companion, he would be sailing it to California. Unfortunately for Samantha, he would be long gone by the time we arrived in Oahu.

Figure16. Honolulu, Pearl Harbour and Gilligan's Island on the Oahu.

Mike and Sam had hit it off big time and I would soon learn the two had already made some loose plans to hook up again. How, where, and when, I could not imagine, as we would not be sailing back Maui's way again on this voyage, and Mike was gone for at least three weeks, and would not be back before Samantha departed for home. From the giddy way Sam had been acting lately, I believed that she was giving some serious consideration to what life with a sea gypsy might be like. They had only known each other for a short while, but I was sure that the "L" word had already been spouted by at least one of them, if not both. I was starting to fear that I may owe my brother an apology; my initial joke about sending him a photo of Samantha waving good-bye from the deck of Mike's boat as they sailed off into the sunset, may actually come true. But I would have to put all the "what ifs" aside for now. I needed to attend to the business at hand, which was getting everyone safely to the next island in our effort to discover for ourselves, the Hawaiian Archipelago.

****

At his first sight of Oahu in 1888, Robert Louis Stevenson wrote:

I saw that island first when it was neither night nor morning. The moon was to the west, setting, but still broad and bright. To the east, and right amidships of the dawn, which was all pink, the daystar sparkled like a diamond. The land breeze blew in our faces, and smelt strong of wild lime and vanilla."

The Beach at Falesa, Island Nights' Entertainments, 1905

Stevenson went on to note:

"The first experience can never be repeated. The first love, the first sunrise, the first South Sea Island, are memories apart and touched a virginity of sense..." In the South Seas, 1908.

Aside from his achievement as a noted writer, Robert Louise Stevenson was also an ardent cruiser and loved to sail and explore; he was arguably the first adventure-travel writer to collect his fodder from the deck of a small sailing vessel, the Casco. For this reason, and perhaps because of my fondness for *Treasure Island*, I feel a unique kinship to this man who sailed the South Seas with his wife and children long before it became fashionable to do so.

In the summer of 1888, Robert Louis Stevenson; accompanied by his wife, Fanny; his mother; and the French maid, Valentine Roch, sailed from San Francisco to the South Pacific in a chartered yacht, the *Casco*, which belonged to his doctor. The *Casco* was not just a small boat, but a 70 ton, 95 foot fore-and-aft topsail schooner. By this time, the 37-year-old Scotsman had traveled extensively in Europe and was already a famous author, having written several popular works of fiction, including *Kidnapped*, *Treasure Island* and *Doctor Jekyll and Mister Hyde*. Some say he was going into voluntary exile owing to his ill health, which had always been poor due to childhood bouts with tuberculosis. Others believed he was simply attempting to live out his dreams of traveling the South Seas under sail. He had never heard of the term "Cruiser" not in the sense we know it today, but he was about to become one.

Stevenson visited the Marquesas, Tahiti, and then spent the first six months of 1889 in Honolulu hanging out with the "royal crowd," before sailing to the Gilbert Islands, Samoa, and Australia. By November of 1889, he was settled in Samoa, where he built an estate, got involved in local native politics; all the while feverishly writing. Stevenson loved the South Seas from the moment he saw its first jewel on an azure sea. When he departed from San Francisco, he had no idea that he would never return to the States, as just six short years later, he would die of a stroke at the age of 44 on Dec. 3, 1894, and would be buried on a mountain top on Samoa.

****

Oahu was next on our hit list. This island is the third largest and most populous of all the Hawaiian Islands and is home to the State Capital, Honolulu, which is located on the southeast coast. Including small close-in offshore islands such as Ford Island and the islands in Kaneohe Bay and off the eastern (windward) coast, the island claims a total land area of 596 square miles, making it the 20th largest island in the United States. In the greatest dimension, this volcanic island is 44 miles long and 30 miles across, with 227 miles of mostly accessible shoreline. The island was born as a result of two separate shield volcanoes: Wai'anae and Ko'olau, with a broad "valley" or saddle, the central Oahu Plain lying between them. The highest point on the island is Mt. Ka'ala in the Wai'anae Range, rising to some 1,220 m (4,003 feet) above sea level.

The island is home to almost a million people, which represent approximately 75% of the population of the entire state with approximately 75% of those people living on the "city" side of the island. Oahu has for a long time been known as "The Gathering Place". However, the term Oahu has no other meaning that I can locate but ancient Hawaiian tradition attributes the name's origin in the legend of Hawai'iloa, the Polynesian navigator who was credited with discovery of the Hawaiian Islands, Hawai'iloa reportedly named the island after a son.

Figure 17. Crossing the Kaiwi Channel with Diamond head to starboard. The Channel (also known as the Moloka'i Channel) separates the islands of Oahu and Molokai, and is 26 miles wide.

The city of Honolulu, which is the largest city on the island surrounds the main deep water marine port for the State of Hawaii. Also located here is Pearl Harbour Naval base and the accompanying Pacific Fleet comprising of everything from submarines to aircraft carriers, fuel and supply tenders, destroyers and a host of other nasty amphibious craft. The extinct volcano Diamond Head is arguably the most well know geographical feature of the island as it lords over the famous Waikiki Beach. It's virtually impossible to locate a postcard of this sandy shore without this South Pacific icon nobly framed in the background. In early 1825, British sailors found calcite crystals in the rocks on the slopes and thought they were diamonds. Following the discovery, the crater was called Kaimana-Hila, literally Diamond Hill.

Diamond Head was purchased by the federal government in 1904, for $3,300. In the 1930s, a couple of gun emplacements for coast artillery defenses were built into the mountainside. After the attack on Pearl Harbor in 1941, further gun emplacements, pillboxes and foxholes were built on Diamond Head to be able to better defend Oahu against future aggression. Many of these bunkers and gun emplacements still remain on the crater rim and one underground facility, the Birkheimer Tunnel, houses the headquarters for the State Civil Defense Agency. Today, the entire mountain and crater is a state park known as Diamond Head State Monument and a popular place to hike and climb.

Today Honolulu, is as frenetic as most any other city and is neither antique nor nostalgic. It has evolved into a tourism and shopping haven, with five million visitors annually comprised mainly of Americans from the mainland, Asians from Japan, along with more than a few chilled-to-the-bone Canucks who flock here every year to enjoy the quintessential island holiday experience. (Five million and four with the arrival of *Maiatla's* crew!)

Oahu was the first of the Hawaiian Islands sighted by the crew of HMS Resolution on the 18th of January, 1778 during Captain Cook's third and final voyage. However, Cook would never set foot here; he was destined to be butchered and served for dinner on a neighboring island. It would be Cook's second in command, Clerke who would first land at the picturesque Waimea Bay.

In 1842, the renowned author of *Moby Dick*; Herman Melville, spent some time here, under arrest. On January 3, 1841, Melville sailed from New Bedford, Massachusetts on the whaler Acushnet bound for the prolific whaling grounds of the Pacific Ocean. He was later to comment that his life began that day, and certainly from a literary standpoint it had. The whaler Acushnet sailed around Cape Horn and traveled to the South Pacific in search of victims to eviscerate and render into oil. Acushnet's captain turned out to be a rather odious fellow who apparently relished making his crew's life miserable. After eighteen hard months, in July 1842, the Acushnet raised the Island of Nuku Hiva in the Marquesas Islands, located some eighteen hundred miles to the southeast of Hawaii.

It took little coaxing from the island's brown skinned and shameless lovelies to convince Melville and a shipmate to desert and jump ship. The pair hid in the forest until their captain gave up searching and sailed away. The two were quickly accepted and lived amongst the Typee natives of the valley who at the time, were known to be cannibals. Melville and his companion not only survived but were actually treated well by the natives. Melville's first novel about south seas island life described a brief love affair with a beautiful native girl, Fayaway, who generally "wore the garb of Eden" and would eventually come to epitomize the guileless noble savage in the popular imagination. The deserters subsisted happily amongst the savages for three weeks until they witnessed a secret late night ceremony and feast centered around a questionable entree.

Realizing that they may be pushing their luck, they signalled a passing whaler and made a dashing escape while pursued by savages bent on stopping them. Apparently, their hosts did not want them to leave. Perhaps Melville's hasty departure ruined their host's future dinner plans.

The mutinous pair crewed on the whaler as far as Honolulu, where they were promptly arrested for desertion. Melville's incarceration was a short one and he was soon released and managed to find employment in Honolulu. It didn't take long for the future famous author to become a controversial figure for his vehement opposition to the activities of Christian missionaries seeking to convert the native population of the South Seas. After working as a clerk for four months, he joined the crew of the frigate, USS United States, which sailed for Boston landing him back on the mainland in October 1844. Melville spent almost three years traveling the Pacific and loved it, but he was destined to never return. However, he would spend the rest of his life writing about his time amongst the isles of Oceania.

Melville was destined to pen fourteen books and numerous articles, all about his favorite subjects; life at sea and the islands and enchanted goddesses of the South Seas. Cook may have discovered paradise and in his own dry and "matter of fact" way, documented it for the world, but it was Herman Melville and a handful of others who romanticized it, introducing the South Pacific fantasy and the idea of the noble savage to the otherwise sexually frustrated and puritanically oppressed cultures of the west.

In just three short years, I too, would sail to the remote cannibal island of Nuku Hiva and trek the now deserted Typee Valley, known today as Controller Bay. In the company of Maui Mike and a beautiful wandering waif, Kelly, we would forge the same streams, swim in the same lagoon and pick starfruit from the jungle as Melville had once done. Unfortunately, my Fayaway was far away, back in Canada awaiting the birth of our second grandchild who would be named Savannah. As we probed the thick bush that revealed stone carvings and footings for the long lost, ancient houses, it was easy to imagine that we were being watched by the very ghosts of Melville's *Typee* cannibals and his long lost island lover, Fayaway. As I have found in all of the tropical isles, Nuku Hiva was truly a supernatural place. However, that's a story for another time.

****

"Where are all the boats? You would think that with a million people living here someone would be out sailing, wouldn't you?" I said, as I scanned the waters about Oahu. My question was aimed at no one in particular, being rhetorical in nature.

The Kaiwi channel was windy and full of great swells crested with white manes; perfect sailing conditions and *Maiatla* loved it as she charged over the waves. I couldn't believe that we had the entire channel to ourselves as there wasn't another boat in sight, not even a sports' fisherman buzzing by; as often the sight of our red and white Maple Leaf would draw them in for closer scrutiny.

We were still sixteen miles out and a little north of Diamond Head, which blocked our view of the lee of the island and Mamala Bay, off of Waikiki. I presumed that we would see more boats anchored and people playing in or on the water; Up to now, we had met no other cruisers like us, and surprisingly, I desired the company. But here, I thought, I was sure to find cruisers either passing through or staying for a while like us. As we rounded Kawaihoa Point off of Koko Head, an explosion of water craft did come into view!

"Hey, Uncle Andy! What is that over there?" I looked to where Samantha was pointing and I was surprised to see that the U.S. Navy was sending out a welcoming committee for us, complete with an armed escort.

It was over 110 meters long, 33 meters wide and it was tearing up the water as it came our way. The Los Angeles-class, 688-class nuclear-powered fast attack submarines form the backbone of the United States submarine fleet and was an impressive sight as it tore through the sea. The Navy reports that they have 43 of these submarines on active duty, making the Los Angeles-class the most numerous nuclear powered submarine class in the world. Except for USS Hyman G. Rickover, submarines of this class are all named after U.S. cities, breaking a long-standing Navy tradition of naming attack submarines after sea creatures, the USS Squalus and the Sailfish being former examples.

Which boat this was I could not ascertain (submarines are boats, not ships); it could be the USS Bremerton or the USS Tucson or one of the other seventeen LA-class nuclear attack submarines that call Pearl Harbour home. Not to be messed with, these boats carry twenty-five Tomahawk cruise missiles, not to mention the thirty-seven possibly nuclear-tipped Mark 48 "smart" torpedoes along with an odd assortment of underwater mines and SEAL Teams for reaching out with a more personal touch. The boats are capable of speeds of twenty knots on the surface and forty knots underwater while diving to almost three-hundred meters. They can go up to thirty years without refueling; which is a good thing because I don't think they could pull up to just any Esso fuel barge and fill up!

Apparently, this behemoth saw us as a threat. No sooner had we spotted the sub, when a call went out over channel sixteen, directed at the fifty foot ketch off of Koko Head. I scanned the otherwise empty horizon around and behind *Maiatla*.

"Well I guess he means us as there ain't nobody else out here. Melissa can you hand me the radio microphone please?" I said.

"This is the Canadian Registered sailing vessel *Maiatla* transiting from Maui to Honolulu, how can I help you sir?"

A little Coast Guard gunboat that was just flying over the water in an effort to keep up with the sub, took up station between us and the submarine. Through binoculars, I could see a guardsman clinging to the handles of the big, bow-mounted machine gun.

My conversation with the authoritative sounding voices was short and left me with no doubt as to their intent and what they required of me. We were firmly instructed to stay clear of the submarine. To give it wide berth of at least one mile. The repercussions of failing to comply were not in doubt, not by me anyway.

After ordering my disappointed crew to stand down from general quarters and informing them that we would not be attacking the sub today, Sam went back to oiling up. Being compliant, I altered course, pointing *Maiatla's* head more towards shore as I placed a request for a cold beer from my mate.

Perhaps in keeping with naval tradition, I should have dipped our colors in salute, but I was feeling just a bit defiant. After all we were a sailing vessel and should have had the right of way as they were far more maneuverable then we were. I think the sub just wanted to throw its weight around. I always hated giving into bullies no matter how big of stick they wield.

"Sam, you better be careful not to get too much sun! The rays are much more intense out on the water!"

"I'm OK, Aunty Jan. I've been using lots of sunscreen. I just want to make sure that I have a good tan for going home." With that, Sam shifted her towel from the shade cast by the mainsail and rolled over.

Our first glimpse of Waikiki Beach was thrilling; the beautiful sand surged with bathers. A gentle surf rolled in to break along the groomed beach in front of the towering waterfront hotels for which Waikiki is renowned. The most recognizable hotel from sea was the four-star Waikiki Hilton with its ground to rooftop, thirty-story painted rainbow, surrounded by a lagoon and private pools. A half dozen docks dotted the length of the beach from which dive charter boats, seadoos and outrigger canoes were launched. I'm not one to be impressed by a city, but; Honolulu, flanked by green volcanic ridges and extinct volcanoes, was breathtaking and more spectacular than I remembered, which is not overly surprising, because my first and only visit here was back in 1967, when I was seven.

****

Oahu and Waikiki beach was one of the stopovers my father had orchestrated on our family's move to Australia, an event that would have more influence on my life than perhaps any other single event.

At the time of our move we were living in Hamilton Ontario where my father was struggling as a bricklayer to support a wife and four children, a common life that perhaps he found more sedate and frustrating than what he could bare. This was not surprising, considering that he spent his teen years growing up in England while world war two raged overhead. He first learned to drive on a steamroller while repairing airdromes after German bombers plastered the runways with high explosives. His postwar military service had him ducking "friendly fire" on his "peacekeeping" duties in Egypt and Palestine as Jewish death squads were running about performing extrajudicial killings and assassinations of fleeing Nazis and other German collaborators. The death squads claimed the moral high ground as they were empowered by biblical justification of "and eye for an eye" and cared little for those that got into their way as they had the duty to kill over six million, just to even the score.

I remember my father telling us about how he was stranded in the middle of a town square in a broken down, lite armored scout car as snipers with armor piercing bullets, poked holes through the vehicle while he and his buddy returned fire while frantically calling for help over the radio. They would eventually be rescued by other British soldiers but not without casualties on both sides. The "friendly fire" incident made brief international headlines, but this event was quickly forgotten as similar clashes continually erupted.

Our father's life, the following ten years in Canada where he was employed first, driving a horse drawn milk wagon in Montreal then laying brick in a Hamilton steel foundry, by comparison, was mundane to say the least. Our father's ensuing mid-life crises necessitated the depletion of his life savings with the purchase of airline tickets that would take us all halfway around the world to a new and hopefully more exciting life. After stops in Vancouver, Oahu and New Zealand, to our mother's dismay, we settled into a sweltering, spider and lizard infested suburb west of Sydney Australia. As a child, I was thrilled with being able to play Tarzan in the real jungle that lay just across the street, all the while being totally oblivious to the deadly reptiles and arachnids that shred our playground. Our immigration to the farthest reaches of the world was short lived as after less than a year in the land down under, heeding to my mother's pleas to retreat north, we were on board a ship, sailing past the Sydney opera house and once clear of the harbour, the ship bore north, with nothing but the great expanse of the Pacific before us. We were headed home, but not without a few detours first.

****

The Ala Wai Harbour channel markers were easy to locate. With shoal water on either side and to the dismay of their crews, we cut between a fleet of four-meter sailing dinghies, that were racing across the channel. We neatly dropped all the sails and throttled up, aiming for the Magic Island fuel dock at the state-owned Ali Wai Harbour, located on the south shore of Oahu between Waikiki and Ala Moana beaches. As noted in all the guidebooks; from any point along this coast, there were stunning views of Diamond Head. The harbour included areas used by the prestigious Hawaii Yacht Club, the Waikiki Yacht Club and the Royal Hawaiian Ocean Racing Club. As we did not have a yacht club membership with any of these highbrow establishments and our Lahaina honorary membership carried no weight here, we would be relegated to the state run section of the harbour. The state harbour can accommodate vessels up to thirty meters in length and with seven hundred berths, I did not anticipate any problem finding a slip.

As we motored past the first set of State docks, we were shocked to see yellow caution tape stuck to many along with signs that read, "Condemned Do Not Use, by Order of the Ali Wai Harbour Authority". Many of the concrete docks sported rotting timbers and crumbling concrete piles. I would later learn that over one hundred of the slips had been condemned and there were no immediate plans to repair any. It was hard to believe that a city as wealthy as Honolulu would permit its public harbour to decay so badly. The sorry condition of the docks was further evidence of state apathy towards the boating community.

The busy fuel dock had just enough room for us, on the end, behind what looked like another cruiser. As soon as we had *Maiatla* secured, I marched over to present my hand. The *S.V. Golden Lion* was a thirteen-meter, center-cockpit ketch and remarkably, was owned by Canucks from our home waters of Victoria, B.C. The father/daughter sailing team had spent the year sailing the South Pacific and were now returning home. It was unfortunate that we did not have more time to converse, but they were just finishing taking on fuel and water after which they would be casting off, starting the long slog home on the same track that we would be taking six weeks from now. This would be their last piece of dry land for the next three weeks.

I helped cast off their lines and watched as they bore down the channel that we had just come up, feeling a sense of deja vu. I would later try and track the *Golden Lion* down, to see if they made it home successfully, but I had no luck in finding them. I do not want to suggest that anything ominous had befallen this vessel and her crew; because if it had, I'm sure we would have heard about it via the coconut telegraph or the tight-knit cruising community. As I watched the *Golden Lion* sail down Ali Wai channel, I suddenly realized why this scene felt so oddly familiar. As I remembered, it was in 1964, that a tour vessel sailed past the Ali Wai Yacht Club and the then Texaco fuel dock, out of this very same channel; only to be lost in a storm with its crew of two and five passengers. The vessel's departure went down in history and became part of the sixties pop culture as it was captured on black and white film. I couldn't believe I was standing right here where it all started! This was the harbour depicted in the TV series, Gilligan's Island! In the opening scenes of the show, you can clearly see the Ali Wai Yacht Club with its flag flying at half-mast, as President Kennedy had just been assassinated. It was exciting to be in the same place as that depicted in a show that was so prominent in my childhood! I shared my excitement with my family; surprisingly, they were less enthusiastic about the discovery than I was.

After topping up all the tanks, I marched up the dock to the harbour office to see about a slip. We wanted to stay a week or two, or at least until Sam's flight departed in six days. Our timing was off and the office was closed but the lady at the fuel dock told us we could spend the night so we were good, for now. We ordered passable fish and chips from the little café attached to the fuel dock and ate at steel tables next to the fuel pumps. We gawked at the fiery sunset as we were being pestered by little birds wanting chunks of French fries.

In the morning, we checked in with the harbour office, and were promptly told that there were no slips available! But after inquiring about alternate dock space, I was informed that we could pull into the space between two condemned fingers and Med-moor between the piles. There would be no electrical power or water and under no circumstance were we to walk on the fingers, but the fee for such a privilege was nominal; actually, really cheap! So the terms were acceptable to me and we would be moored at the very heart of Waikiki Beach and unlike Lahaina Harbour, we wouldn't be harassed by the ocean swells.

There was plenty of room between the piles and it was easy to slide *Maiatla* into a space originally meant for two vessels. One of our piles was guarded by what I would later learn was a Cattle Egret from Micronesia. The regal-looking, tropical Heron, in its all-white plumage, supervised the docking. Finally after being un-nerved by the tossing of lines about his pile, he was spooked into flight. After setting up a spider web of lines to secure us in the center of the piles, I jumped the gap between the bowsprit and the concrete pier. I combed the docks and managed to locate a long, wooden board, which became our gangplank; the narrow, springy bridge from *Maiatla's* bow to the pier. The scarred and splintering plank provided access to and from *Maiatla*, without leaping across the encompassing moat. We were neatly tucked in between a towering, old cabin cruiser and three slips down, a scraggly looking fifteen-meter ferro-cement ketch. The owner of the 1950s cabin cruiser was a young local who lived aboard. He graciously permitted us to run an electrical extension cord over to his boat so we could plug in: giving us - I'm sorry to say - TV and unlimited internet, courtesy of the harbour.

Melissa wasted no time in sending off a flurry of e-mails, bent on finding out what she had missed during our latest passage. And unbeknownst to us, she was asking her friend's parents to put her up for the rest of the summer, that is, if she could convince us to send her back to Canada with her cousin Samantha when she departed in less than a week!

We would not see our young neighbour much, but he and a friend would often entertain ladies down below. It didn't take me long to learn that if the music was playing on his boat, so was he. The big, black, cement boat on our other side, was a cruiser; a single handler by the name of Leon, who hailed from the west coast of Australia. This little fellow with his Aussie accent, was quite personable and reminded me of Steve Irwin, "The Crocodile Hunter", and he was eager to tell his story, which had really just begun, but it was already a good tale. I'm not sure who said it first but the quote is: "Bad decisions make for good stories." and I would soon learn that Leon may exemplify this.

Figure 18. Samantha (on plank) and Melissa going ashore at Waikiki Beach while tied to the condemned docks of the state harbour.

Over a beer in our cockpit, Leon was anxious to tell of his adventures to date. He had always dreamed of sailing the South Seas (his wife not so much), so he flew to San Diego and found an old but serviceable cement boat. After a brief refurbishing, more jury-rigging than repair, from the sounds of it, he sailed to Mazatlan, Mexico, where he spent three more weeks jury-rigging all the gear and rigging he broke on the way down the coast. When he thought he was ready, he departed for Hawaii, but just three days out, both his backstays failed and he was suddenly faced with the possibility of his mast coming down around his ears! He made repairs, but having no confidence in his rig, he hoisted only a small headsail and continued on to Hawaii. Apparently, turning back was not an option for him as it was "go west or die!" Due to shifting winds, he missed his intended landfall on Hawaii then missed all the other islands as well and only just managed to sail close enough to Oahu to motor in on the last of his fuel. A voyage that should have taken twenty-one days, took almost three times that... Leon's voyage from Mexico to Hawaii took a gruelling, seven weeks! His first landing after almost two months at sea was at the Magic Island fuel dock where he dutifully called the U.S. Customs.

When the customs officers arrived to inspect Leon's boat, not only were they shocked at the condition of the vessel but also at the sight of its lone occupant. Poor Leon was, malnourished and dehydrated; all skin and bones, as he had run seriously low on food and water. He was exhausted because his self-steering gear had failed, weeks previously and his face was wind burnt, peeling and blistered from spending all his time on deck, hand steering. Needless to say, he must have made quite a sight; looking more like a wreck survivor or castaway than a successful trans-pacific navigator. Suffering from food poisoning, Leon was rambling deliriously, the officers believing that Leon had some sort of communicable disease or scurvy, or was just plan crazy, he was taken into custody and quarantined for three more weeks in hospital. His boat was impounded where it sat at the fuel dock, until his eventual release.

"But I'm OK now!" Leon finished his story, with a big grin.

By the time we met, Leon had been free for almost a month and he had been quite diligent in getting himself healthy and his boat ready for the next leg of his voyage down to Tahiti. Over the next six months, his plan was to sail the rest of the way across the Pacific, over the top of Australia then south and finally home to Gladstone, Australia. Over seven thousand nautical miles - two and a half months at normal cruising speeds - through the most poorly charted and reef-infested waters of the world - and all single-handed in a boat that would better serve as an artificial reef, in my option anyway.

Leon also informed me that his wife and fourteen year old daughter were flying in for a visit, and would be staying with him onboard for the next two weeks, until his departure. I perked up at hearing that Leon's family was arriving, as it meant that Melissa would possibly have another boat kid to hang out with if she chose to and Jan and I could mingle with the other adults. I was content for the moment; we had indeed arrived in Waikiki World and we were eager to explore.

Chapter #17

"That is Gilligan's Island!"

But let there be spaces in your togetherness and let the winds of the heavens dance between you. Love one another but make not a bond of love: let it rather be a moving sea between the shores of your souls.
  Kahlil Gibran

It didn't take Samantha and Melissa long to discover the high-end boutiques lining Kalia Street, that ran behind the grand waterfront hotels. While the girls were off shopping, I went about renting a car so we could see Oahu from the perspective of a land based tourist. I had planned to circumnavigate the island by boat as there were many neat little bays to gunkhole, but I learned that local boating restriction and required permits virtually made this impossible.

In Hawaii, commercial and pleasure boats are regulated by the Department of Lands and Natural Resources and the ensuing documents and draconian regulations total in the hundreds of pages necessitating a background in Maritime Law to ensure that you were in full compliance. As a transient vessel, we were required to apply for a liveaboard permit. Local boaters had to show cause why they needed to live-aboard their boats and there were only two harbours in the islands that allowed full time live-aboards, Ali Wai Harbour being one of them with a pre-set limit as to how many could live aboard and they were already at the maximum.

The rest of the locals had to limit sleeping aboard their yachts to three nights a week or an aggregate total of thirty days a year. A vacation permit was available if they wanted to holiday aboard their boat and if they actually wanted to leave the harbour to cruise around the island, more permits were required and had to be applied for in advance. To make matters worse, most of the best bays for anchoring (with a permit of course) were either day use only or had a seventy-two hour limit. Apparently, if you moor on a state owned mooring ball in a marine park, you could be kicked off after two and a half hours, if another vessel wanted to use it.

The Island of Oahu is surrounded by a complex array of overlapping no anchoring zones; no overnight anchoring zones; ecologically sensitive zones; military zones and don't even think about coming in here zones, all of which came with hefty fines if the rules were breached. Thankfully, the fines were not to exceed $ 10,000 per violation!

Not long after arriving back in Canada, I learned that things were about to get even uglier for both local and transient boaters alike, new rules had been proposed. The Recreational Boaters Renaissance plan, a grand name for the Departments of Lands and Natural resources latest scheme to fleece boaters and to kill the recreational industry in the islands, was draconian to say the least. The worst of the proposed changes would instigate a new transient mooring fee of $2 per foot per to moor at a government dock in any harbour or $1 per foot per day to anchor out in any of the designated mooring zones or anchorages, whether there were services available or not. I'm afraid I would refuse to pay or even to stop at Ali Wai if the fee for *Maiatla* was $104 per night. Just to hang out offshore shore at Lahaina would cost us $52 per night if these new regulations came into effect.

It was also proposed that an itinerary of all intended stops would be required and all mooring fees were to be paid in advance, with no refunds if plans changed, even if the weather made changes necessary. To just show up in an anchorage without advance notice could result in heavy fines and it was proposed that reasons of fatigue, mechanical failure or weather would not be accepted as an excuse for the violation of these rules. I couldn't help but to feel pity for any cruiser who visits these magnificent islands if the proposal is passed into law, as they would be at the mercy of unscrupulous xenophobic island dictators who hate boats, but love money. Land of the free, my ass!

Apparently, we had already been in violation of some of the old rules, many times since reaching the islands by anchoring overnight in day use only zones, but either no-one of authority noticed, or no-one really cared. But, with big money at stake that would likely change in a hurry. At present, to sort out where we could go and for how long and arrange all the necessary permits, would have taken longer than we planned on staying in Oahu and cost us a few hundred dollars, so Jan and I were off to Budget Rent-a-Car to acquire our sub-compact land transportation.

Surprisingly, aside from the sole cruiser, *Golden Lion,* that we encountered at the fuel dock on our first day in Honolulu and of course the crazy Australian, Leon, we had not met any other foreign cruisers. But as we sped our way into to the Ali Wai parking lot, we had no idea what surprise was waiting for us.

I had just pulled into a vacant stall next to a rag-topped jeep with surf boards strapped on top; no sooner had we opened the car doors than I noticed a tiny woman with a tight, blond perm trooping down the pavement and she was making a bee line straight for us. She marched with purpose and what first struck me was her great cheek splitting grin, but as she closed the distance, I noticed that behind her wire-rimmed glasses were eyes afire with the look of recognition. I had a strange feeling that I knew this woman from somewhere, but from where or when I could not be certain. Fortunately, Jan had no problem dipping deep into her well of memories and found the connection.

"Andy! Look who it is! It's Lorraine from *Sea Niddry*. What's she doing here?" As soon as my dear heart mentioned the name, I instantly knew who I was looking at. While still separated by ten paces, arms flew open and seconds later there were hugs all around. One of the great things about cruising is that you never know who you will meet and where. Even though Honolulu wasn't exactly the deepest and most remote backwater of the world, it was still surprising to encounter not only an old friend but an old cruising friend way out here in mid pacific.

We had first met Lorraine and Henry on their boat, *Sea Niddry* back in 2001 while anchored in Richardson's Bay in San Francisco, where the Canadian cruising fleet had congregated after the long seven-day passage down the coast from British Columbia. The gregarious Lorraine and her significant other Henry, who just happened to be fine pianist and musician, anchored nearby. In a very short time, we became fast friends; we would spend the better part of the following nine months celebrating birthdays and enjoying potlucks, while harbour-hopping down into Mexico and then up into the Sea of Cortez to La Paz. Sorely, we broke company in May of 2002, when we sailed back to Canada while *Sea Niddry* prepared to summer in the Sea.

As usually happens to friends who are traveling on different tacks, we eventually lost touch. We had heard through the cruisers net, which is nothing if not efficient (efficient in propagating stories whose accuracy is not necessarily of principal concern), that sometime later, the couple had separated on amiable terms. Henry remained in La Paz, building a new life, earning his living by working the cantina circuit with his piano. After the break-up, Lorraine first signed on aboard a twelve-meter yacht bound for the South Pacific, after which she began to hire herself out as a delivery crew, which would keep her away from home for years. Her lust for travel under sail would take her all throughout the South Seas and she experienced many exotic sights and stops such as Bora Bora, Tahiti, the Marquesas and not to mention the Moai, the monolithic human figures carved from rock, which infested Easter Island. After five years of voyaging in Oceania, here she was now! Our wakes had indeed crossed once again.

"Hey guys, I was just at your boat looking for you. When I saw her I knew instantly it was *Maiatla* and I was hoping that you still owned her," Lorraine said, as she gave me another hug. "When did you get in and where did you come from?... Mexico?"

I think she was as excited to see us as were where her.

"Are you here on *Sea Niddry*?" I asked, being careful not to ask about Henry, as I wasn't sure if what I had heard was true and I didn't want to unnecessarily upset our friend. But, I was sure that she would fill us in about their break-up in her own time.

We moved to the side of the busy parking lot to do a little catching up. She didn't have much time as she was on her way to meet someone, so we took turns and quickly gave the Reader's Digest version of our stories since we'd last been in each other's company.

For Lorraine's part, she was on a delivery and was supposed to be delivering a small yacht to the Pacific Northwest via Hawaii, but apparently, the boat owner's plans had started to unravel shortly after purchasing the boat in Mexico.

"We got in a few days ago and we have been cleaning the boat up for the owner. He took off after hitting the dock and disappeared for a few days without telling us anything," Lorraine said with a chuckle.

As usual, her story proved to be an interesting one and Jan and I hung on every word. Lorraine suddenly became animated.

"Well, I had been sailing the Sea of Cortez by myself on *Sea Niddry* for a while, when a friend, who I had done my first Pacific crossing with, invited me to join his delivery crew. My friend picked up the gig in Mazatlan, when he got to know a fellow anchored-out in the old harbour. Apparently, this guy he met, had just learned how to sail on a course he took in San Carlos, up in the Sea of Cortez. He bought a boat a month or so later and intended to sail, who knows where, with his fiancé." She paused a moment to search her memory.

"Anyway, after a couple of very short day trips outside of Mazatlan Harbour in open water, his fiancé jumped ship and fled back to the States. Apparently, she had decided that she didn't want anything to do with cruising stuff. Anyway, this new sailor decided it would be best to take the boat to the U.S. mainland and perhaps he could ease his fiancé into sailing in more protected waters. He obviously didn't have the expertise to cross oceans by himself, so that's how this delivery came about. We decided that the best route to take would be the old clipper route, so our first leg was to Hawaii and then we'd see how the boat handled and we could reassess our situation here, whether to carry on north or not."

"What do you mean that you had to reassess your situation?" I asked. "Were you concerned about the boat making it or the crew getting along?"

"Oh, no, it wasn't that, I forgot to mention that I had fallen aboard *Sea Niddry* sometime earlier and had torn a muscle in my right arm. I wasn't sure I could handle a rough voyage north." A pained expression cut Lorraine's face as she held out her injured arm.

"Today is the first day I haven't worn my sling. Feels a lot better, but I have little strength in it. I'm having trouble cranking on the winches." Quickly she checked her watch.

"Anyway, I was lucky! It was the easiest ocean passage that I have ever made; relatively flat, well off the wind or downwind almost the entire way and therefore not fast, but very comfortable, so my arm was not an issue. On the voyage, it soon became apparent that this was not what the owner had in mind. I don't know what he was expecting but whatever it was, this was not it. I don't know what he was struggling with, boredom, too much sail tending because of the light winds or lack of sleep and privacy, confinement, likely all those things, but his attitude tainted the cruise. Everything was not very copacetic on board. Anyway, as soon as we cleared U.S. customs and we were tied up in a slip here at the Ala Wai, the owner was packed and off the boat within an hour. He returned several days later, to say the boat was up for sale, but that we could stay aboard until we were ready to leave. He had no further interest in the boat and that was the end of it, really! No great adventure there."

"So what now, are you flying back to Canada?" Jan asked.

"Well, we can stay on the boat for a few more days but we will have to get off. The "For Sale" sign is already stuck to the pulpit, so if I can't find another paying gig going north, I will fly back. Haven't been home in years, so I guess it's about time."

After vowing to get together again in the next couple days, we went our separate ways and despite all our desires and good intentions, it would be another four years before our paths crossed, and once again it would be in a most unexpected place.

Later that same day, our first jaunt in the car was over to the Waiakamilo Shopping Plaza which was just a few miles west of the harbour down the Nimitz Highway and over the fish filled Kapalama waterway. We had looked up the address of a local sail maker, so we dropped off our number-one headsail. We had blown out the stitching at the reinforced clew, while doing battle with the strong tradewinds as we raised Hawaii. The man in the loft assured me, that our repaired sail would be ready within a few days. Our sail wasn't the only repair that we required; the shroud that we had broken off the Washington coast on the first week of our voyage was still a worry. The sail maker recommended a rigger in the same building, so we placed an order for two new lower shrouds, and again, I was assured that they would be ready within the week. By the time we arrived back at the boat, the girls had returned. We formed a chain to pass all the groceries over *Maiatla's* springy gangplank. Amazingly, my boat chore list was short, so we could focus on having fun, which included an around the island drive and we would leave in the morning.

First thing in the morning, attempting to organize three women that must share a single tiny bathroom can be frustrating, (I would have been smarter to retire to the cockpit and wait them out, but my captainitus had kicked in). By 9:00 a.m. and after some hair pulling on my part, we were happily packed into our tiny car, weaving eastward through the tourist-lined streets of Waikiki. We weren't particularly interested in the sites of the city, not to suggest that the drive wasn't interesting through the maze of hotels and waterfront parks, but we wanted to explore the shoreline and countryside beyond Diamond Head. It was a beautiful day with the paved road surprisingly clear of traffic for a Wednesday, or was it Sunday? I wasn't sure and I guess it really didn't matter anyway! One of the perks of cruising is the ability to lose all sense of time without having to suffer through the consequences of doing so. As we snaked our way along the waterfront, the hotel high rises quickly thinned until we were coursing our way between upscale homes with the Wiliwili trees, Tiger's Claw, Indian Coral Trees and coconut palm trees sprouting from the manicured lawns.

After twenty minutes or so of ogling the upscale houses and miniature tropical estates, the houses all suddenly vanished, revealing a spectacular ocean view to the right of the car; A vista that nearly took our breath away. The road had been cut from the side of the extinct Diamond Head volcano, and over fifty meters below, the submerged coral and turquoise waters stretched out for hundreds of meters before reaching the deep blue of the deep water drop off. Amongst the breaking waves, pods of surfers could be seen astride boards; off to the sides other surfers were lazing like seals on the crystalline water.

Once clear of the green canopy, the temperature rose; the now bare volcanic rock radiated the warmth that it had already absorbed from the hot morning sun. The heat would have been rather uncomfortable if not for the constant trade wind breeze, that was now coursing along the coast and whipping into the car's open windows. There were many stops of interest and lookout points to take advantage of, one of which is the Honolulu lighthouse on the point, a local landmark and edifice set in a park-like setting.

A lookout tower was first established here in 1878 on the seaward slopes of Diamond Head for spotting and reporting incoming vessels. A local, John Charles Petersen, a mariner born in Sweden, was the first watchman at the station and was paid $50 per month to man the tower. After his arrival in Hawaii, Petersen married a native girl who died just four months after the birth of their daughter, Melika. Diamond Head Charlie, as he was known raised his daughter at the isolated station where he served for thirty years until his death in 1907. It wasn't until the grounding of two separate steamers upon the reef in 1893 that the federal government decided to upgrade the lookout station and began the construction of a newer more modern light house which wasn't completed until 1899. The selected site was just 250 yards west of Charlie's lookout tower. The original structure was a forty-foot-tall, iron, framework tower built by Honolulu Iron Works but due to concerns over the stability of the erection, the open framework was enclosed with walls constructed of coral-rock, excavated from a quarry on Oahu.

The Lighthouse Board took control of all aids to navigation in the Hawaiian Islands in 1904 and in 1917, after cracks were found in the base of the structure; funds were allocated for constructing a fifty-five-foot tower of reinforced concrete on the original foundations. The complex has grown over the years to include a keeper's home with various outbuildings. The lighthouse has played a key role in ensuring mariners safety in both peace and wartime.

However, what interested me most was that this lighthouse was also used as the official finishing line for the Transpac Yacht Race held bi-annually from California to Honolulu. In just a few days, we would see the first of this year's race contestants charge across the finish line, with billowing spinnakers flying. It was humbling to see that the fastest of boats, hybrid, racing sleds, complete the course in less than eight days. Remarkable, considering that it took *Maiatla* 21 days to cover the same distance. That is not to suggest that we were slow, not at all; Some of the more normal racing boats took 19 and 21 days to arrive in Hawaii, several never made it at all and had to turn back due to crew, gear or general boat fatigue or failure. Or perhaps they simply got lost! After all, it is immensely easier to find the North American continent then a tiny speck of land hiding in the great expanse of the Pacific. The fact that we were here to even witness the arrival of the racers makes a bold statement about the capabilities of *Maiatla* and her crew! (OK, blowing my own horn!)

We did as most of the other tourists on the Kaalawai Road were doing; pulling over for a few minutes, snapping some pictures, only to pile back into the car and shoot back onto the busy road, carefully timing our merge into the now-steady stream of cars and tourist buses. We would often see the same groups of people along the way, grey-haired retirees and families with young children at the next stop around the bend; after a while, we would exchange curt nods of recognition as if somehow we had been acquainted. The groups being mostly exclusive in nature, with whites only acknowledging other whites and Asians likewise bowing to their own with the twain infrequently mixing. I found all the dramatic landscape very interesting but I was eager to move on to a very specific lookout point down the road.

Once past Diamond Head, the road turned back inland and we found ourselves in amongst what appeared to be more modestly kept homes of Oahu's upper-middle class. A few tall high-rise apartment blocks dotted the otherwise unassuming landscape. If it were not for the reaching palms or the odd sprawling banyan tree we could have been traversing on the fringe of most any metropolitan city in North America with the Golden Arches and 7-Eleven's with their ubiquitous Coke Slurpees on every other street corner.

As we drove along, I started to notice something that I had not expected to find in what I thought to be a primarily affluent city and state; the signs were subtle and could be passed over by the unwary or unobservant. Here, as in eastern part of Honolulu, there were signs that a disgraceful condition existed, a human condition like I had never seen anywhere else I had traveled and it was evident in virtually every city, town and state park we would visit on Oahu. The condition was evident in the dank alleys of the City, as well as the secluded back roads of the mountains or quaint coastal villages. For the most part, the locals seemed to ignore this shame and even appeared to condone it, as they left it unmolested and it had long since become part of the very fabric and a necessary measure of island life.

Its goes without saying that every city has its seedy side. Illegal drug use in all its forms goes along with needles and dealers and the associated crime required to support such habits. Prostitution swept ashore in Hawaii over three hundred years ago, just moments after the first member of Cook's crew traded a single nail for a sexual favour (A shiny penny offered to a native got you more than just their thoughts) and it was not long after that the first Hawaiian "Son of a Gun" was born.

(A Son of a Gun is thought to originate within the British Navy when "ladies" of the working variety, were either permitted or sneaked aboard war ships. Copulation was often performed between the cannons on the gun decks. Most offspring conceived in this manner were often fatherless as the sailors had long since sailed away. This child would often be referred to as a "Son of a Gun" due to their questionable parentage.)

Today, the illicit trade in flesh still flourishes within Honolulu's strip clubs, massage parlors and back alleys. The sex trade, whether organized or less formal with the freelance practitioners, has changed little in the islands, only the manner of payment has been refined and exorbitantly inflated.

The aforementioned elements, I had expected to see in Hawaii, but this? What I was now seeing? I said nothing to Jan about it, as part of me didn't want to spoil the paradisiacal illusion. But, I should have known that I couldn't keep anything from Jan for long… soon she too would notice what I had seen. However, more on this condition later.

THE TAHITI SYNDROME-HAWAIIAN STYLE

I stepped on the gas and made my way back to the Kalanianaole Highway that led past the Niu Valley to my first real stop of interest. Estimated to be over 800-years-old, the ancient Hawaiian kuapa (walled) fishpond of Hawaii Kai located just six miles east of Diamond Head and in the western shadow of Koko Head Crater, is a must see. Hawaiian fishponds represent the remarkable engineering and aquacultural skill of the ancient Hawaiians who constructed two types of ponds that extended from the natural shoreline: loko kuapa (walled ponds) and loko `ume iki (ponds that draw little). Loko kuapa were the most common type of fishpond in ancient Hawaii and were highly reliable in providing food from the sea.

Approximately 127 of these ponds were built throughout the islands over the centuries, becoming cultural community centers. Constructed in shallow waters, loko kuapa are formed by a rock wall that encloses a portion of the ocean. These ponds were built on the command of local chiefs with labor contributed by the families over which he ruled. After construction, a caretaker would be appointed to maintain the fishpond and protect it against poachers from rival villages and islands.

The massive stonewalls of a loko kuapa enclosed a shallow bay or inlet or extended out in an arc between two points of land. Walls were constructed of coral and permeable rock such as basalt to allow the wall to absorb the pounding action of the water. These materials also allowed water to flow into the pond to reduce stagnation. The walls were designed in a curve so prevailing currents pushed sand and debris around the wall rather than collecting it at one side. Stones on the outer wall were placed without mortar and angled downwards so wave action worked to pull them tighter. Wall height, width and length varied depending on the size of the pond. The longest wall of any fishpond is located on Oahu's North East corner at He`eia. This pond's seawall is 5,000 feet long and encircles 88 acres and is still intact to this day and for a ridiculously high fee, a tour can be had.

A distinctive feature of the loko kuapa is its sluice gate. A grate of vertical wooden sticks built into the pond walls permitted small fish to enter from the open sea and prevented larger fish from leaving. The wooden grates aided in water circulation, fish harvesting, stocking, and silt removal. Ocean currents determined the location of the gates with placement chosen to maximize circulation within the pond.

The second type of shore pond was the loko `ume iki which were built into the ocean on coral reefs. These ponds are found primarily on Molokai and Lanai. As with the loko kaupa, a wall of coral and or basalt is built in an arc from the shoreline, but this wall is not continuous. Instead, it is broken up by stone-lined lanes leading into and out of the fishpond. These lanes were placed to take advantage of ocean currents and tides to flush the pond with fresh water and fish. The loko `ume iki was used like a large scale fish trap: During the tidal flux, a fisherman would catch fish by walking to the end of one of the pond lanes and casting a net over the mouth of the lane from a platform built there.

The Hawaii Kai fishpond we were now headed for, was of the walled variety but little of the original structure remains today. After the decline of the native population, the pond fell into disrepair until a twentieth century visionary discovered its marshy remains. Born in 1882, Henry John Kaiser was an American industrialist and a philanthropist who became known as the father of modern American shipbuilding. He established the Kaiser Shipyard, which built Liberty ships during World War II, after which he formed Kaiser Aluminum and Kaiser Steel. True to his philanthropic tendencies, Kaiser initiated health care for his workers and their families. He led Kaiser Motors automobile company which was known for the safety of their designs. Kaiser was also involved in large construction projects such as civic centers and dams, (think Hoover) and invested heavily in real estate. With his acquired wealth, he initiated the Kaiser Family Foundation a charitable organization often seen promoting on public access TV. While living in Honolulu in the late sixties, H. J. Kaiser developed an obsession with perfecting urban landscapes and the result of which can be seen in the community of Hawaii Kai, at the site of the old loko kuapa fishpond.

The modern Hawaii Kai development is a largely residential area located in the City & County of Honolulu and the development is the largest of several communities at the eastern end of Oahu. The area was principally developed by Kaiser around the ancient Maunalua Bay fishpond. The Hawaii Kai or Koko Marina was dredged from the kuapa pond starting around 1959. Dredging not only transformed the shallow coastal inlet and wetlands into a marine embayment, but was accompanied by considerable filling and clearing of the pond's margins. In 1961, Kaiser entered into a lease agreement with the landowners, to develop the 521-acre fishpond into residential tracts with a marina and channels separated by fingers of land and islands upon which house lots and commercial properties would sit. Not unlike parts of Venice, except with a Polynesian flair, with out-rigger canoes instead of sweeping gondolas.

Nearly all of the low-lying lands surrounding the marina have since been developed, and neighborhoods now extend back into several valleys and up the separating ridges. I found it interesting that all the resident's need's, everything from groceries to attending movie theaters can be accessed from the water. Virtually all the waterfront residents boast their own docks and boats for zipping around the waterways, gaining access to the malls though the public access docks. For those who don't have their own boats, a well-organized fleet of water taxis can be called up on demand or like a bus, met at one of the many loading docks strategically placed amongst the waterways. If you navigate the waterway that passes beneath the Kalanianaole highway, it leads to the protected anchorage in Maunalua Bay in the volcanic shadow of the Koko Head Crater.

From the road on the causeway I could see several small sailboats and out-rigger canoes lying peacefully on their moorings as the subdued tradewinds rippled the water.

"Looks awfully shallow!" Jan said, as I pulled the car over to the side of the road for a better look. "Can we get in there behind that reef? The channel looks pretty narrow."

As everyone piled out of the car, I scanned the bay. The dark green of the reef stood out in stark contrast to the white sandy bottom of the bay and in the distance, a school of baitfish that was perhaps chased to the surface by some unseen predator was being harried by flock of swooping gannets. Perched atop a nearby channel marker looking like a wobbly crucifix, a disinterested looking cormorant dried his outstretched wings in the late morning sun.

"Well, I think so." I said, as I wracked my brain in an effort to remember what I had read. "The guidebook said there is a cut in the reef with three meters of water at low tide and it is supposed to be well marked, I can see the piles that indicate the channel from here."

"How much tide is there, can't be much here." Jan squinted against the sun, shielding her eyes with her hand.

I looked at the beach for the high water mark but it was difficult to tell just how low the water went.

"I think an extreme tide is less than three feet. Typical tides here are stated in fractions of a foot with daily fluctuations of six to ten inches being the norm."

"Well that ain't going to help us much to get over the reef. At least the water is clear so we can see the bottom coming up!" Jan scoffed.

Back home in Canada, we were used to dealing with average tides that ran between three and five meters (9 to 15 feet) which can make for wicked tidal currents in the narrow passes and exciting nights if you just happened to have anchored near a shallow spot that wasn't marked on the charts. More than once while navigating the remote parts of the British Columbia coast, we stopped for the night in what looked like a bay clear of obstruction only to see in the morning pointy rocks poking through the surface of the water uncomfortably close. If you really screwed up you could find your boat on her side sitting on a rock ledge a couple of meters above the water. But here that would not be a problem; I just needed to get over the typically shallow barrier reefs that line most of these shores.

Hawaii Kai looked like a fun place to explore from the boat and I was looking forward to bringing *Maiatla* in here once we had had enough of the excitement of Waikiki. It was nice to see a community, especially in Hawaii that actually catered to boaters, if not cruising boats, at least small runabouts, kayaks and canoes. After making some mental notes and taking a few pictures, we moved on up the road to perhaps the prettiest little unspoiled bay on the island.

As you broach the crest of Koko Head Crater, a pullout on the right beckons you to turn into the Hanauma Bay parking lot. The view from the eastern rim of Koko Head is nothing if not spectacular in any direction that you happen to glance. Before you now is a crescent-shaped bay surrounded by dense forestation and far below is the strikingly white sand beach of Hanauma Bay. This entire area is a protected marine life conservation area and underwater park and was made so way back in 1967, which explains how this little piece of wilderness remained so pristine. All the guidebooks declared that this is the best protected cove on Oahu with a diverse population of marine life and a large, rich coral reef. The bay floor is actually the crater of an ancient volcano that flooded when the exterior wall collapsed and the ocean rushed in over the eastern rim. It is a popular spot for both locals and tourists alike, and the large sandy beach is perfect for sunbathing, relaxing and picnicking.

Several hiking trails extend along the coastline or the narrow ridge overlooking the bay providing breathtaking lookouts. One trail on the north side of the bay leads to what is called the Toilet Bowl which is a natural spa-like tub that swirls and flushes with the cycles of the swells and tides. However, recently the Bowl has been closed to the public due to injuries suffered by visitors who liked to get flushed.

Darting songbirds abound in the Paper Bark Eucalyptus and Monkey Pod Trees as legions of geckos scamper and bound over the lava rocks lining the parking lot. Other forms of animal and bug life could be seen scurrying around the grounds as well, with the most objectionable not being the lizard or creepy bug variety, but the feral cats that seem to be everywhere in the islands. Here, a pair of semi-tame, scruffy looking felines begging for handouts next to a trash bin stuffed to overflowing with McDonald's wrappers and paper coffee cups from a local java shop.

The curvature of Hanauma Bay usually provides protection from large ocean waves and allows swimmers a terrific opportunity to view the marine and reef life in a safe, protected environment, just so long as you didn't mind sharing it with the large population of Green Sea Turtles that have laid claim to the area. It was one of the bays I had originally looked at as a possible anchorage for *Maiatla* but I was quick to learn that this was one of the "No anchoring or don't even think about coming in here zones" I mentioned earlier. As the Park charged a day use fee that seemed a bit pricey, we would have to be content with gawking for a few moments at the aqua waters and frolicking bathers from above.

Despite the Park's protected status, the surrounding area wasn't so peaceful. As we commenced to climb back into the car, the sudden chatter of heavy machine-gun fire filed the air. It sounded close, too close for my liking, just over the hill behind us. In an adjacent parking stall, what looked like a local couple were likewise entering their vehicle when the shooting started, but they did not appear to be the least bit concerned by the skirmish unfolding nearby. Perhaps it was Brian and his band of eco-terrorists from Maui attempting to reclaim what they thought was theirs! I called from my open window to the adjacent car.

"Hey, excuse me! Do you know what all the shooting is about"? Sounds awfully close!"

The tanned middle-aged man looked over his right shoulder as if he had just heard the continuous gunfire for the first time. His perplexed look melted away to one of recognition.

"Oh, that! There is a military small arms firing range just over the hill. But don't worry, they are shooting the other way, towards the mountain."

I thanked him and we both drove off.

Jan looked at me with some concern.

"You wouldn't think they would be allowed to have a firing range so close to a recreation area would you? There are hiking trails here and what if someone gets lost? If they went down the wrong trail couldn't they get shot?

"Ya, it is odd that they are shooting right next to a picnic area, but I would assume or hope anyway that they have the firing range all fenced off so it's probably not a real danger. But man, all that noise."

"I wonder how often they use it?" I also wondered what the life expectancy of a feral cat would be that was foolish enough to ignore the No Trespassing signs posted all along the roadway.

We sped off down the road headed for the distant point and the spot I'd been anxious to get to ever since our landing on the island: Makapuu Point Lookout that overlooks Waimanalo Bay is typical for this stretch of the coastline. The vista offers a seemingly endless ocean, jagged cliffs with sprawling sand beaches at their bases and clear waters with a delicate maze of underlying coral reefs. But, this point was special, to me anyway as memories leaped straight out of my childhood.

"Come on everybody, out of the car and let's line up along that rock wall along the edge!" I said, with much excitement.

As everyone piled out of the car, the full force of the northeast tradewinds that were whipping down Kaiwi Channel instantly buffeted us. The winds were well up in the 30-knot range, made the sea before us white with breaking waves.

As the girls lined up along the lava rock wall, Melissa squealed and laughed as she had to fight to keep her short pleated skirt from blowing up in the strong swirling winds. To make matters worse, her long, unrestrained hair kept whipping around, burying her face. The girls were all laughing and giggling about Melissa's plight and I had to prod them to hold still long enough for me to get some pictures, all of which showed Melissa with one hand clutching tuffs of hair and the other clenching tight to her skirt. After several attempts, I did manage to get everyone lined up, but as I did, a bus load of tourists pulled up and it didn't take long for a group of teenage boys who just exited the bus to notice our beautiful daughter's dilemma. Now that we were all in position, I asked a passing woman to take the shot which she happy did. As she snapped away, the tight knot of boys seemed to be migrating in our direction, however, to the obvious disappointment of the boys, as soon as the woman passed me back my camera, Melissa bolted for the security and cover of the car.

"OK! So what's so special about this spot that we had to get a picture with everyone?" Jan asked, after we had all had crammed back into the car.

"Well, as you all know, back in 1967 when my family flew to Australia, we spent some time on Oahu. Well, my Dad hired a taxi to take us on a tour of the Island and this is one of the places we stopped. Dad had us all line up against that same wall right there where we were just standing and he had the cabby take the picture. That picture is in my parent's family photo album and I thought it would be so cool to take the same picture with all of us at the same spot almost exactly 40 years later."

I don't know why, but that day way back then was forever burned in my memory, having stored it in my special repository, a memory that I had fondly recalled and replayed many times over the years. I recalled the cabby grinning from behind his dark sunglasses, pointing to the distant islands and saying to my brother, Steve and I, "And that island there is where they filmed the show Gilligan's Island!"

Perhaps that declaration was the key element in this memory, the common denominator, Gilligan's Island was the catalyst that triggered my mind to ensnare that memory and ear-mark it for future retrieval. The cabby's simple statement tied a favourite TV show of my childhood directly to my family and this spot, all three ultimately coming together in one specific place and location in the middle of the pacific, here on Makapuu Point.

My family's Australia trip had been the single biggest influence of my life; it not only opened my eyes to a vast world and all its possibilities, it more importantly brought me closer to a father that for most of my life had been absent, as his work frequently took him away from us. For the first time in our lives, my siblings and I had our father's undivided attention and we made the most of it, if only for a short year.

I now suspect that what I was doing here and now was an attempt to forge tight and pleasant memories with Melissa, with the hope that she would do as I had, and place these memories in her special repository so that 40 years down the road, she could call upon them. I wanted her to have the types of memories that could comfort her in times of trouble and I wanted her to be able to pull *me* out of the dust, in her times of despair and smile when her mind's eye sees me! I wanted her not to forget me; I wanted not to be forgotten!

I see now that I had consciously and secretly hoped that this voyage with Melissa would impact her the same way the one that I made 40 years ago had done for me. Although I was nearly an adult before I fully realized how deeply it affected me.

However, that is not what appeared to be happening here for Melissa. Our daughter was struggling emotionally - internally tortured - which closed her off to all that was going on around her. I was worried that Melissa's protracted illness had been hard on her and I felt that it had jaded her to life in a way that no teenager should know, skewing her priorities and outlook. I also feared that steeling my emotions in an effort to cope with her illness had actually created a rift between us instead knitting us tighter together and I now began to fear that by my dragging her along on this voyage, forcing her to be where she did not want to be, was having the exact opposite effect than intended.

Figure 19.

Janet, Andrew, Melissa and Samantha standing at the same windy wall at Makapuu Point I had done forty years earlier with my family.

As I looked at Melissa through the rear view mirror, the reluctant passenger, the unwilling participant in this adventure. I felt sick in my heart and I feared that if I had not already lost her, I would soon, if we or I, didn't do something different. I needed desperately to find a way to reach her, but my time and opportunities were running out.

In the back seat, Melissa was smiling and jostling about with Samantha, as they made fun of the teen boys by the curb. Melissa was happy for the moment and I was glad for that. The cabby was wrong, we weren't looking at Gilligan's island from that point, but we were not far from it. In actuality most of the show was filmed on a stage set in Los Angeles; the few out door scenes were either recorded here in Hawaii, as in the opening shot of the show at Ali Wai Harbour or on a beach in California. The distant island depicted in the start of every show is here on Oahu and just around the corner. Gilligan's Island is really called Coconut Island, or Moku o Loʻe, by the Hawaiians and is a 28-acre palm covered isle located in Kaneohe Bay on the east shore of Oahu and the island is now owned by the state and is the facility for the Hawaii Institute of Marine Biology, part of the University of Hawaii. I assume Gilligan's professor would have approved.

We drove on to Kaneohe Bay and after snapping a few pictures of a rather unimpressive little island that didn't resemble the fantasy of my boyhood; the isle of exile for the S.S. Minnow's castaways. We turned around and retraced our route back to Honolulu and our waiting *Maiatla,* but not before hitting McDonald's for dinner.

Chapter #18

Pearl Harbour

Yesterday, Dec. 7, 1941 - a date which will live in infamy - the United States of America was suddenly and deliberately attacked by naval and air forces of the Empire of Japan.
Franklin D Roosevelt.

Our fourth morning at the Ali Wai boat basin was a busy one as we prepared to load up the car and head out to visit Pearl Harbor and the Arizona Memorial. The car would be extra crowded as we had invited some friends along for the day. Our guests were Leon, an Australian Caucasian, his wife Kim, of Chinese lineage, and their thirteen year old daughter Melanie, a visually pleasing blend of the two races augmented by a personable disposition. What I have always found remarkable about cruisers is how quick they are to accept an opportunity to get to know other people regardless of their ethnicity or disparity in economics. And what better way to get to know someone than to sit upon a stranger's lap when you cram five adults and two teens into a sub-compact, with arms dangling out the windows, barrelling down the highway!

The typically gregarious nature of cruisers notwithstanding, I would like to point out that camaraderie and the desire to mingle with like-minded souls may not be the first motivating factor behind this cuddling phenomenon that cruisers normally display. (Even power boaters are routinely included without prejudice). Despite what appears to be altruistic motives and a real desire for human companionship, more often than not, frugality is usually the overriding factor in such behavior; it is well documented the world over, that cruisers are notoriously cheap and the offer of a free ride or a piece of the day's catch is rarely declined and readily accepted with a friendly smile!

As I peered into the rear-view mirror at the collage of smiling faces, I felt compelled to warn everyone.

"OK, I know it's a tight fit back there but if we see a cop and I yell, at least two heads must disappear, OK? If we get caught, some of us will be taking the bus home and I don't mind telling you that I won't be one of them as I have the keys!"

My comment triggered another round of giggles as Leon took my warning seriously and declared that he had found his hiding spot as he attempted to fit his head into the front of his wife's blouse. Melanie rolled her eyes while giving her parents a disgusted look. The rest of us just laughed. Apparently embarrassing your teenager is a parental right that is not limited geographically. With the ground rules set and while receiving more than one disapproving or confused look from other morning commuters, I pushed my way onto the busy Ala Moana Boulevard, bound westward for Pearl City.

It was the afternoon before that I had informed the crew that if nothing else, I wanted to visit the site where W.W. II and the War of the Pacific, for the Americans anyway, had started, in 1942. The British and Canadians at that point in time had already been shooting it out with the Germans in Europe since 1939 and Japanese in the western Pacific since 1941. Jan and Samantha were all for a visit to the memorial, but Melissa, appeared rather lukewarm on the idea of spending the day at an old navy base. I attempted to excite her by regaling her with stories of the bold attack and informing her of the historical significance of the events that unfolded at Pearl Harbour. I went on to describe the great tragedy that befell the crew of the Arizona and how so many men became entombed in their own ship and that most of the bodies were never recovered. But, the more I talked, the less she seemed to be interested. Melissa didn't say that she didn't want to go to Pearl, but her posture betrayed her feelings on the subject. (Or perhaps she was feigning a disinterest just to bug me). Whichever the case, I was thankful that she was coming but if I thought I had my last confrontation for the day with her, I was sadly mistaken. Later that night just about the time Jan and I were about to head off to bed and after Melissa had sent and received a flurry of emails, she stormed the salon where Jan and I were sitting and made an announcement.

"Dad, I talked to David's parents and they said I could stay with them in Mission, you can call and talk to them if you like, but can I please go home with Sam next week? I really don't want to be here!" Our daughter was more pleading than demanding and the site of her being so unhappy most of the time broke my heart. I turned to look at Jan who just stared blankly back at me. I couldn't help but expel a relenting sigh as I felt all my resolve melt away.

"Tell you what I will do Melissa, I will phone his parents after we get back from Pearl Harbour but no promises, your Mum and I will have to think about this for a bit, OK?"

Melissa retreat to her cabin with a smile on her face and moments after closing her door I could hear the rattle of her laptop keys as she relayed to her friends that she thought she had worn us down and that she might coming home after all. I didn't sleep much that night and I suspect, neither did Jan.

Pearl Harbour was as expected and well worth the visit and if the tomb at the

Arizona Memorial and reading out the names of the dead as scribed upon the wall doesn't bring a tear to your eye, then I would suggest that perhaps you may well be a sociopath, unable to feel the pain of others. Despite the otherwise tragic surroundings, all seemed to have had a good day as we wandered about with Leon and his family. After visiting the Arizona, we returned to shore on the big, water taxi and commenced wandering around the other exhibits. Big guns and pieces of submarines were set up and not only the kids took great delight in being able to climb upon and work the controls of the historic tools of war.

Jan and Samantha laughed themselves silly as they braced themselves for battle, first at the controls of an anti-aircraft gun with their target being a commercial jetliner foolish enough to pass over head. Then again while peering through periscope of a submarine's conning tower, firing torpedoes at an imaginary foe in the harbour. Melissa and I stood nearby, looking at a plaque depicting Japanese dive-bombers making a run at the U.S.S. Nevada as it attempted to flee the harbour, all the while pretending not to know the giggling pair yelling orders, complete with battle sound effects.

On our way home, we made a side trip to a beautiful waterfront park located adjacent to the airport after navigating through a rather dirty looking industrial area. Sand Island State Park is a 140 acre, landscaped coastal park that provides a fine view of the Honolulu coastline from the harbour to Diamond Head and is deemed to be one of the best places to view Oahu's stunning sunsets. This is a large park directly on the ocean, which boasts spacious grass lawns with medium-sized ironwood and seagrape trees, and a fringe of palm trees lining the long, uncrowded sandy beach. The Park caters to mostly locals, but the occasional tourists also drop by, mainly for the historical significance of the place or after taking the wrong exit off the Nimitz Highway.

Sand Island's military history dates back to W. W. II; it was the first line of defence for both Pearl Harbour and the City of Honolulu just beyond. Historic Hickman Field is also located just west of Sand Island where a handful of American fighters managed to get airborne despite having the field decimated by the Japanese. As we entered the park, several abandoned concrete bunkers and rusting, lookout towers came into view and it was easy to imaging anti-aircraft guns firing up into the sky as wave after wave of Japanese bombers roared overhead. The park, with its incumbent ghosts, still possessed that battlefield-feel and I suspected the place would feel creepy after dark.

What we also noticed here was not a wartime relic or of our imagination, it was evidence of Hawaii's little spoken of and ever present shame. On our travels up the coast a couple of days ago to Gilligan's Island, I noticed them in several back streets on the way out of Honolulu and again on some of the roadside pullouts and in parks. And here they were again, at Sand Island; making busy as they went about their daily lives as if this was the way it was supposed to be.

Jan pointed to a middle-aged couple, well-groomed and reasonably dressed as they stood next to a cloth-covered picnic table. They had set up a camp stove and the woman was stirring a steaming pot while her mate sat at the table reading the newspaper in the shade of a great palm. The sight would not have seemed out of place for a State Park except that the new Ford Econoline van that was parked next to them that appeared to be filled to the brim with all this couples' worldly chattels. Jan noted, as I had a few days ago, that these people were neither vagrants nor destitute; but they were, effectively, homeless.

It would be a sight that we would see countless times around Oahu and later, on Kauai. We would witness entire families, whites and natives alike, living in vans, VW buses or Corollas, under tarps or just stretched out on the grass. They would set up sleeping and dining tents in parks and in the bushes, on streets and in back allies. They set up their Coleman stoves, refrigerators and stereos all hooked up to big gas generators, powering TVs as well as laptop computers.

If the children were old enough, they attended local schools and both parents worked to support the family. It was not unusual to see an entire family of four living in the park, sleeping in tents next to a brand new Chevrolet Tahoe and in the morning, Mom walking the kids to the end of the road to catch the school bus. I was surprised to learn that many of the people that were living this veritable gypsy life lifestyle, were skilled tradespeople or domestics for many of the upscale households or hotels of the Island.

Later, as we explored the western end of Oahu, the island's leeward coast, we found the other side of paradise. There, on sixteen miles of beautiful beaches and several beach parks that stretch beneath the sweeping Waianae Mountains, we found small "tent cities", wooden containers, vans and simple tarp overhangs, that are the residences of many more of Oahu's homeless population. The subject of the homeless is often in the papers, but always in the back pages. Officials, aware of the problem but at a loss as to what to do about it, estimate the number of the Island's homeless is well over four thousand, with another two or three thousand on the other islands, and this number is growing every year. I guess if you must be homeless in America why would you choose Alaska over Hawaii? We would see many more examples of Hawaii's working poor, struggling to overcome their homelessness while living in what we thought was paradise.

After a few well-placed questions, I learned why these people were living and raising families the way that they were. For many, the availability of suitable housing and the extremely high cost of realestate and goods was to blame. Living in Hawaii is expensive with the high cost of housing leading the way. In 2007, the average cost for a single-family home in the islands was $625,000 with condos selling for an average of $309,000. This is considerably higher than the housing cost in most cities on the U.S. mainland and, it's not only owning a home that is expensive; rent is comparatively expensive also. But I did find a nice little fixer-upper, a nine hundred square foot bungalow, in Kailua on the east coast, a mile or so away from the beach for only $920,000.00 USD. What is also exasperating the problem is the typically low wages and the lack of fulltime jobs. Most working class people hold down two or more part time jobs just to make end meet, all of course with no benefits.

Although the working poor do make up a large percentage of Hawaii's homeless people, many are also on welfare, have mental or drug addiction problems, so it's a mixed bag of humanity and you never know who may be sleeping in the park under that tarp or in the back seat of that Chevy, a crack addict or your dental hygienist.

No matter who it is, the odds of them possessing a valid camping permit is next to nil.

I have found out in later years that we were very poor, but the glory of America is that we didn't know it then.   Dwight D. Eisenhower.

We spent three more days hanging about Ali Wai, doing boat chores or playing tourist. One afternoon I took our dinghy, *Fish Killer,* out the channel and headed for a distant marker, the first of the many sentinels guarding the outermost part of the reef. The water was warm, clear and surprisingly calm. Once clear of the channel, the boat traffic dropped off enough for me to feel it was safe enough to jump in for a swim. I donned my snorkeling gear, tied a twenty-meter-long rope to my waist so I could tow *Fish Killer* behind, and I rolled in. The bottom, 10 meters below, was a mixture of white sand patches and coral outcroppings, all infested with reams of tiny darting fish of all colours. I had brought my speargun along, in hopes of skewering dinner, but there was nothing big enough to shoot, so I left the gun in the boat, which was perhaps best, as I later learned that this whole area was a marine preserve. There were quite a few turtles lounging on the bottom and I even had a small school of barracuda, part to pass around me, as they headed inshore on what I could only assume to be a foraging trip.

My jaunt along the reef was an easy one as there was a strong current setting me to the east so all I had to do was laze on the surface and watch the undersea garden cascade by. I wasn't in the water but a few minutes before I saw the first of many sharks that would slip effortlessly by, as they cruised along looking for an easy meal. The two-meter Whitetip sharks paid no attention to me, but I most assuredly kept an eye upon them!

On the surface, with my head just barely above water I had a unique view of the busy Waikiki Beach, just a kilometer away with its thousands of splashing bathers and dozens of roaring Seadoos. As another shark passed beneath me, I had to wonder what the people on the beach would do if they knew just how close or how many sharks were swimming amongst them.

In less than an hour, the current had taken me a good two kilometres and aside from being buzzed by the odd sailboat and a tourist sub passing directly below me, it was a peaceful and soul soothing swim and if I had any cares at that moment, I was blissfully ignorant of them. While in Hawaii, I would regularly take long, solo snorkeling trips lasting many hours, hunting and exploring for miles along the coast of these incredible islands. Some people meditate - I swim.

Most nights we walked the beach under moonlight, or sat in the cockpit with Leon and his crew sharing a glass of wine. Samantha likewise spent her time just wandering about, looking into shops, and finding new places to take pictures around the city. Melissa, on the other hand had decided that she was done playing tourist and after returning from Pearl, she refused to leave the boat or at times, even her cabin. It would seem no matter what we said, we couldn't entice her to get off the boat. One morning, young Melanie came aboard, all excited about meeting some local boys on Waikiki Beach; they want to teach her how to surf and she wanted Melissa to come along, but our distraught daughter would have none of it. She wouldn't even come out of her cabin long enough to say, "no thanks."

I walked Melanie off the boat and when I returned, Jan was right behind me.

"Well, what are we going to do about our daughter, she is not happy just making herself miserable she has to make everyone else miserable as well. Sam is leaving in a few days, I don't want to spend another month on our own with Melissa, not when she is like this."

Jan paused to gauge my reaction. When I said nothing, she continued. "Perhaps she needs to go home to see for herself that she isn't missing anything, but I think we need to let her make her own decision, what do you think?"

Figure 20.
A happy Andy and Melissa moment at the Arizona memorial-Pearl Harbour.

I have always believed that children need to be permitted to make some decisions for themselves. If a person doesn't learn to make good decisions as a child, how could you expect them to make good decisions as teens or adults? Against all parental instincts, sometimes you must let children fail, to fall flat on their faces and hope they learn from it. We have always let our children make some decisions for themselves. It can be tough to know which choices are safe to let your child make. The criteria, which we apply when deciding whether to let our child do something or not, has always been a simple one. We ask ourselves, "Is what they want to do life threatening morally threatening or permanent?" If the answer to all three is, "No!", then perhaps you should let them do it. In grade eight, Thomas' orange hair eventually reverted to blonde, and at age ten, Melissa realized that Mum was right when she said that flip-flops were not the best choice of footwear for school, during a B.C, winter. Lessons were learned with only minor, non-permanent consequences.

I felt sick to my stomach over the prospect of letting Melissa go and there was a lot to consider. Should we let our child make a choice that we knew she would someday regret? Could I really trust the people I would be passing her on to? Would they ensure that she did not go wild and do something really stupid in our absence? Was it fair to even ask them to become responsible for our child for a whole month? Did they agree to take her, just to please their own child, with a secret hope that we would not permit it, saving them from looking like the bad guys?

Could I really enjoy our remaining time here without Melissa or would our guilty conscience haunt us and prevent us from having fun? And, if we did have fun, would we later feel guilty about that? I undertook this voyage with the belief that it would draw us closer as a family, build tighter father/daughter bonds, but it seemed to have the opposite effect, and I was at a loss as to what to do.

The realization that there was nothing more I could do for Melissa had finally sunk in; against my better judgment I bowed to her conviction that she must go. She had made up her mind and there was no changing it. All I could do now was take care of Jan and make sure that she enjoyed the rest of this voyage, which would last another month or so, for her. Jan had earned this time, and we both desperately needed it. I was going to make sure that it was memorable for her. I hugged Jan so she couldn't see the tear rolling down my cheek.

"I'll call Dave's parents to make sure it's really OK for her to stay with them. And if it is, I will see if I can get her on the same flight as Sam, OK?"

We spent a total of seven days at Ali Wai and Waikiki and we departed with mixed feelings about the place. We had decided to run back up the coast, to Hawaii Kai and Kaiser's converted fishpond where we would spend Sam and Melissa's last few days in Hawaii, before putting them both on a plane headed north.

Chapter #19

Tiger Sharks Eat Sea Turtles, Don't Ya Know?

I travel not to go anywhere, but to go. I travel for travel's sake. The great affair is to move.
                                              Robert Louis Stevenson.

We quietly slipped *Maiatla*'s moorings just after daybreak to motor out of Ali Wai channel, nosing into a gentle swell and a windless sea. The tradewinds had vanished on this part of the coast and the sun hadn't had time to warm the land, to build the onshore breeze. Sam took up her usual station on the cabin top to sun herself while a surprisingly chipper Melissa came topside to take pictures of a retreating Honolulu skyline. Once we told Melissa that we had decided to let her fly home, she became animated and was actually fun to be around, as she finally allowed her playful nature come out. I tried to joke with her, but my heart really wasn't into it.

"Sam, you better be careful to not get too much sun today; remember it's much more intense on the water." Jan said, in her mothering way.

My plan was to see if we could get in behind the reef at Hawaii Kai, spend the next two days exploring the waterways and just hang out until the girls departed. The motor up the coast was scenic, utterly windless, and uneventful until we attempted to anchor just beyond the channel marker at Hawaii Kai. The narrow cut through the reef looked awfully narrow and shallow so I decided to anchor on the outside of the reef. If we could get close enough to shore we would be out of the wind and most of the swell that rapped around the point. But after several attempts to set the hook without success, I finally had to jump ship and go for a swim to see what the problem was.

As I clambered back aboard, Jan asked, "Well, what did you see? Any sand patches?"

"Not a one! The whole bottom here is flat rock covered with a thin layer of coral, no place to set the hook. Further out there is sand but when the wind picks up it will get rough."

"So, what do you want to do then?" Jan queried.

"Well, I guess we need to find our way in through the reef today while we still have light. All I know is we can't stay here and I don't want to go back to Ali Wai, so it's in we go! OK, Babe?"

"The pass looks even shallower from here than it did from shore." Jan offered as she sighted down the very narrow channel that had deep green tuffs of coral marking the shallows on either side.

With few options, the girls help me launch the inflatable and with my snorkeling gear in hand, we motored over to the pass to reconnoiter the situation. The minimal tide was flowing in. I jumped overboard to sound the pass for depth and to look for any obstructions that would prove to be a problem. The water was clear and the coarse, sandy bottom was thankfully level. Using a two-meter long Hawaiian sling fishing spear as a gauge for depth, I swam the entire pass, three separate times before returning to *Maiatla*.

"Well Babe, the pass looks clear enough, but we will have to cut it very close to that second marker as the channel is too shallow on the opposite side."

"Is there enough water all the way through? We are not going to hit bottom and get stuck are we?" Jan asked.

Jan's concerns were valid ones. It was going to be tight in the pass and it would be difficult to turn around if we needed to retreat; making matters worse, the hard ocean bottom would only be a few inches beneath our keel.

"No. I said. I think we will be fine, but we better get going as the tide will only be flooding for the next two hours; if we do strike bottom, it better be on a rising tide, not falling."

Our transit of the pass was a little nerve-wracking. I think we brushed some of the barnacles off the bottom of the keel a couple of times, but once inside the reef, the seabed left us alone and retreated to give us a more comfortable three-meters of clearance. With the anchor down and set, we settled in for a comfortable night and to celebrate, I barbequed some steaks and after returning from the cellar, I tapped another keg of our imported red wine to dine with this evening. (I pulled a cardboard box out of the bilge and twisted the plastic cap off of the bladder of my seven-week home brew!)

"Oh, Sam! That looks really bad, does it hurt?" Janet blurted out, as she saw Samantha emerge from her cabin in the morning.

"It really stings, Aunty Jan! Do you have anything to put on it?" In her effort to ensure she went home with a good tan so everyone would ask where had she been, Sam had overdone it on the cabin top the previous day; she had seriously burned her face.

"Oh, Sam! You have some good blisters coming up there. I have some

Burnfree! Come into the head and I will help you put some on."

Over the next few days, Sam's face continued to blister and then began to peel in great sheets, leaving her looking not unlike the blotchy lepers of Molokai. We felt horrible for her, but she did ignore Jan's multiple warnings. For Sam, her time for sightseeing had passed; she would spend her last day in Hawaii, hiding from the sun, inside the boat with a beet-red face, looking like a glazed donut from all the salve Jan had applied. With Sam out of action, the rest of us decided to spend the day aboard relaxing. and it gave the girls a chance to finish packing, as they would be leaving early the next morning for the airport.

We awoke at daybreak the following morning to find a heavy, rainsquall buffeting the harbour. The rain was blowing horizontal. With the large waves in the bay, I knew it was going to be a wet, 300-meter ride to shore. I was surely glad that we hadn't decided to stay anchored on the outside of the reef but in some respects, I was glad that the wind had gotten up as it tested *Maiatla's* anchor set while we were still aboard, so I felt confident to leave her now unattended while we took the girls to the airport. If we didn't drag anchor in these windy conditions, we probably wouldn't.

While swaddled in rain gear, we placed the girl's luggage into plastic garbage bags before jamming them into the bow of the dink, then we motored for the beach. I caught hell from everyone for the odd wave that broached the dinghy's sides as we roller-coastered along. I had gone ashore alone late the previous day to arrange for a rental jeep and after securing the dink to a nearby palm with lock and chain, we were westbound for the Honolulu airport.

It all happened far too fast, and before we knew it, we were watching in silence as Samantha and Melissa passed through the airport security. They were instantly gone, leaving us utterly alone. If Melissa had any remorse about having made the decision to leave, she did not show it as she hugged us both goodbye.

"Did you see that?" Jan asked, with tears in her eyes. "She didn't even look back, she just went!"

It was a good thing it was raining outside, as it hid my tears well. Winter had just dripped back into my soul.

Our drive back through the streets of the city was done in silence, as the meaning of our girls' departure, slowly sunk in. I think I was more upset than Jan, but it was hard to tell. Jan was very good at hiding her feelings, but I knew she was hurting just the same. Nevertheless, the reality was that we were now effectively empty nesters and we had our boat in Hawaii and a full month together to romp, explore, and cuddle! (Or whatever!) We would make the most of our new found freedom and since we had the jeep and the squall suddenly vanished leaving a fresh scent in the air and blue skies to entice us, it was off into the hills to see what lay beyond.

We had already covered most of the east coast with the girls when we oversaw Gilligan's Island, so we decided to cut straight across the Island. Our course led us northeast, up the old Pali Highway, to pick up where we had left off with the girls at Kaneohe Bay, on the windward side of the island. The drive looked promising as the four-lane road wound through verdant hills, great green forests and passed through a couple of long tunnels that cut through the mountains to the Koolau Ridge. Up at that altitude, the air was fresh and cooler than down in the valley. A delicate veil of clouds clung to the summit, filtering the sun. Perhaps the most interesting aspect of the drive was that the road passed directly through an old Hawaiian battlefield where King Kamehameha fought to gain control of the entire Island Chain; many died horribly here.

As we climbed to the summit, I pulled into a lookout parking lot. Jan and I got out of the car and were instantly buffeted by the winds that rolled over the mountains from the windward side of the Island. The brisk winds caused the ironwoods, albizzias and gunpowder trees, some with dazzling colours, to rustle as if each leaf bore the soul of an angry ghost; considering how many perished here, one spirit per leaf seemed reasonable to me. A plaque on the trailside gave a brief overview of the battle and history that led up to what would be the climactic struggle to control all of Hawaii.

> The plaque read:
> *BATTLE OF NU'UANU PALI: Uniting of the Islands*
> *In the late 1700s, King Kamehameha I, from the island of Hawai'i, sought to unite all the Hawaiian Islands under one rule. The battle for Oahu began with the arrival of his forces at Waikiki in 1795. Oahu had been defeated by Maui forces a decade earlier and Maui's chef Kalanikupule now lead the forces on Oahu against Kamehameha. After many hard fought battles, Kalanikupule was driven up the Nu'uanu Valley to this location. Both sides fought with Hawaiian spears and western firearms but Kamehameha's canon gave him the winning advantage. The battle called Kaleleka'anae (leaping of the anae fish), refers to the men forced off the cliff during the fighting. An estimated 400 warriors died in this battle. With Kamehameha's victory on Oahu and the signing of an agreement with Kauai, he became the first king of all the Hawaiian Islands.*

While doing my research for this book I discovered that Mark Twain, who spent six months in the islands back in 1866, almost 80 years after the epic battle, scaled this very mountain. On horseback Twain visited the battlefield but the site he saw was much different than what greeted us today.

Twain, wrote: *"out of the shadows of the foliage the distant lights of Honolulu glinted like an encampment of fireflies. The air was heavy with the fragrance of flowers. The halt was brief.— Gayly (the guide) laughing and talking, the party galloped on, and I clung to the pommel and cantered after. Presently we came to a place where no grass grew—a wide expanse of deep sand. They said it was an old battle ground. All around everywhere, not three feet apart, the bleached bones of men gleamed white in the moonlight. We picked up a lot of them for mementoes. I got quite a number of arm bones and leg bones—of great chiefs, may be, who had fought savagely in that fearful battle in the old days, when blood flowed like wine where we now stood—and wore the choicest of them out on Oahu afterward, trying to make him go. All sorts of bones could be found except skulls; but a citizen said, irreverently, that there had been an unusual number of "skull-hunters" there lately—a species of sportsmen I had never heard of before. Nothing whatever is known about this place—its story is a secret that will never be revealed. The oldest natives make no pretense of being possessed of its history."*

"They say these bones were here when they were children. They were here when their grandfathers were children—but how they came here, they can only conjecture. Many people believe this spot to be an ancient battle-ground, and it is usual to call it so; and they believe that these skeletons have lain for ages just where their proprietors fell in the great fight. Other people believe that Kamehameha I. fought his first battle here. On this point, I have heard a story, which may have been taken from one of the numerous books which have been written concerning these islands— I do not know where the narrator got it. He said that when Kamehameha (who was at first merely a subordinate chief on the island of Hawaii), landed here, he brought a large army with him, and encamped at Waikiki. The Oahuans marched against him, and so confident were they of success that they readily acceded to a demand of their priests that they should draw a line where these bones now lie, and take an oath that, if forced to retreat at all, they would never retreat beyond this boundary. The priests told them that death and everlasting punishment would overtake any who violated the oath, and the march was resumed. Kamehameha drove them back step by step; the priests fought in the front rank and exhorted them both by voice and inspiriting example to remember their oath—to die, if need be, but never cross the fatal line. The struggle was manfully maintained, but at last the chief priest fell, pierced to the heart with a spear, and the unlucky omen fell like a blight upon the brave souls at his back; with a triumphant shout the invaders pressed forward—the line was crossed—the offended gods deserted the despairing army, and, accepting the doom their perjury had brought upon them, they broke and fled over the plain where Honolulu stands now—up the beautiful Nuuanu Valley—paused a moment, hemmed in by precipitous mountains on either hand and the frightful precipice of the Pari in front, and then were driven over—a sheer plunge of six hundred feet!

The view overlooking the Kaneohe Valley is nothing if not spectacular, and I know of no words that could possibly begin to describe what was laying before us. Even sublime is woefully inadequate. As you peer over the edge, if the howling tradewinds rushing over the mountaintop don't take your breath away, the thought of hundreds of men tumbling off this kilometer high precipice, would. To the right of the lookout, the old decommissioned Pali roadway, constructed around 1930, winds precariously down the mountainside. Now partially over grown with numerous tiny streams coursing across the pavement, it makes for a beautiful hike into the valley below. Jan and I navigated the roadway for a kilometer or two, but when an old landslide partially blocked our path, we decided not to do as others had and clamber around. We returned to the parking lot. This old road would be perfect for mountain biking; peddling would be made redundant by the steep incline, but one would have to make sure that the braking system was functioning correctly, or the rider would likely go the way of the ancient warriors and take the short cut down to the bottom.

Over the following few hours, we wound our way down the mountainside, through the deep valleys of the windward side of Oahu until I began to recognize geographical features I had seen depicted in so many of the movies and TV shows that had been filmed locally over the decades. In Kaneohe Bay we saw the waterfront home of *Magnum P.I.* and the beach with the view of Chinaman's Hat that Kirk Douglas romanced a married women in the opening scenes in the movie,

In Harm's Way, just to name a couple.

We had lunch at a roadside snack shack, which was located alongside a freshwater shrimp pond. It seemed like a good idea, but the best part of the very expensive shrimp meal was the overcooked fries. After expressing our disappointment to each other, we continued our drive down the coast which consisted of a series of small, working class communities with less than interesting architecture. We followed the road past Kawela Bay and then around another bend where the vista to our right opened up, exposing a beautiful beach with waves breaking over the reef, off in the distance.

"Look Andy! There's a bunch of people gathered on the beach next to a long, yellow "caution" tape. What do you think is going on? Can we stop?" Jan asked.

I pulled over next to what looked like a bunch of rental vehicles and we clambered out. Jan grabbed the camera and headed for the sandy patch between the sloping palms that led onto the beach. By the time I caught up, Jan was busy snapping pictures of dozens of great green sea turtles that appeared to be doing nothing other than lounging about in the sun. The turtles' sunning spot had been cordoned off with wooden stakes and yellow caution tape, in an effort to keep the tourists and the normally lethargic animals apart. A big man, who later identified himself as being from a local wildlife protection society, had a crowd gathered around and was giving a lecture on the life and breeding cycles of the turtles. I noticed that several of the larger animals sported great tumors, some the size of grapefruits, just as we had seen on the Maui turtles.

Although I found the lecture interesting, I was starting to get over-heated in the noonday sun. I looked around at the blue water. The bay had a beautiful sand beach and approximately 200 metres offshore, I could see a shallow reef that broke the backs of the ocean swells. Jan was nearby, trying to get our still camera to take video of subjects that really weren't too intent on moving. Just every once in a while one would stretch its neck and take a big gulp of air, then go back to napping.

"Hey Babe, if you're going to be a while I'm going to grab my mask and fins and head out to the reef. OK? Just wave me in when you want to go."

"OK. See you in a bit." She said, without looking away from the viewfinder.

After grabbing my gear, I skirted around some kids swimming in the shallows and headed offshore. As usual, the water was warm but there must have been a stream or river nearby as the water was murky, giving me no more than three meters of visibility. If the clarity wasn't disappointing enough, I found the inside of the reef devoid of the typical throngs of fish that I would normally see in places like this. Undeterred, I finned my way over the crest of the reef, which was barely a meter or two below the surface and headed for the drop off. I was hopeful that the ocean-side of the reef had clearer water and more marine life but on one account I was again disappointed. There were more fish on the outside, but the visibility remained abysmal. I went about peering into holes and chasing schools of small, brightly colored fish about the coral. The reef stretched for about two kilometres in either direction, reaching between two points of land creating a natural fishpond. The outer rim of the reef dropped off abruptly with the submerged wall disappearing below me into water that was hundreds of meters deep. As I moved along the drop-off, I spotted numerous old tunnels or lava tubes, and if they weren't too deep I would dive down into them; many would be hiding the bigger fish of the reef, some of which were a meter long and weighing close to twenty kilograms. I was starting to regret not bringing my spear gun.

Occasionally while on the surface, I would throw a glance shoreward to see where my wife was. Jan had moved little and was still keeping herself occupied taking pictures of the turtles, flowers or whatever she found fascinating on the beach. After an hour of picking about the outer reaches of the reef, I finally made my way back to the beach where I found Jan engaged in conversation with the conservation fellow. With my fins in hand, I sauntered up next to Jan and began listening to their conversation. Apparently, they were talking about why it was necessary to put up the barricades around the turtles.

"It's amazing how many stupid idiots try to sit on or over turn the turtles," the fellow said with more than a hint of disgust in voice. "I've caught people spray painting them, carving their initials in their shells and I even caught a teen last week hitting a turtle over the head with his Boogie Board."

Despite heavy fines imposed for harassing the turtles, some people still felt the need to torment the poor beasts and considering the herpes like virus that has infected the animals, you would have to wonder what else they have been subjecting the animals to? Jan and I both expressed our concern for the animals as well as our approval for the role his group was playing in not only the protection of the turtles but also the education of the people who encounter them. I was starting to wish I had hung around a bit longer to hear this guy's whole spiel, instead of swimming off, as I now had a bunch of questions of my own.

"I know you probably already told everyone else but, why are there so many turtles here on this beach now? It's not breeding season is it?"

"Oh, no! It's not mating or egg laying season," he said with authority. "You see, these turtles are the natural prey for tiger sharks. People think that their hard shells will protect the turtles from shark attack, but an average sized tiger will bite right through the shells as easy as you can bite through an apple." He paused to demonstrate how a shark bites down by moving his arms up and down in a scissoring motion with his stiff spread fingers representing teeth. After thinking for a moment about what he had just said, I started to feel just a little uncomfortable about my next question, but I just had to ask.

"So are you saying that a tiger shark chased these guys in here? That they came in here to get away from a shark?" The fellow smiled and his long pause unnerved me even more.

"Not just one shark! Dozens have congregated off this beach, just beyond the reef," he said pointing out, towards the water, "and they have been here for several days, looking for food, looking for turtles. One local claimed yesterday that he saw an 18-footer out there. But you know how fishermen are. He was probably exaggerating it; was more likely only 10 or 14 feet long."

I had read up on all Hawaii's sharks before arriving and what I had read said that tiger sharks up to seven meters (21 feet) have been sighted, so the fisherman's tale was not only possible, but highly probable and if he fished commercially for a living I would have little reason to doubt what he had claimed to have seen just beyond the reef. My reef!

"Beyond the reef?" I said, as I pointed to the distant breaking waves, "out where I was snorkeling just a little while ago? That side of the reef?"

He looked to where I was pointing.

"Yeah, out there! The big sharks either don't like crossing the reef for fear of injuring themselves on the coral, or they haven't been able to find their way inside yet."

It must have taken a few seconds for either my line of questioning or the tone of my voice to sink into this fellow's brain, but eventually he finally realized where I was headed with my questions.

"Oh, but don't worry, tigers don't usually attack people around here, there is too much else to eat around here, too many turtles for food."

I would like to say that I found comfort in his final remark, but I didn't, and I guess it was my own fault for not talking with him more before heading out into deep, dark water. Guess I was lucky this day that I hadn't encountered a very hungry or nearsighted tiger that could mistake me for a turtle in the murky water. I learned my lesson; before entering the water, I would look for turtles on the beach and other swimmers in the water. This is perhaps a good example of how local knowledge can be so important. Duh!

Our next stop was the famous north shore destination, Waimea Bay, where surfers come to challenge the wave breaks and where Captain Charles Clerke aboard HMS Resolution stopped on 28 February, 1779 to take on water. Clerke had shortly before taken command of the ship after Captain James Cook was killed at Kealakekua Bay, on 14 February, making Waimea Bay the only Oahu anchorage visited by Cook's expedition. Waimea Valley was densely populated by natives and a major center in the pre-contact period. The remains of Puʻu o Mahuka, an important heiau (Hawaiian temple) can still be seen above the bay. In summer, Waimea typically has clear and calm water but in the winter months, Waimea and other north shore locations such as Banzai Pipeline and Sunset Beach host a number of surfing contests because of the large waves typically found along here. These big waves are generated by winter storms high in the North Pacific, and their arrival on Oahu's north shore are typically forecast accurately several days in advance.

The surf break at Waimea Bay was significant in the development of big wave surfing – waves at least six meters (20 feet) high. Larger surf at the bay went un-ridden for years until November 7, 1957 when a handful of surfers finally paddled out and rode the giant waves that break off the northern point of the bay. While the surf only breaks big a few times a year, Waimea was the most prestigious big wave surf break in the world for decades and still holds a significant place even in today's world of big wave surfing.

Waimea Bay was made famous to the public in the 1964 film, *Ride the Wild Surf* and in the Jan and Dean song of the same name, the movie's theme song, which played at the end of the film. Many other musical artists have songs about Waimea Bay, such as The Beach Boys and my favorite, Jimmy Buffett. Waimea Bay was also one of the filming locations used for the television series *Lost*, which was an

American drama-adventure television series surrounding the survivors of a plane crash on a mysterious tropical island.

Now in the summer, Waimea Bay is a playground of fun for freedivers, SCUBA divers, and those who desire to jump off "da Big Rock" or "Jump Rock", a rock that is perfectly positioned in the bay. We stopped to watch a group of young people (obviously without fear) climb and leap off Jump Rock, into the sea. Due to the large crowd already frolicking in the water, Jan and I pressed on to the more remote and less inhabited part of the island on the most north-western tip at Kanea Point. To travel any farther west from here is to drown. The surrounding Kuaokala Mountains slowly creep towards the beach until the road is thrust up against the seashore. At this time, the waterfront road was mostly deserted which I found surprising considering the masses of people we had just left back at Waimea. Along the way, there were many little private beaches and one with a couple of turtles grazing on algae in the surf compelled us to stop.

It was late in the afternoon so it was time for a skinny dip and a few beers, which gave us time to admire the view as well as the antics of a couple of kite surfers down the beach. As the wind here was strong and blew parallel to the shore, the surfers could travel for miles without having to be more than a fifty meters from the beach. They were amazing to watch as they achieved incredible speeds and when the opportunity presented itself, they would launch themselves from the waves letting the kites take them 30 meters or more into the air. More often than not, they would wipe-out upon landing. One surfer raced over our way and after wiping-out, with his kite in hand, paddled to the beach near us. As he gathered his gear to haul it up to his car, which was parked near ours, I noticed that this obviously very athletic fellow wasn't some young kid. In fact, this high speed daredevil sported a thick mane of grey hair! I approached him to ask if he knew of another way around the point as the road ended just up ahead.

His name was John, friendly to strangers and a business owner from the island of Kauai.

"You can't drive much further as the military have the road blocked off. You see, that is all government land, you can hike up there on the weekends but not on week days," he said as he swept his hand across the landscape.

"There is an old rail bed that starts just up the road," he added, "and you can walk on it all the way around the point, past the lighthouse to the west side of this ridge, but you must be careful as several landslides have taken out the path and you must scale the cliff or climb along the rocks at the surf line to get around." He continued as he wound up the lines for his kite.

"Every year the coast guard or the wilderness search and rescue team pull people and bodies out of there," he said.

He paused for a moment to assess my attire as I stood there, shirtless in khaki shorts and sandals clutching a can of Coors, obviously attempting to gauge my capabilities.

He smiled, then said. "If you go up there, you need to be prepared and take a pack with food and water and let somebody know you are going."

"So if you live on Kauai, what are you doing here? On a business trip?" I asked.

"No, Kauai can be too quiet for me, I just needed to get away, needed a break."

As he pulled away in his Subaru hatchback kicking up a dust storm, I thought it strange that an islander would travel to a nearby island for a holidays. Is Kauai that much different from Oahu? Smaller? In hindsight, I realized that I had posed a stupid question, as I already knew the answer. Just as each child of the same father bears their own distinct character, charm and personalities despite their common genealogy; so does each island in this archipelago. Each island is unique with its own character, flora and fauna and Kauai would not be an exception.

The 830 Highway connected to the H-2 Interstate, which took us back into Pear City in very short order. We took the by-pass around Honolulu as we were exhausted; all Jan and I wanted was to go to bed. It was almost midnight before we rounded the last bend to see *Maiatla*, illuminated by nearly a full moon, riding peacefully at anchor right where we had left her at Hawaii Kai.

"You forgot to leave the anchor light on this morning when we left," she said, as she placed her bag in the bow of the dinghy.

I unlocked the chain and untied the painter from the tree that sat scarcely above the high tide mark and began to drag *Fishkiller* into the water.

"Yeah I did! It's right there!" I said, as I pointed up into the sky. "I switched the moon on before I left the boat, but it was daylight so you didn't see it!"

We spent the next day retrieving our headsail from the sail loft and new rigging and installing them on the boat. I was thankful the rigger had done a good job and the stainless steel wires with swaged ends actually fit. We also spent several days playing tourist, driving about, covering most of the island's hinterlands. We swam at isolated beaches, bought leis and postcards at tourist shops and ate Kalua pork wherever we could find it.

The word "kalua" is a Hawaiian word that refers to cooking in an underground oven or Hawaiian "imu". Normally, a large pit is dug in the ground, and lava rocks are heated over an open flame until they are extremely hot. The rocks are placed in the pit, which is lined with greenery such as banana leaves or ti leaves. The leaves insulate, aid in the steaming process, and add flavor. A cleaned, whole pig (seasoned with Hawaiian sea salt) is placed inside the hot pit and then covered with more greenery for insulation and flavor – it is then covered with a protective covering, more soil, and left to cook throughout the day (about 8 hours).

Kalua pork (cooked in the traditional method) is served at Hawaiian luaus, or family gatherings or parties. One can also find kalua pig in restaurants were it is typically smoked in a traditional smoker or oven and then served with steamed white rice and /or poi, a taro root paste. The pork meat falls off the bone, and is characteristically very tender and moist, with a slightly salty, smoky flavor, that is just delicious.

It was almost August, and a full week after the girls had departed. We had talked to Melissa on the phone several times since she had been home and whenever we asked what she had been up too, her reply was always the same "Not much, just stuff."

It took a bit of prodding on my part, but when I asked her if she had been hanging out with her girlfriend, Nicole, the person she was most eager to go home too, she said she hadn't seen Nicole much since being back. Apparently, Nicole had a new boyfriend and he didn't want Melissa hanging out with them. Nice friend, I thought. She goads Melissa into coming home, then dumps her! Melissa sounded a bit homesick and I think she was disappointed with what she had been doing since arriving back home, but if she was, she wasn't about to admit it, not now anyways. I missed her.

On our last day anchored at Hawaii Kai, we couldn't sleep late as we had a rental jeep to return and after taking the dink into the inner pond for some final shopping at Costco, I brought the *Fishkiller* aboard and secured it to the foredeck in preparation for an early morning departure. We would weigh anchor in time to ride the slack-tide down the channel; bound for our last, brief stop on Oahu before setting our sights on the Garden Isle: Kauai.

Chapter #20

The Dead Leap into the Western Sea.

Sometimes we are lucky enough to know our lives have been changed, to discard the old and embrace the new and run headlong down an immutable course. It happened to me… on that summer's day when my eyes were opened to the sea. -Jacques Yves-Cousteau

Our departure from Hawaii Kai on the 25th of July was uneventful for the most part. We rose just after first light. I cooked French toast with bacon for Jan and I, poured the tea and we ate in the cockpit while watching the first signs of life stir ashore. It wasn't long before the first outrigger canoe raced past *Maiatla,* the crew on their morning practice run in preparation for a competition to be held on the weekend. From our vantage point, we could see several paddlers in their sea kayaks out for a little exercise presumably before heading off to work. The Hawaiians, both haoles and natives alike truly seemed to love their outdoor activities and in particular, their water sports, just so long as it didn't include a cruising boat or involve gunkholing about the islands.

Our departure was routine with only one exception - I no longer had a crew to work the boat. With Melissa and Sam gone, Jan and I were forced to get *Maiatla* underway all by ourselves, as there wasn't anyone to shout orders to! Jan manned the wheel and throttle as I recovered the ground tackle; a gruelling job, necessitating the removal of the chain snubber and pushing the "up" button on the electric windlass while cleaning off whatever debris was clinging to the chain as it came up. In the past, items we have hauled to the surface included everything from old crab traps and fishing gear, to lost anchors and a 15-meter timber log, a full meter in diameter (B.C. waters are full of sunken logs!).

Anchors are designed to hook the bottom of the sea; as a result, they are very efficient at snagging whatever else is down there. There have also been times when the anchor just refused to surface at all, and I was forced to don my diving gear in order to recover our very expensive tackle that was hooked in a rock crevice or the window of a 57' Chevy. OK, usually it's not so gruelling, but I would often spill my morning cup of tea while performing this operation!

This would be our first departure since dropping off the girls and it felt odd leaving harbour without them, especially Melissa.

We managed to get back over the reef without bumping bottom and Jan set us on a course directly offshore in an effort to pick up the tradewinds that would fill in once we cleared the shadow of Koko Head. Before long, we were sailing magnificently; wing-and-wing, with the headsail poled out to starboard and mainsail boom-vanged to the port rail. First, we hit six knots, then seven and eight; the wind continued to build as we worked our way clear of the land.

We had all day to complete a run of 38 miles; 22 miles along the south shore passing Diamond Head, Honolulu, and Pearl Harbour then on to the industrial corner of Oahu, Barbers Point. From there, we would bear due north and sail another 16 miles to Pokai Bay.

Barbers Point is located on the southwestern-most corner of the Island, where the Chevron and Tesoro Oil refineries are situated, along with the old Honolulu International Airport and a metal-shredding facility surrounded by a mixed bag of industrial enterprises. Thankfully, all downwind of Oahu's residential communities.

At Barbers Point, we turned right, putting *Maiatla* on a fast, beam reach; powered by the stiff tradewinds, aided by the flat seas in the lee of the low shore. We had just gybed the headsail as Jan altered course to the north with the tanks of the Chevron Refinery to our starboard beam, when I realized that I hadn't put out the fishing gear. After trimming for a beam-reach, I went aft to throw the meat hook over the side.

"Hey Babe, how about mahi-mahi for dinner?" I asked Jan, as I crawled back into the cockpit.

Jan was having a bit of trouble getting Auto to settle down on our new heading as we were a little overpowered, but since we only had 16 miles to go, I decided not to throw a reef into the sails.

"You haven't caught anything on the meat hook since we have been in Hawaii! What makes you think your luck has changed?" Jan asked, as she continued to play with the autopilot controls.

"Well, I'll just do what Bert and Ernie off of Sesame Street do!" I said.

Jan looked puzzled by my comment but before she could ask, I cupped my hands about my mouth and began to call loudly.

"Here fishy, fishy, fishy! !Here fishy, fishy, fishy!"

The less affluent, west coast of Oahu is far removed from Honolulu and we were told that it boasted its own character which manifested itself in the form of hatred for change and distrust of strangers as exhibited by the residents. Few tourists typically make the journey to this side of the island as resorts are few (but that is changing) and a trip there would entail renting a car.

Once clear of the industrial complex at the Barbers Point, there is a luxury hotel and marina, permitting well-heeled tourists to wallow in slutish comfort with four man-made lagoons to provide calm waters for swimmers when the waves are normally breaking big. A large reef system extends for virtually the entire length of this coast, extending more than 20 miles from Barbers Point all the way north to Kaena Point. Large-scale tourist development here is minimal, leaving many public parks and secluded sandy beaches which are heavily used by locals. During the winter storms, the surfing is as fine here, if not better than at Waimea. The communities along Oahu's leeward shore consist of mainly blue-collar workers living in one and two-story structures, with a few low-rise apartment blocks to perk up the population density. Most of the apartments and homes alike were in need of a bit of TLC.

That said, even from the deck of *Maiatla*, we could see the telltale signs of Oahu's homeless; in virtually every park, tarp encampments covered the fields, smoke from cooking fires wafted skyward and RVs, SUVs and wagons of all sorts dotted the landscape. It was easy to assume that the bulk of Oahu's 4000 homeless, and down and outs resided here as there are few if any options.

I had planned to anchor offshore for the night at Pokai Bay, at the town of Waianae, where there is a small boat basin and park; but when I informed the harbour master at Ala Wai of my plans, he warned me to anchor well offshore as there were a lot of "low life's" there, and to be wary of boarders (would be Pirates) during the night as some of the locals will steal anything! Well, if that wasn't a ringing endorsement for the place! Apparently, this part of the Island is fertile hunting ground for TV's, *Dog The Bounty Hunter*; because as most wild animals do when wounded or pursued, they run home to hide.

Despite being one of the most productive sport fishing grounds in the islands, our troll up the west coast was fruitless and my meat hook had failed to deliver.

"I think you better find another fishing song!" Jan said, laughing as I pulled in the fishing gear, in preparation for anchoring at Pokai Bay.

From our anchorage offshore, well offshore, the town of Waianae appeared peaceful enough and with the arid-looking, kilometer high Waianae Mountains in the background, the place almost looked enchanted. The sky above was deep blue as it reflected the sea; the only sign of clouds hung like cotton candy on the crown of the coastal mountains. In the lee of all the mountain ranges, the west coast of Oahu is substantially dryer than the rest of the Island and from the parched, tanned landscape, this was obvious.

"Well, the few natives I see on the beach look harmless enough; some fishing, others just sitting in the shade looking bored,. Do you want to go ashore?" I asked Jan, as I continued to peer through the binoculars, scanning the shore and park on the point, looking for hostiles.

"No, I don't think so, the harbour master wouldn't have said what he did if there wasn't a risk here. You go, I'll stay and watch the boat and since you got skunked fishing, I'll pull some chicken out of the freezer for dinner later. You can barbeque!"

It was only two in the afternoon, so doing as Jan suggested, I launched the dink, intent on making a covert landing then prowling the park and waterfront. I landed *Fish Killer* behind a riprap breakwater next to a park that sat on a point which jutted out into the sea. There were a few people wandering about the grasslands, but ostensibly, I had succeeded in landing undetected.

The beach here is expansive, long, and wide with an ever-so-gentle slope, making it possible to wade out a long way before having to start swimming. The town of Waianae, the largest residential community on the leeward coast, was prominent on the bay, with what looked like a well-kept public marina behind a breakwater located at the north end of town. The town itself was that of a working class community but it was obvious that at least some of the residents took pride in their community as revealed by the tiny but neat rock gardens some yards displayed. And why shouldn't they be proud of their town? It truly was a beautiful spot and we would soon see that when the sun began to set in the western sea; the fading light would set the already parched Waianae Mountains afire with shimmering reds and golden browns before fading to black and releasing the stars.

As I commenced to wander about the park, I was suddenly and aggressively approached by several of the locals who just materialized from a clutch of dense coconut palms. I then realized that I had indeed been spotted as I came ashore. I froze as the group encircled me, apparently sizing me up, milling about with their eyes fixed upon me and my camera bag as it hung on my shoulder. As it always is with these urban gangs, there is always a leader, an instigator that the rest all follow and in this group, it was a big, black slug with white hair sprouting from his chest.

He was the bravest of the group and it was him, the alpha male of the pack, who closed in on me first. As he approached, I held my ground and braced myself as without any hesitation, he lunged forward, passing between my legs. Later, I would count over 30 feral cats in this park alone! They were very skilled in tracking down anyone who carried a bag that might conceal food, and I guess my camera bag qualified. From the number of empty cat food cans spread about the park, it was apparent that someone regularly fed these semi-wild animals.

In the center of Kaneilio Point Park, there is an odd collection of coral blocks, each weighing many tons, piled high, forming a platform. The ancient Ku'ilioloa Heiau built in the 15th or 16th century was used for a variety of sacrificial, healing and swearing–in ceremonies by the Hawaiians. It is also suggested that this site was likely a navigational training center as it was a good location for viewing the heavens. It is said that the western shores of all the Hawaiian Islands was the location that the recently departed, their newly freed spirits came to take their final leap into the sea. An act that was necessary for their spirits to pass into the next world. A common Hawaiian saying for someone who had recently died is that, "He went west". It is also interesting to note that after 1819 when the kapu (Taboo) system was overthrown, Ku'ilioloa, this site was one of the few heiau which was still used by the community to practice ancient Hawaiian rituals as the Wai'anae area, in which this alter sits was one of the last places on Oahu that accepted Christianity.

The paved parking lot of this quaint park gave me my first up-close look at the homeless encampments that we had seen from offshore. Aside from the usual, middle-class families with tents, caravans and generators that we had seen elsewhere, here were the "others" as well; the welfare and down-and-out set, the absolute bottom rung of Hawaii's extremely lofty ladder. Next to an exceptionally disgusting and abused stone public restroom house, there were several shopping carts full of bottles and other valuable refuse. The commonly seen buggies being pushed about by street or bag people. The parking lot was congested and I estimated that there were close to 100 lost or displaced souls, the people of Hawaii's shame.

I clung to the water-side of the park, where I was surprised to find dozens of camping chairs lined up along the beach, and beside each one was a fishing rod in a holder pushed into the sand. Taught lines stretched out into the nearby surf. My first thought was that the homeless were attempting to catch lunch, but later I would learn of state park rule that these homeless people exploited. Normally, the Hawaii State Parks do not permit anyone to stay overnight in a day-use-only park. The only exception is that if you are fishing for food, you can spend the night; so to take advantage of this loophole in the rules, many validate their presence by casting a line into the water, the pretense of fishing.

I survived my excursion ashore but came back with a new appreciation for the lives and struggles of the inhabitants. A paradise isn't always as it seems; people live, work, suffer and even die here, just as they do in any other place in the world. As I looked back ashore, I felt no envy for the residents of this community, but perhaps just a little pity.

Back onboard *Maiatla,* I hoisted aboard and secured *Fish Killer* to the foredeck in preparation for our next intended offshore passage. After a dinner of barbequed chicken, Jan and I watched the sun set and the new moon broach the hills in the distance. We pulled up the ground tackle just after dark and set off on our overnight sail that was required to cover the 100 miles of ocean that separated Oahu and Kauai; and our next destination - the harbour of Nawiliwili.

Chapter #21

The Little Pigs of the Huleia River.

There is nothing like lying flat on your back on the deck, alone except for the helmsman aft at the wheel, silence except for the lapping of the sea against the side of the ship. At that time you can be equal to Ulysses and brother to him. -Errol Flynn

As the mountains set below our taffrail, we sailed still further to the west, I noticed that we were fortunate to have a new moon over head as we bore away from Oahu; the light from the heavenly sickle was sufficient to illuminate the deck, enabling me to set the whisker pole on the genoa without the aid of the spreader lights. However, more importantly, the moon was not so bright as to overpower the billions of points of light in the sky, a stadium of stars. Off of to our starboard stern-quarter, partially sunken in the sea, I could see Ursa Major (the Great Bear) which contains the group of stars commonly called the Big Dipper. The handle of the Big Dipper is the Great Bear's tail and the Dipper's cup is the Bear's flank.

There are 88 recognized constellations which cover the world's skies. About 80 of them can be seen from Hawaii at various times of the year. If you are in the Northern Hemisphere, you can use the Big Dipper to find all sorts of important stars and if you draw an imaginary line though the two stars that make up the end of the "cup" and travel for about five times the distance between these two stars, they point to Polaris, the North Star. Low in the south, just barely peeking over the horizon, were the five stars of the Southern Cross, now visible off our port bow. Just as navigators use Polaris to locate the celestial north pole, the Southern Cross likewise points to the celestial south pole. Moreover, directly above our gyrating mast, high above us slashing across the heavens like a lit up freeway and the galaxy of our home, containing over four-hundred-billion stars - the Milky Way. You haven't seen the heavens unless you've seen them from the deck of a ship upon a barren sea.

It felt good be at sea again, to feel *Maiatla* alive beneath me. She seemed to know when we sailed off into blue water, where depth is measured in miles, as opposed to meters or the more traditional fathom. Yes, it felt good to leave the cities and the land, the netherworld behind, although just for a short while. Shore side life is far too busy and encumbered with too many trivial details that seem so necessary if you want to engage society, the plight of Oahu's homeless being a case in point. A few hours after sunset we were directly downwind of the Island. Her garden scent came wafting across the night; it was a thick and fleshy; a musty vegetable fung and floral soup. The earthy air was accented with just a hint of sulfur from the oil refinery, one of the many exhausts of the Island's industry. The aroma of Oahu and its inhabitants was noticeable long after the land had disappeared.

Figure 21. Kauai, *Maiatla* made two complete circumnavigation of the island over the month of August

Ancient voyagers sailing in outrigger canoes, seeking new lands could not only "smell" the islands for up to one hundred miles away, they were also able to discern the changes in wave patterns as the deep ocean swells rebounded off the rocky shores. It was also said, that they could even taste the earth of nearby land or the decrease in the ocean's salinity which could indicate the existence of a great freshwater river flowing into the sea, all simply by sampling the sea water. The voyagers would also be casting an eye skyward in search of sea birds that normally rest ashore, paying close attention to the direction from which they had come in the morning and to where they retreated to at sunset. The navigators were also mindful of floating debris washed from distant beaches, drifting coconuts and palm leaves being the most common signs of land. And of course, they would also be gazing at the heavens, not just at the one-hundred and fifty stars that they used for navigation, but for the glow of the moon as it reflected off the clouds that constantly crowned Oceania's volcanic peaks or during the day they would see a lagoon's turquoise reflection on the underbelly of passing clouds. The ancients would follow these telltale signs until the mountaintops pierced the horizon.

Navigation was not the science back then as it is today, but an art form comprising of perceiving subtle details in the wind, weather and marine life, minute changes in the environment. Perception and understanding of the physical world were the tools that they used to find their way around the vast Pacific. Maps were constructed by twisting and tying together sticks to create a web with tiny seashells secured to the branches to represent the location of islands as they related to one another. They used these tools of the senses, coupled with the help of some benevolent gods, of which they had many, along with perhaps a measure of dumb luck. Chance would certainly have played a roll, as much of the ocean is so vast they would just have to stumble into the shadow of land before any of these telling signs would even materialize. Perhaps if Magellan were more of a natural sailor he would not have crossed the entire Pacific without sighting any land.

The crafts of these early voyages were just as remarkable, catamaran-like structures with cabins build on a platform straddling the twin hulls carved from single trees, with woven leaf sails of hala tree. Some of these watercrafts were in excess of 30-meters long and could travel at twenty-knots or more while carrying whole families with all the necessities to start anew in a foreign land. They even brought their livestock with them in the form of goats, pigs, chickens and dogs along with coconuts and breadfruit seedlings to transplant after spending more than a month at sea and sailing thousands of miles of uncharted ocean. These were great navigators and I like to think that they are the ancestors of modern day cruisers, if not in genealogy, certainly in spirit.

I had timed our departure and passage from Oahu so we would have a daylight landing on the island of Kauai and our port of entry, Nawiliwili. Kauai is geologically the oldest of the main Hawaiian Islands at approximately six million years of age with an area of 562.3 square miles making it the fourth largest of the main islands in the Hawaiian archipelago, and the 21st largest island in the United States. Known also as the "Garden Isle", Kauai with a population of about 60,000, lies 90 miles across the Kauai Channel, northwest of Oahu. Kauai and its closest neighbor, Niihau to the west, are the only islands that cannot be seen from the rest of the main islands in the chain, which have no more than 27 miles or as little as eight miles between them.

The highest peak on this mountainous island is Kawaikini at 1598 m (5243 feet). The second highest peak is Mount Waialeale near the center of the island, 1569 m (5148 feet) above sea level. Kauai has the dubious reputation as being one of the wettest spots on earth; on the east side of Mount Waialeale the annual average rainfall is 1200 cm (460 inches-that's more than 38 feet of rain!). The high annual rainfall has eroded deep valleys in the central mountains, carving out canyons with many scenic waterfalls. On the west side of the island, Waimea town is located at the mouth of the Waimea River, whose flow formed Waimea Canyon, one of the world's most scenic canyons, and which is part of Waimea Canyon State Park. At 914 m (3,000 feet) deep, Waimea Canyon is often referred to as "The Grand Canyon of the Pacific". On the western shore is the rugged and nearly impassable Na Pali Coast, which is a center for recreation in a wild setting that will challenge the most energetic outdoor sports enthusiasts, on land as well as the water.

One of Kauai's best beaches is also home to the U.S. Navy's "Barking Sands" Pacific Missile Range Facility which is located on the sunny and dryer western shores, at the southern end of the legendary Na Pali Coast. Waimea, on the south west coast, was the first place in Hawaii visited by Captain Cook in 1778 where he took on water.

Kauai also has its own distinct flora and fauna. Anyone who has ever visited this island has seen the great flocks of wild chickens that roam freely about the island. Kauai is home to thousands of feral chickens, which have few natural predators, (however, the feral cats do give the chicks a hard time). Kauai's chickens originated from the original Polynesian settlers, who brought them as a food source. They have bred with European chickens and after several chicken barns blew over in a hurricane, the roaming gangs of birds have now taken over the parks and hinterlands and are often seen dead after being clobbered along the roadsides and Iniki is solely to blame.

Hurricane Iniki, was the most powerful hurricane to strike the U.S. State of Hawaii in recorded history. The strong El Niño years between 1991and 1994, spawned Iniki as well as other Central Pacific tropical cyclones during the 1992 season. Iniki attained tropical storm status on September 8 and grew into a monster hurricane within 24 hours. Iniki struck the Island of Kauai on September 11, with peak winds of more than 145 mph (235 kmh), developing into a category 4 hurricane with unimaginable destructive power.

This was the first hurricane to hit the state since Hurricane Iwa in the 1982 and the first major hurricane since Hurricane Dot in 1959, the year of my birth. Before blowing herself out a week later in the cooler waters to the north, midway to Alaska, Iniki had racked up $1.8 billion in damages and claimed six lives. Kauai was the worst hit in the Hawaiian chain where the winds destroyed over 1,400 houses and severely damaged over 5,000 more. Iniki remains one of the costliest hurricanes on record in the Eastern Pacific. Many of the locals say that it would take another category four storm to blow all the chickens off the Island as they have become a real nuisance; but many more just dutifully feed the fowl but their motives many not be fostered solely by concern for the birds' welfare, as often the least wary of the feathered vagrants are invited for dinner.

Our passage across the Kauai Channel was a fast, but comfortable ride with nighttime temperatures only dropping such that a light sweater was required to fend off the chill. Jan and I stood watch all through the night; only going below long enough to make tea or a sandwich. We took turns babysitting *Maiatla* and Auto, giving each other a chance to take short naps, stretched out on the cockpit bench next to the helm. We didn't talk much which was a little unusual for us. Who would have thought that after almost 25 of marriage… yes to each other - that we would have anything left to say. On the other hand, we never argued any more as we had nothing left to argue about.

It had been a busy week since the girls had departed and this was the first time we really had nothing other than managing the boat, to distract us and I think we were both enjoying the quiet time together. Our first indication that there was something ahead of us was the flashing light, which we assumed to be the Ninini Point lighthouse as it was reported to be visible up to 24 miles out to sea. According to the GPS, we were only 20-miles from our destination, the entrance of Nawiliwili Harbour and thankfully the GPS bearing matched that of the flashing light.

"Jan, can you pass me the stopwatch? I want to time the flashes just to make sure it's our light."

Jan slipped down below and retrieved the timepiece. Using a headlamp, she wound the watch and tested the function.

"OK. Ready," she said. We timed the light several times and came up with an average of fifteen seconds between flashes.

"According to the chart that is our light, we are right on course, Babe!" I said.

"Can't you pick it up on radar yet? See the harbour?" she asked, as she stared off at the distant but intense light that gave the impression that it was a lot closer than it was.

I glanced at the radar screen to watch the next series of sweeps.

"No, can't see a thing other than the tops of the mountains back from the coast." I replied. "We are still too far way and the coast is still below the horizon, won't be able to see the shore line for at least another ten miles."

It was three a.m, and we were still a good three to four hours out, and still two hours from the first streaks of daylight. Jan took over the helm while I reclined for a nap in preparation for our landfall.

As the dawn swept over us, the great green island materialized directly off our bow. Approached from the east, Kauai is grand, incredibly rugged and hostile-looking. When you first draw near the Island, there doesn't appear to be any place to land, nothing at all welcoming. All that is seen is mountains of rock with dashing seas at their bases. As the distance closes, you begin to see low lying sections of land with what appears to be a cut leading inland and if the chart is believed, that is where Nawiliwili is hiding, to the left of the tall, whitewashed lighthouse that we had been fixated on for the last few hours. The south side of Nawiliwili Harbour was constructed by the placement of black lava block and stones to form a large breakwater. |On the right, a natural point of land, grass covered with scatted coconut palms, thrusts seaward where a red channel marker warns of the shallows off its point.

Nawiliwili was an impressive bay to sail into and we weren't the only new arrivals this morning; our old friend, the *Pride of America* was secured to the cruise ship dock and had already began to disembark her passengers for a day of sightseeing. We waited until we were completely behind the breakwater and out of the swell before we quickly furled the headsail and brought *Maiatla* into the wind; Jan fired up the engine as I dropped the mainsail into the lazy jacks while cinching it tight with the sail ties.

"Where do you want me to go?" Jan called out, as I threw the last of the sail ties onto the mainsail.

"Just head over to that group of boats on the south side by that cliff, we will tuck in on the outer edge of them. That way we shouldn't be in the way if that cruise ship decides to leave," I said, pointing the way.

We went from transoceanic sailing conditions to being peacefully at anchor in a tranquil bay all within 40 minutes; such is the reality of cruising the Hawaiian Islands. It was 7:00 a.m. August 2nd, and we were finally on the island of Kauai.

"Where do we have to check in?" Jan asked, as she scanned the harbour for any official-looking buildings. Before I could answer, she found what she was looking for.

"Oh! I see the Coast Guard station, to the right of that looks like the harbourmaster's office. It has a flagpole and a big sign on the building. Think that's it? No sign of life though, guess it's still too early. Is today Sunday or Monday?" she asked, sounding a little puzzled and turning back to look at me as I finished shutting down the engine.

"Monday, I think, but it doesn't matter because if they are closed because it's actually Sunday, we'll just clear in tomorrow," I said, "shouldn't be a problem."

We were all settled in, but playing tourist would have to wait. I cooked a nice breakfast of eggs and bacon with toast then Jan and I crawled into bed for a sleep. My normal arrival manic state did nothing to prevent me from falling asleep right away.

I was still semi-comatose when I heard the first set of horn blasts that, after the fog in my head cleared, I presumed came from the cruise ship. Jan rolled over to peer out the stern windows in an effort to see what was going on but *Maiatla* was pointing the wrong way. All she could see out the window was a nearby rock wall and a couple of old fishing boats on mooring balls.

"Can't see anything!" she said, sounding a bit flustered.

"Three short blasts, Babe, means he's going astern. I guess he's leaving!"

"Already?! What time is it?" Jan asked.

I checked my watch and was surprised to see that it was already two in the afternoon. Jan was up, so I knew my nap was done; I rolled out of bed to head topside to see what was going on. Jan was right behind me. For a vessel *Maiatla's* size, the harbour was large with mostly deep water in excess of ten meters, but for a vessel that is over 250 meters long (800 feet) with a draft of four to five meters (13 to 16 feet), Nawiliwili was tight both in breadth and as well as depth. For the *Pride of America*, it was a very tight fit. We stood on *Maiatla's* bow and watched with awe and respect, the ship first maneuver backward then sideways, slipping away from the dock and once they decided that they had enough swinging room, the ship, using bow and stern thrusters spun around to point herself towards open water. And, of course, the whole operation was closely scrutinized by the three Coast Guardsmen hovering nearby in their little red gunship. I could only assume that me, clad only in jockey shorts and Jan in her nighty, an oversized t-shirt were perceived to be of the greatest threats at the moment. Once again, the gunship took up station between the cruise ship and the sinister-looking, foreign vessel, *Maiatla*.

The huge vessel swung her stern; towering over 20 meters above us, it came surprisingly close to not only us, but the couple of dozen other vessels that were anchored nearby. There were passengers on the stern waving good-bye to both dock workers and passerby alike; many looked like they were waving to no one in particular. They even waved rather enthusiastically at Jan and I as the ship's stern came within 20 meters of *Maiatla*, which was just over one *Maiatla* boat length away and a lot closer than I felt comfortable with.

I was a little nervous, at first, at the close proximity of the cruise ships, but for the three days we were anchored in Nawiliwili, the show repeated itself twice a day as a new ship would arrive and then depart. Each time, there was more waving goodbye, the cruise ship's "swing", that always came precariously close with the ships' wakes rebounding around the harbour for several minutes afterwards, buffeting us from all sides.

"So you wanna head to shore and see if we can check in?" I asked. I thought it best to make an attempt at checking in to announce our presence to the officials.

"Sure. Why not? I'll take my shopping list just in case we see a store," Jan said, as she slipped back down below to get herself ready.

I hung out top side to launch the dink and to take in the view that was at least as impressive as any we had already had seen, well for a harbour at least. Nawiliwili Bay was surprisingly quiet, with only a couple of seadoos tearing up the water in front of the sprawling five-star Hotel Marriot on the far side of the bay and a few people making busy at the now empty cruise ship dock. The gunship had quickly retreated to its dock and I could see the guardsman tidying up the boat, but over at the harbour master's office and the surrounding park it was absolutely dead, no movement at all, neither aquatic nor terrestrial.

"I think I'm going to like here," I said to myself.

Fishkiller made short work of the half mile to the inner harbour, the State owned docks and waterfront park. We tied up at a small dock next to the loading ramp, walked past the now deserted CG station and a clutch of wild chickens tearing up the grass of the cottage-like building. Three steps led up to the covered porch where we found an empty office behind a glass door. The hours of operation for the harbour master's office were stuck to the glass, I checked my watch, then again the sign.

"Well, Babe they either left an hour early or it is actually Sunday. What do you want to do now?" I asked.

"Well, if these guys are closed, I don't think we will have much luck finding an open store," said Jan.

As we discussed our options while sitting at a nearby picnic table, Janet stopped talking as she heard a cat crying.

"Where is that coming from?" she asked. But before I could answer, she was off tracking down what definitely sounded like a cat in distress. Jan followed her ears which led her around the back of the harbour office where sat a green sea can of the type containerships use to ship cargo.

The single garage-sized can, with several old oil drums alongside was obviously being used as a storage shed of some sort. We encircled the can and then came to the conclusion that the wailing cat was inside the container. Jan began to call to the cat, which seemed to upset it even more. She checked the door and it was padlocked. We could now hear the cat right behind the door attempting to claw its way out.

"Oh, the poor thing is trapped inside we have to get it out!" Jan declared.

"Can't see how Jan, it's locked!"

Jan moved around the unit and found a small hole at one end right in the corner just big enough for a cat, but it was covered with a heavy wire mesh. Jan called the cat again and almost instantly a little furry face appeared and a single paw slid through the mesh as if desperately trying to make physical contact.

It was a pitiful sight and reminded me of an old movie when there was a condemned prisoner who was begging through the bars of his cell, pleading not to be taken to the electric chair. There wasn't anything we could do for the poor creature. I took the phone number of the harbour office from the sign in front and using my cellphone, left a message concerning the cat. Jan felt bad leaving it to its fate, but we had to go.

"Hey Jan, just around the bend is the start of the Huleia River, you remember, we read about it in the guide book, let's take the dink up there now and have a look, OK?

Jan was still a little rattled by the trapped cat but she agreed, so up the river we went.

Kauai's Huleia River or stream as the locals called it, starts its life only a few miles away up in the steep valley to the west of the port. Its banks consist of dense mangroves and mud and only navigable by small boat or kayak for about two miles. On the northern side of the stream that is barely 30 meters wide over most of its length, is a rock wall caked with mangroves. The wall separates the slow moving stream from an eight-hundred year old fishpond. The Menehune Fishpond also called Alekoko(Rippling Blood) is said to have been built by mythical 'little people' (Hawaii's version of leprechauns) in one night, long before Hawaiians arrived at the islands. The pond is said to have guardian spirits for protection and for Hawaiians, it was a scared place and Kapu, and for commoners, forbidden. This structure, consisting of a 900-foot-long stone wall alongside the Huleia stream has two holes or gates to let the tide flush the pond. The fishpond has long been out of commission as a fish corral, but it now serves equally well as a refuge for rare native Hawaiian waterfowl, and it was here somewhere along this stream, under a great mango tree on the ponds bank that *Indiana Jones* swung from a vine in the opening scene of *Raiders of the Lost Ark*.

If you carry on, the shoaling creek forces you to walk and if you hike another 2.5 km (1.5 miles) through leafy forest, you will discover the wide watery curtain of Kipu Falls with all lands just north of the stream and path being part of the Huleia National Wildlife Reserve.

As it was already getting late, we would only explore for about half the streams length. The mangrove jungle clung tightly to the edges of the watercourse and as we slowly motored along, Jan began to spot egrets and other exotic looking birds sitting or darting between the branches of the mangrove trees.

"What is that there Andy, floating in the water?" Jan asked, pointing just a head of the dinghy, close to the bank.

"Looks like a fishing float or something I guess, I'll pull alongside and you grab it, OK?" Jan did as I instructed and grabbed the small block of wood that had a light cord rapped around it.

"It's not very heavy and look! Something is coming up!" Jan said rather excitedly.

The water could not have been much more than a meter deep here and the little cage broke the surface covered in a layer of what looked like eelgrass.

"Looks like a little crab trap," Jan said, as she turned round to show me, "but can't be for crabs, the hole to get in is too small."

We would see dozens of these tiny traps along the stream, usually close to the bank or in amongst the roots of the mangroves and we would later learn that they were set by the locals to catch the red, freshwater shrimp that inhabited the shallow stream. At certain times of the year, the stream is choked with these little shrimp, which is the origin of the name "rippling blood". We motored past the two openings that led into the sacred fishpond, I gunned the motor but the out flowing tide was too strong for our little Mercury. The pond definitely looked intriguing.

"We will have to come back tomorrow at slack tide," I said to Jan.

We continued on for another mile to a spot in the stream where it narrowed and on the bank, next to a big tree was a muddy landing spot and a trail that led off into the jungle. I didn't know it then, but while researching the river further for this book I learned that we may have actually landed next to Indie's tree. We pulled *Fishkiller* up onto the bank and secured her to a great exposed tree root, then we headed up the meandering trail.

The jungle canopy was thick, not only with vegetation but thick with humidity that clung to our skin; the air was heavy with the pungent odor of compost. With the sun well in the western sky, it was already quite dark and just a bit creepy as the thick foliage cast deep shadows that seemed to move when seen out of the corner of your eyes. Here it was easy to imagine legions of night marchers trooping trough the bush by torch light. The sounds of birds could be heard overhead and a bit further off the thrum of machinery, a tractor perhaps labouring away. From my map of the Island, I knew that there were some farms surrounding the stream, but how far away I did not know. Jan stopped to listen, first to the tractor then to the rattle of a truck bouncing down a rough road, which sounded like it came from just beyond a nearby clump of trees.

Looking a little worried, she asked, "Do you think we're trespassing on someone's property? We could get in trouble if we're caught, don't you think?"

"I didn't see any signs where we came ashore or on the trail so I think we're OK. What can they do other than ask us to leave, right? It's not like they are cannibals or something."

"I guess. But remember we haven't checked in yet!"

While Jan was fretting about trespassing, something a little further along the path caught my eye. The ground was soft, almost spongy and muddy where something had torn up the ground apparently looking for roots to eat. I knelt down to have a look at the tracks left in the soft mud.

"Hey Babe look, boar tracks! From the size and number I would say that somewhere around here is a big mama and a bunch of little piglets."

"Mom with babies, she could be dangerous, we should go back!" Jan said as she began to scout the underbrush for a snarly tusk ridden pig that may weigh in at over 200 kilos (440 pounds).

The words were hardly out of Jan's mouth when we heard the bushes just down the trail commence to rustle. I put my finger to my lips and whispered to Jan to be very still and quiet. As we stood utterly motionless, several small pigs wandered out onto the trail not more than 10 meters before us. They were cute little things and they were rooting about looking for something worthy of eating. They didn't seem to notice us so we just stood and watched them for several minutes while they snorted and scurried about.

"Where do you think Mum is?" Jan asked in a whisper.

"Don't know, but if these little guys make this much noise, mummy would sound like a bulldozer coming through the bush, I don't think she's about."

Jan cooed, "Oh, they are so cute!"

I chuckled. "Yeah, cute and barbeque size. I wish I brought my shotgun."

"You wouldn't shoot one of them would you? You can't! Someone would hear the shot then we would get into trouble."

"OK, the shotgun might be a bit of an overkill, but wish I had my bow. Then I could take one easily at this range."

"Well you don't have either, so I guess you will just have to leave them alone won't you!"

Jan was right, I was affectively unarmed and just when I thought my Hawaiian boar hunt and pig roast was over before it began, I suddenly had an idea.

"Hey I know, I'll get my spear gun and use that!" I triumphantly declared. "At least it would be quiet!"

Jan gave me a disgusted look, "You can't shoot a wild boar with a spear gun!"

I thought about it for a moment, "Yeah, you are right it would be too noisy, someone would hear it!"

Jan again gave me a puzzled look.

"Too noisy? Hear what?" she asked.

I couldn't resist.

"They would hear the boar!" I declared while brandishing a big grin.

"If I used the spear gun it would probably squeal like a stuck pig!" I explained.

A we made our way back to the dinghy, Jan said nothing more about my stuck pig joke, as she always thought it unkind to tease the insane, but I couldn't stop laughing… for days!

Chapter #22

Kauai, An Island Unto Itself!

The sail, the play of its pulse so like our own lives: so thin and yet so full of life, so noiseless when it labors hardest, so noisy and impatient when least effective.
  -Henry David Thoreau

We awoke early the morning after our river trip as we had big plans but the first order of business was to check in with the local harbour master, then a small boat chore would demand our attention. We had been surprisingly lucky since arriving in the islands, *Maiatla's* systems gave us relatively little trouble, that is until the tensioning arm for the house alternator developed a crack. I noticed it the morning before while checking the engine oil and for any other bits that may have dropped off. It was not serious for the moment but would have to be tended to before departing for our around-the-Island cruise. It appeared that at least some of our little gremlins had awakened and started to get up to no good. Perhaps they could sense the presence of their kin, Kauai's Menehune.

We tied *Fishkiller* up to the same little dock, but unlike last time, we were being watched by several guardsmen in flack vests as they were preparing one of their little gun ships for the arrival of another cruise ship this morning. I could see the massive liner approaching off in the distance. This one proved to be the *Pride of Hawaii* with a gaudy Hawaiian floral scene and hula girl painted along her sides and bows. I was rather surprised to see that one of the coast guard crew, the helmsmen, was a rather attractive young brunette woman in her mid-twenties, built like the type you used to see on Bay Watch, bouncing down the beach in urgent need to save someone. I'm not sure whether it was her pleasant smile and bright I eyes I found most appealing or perhaps it was that she was dressed goth-like, all in black with a big 9mm Glock slung in a quick draw holster strapped low on her thigh, midway between her ample right hip and knee. The dark vixen looking strikingly like Laura Croft from the movie *Tomb Raider*.

"Andy, you are not wearing your life jacket and you drove right past them, can't they give us a ticket or something?" Jan asked, shaking me out of my impromptu leather fantasy.

"They look too busy to concern themselves with us, they are looking for terrorists, cocaine smugglers or alien traffickers and American boaters who look like they are having too much fun. Besides I am sitting on mine," I said as I pointed to makeshift seat cushion.

The harbour office was now open as it was after eight and the rather rotund, sooty skinned Tonga warrior type came out from behind his desk to greet us with an "Aloha", followed by a big smile and a hand shake.

"You must be from that Canadian boat out there," he said as he took my hand.

His name was Al and he seemed genuinely happy to see us.

"I heard that you arrived yesterday so I was expecting you today, Al said, "oh, and I got the message about the cat, we got him out this morning."

The big man was dressed in a red and while floral shirt, blue jeans and open-toed sandals. If he had been Caucasian, we would have said that "he had gone native", but this man was obviously born into his skin. There was something deeply respectable and orderly about him. He was neat and dapper in a colorful pansy kind of way with an inner grace that seemed to smooth out his bulk-hindered movements as he awkwardly slid back behind his desk.

"It's a good thing you came in as I have some information for you as to where you can go on your boat, you know, the rules!"

As everywhere else that we had landed, our arrival had not gone un-noticed. I would have nearly daily encounters with this fellow and he would later tell us that someone had phoned him late the previous evening to report our arrival. I can only assume that this someone wanted to make sure that we were given the "rules".

Nonetheless, I was expecting this, a list of dos and don'ts, as I knew Kauai had tougher regulations for visiting boats than Oahu. The Governor of Kauai has stated publicly, numerous times that they did not want transient boaters visiting their Island. Not outside their official harbours anyway. What was her motivation or concern? I was not sure, but I suspected that it had something to do with the people who own ten million dollar homes along the shore who hated seeing boats, especially other peoples boats, cluttering up their expensive scenery. I also suspected that they resented boaters who can have the same view, even if it's just for a short while, without having to pay for it.

I thanked him for the welcome as it was a surprise, then I showed him the cruising permit that we had received in Maui when we landed along with the Customs papers. He then informed me that I did not have to contact Customs now, but would have to when it was time to leave. Seemingly, I needed permission to depart from the USA. I found this odd as I didn't have to get clearance to leave Canada; they only seemed to care when I came back.

Appearing satisfied that we weren't actually undesirables and attempting to sneak in under the radar, he charged us a nominal fee for anchoring and then he pointed to a rack of tourist brochures that was screwed to a nearby wall. As Jan moved over to check out some of the flyers, which included river kayaking and whale watching, Al handed me two sheets of paper, a list of where we could and could not anchor.

Kauai had similar rules to Oahu concerning locals wanting to live or play on their boats about the island, but when it came to cruisers, there were definitely more rules. Reviewing the document, it became very clear that someone wanted it to make it as difficult as possible to enjoy the island from a vessel other than a licensed high-speed charter boat.

For us cruisers, it stated that there were only two official harbours and one bay on the Island where we were permitted to anchor overnight for more than 72 hours. Nawiliwili, here on the east shore, Port Allen on the southwestern side of the Island and Hanalei Bay on the north shore. Moreover, anchoring in Hanalei Bay was only permitted during the summer months (under permit) as the winter storms pound directly into the bay. Most of all the other bays, inlets, reefs, and parks were designated as "day use" only. With the exception of a couple of other bays where the three-day anchor rule applied. We definitely felt we needed a scorecard to keep track of all this.

Considering that there are almost 50 km(30 miles) between Nawiliwili and Hanalei Bay and another 50 km to Port Allen via the rugged Na Pali Coast, making a daytrip to any of the more remote bays and being able to return to an approved anchorage while it was still daylight, was nearly impossible, for a slow moving sailing vessel at least. With just 12 hours of daylight and a minimum transit time of five to six hours, that left only half the day to enjoy the magnificent bays and reefs, a fact, I am sure that did not escape the Governor's notice.

We talked some more and Al was more than willing to divulge the locations of the best swimming and snorkeling beaches. I told him that I might be writing a book about our visit to the islands.

He looked at me with some concern.

"If you write about this island, be careful about where you tell other people where to swim and surf. The currents can be dangerous around some places and other writers have told people where to go and they drowned."

Al appeared to be truly concerned.

I assured him that I would take care about what I would write. I thanked big Al for the information and for the address of a welding shop that could fix my alternator's tensioning arm. As we were leaving he called after me.

"Hey, we do have a boat that normally patrols around the island, but it has engine problems and won't be fixed for a while," he said with a smile. "No money in the budget".

It would seem that the Governor's reluctance to spend money on the State's harbours and their infrastructure, may have had some unforeseen consequences.

"Well doesn't that little gun ship out there patrol the Island?" I asked while jabbing a thumb over my shoulder, pointing at the Coast Guard gun ship.

"Not really, they are here mainly for show. You know, to protect the cruise ships from terrorists."

I thanked him again, but as I walked back down the paved road towards town, it suddenly dawned on me that perhaps big Al was trying to tell me something. I suspected that maybe he didn't share the Governor's Department of Land and

Natural Resources views concerning boaters. I wasn't sure, but at the very least I had decided to test the State's resolve in enforcing the "day use" only restriction, because, after all, I had not sailed over 3000 miles of ocean to spend my nights in rundown harbours when a beautifully secluded bay was just around the corner.

The sky was overcast but it was still very warm and rather humid, making the walk into town and to the budget car rental agency, a bit of a trek. After seeing the sweat roll off Jan's brow and the steely looks that she was shooting my way as she dragged herself up the hill behind me, I began to feel just a bit guilty for not calling a cab. But, we were now close and I was sure that we had the resolve to complete the journey. (Remember? Cruisers are cheap!)

After picking up the spanking new PT Cruiser, we found the welding shop and explained our predicament while playing up the visiting bluewater sailor angle. Often when people learn that we have risked life and limb, crossed whole oceans to get to our destinations they are suitably impressed and are eager to help, which often takes the form of cheap or even free goods or services. The fellow behind the counter, dressed in soiled welding leathers was not only un-impressed by our exploits, but it somehow encouraged him to take advantage of us. I guess I should have gotten a quote first, but how expensive would two tack welds be? He wasn't gone more than 10 minutes when he returned with my tensioning arm still smoking, held in a grimy welders' mitt.

"With taxes that will be 200 dollars please!." He said.

I could have objected to being fleeced, but since he still held my part in his hand for ransom and all I could do was to threaten to withhold my repeat business, there was little else to do other than to pay him. Any real fight that I may have had, vanished somewhere between Maui and Kauai; a lazy sort of boredom had invaded my soul, a South Pacific malaise that cruisers all too often become afflicted with.

As we left the shop, I was grateful that at least he was polite when he mugged me. Welcome to Kauai!

I had a list of places and bays to visit around the Island before we made our circumnavigation in the boat. Some of the bays located on the charts may appear inviting but in reality, could be extremely dangerous to approach, so I thought it best to view as much from shore as possible before committing the mother ship. Our first stop after bidding adieu to the our welder friend, would be just around the corner at Hanamaula Bay, located three kilometers (2 miles) north of Nawiliwili and a coconut toss from the Lihue Airport. This airfield is where Kara and Mike would fly in to rejoin *Maiatla* in about three weeks' time. This is also the airport that Jan would be flying out of in less than four weeks to head home, leaving just the three of us to make the long voyage back to Canada.

Finding Hanamaula Bay was a little bit of a chore, as there wasn't an exit off of the main highway to get down to the bay, we had to first head west then, pull a U-turn in town to get to the river road that follows the Hanamaula stream that empties into Hanamaula Bay. The river road was actually a pleasant drive through dense foliage with the lazy stream on the passenger side. We passed under the old concrete overpass that had long since been de-commissioned and reclaimed by tall grasses.

"Hey Jan, I think we should bring the dinghy up river, would be cool to explore the bush, what do ya think?"

Jan consulted the map, which she held.

"I don't know, from the looks of the river it doesn't go very far inland. Maybe another mile where it would be deep enough for us. Then it looks like it cuts straight through a town. But we can give it a try if you like."

There were several teens leaping in to the stream from various parts of the abandoned structure, they stopped to watch us drive by.

"Looks like the local swimming hole, hey Babe?"

"Yes, and I don't think they get many tourists down here," Jan said as she snapped a couple of pictures. "Those kids probably don't recognize the car."

Hanamaula Bay Beach Park is located on the south side and it was possible to walk out along the rubble breakwater that enclosed part of the bay. There were a few buildings visible over the treetops beyond the very head of the bay which contained a beautiful sand beach. I was surprised to see that the shoreline had not been developed, what with it being so close to the commercial and residential center of the Island. The large bay made a nicely protected anchorage but what really caught my eye was the old concrete wharf and pilings that used to support warehouses; the Ahukini Pier was originally used by overseas and inter-island vessels importing and exporting goods to and from the Island. After WWII, all shipping activities were relocated to Nawiliwili Harbor and eventually the pier was dismantled and abandoned. The buildings are long gone, but the complex array of piles and supporting members made a intricate underwater maze, a perfect fish habitat that was ripe for exploring.

As I retrieved my snorkeling gear from the car, Jan, who was busy snapping pictures of the flock of chickens that had surrounded our car looking for food, came out from behind her lens long enough to see what I was up too.

"What are you going to do with that?" she asked as she kicked at a bold hen that came a bit to close.

"I'm going for a swim under the dock, you wanna come?"

"You can't, didn't you read the sign at the head of the dock?" she asked while pointing to the official looking sign as big as a full sheet of plywood. I looked again at the sign that stated in big black letters:

AHUKINI PIER

NO Open Fires.
NO Net Fishing.
NO Animals allowed.
NO Swimming or diving from pier.
NO Snorkeling or Scuba Diving.
NO Bicycles/Motorized vehicles/Equipment
NO Boat Mooring.
By order of the Department of Lands and Natural Resources.

Looks like they had said it all except, NO Trespassing. That must be a loophole meant for me. I thought that if I was going to challenge the State's authority, this was a good a place as any.

"Ah, they don't mean us, that sign is for the locals. Sure you don't want to come in? Water looks warm?"

"I'm sure it is but somebody will need to get you out of jail."

"OK Babe, I won't be long."

I walked out along the old boardwalk, donned my gear, and leapt.

The underwater scene beneath the coral encrusted piles was amazing, huge schools of tiny, brightly colored fish darted amongst the shadows as intense bolts of sunlight streaked between the old wooden beams. There were concrete tunnels, beams and pipes lying on the bottom or leaning perilously against rocks or piles. Old cables slashed this way and that with old bits of machinery scattered about. Engines, air compressors, winches, and electrical wiring all appeared to have been submerged for over half a century or more. It was a veritable death trap for swimmers and I had a blast exploring. After two hour of chasing the bigger fish through pipes and between piles, Jan who had tired of pictures of land and seascapes, beckoned me to come out.

Reluctantly I returned to the car and towelled off. During my time in the water, many people had come and gone from the park, and I would hazard a guess that all saw me in the water.

"See Babe, no cops, nobody really cares."

This was my first joust at Kauai's' bureaucratic windmill and I was sure it wasn't going to be my last. As for an anchorage for *Maiatla*? Hanamaula Bay was too close to town and the harbour offered little advantage to stop here but after having another long look at the peaceful bay, how could we pass up such a beautiful spot? I didn't need to decide right now, but the more I thought about it, the more I felt compelled to anchor here, even if it was for just one day. It would do nicely and fortunately this was one of the bays that came with a three-day anchoring limit.

We spent the next two days exploring the coast for suitable anchorages - there were very few. Some of the bays discovered along our drive were nothing more than deep indents in the land, providing either a windbreak or a place to hide from the swells but rarely both. A few others offered complete peace and tranquility with hardly a ripple to tickle the hull. After passing through several quaint little communities reminiscent of the 1960's, rural farms, cattle ranches and Taro plantations, we discovered the town of Kilauea which, perhaps not so coincidently, shares the name of the active volcano, Mt. Kilauea on the Island of Hawaii.

The name Kilauea literally translates to "spewing" or '"much spreading" in Hawaiian. How this would translate to the tiny community of Kilauea is a bit of a mystery because at only 2.5 square kilometers (1.5 miles) in size with a population of 2300. The town is neither spreading nor spewing (might refer to the tourists that gorge themselves at one of Kauai's many festivals). Kilauea was also referred to as the "Guava Capital of the World" because it was home to the Guava Kai Plantation, reputed to have been the largest guava plantation in the world, however all good things must come to an end, and the Guava Kai Plantation closed in late 2006.

As we cruised through the otherwise tranquil community, Jan noticed signs that pointed the way to an old church, which I dutifully followed. Beyond a curve, the Kilauea Church surrounded by its park like setting rolled into view. The quaint church, built in 1935 was constructed with black lava rocks after the Kilauea Sugar Company deeded the land and provided the stone. The building had been slowly going to ruin until 1968, when an effort was made to restore the old church to its former glory, which included the importation of magnificent stained-glass windows from England. While Jan snapped pictures of the windows I wandered around the corner to the old cemetery where I found numerous graves dating back more than 100 years; however several grave sites had no headstones making it difficult to determine the real number of people buried here.

Our tour of the north coast was as beautiful as it was enlightening from a navigational standpoint as we were able to strike many potential bays off our list. However, we did manage to locate a few spots that took our breath away. The first being Kauuapea Beach (Secret Beach) just west of the Kilauea Lighthouse and the other being the very well-known Hanalei Bay. Another such bay located almost directly between the last two was Kalihiwai Bay.

The coastal road to Kalihiwai Bay passed through a dense crop of ironwood trees that partially shielded us from the hot afternoon sun. The winding road cut sharply to the left at a point of land and at the guardrail, there was a tiny pullout. We couldn't see much from the road other than a flash of blue ocean through the trees but when we exited the car and walked to the small clearing, the earth suddenly fell away and a magnificently tranquil bay came into view. We were over 30 meters up a sheer black basalt cliff and directly below us the ancient lava flows were being dashed by breaking waves. At the far end of the sweeping beach a meandering stream flowed against black boulders before cutting through the sand. In the center of the beach, a dense jungle of great trees lined the shore while partially obscuring what looked like a public park or camp ground. Bordering the bay, the reef was alive with fish and in the center of it all was a great patch of sand, perfect for anchoring *Maiatla*.

"Well, I think we need to come here, what do you think Jan? We could anchor right there," I said as I pointed off to a spot where the river formed a sandy hook.

Jan was obviously taken by the place as I was. She gawked at the scene for several seconds before replying. "Looks beautiful and look at that beach! Is that a river coming into the bay?"

"Yep, and according to the guidebook you can take a small boat up the river for a few miles, passing through dense foliage and a bird sanctuary, then the bush gets really thick. Would be cool to take the dink up there wouldn't it?"

"Yes, it would but look down there, it looks like someone is having a party down in the park," Jan said as she gestured to a large tent with many people milling about.

"Let's head down there and see what's going on," I suggested.

The Kalihiwai Bay beach public park was free to enter as all are in the islands and if I have anything to say about the State of Hawaii, it's that they do place their public parks on some of the best real estate in the islands, in an effort to make sure everyone has access to the ocean and beaches. As we slowly drove through the park, we noticed some of Kauai's other residents, just as we saw on Oahu. A VW buss with a camping stove placed outside and a newer SUV similarly filled with the couple's worldly possessions were parked off at one end of the park. We had seen some of this islands homeless but nowhere near as many as we had seen on Oahu. I pulled the car over near the party tent that had a set of big speakers supported on tripods and between them stood a microphone. A table of food had been set out and many chairs were placed facing what looked like center stage.

"Do you think it's a church revival meeting or a Jehovah Witness retreat?" I shot at Jan as I slowed the car to a crawl.

"No, it doesn't look like a church social but then again it is Saturday so your Jehovah's guess might be on the mark, or it could just be a big family BBQ," Jan offered.

As a small group of what looked like happy locals passed by, I rolled down the window and spoke to them.

"So what's the occasion here, is it someone's birthday?"

A tall bearded man in his mid-thirties stopped to talk. He was neatly but casually dressed in the usual Hawaiian theme shirt. He waved his companions on as it now became obvious that something was about to commence over at the tent.

"Hi and no, it's not a birthday," he said as his happy demeanor suddenly slipped away. "We have come here today to celebrate the life of a friend who committed suicide last week."

He paused to allow what he had just said sink in.

"She had been depressed for a while so she finally jumped from that cliff over there; she died on the rocks by the shore."

I felt a little taken aback and I wasn't sure what to say other than sorry, which seemed at the time woefully inadequate. But, what can you say about the death of someone you knew nothing about? I couldn't help but flashback to the little pull off on the cliff and remember looking down on the rocks below thinking how beautiful a site it was, but that site was the last that women had seen on this earth. If he expected me to say anything, he didn't give me much of a chance.

As I looked at Jan, hoping she would say something, he continued. "That is a popular spot for jumpers as it's hard for rescuers to get to the bottom. If they aren't killed instantly, they die long before anyone can reach them."

Jan and I expressed our condolences and moved on to the beach leaving the mourners to their thoughts. We reached the water's edge and gazed out over this beautifully peaceful scene. The sea breeze was fresh and alive, causing the trees behind us to rustle in such a way as it sounded like they were whispering. A flock of snowy white Hawaiian geese milled about at the river's mouth near a threesome of young children, frolicking on the beach as if they didn't have a care in the world.

I took Jan's hand. "Why would anyone who lived in paradise commit suicide?"

Jan looked about the bay, from the breaking waves at the point to the slanting palms reaching over the water then again, over her shoulder at the homeless man sitting in a tattered garden chair outside of his rusty VW Bus. She gave my hand a great squeeze

"It's not paradise for everyone, Dear."

After passing through several tiny villages, including the beautiful Hanalei Bay, the coastal road came to an abrupt halt at the extreme northwest corner of the island. We knew we could anchor at Hanalei Bay so since we were running out of time we were forced to by-pass the spot for now.

It was at the end of the road where the mountains climb directly out of the sea, some up to 1000 meters tall, but not without challenge. The torrential rains along those shores have over the eons slashed and cut deep canyons that stretch from the interior all the way down to the sea creating a series of knife edge ridges, all carpeted in jungle greenery of every shade imaginable. This is arguable one of the most beautiful vistas in the world: 18 miles of nearly impenetrable coast, only accessible by a laborious hike or by boat. I knew how we were going to see it, but not before one more day tripping about the Island in the car.

There was at least one site that could not be viewed from the deck of *Maiatla* and that was the Grand Canyon of the South Pacific, the Waimea Canyon. But that would have to wait for another day. It was getting late and we had to be heading back. It was a three hour drive and it would be close to midnight before we were again aboard *Maiatla*. I turned us around and began to retrace our route along the windy coast road past Hanalei Bay where numerous old sea caves sit high and dry on the inland side of the road. Their gaping mouths often partially concealed by the dense foliage. As we swept around another corner, a pedestrian came into view. She was wearing a green and white sleeveless sundress that had obviously been around a while. Her long brunette hair was pulled back from her face, tied back with a ribbon and she sported the tan of someone who had spent years in the tropics. She possessed not the color of someone who worked in a surf shop or tanning salon, but of one who lived and laboured routinely in the sun. A backpack rested at her feet and what looked like a young boy of about two years of age wearing nothing but a pair of shorts, rested upon her hip and cradled in her arms. As we approached, she thrust her thumb out.

"Why don't you pick her up"? Jan suggested. "She's carrying a baby."

Her name, I think, was Laura and she and her little boy quickly made themselves at home in our backseat. No sooner settled in she reached into her bag and retrieved and orange which she offered to us, both Jan and I declined with a thanks. She began peeling the fruit and commenced to share it with her boy. His naked chest was quickly covered in running juice but the cute little guy didn't seem to mind. She was one of those people with an ageless face, it was hard to tell how old she was. At first sight, I thought she was in her late teens, but as I watched her through the rear-view mirror, I changed my mind and put her in her mid-twenties.

Laura was pleasant and grateful for the ride but the moment the pair entered our car I was surprised that this beautiful girl smelled as if she had been living in the bush for weeks. I took another cautious breath and discovered that she was definitely a stream bather without the benefit of deodorant or razor as indicated by her unshaven pits and legs. A true child of nature, both her and her boy. Without a word passing between us, Jan and I both quickly rolled down the windows in an effort to ventilate the car. If Laura thought there was any connection with her arrival and our sudden need for fresh air, she didn't give any indications of it.

"So where you headed to." I asked, secretly praying that she would want dropping off just down the road.

"We are heading to a community farm on the other side of Kilauea, up in the valley. There is a farm where we can stay and all we have to do is work the land for four hours a day," she said, with all the excitement as if they were headed to Disneyland.

She paused long enough to wipe the juice from her son's chin with her hand then shove another slice of orange into his mouth.

"We can live there until after harvest and that will give me time each day to work on my crafts."

From her excitement, Laura obviously saw this farm as a step up in the world.

As we drove along, as typically happens when travelers with many adventures to tell of, get together for just a short time, the stories gush out so over the next few miles we were treated to more than a sampling of hers.

She was from California originally, and after high school she came here with her boyfriend to hike about the islands. That was eight years ago and she had never left. She had just recently moved from the Island of Hawaii where she lived for two years in a tent in the jungle raising her little boy. She earned an income by taking odd jobs and making necklaces and bracelets from nuts and shells strung on fishing line. That is what she was doing this day, selling her crafts to tourists at the beach. She showed Jan her wares that she had remaining and Jan paid her twenty dollars for two beautifully made necklaces. She made no mention of what became of her boyfriend or who the father of her child was. I couldn't bring myself to ask, not wanting to pry too much. She said that she was thinking about returning to the California for a visit so her parents could meet their grandchild. I couldn't help but wonder what they would think of their daughter and grandson living like Jane and "Boy" in an old *Tarzan* movie? I began to think of my own children who were also far away. I thought of Melissa and began wondering what she was doing.

Where she wanted dropping off was only about 30 minutes up the road, for that I was grateful if for the smell alone, but by the time we had left her on the roadside and waved goodbye, I wish I could have spent more time with her as she seemed to be living the life belonging to a different era. She was living a nomadic life where she carried all her positions and family with her while living off the land. She obviously owned or required little, but enough for today, not unlike the original Polynesian navigators who settled these very shores. I saw no remorse or regret in her; for all outward appearances, she seemed happy and content.

Chapter #23

Painted Canyons and the Ends of the World.

The traveler sees what he sees, the tourist sees what he has come to see.
G. K. Chesterton

Our last full day of touring the Island by car commenced by heading west from Lihue on the Kaumualii Highway into the interior which is comprised of low flat lands nestled between the Kilohama Crater to the north and the Puhi Mountains to the south. The broad flatlands reminded me of an African savanna with waist high grasses rustling in the breeze and the tall Kapok and African tulip trees reaching up into an eternally blue sky, a scene straight out an old safari movie. The only thing missing from what we saw out the windshield was a lioness resting over its most recent kill, baboons picking lice and a horny rhinosorius looking to give a few lumps to a trespassing Range Rover.

As we proceeded down the road and made a turn in the direction of the wetter coast, the lush mountain vegetation on either side slowly progressed down the slopes until it challenged the grasslands. The road curved to the left then suddenly we were enveloped in a green canopy. Kauai's great eucalyptus tree tunnel is as beautiful as it is fragrant and is thought to have been intentional planted between 100 and 150 years ago. The origin or intent of the planters is uncertain but it is generally believed that the tunnel was designed to be a windbreak that ran down the center of two great sugarcane fields. Others believe the trees were planted purely for aesthetics alone but whichever the case, the result is spectacular as the jungle swallows up the pavement and we found ourselves driving beneath a thick canopy with a kaleidoscope of darting shadows.

The coastal communities of Koloa and Lawai had an American frontier atmosphere about them, with their colorfully painted, single-story clapboard buildings with great verandas and porches to offer relief from the intense sun. Each community claimed their own general store, post office, and trading post disguised as gift shop next to dangling Monkey Pod trees with their phallic like seedpods. All reminiscent of the last century with a pace of doing business that would be considered painful in other parts of America, but seemingly quite appropriate here. Koloa opened its first sugar mill in 1835 and set the precedent for commercial sugar production across the islands. The sugar era opened the door to a wave of immigrants that make up Hawaii's multicultural population today. However, with the decline of the sugar industry, tourism has become the new cash crop, which the locals seemed to have embraced. If anyone here resents the intrusion, it was not evident as we were made to feel quite welcome as we stopped for a cooling treat at Lappert's Ice Cream Store. We made ourselves comfortable at the side of the store on wooden picnic table shaded by a big Budweiser umbrella, mostly in silence we sampled each other's cones while admiring the sights.

Life in this little community had apparently changed little in the past 100 years or so, for the white population at least. However, for the native Hawaiian, the past century has not been so forgiving. Charles Bernard Nordhoff was an English-born American novelist and traveler, who in 1873 wrote of the daily life of the Hawaiians:

… if he lives (the native) near the sea coast and is the master of his own life, is divided between fishing , taro planting , poi making, and mat weaving , All these but the last are laborious occupations :but they do not make hard work of them. Two days labours every week will provide abundant food for a man and his family. He has from 5 to $10 dollars a year in taxes to pay, and this money he can easily earn. The sea always supplies him with fish, sea moss, and other food.

He is fond of fussing at different things; but he also lies down on the grass a good deal why shouldn't he?-he reads his paper, he plays at cards, he rides about a good deal, he sleeps more or less, and about midnight he gets up and eats a hearty supper. Altogether, he is a very happy creature, and by no means a bad one. You need not lock your door against him; and an election or Luau occasionally give him all the excitement that he craves, and that of not an unwholesome kind.

Several people who looked to be of Hawaiian origin passed by; compared to Nordhoff's description, their lives have de-evolved into a more frantic one.

As Jan and I sat watching a few people who looked like tourists drift by, I decided to call Melissa just to see how she was doing. We hadn't talked to her for a few days and I was starting to feel a bit guilty, not just for not calling, but because I was actually having fun without her.

"Hey Jan, you got the cell phone? I want to call Melissa."

Jan pulled the phone from her pocket and gave it to me.

"Ask her if she has gotten any of her stuff for the school yet, you know her course schedule. She should be getting it soon if not already."

I was glad to hear Melissa's voice and happy that she was OK. We padded around with small talk for several minutes but I could sense that she wanted to tell or ask me something as she was unusually vague or evasive about what she had been doing. I pushed a little and after a couple of prods, she broke, sounding more than just a bit mad. Mad at who I wasn't sure, but I was about to find out what was on her mind.

"Dad, I really haven't been doing anything, just hanging with Dave! I haven't seen Nicole at all because of that boyfriend of hers!"

Melissa sounded frustrated and perhaps a bit confused. I wanted to console her but I wasn't quite sure what to say. Her voice suddenly changed in tone, she went from being angry and confrontational to sounding dejected and resigned.

"Look Dad, can I come back to Hawaii for the rest of the summer?"

Well, there it was! She said it. She didn't come right out and admit that she made a mistake but her asking to come back was about as close as she would ever come to it. My first reaction was one of relief and joy at the prospect of having her come back to us, but then I suddenly realised that perhaps I shouldn't let her off so easily. She had been putting us through a lot of grief, which started months before when I first announced this voyage. I probably paused longer to respond than she would have liked because she repeated her question, but this time she was more pleading.

A barrage of thoughts raced through my mind and I struggled to grasp at the most logical. After what seemed like minutes but in reality only seconds passed, I responded.

"Well, I'm not sure, Honey. I will need to discuss it with your Mum, OK? We will let you know tomorrow, I'll call, OK? And, Oh, your Mum wants to know if you have your course schedule yet? Here, talk to your Mum."

I was starting to choke up, so I passed Jan the phone as I was done talking.

Jan took the phone and repeated her scheduling question but Melissa quickly turned the conversation back to her rejoining the boat. I heard Jan tell her what I had, and that we would have to talk about it and we would get back to her.

I could hardly speak when Jan held the phone out so I could say goodbye.

For most of the day when we weren't ogling at the scenery, Jan and I discussed Melissa's request. I desperately wanted her back but the power of this lesson for her was unmistakeable. She had made a choice and as adults, we must live with them and the consequences that come with those choices. Jan and I waffled back and forth most of the day but the ultimate argument didn't come till late in the afternoon which came from Jan.

"Look, I would like to have her back as well, but she had her chance and she made her choice. She made herself and us miserable when she was here and what's to say that she won't do that again if she were to come back? There is less than three weeks of her summer left, and it's been great just being the two of us for a change and we deserve this time. You've worked hard to get us here and we earned the right to be just a bit selfish. I want to spend what time we have left together, just us, OK?"

Jan was right, and I felt much the same way but I just needed to hear it from her. We were both torn, but I think united in what we needed to do. I have had to make a lot of painful decisions in my life and this was definitely one of them. Now that it had been decided, all I had to do was tell our darling daughter and I wasn't looking forward to that.

"Tomorrow I will call "M" and tell her that we won't be bringing her back, OK?"

Surprisingly, the following day when I told her, she didn't burst into a tirade, she respectfully asked why. I think she had anticipated our answer and had already steeled herself to hearing what she didn't want to hear. Her not exploding perhaps was sign that she had grown up, if even just a little and had learned something valuable from all this. I had tears in my eyes when I hung up.

There was much to explore on this side of the island but our time was limited so we made brief stops at sites we had previously selected. The highway took us on down to the only real port or harbour on this side of the island, Port Allen. From our first glimpse of the town, it was obvious that this was an industrial and commercial boating centre and it was one of just a handful of places that didn't come with a tongue-twisting multi-vowel, Hawaiian name. Six great smoke stacks surrounded by three or four tan colored warehouses and workshops, all a full football field long came into view as well as an equally great warehouse that sat atop the concrete quay that stuck out into the harbour. Off to the right of the quay were several serious looking work boats in the 25 meter range. I had seen similar vessels in Tuktoyaktuk working as oil rig tenders in the high artic, in the Beaufort Sea. Then finally on the western side of the bay were the sorry looking public docks managed by the state. Port Allen is also the home to the many high speed, rigid inflatable charter boats that make daily the 25 mile run to the start of the Na Pali Coast, past the Barking Sands Missile Range Facility with its vessel traffic exclusion zone.

There was a small harbourmaster's office surrounded by a tidy little park but most of docks were hardly fit for the birds that were nesting upon them. Less than half of the facility was usable; the rest of the wooden docks were either rotten or partially sunken. Despite the dilapidated condition of the harbour, the bay was protected behind a great rubble breakwater that succeeded in calming the waters within the bay, making for a fine anchorage. We would bring *Maiatla* here if just for a few days to take on water, fuel, and provisions. While holding hands, we took the time to stroll down the long quay as I was curious about who owned the tall masts that were visible above the warehouse. We found a pair of large catamarans alongside the concrete dock with nattily dressed crews cleaning up the boats after spending the day upon the sea.

A young man in his mid-30s left the command bridge of one of the charter cats and came down the gangway, headed for a van with Holo-Holo Charters, scrawled along the side. I went up to introduce myself in hopes of picking his brain about some of the better places to go. After he took my hand, I went on to explain who we were and how we got there and I guess I should have not been surprised that he had seen *Maiatla* with our big Canadian flag flying in the harbour at Nawiliwili. Dave, was the captain of the *Leila*, a beautiful 50' sailing catamaran that routinely took tourists out on snorkeling and sightseeing tours and he proved to be very helpful as to which bays along the Na Pali Coast were best and what signs to watch for concerning the weather.

"If you start to get a big groundswell or see a front coming out of the southwest, a Kona wind, get the hell out of there," he said with all seriousness. "You don't want to be caught with the Na Pali as your lee shore during a blow!"

Our new friend was waning us. Kona is a Hawaiian term for the stormy, rain-bearing winds that blow over the islands from the SW , in the opposite direction of trade winds. The western or leeward sides of the islands, then, become windward in this case, as the predominant wind pattern is reversed. Although strong Kona winds usually don't last for more than a day, during this time they can cause considerable damage to boats caught in the open ocean or in an exposed anchorage.

I asked him about visiting Niihau, the Forbidden Island.

"Yeah, that place is strictly off limits, can't land without permission but we do take divers out there, drop them in the water off Lehua, that little crater off the north end, great diving there but deep. We have anchored off the beach and put snorkelers in the water in the Lehua Channel and no one has said anything, just can't go ashore."

"Sounds great," I said. "I think we will try and get out there and stay a night or two." I thanked him and was about to walk away when Dave appeared to suddenly remember something.

"If you get out to Lehua, we have a submerged buoy on the west side just off a partially submerged cave, you can tie to that if you like. We have no plans of going out there anytime soon, so you can moor for the night on it if you like."

Again, I thanked him and Jan and I moved on as the day was getting late and we still had much to see. After making a mental note of where I would anchor upon arrival in Port Allen, we moved on down the coast road to our next point of interest.

The Old Russian fort that dated back to 1815, was located on the southeastern shore of the mouth of the Waimea River. Aside from a few crumbling walls that now only served as roosts for some feral chickens, there was really little to look at, but from the grounds of the fort's ruins, the site where captain Cook first landed on the Island was visible. Jan and I walked down to the water's edge to admire the view. From our vantage point, an expansive beach stretched out to the west to where the town of Waimea touched the shore. A long fisherman's pier breached the gentle surf and between us and the pier, several surfers were riding that break that led them to the very mouth of the river. I could well imaging Cook's marines standing guard on this very embankment as they watched the crew fill the ships water casks with the red muddy waters that were now flowing out into the bay.

A copy of an etching done by one of Cook's artisans depicts this river as they saw it, as viewed from the opposite shore, showing the very bank upon which we now stood. Aside from the historical landing of Cook, this beach had another little know claim to fame; it is the Nagasaki of Hawaii, ground zero for the explosion of venereal disease that like nuclear fallout, spread throughout the islands. Against Captain Cook's direct orders not to copulate or trade with the natives, the men planted the seeds that would render a sizable portion of the populating infertile. After spending a few months island hopping and provisioning his ships, Cook departed for northern climes in search of the Northwest Passage.

Winter set in before he could make this great discovery so he returned to Hawaii to re-provision and to wait out the winter before sailing back to the Bearing Sea. When Cook's ship sighted Maui again, Cook, who had learned from his previous error refused to land, and to the frustrations of his men, he stayed offshore, within sight of land for two months. He only closed on the shore long enough to trade for supplies that the Hawaiians brought out in canoes and no women were permitted on board. No doubt, frustrating for seamen who had not the companionship of the island's women for over eight months.

Edward Riou, a midshipman on the Discovery wrote on November 29, 1778 in his journal: *"I heard that many of the natives (that came out to trade) had been complaining yesterday onboard the Resolution of the Venereal disease… & said a great many men & women were afflicted with it on Shore, and spoke of the Isle Atowi, (Kauai) as if we had left it at that place the Last year… it will appear it has been we ourselves that has entailed on these poor, Unhappy people an everlasting and Miserable plague."*

"There you can see the start of the Waimea Canyon, that's where we are going next," I said to Jan as I pointed off to the distant hills.

We took the well-paved road up into the rugged hills, entering the Waimea State Park. It was a beautiful drive with great vistas at every crest and bend. Ahead were the painted hills with deep unforgiving gorges and the higher we climbed, the cooler the air became until a jacket was necessary to leave the vehicle when we stopped to take pictures of cascading waterfalls or the winding river far below. Waimea Canyon, also known as the Grand Canyon of the Pacific, is approximately 16 kilometers (10 miles) long, 1.5 kilometers (1 mile) wide and up to 900 m (3,000 feet) deep, located on the western side of Kauai. Waimea is Hawaiian for "reddish water", a reference to the erosion of the canyon's red soil and as we saw down on the coast where the canyon sediments were being deposited. The canyon was formed by all the rain that falls upon Mount Waialeale, the wettest place on earth, cutting into the soft volcanic earth, but the rainfall could not claim all the credit for what we were seeing now. The canyon was also formed by a catastrophic collapse of the volcano that created Kauai. Like the other Hawaiian Islands, Kauai is the top of an enormous volcano rising from the ocean floor.

Waimea Canyon State Park encompasses 7.5 km² (1,866 acres) and is an extremely popular tourist attraction on the island that provides a wilderness area with numerous hiking trails and vantage points to marvel at the shear vastness and beauty. When we cast our a gaze to the southwest, the forbidden Isle of Niihau was visible on the horizon like a sulking child hiding in the shadow of its bigger sibling.

We took the road that travels for several miles right along the knife-edge rim of the canyon until stopping dead at a small parking lot. We exited the car and made our way down a trail that led to a waist high chain link fence with a steep drop off beyond. What lay before us now was the entire jungle carpeted Na Pali Coast with the dashing surf, rioting at its base. We stood for a considerable in silence just trying to grasp the enormity of it all.

The cold blustery winds pulled at our clothing as we stood on the very brink of Kauai. From here, it was easy to imagine what the ends of the earth looked like, as you gazed off at an utterly limitless horizon. As we stared off, across the ocean, I found it utterly mind boggling to consider that the next significant landfall was still over 3000 miles away to the northwest in Japan, and over 4000 miles directly west in Taiwan or the Philippines.

Cuddling to stay warm, we stayed to watch the sunset.

Chapter #24

First Time Around & Shark!

People travel to wonder at the height of the mountains, at the huge waves of the seas, at the long course of the rivers, at the vast compass of the ocean, at the circular motion of the stars, and yet they pass by themselves without wondering.

-St. Augustine

We departed from Nawiliwili after saying goodbye and mahalo to harbourmaster Al. As I visited him for the last time, he inquired as to where we were headed next. I informed him that Hanalei would most likely be our next stop. Considering it was the only place we were permitted to anchor for any length of time, I thought it best to just lie to him, for his own protection of course.

"OK, when you get anchored you will have to check in with the harbourmaster there. He doesn't have a boat so you will have to look for him along the shore as he patrols there each day. He has a small office near where the Hanalei River runs into the bay but he's not there much" Al said. "You can pay him the anchoring fee then, OK?"

"No problem Al, I will do that."

I thanked him again but just as I was ready to pass out the door, he suddenly called out after me.

"Hey! Here, this may help you when you write your book about the Island," he said as he handed me what appeared to be a large text book.

I was surprised to see that it was a copy of Hawaii Administrative Rules for Small Boat Harbours, Volumes one through three and collectively they were over 75 millimeters (3 inches) thick! (As I looked at the mass of pages, I wondered how it would it be possible to be a boater in Hawaii and not run afoul of at least some of these collections of ponderous regulations. And as always, ignorance was no excuse.

We left the harbour just as the latest cruise ship to arrive, the *Pride of something or other*, began to disembark its passengers for their morning romp ashore.

Our excursion out of the harbour was a short one as we just motored the three miles or so around the corner to Hanamaula Bay where we anchored close to the ruins of the old Ahukini Pier. I thought it would be a good place to just hang out on the hook, get caught up on some reading, and explore some more of the waters around the bay. The bottom provided good holding but we had to move in a little closer to the south shore, even closer to the old pier as the ocean swell still managed to wrap itself around the breakwater to set *Maiatla* a-rocking. Not a serious roll, but just enough to be aggravating as every now and then, the boat would swing on the hook to line up to the perfect swell that would send an unattended cup skating across the galley table. It only took the loss of a single glass of wine to initiate the up-anchor-and-relocate sequence. The setting of the stern hook was the final tactic that was deployed to stabilize our world. (At the Admirals insistence!)

By most accounts, it was a beautiful spot but if Hanamaula Bay had any drawbacks it was its close proximity to the busy airport, as the normal flight path passed directly over the top of our mast.

"Why didn't we notice the low flying plans when we drove here?" Jan asked as she stared at what must have been the third 737 to thunder by within the hour. We were trying to have a peaceful dinner in the cockpit, but I found it rather difficult eating while being watched by hundreds of faces pressed to the windows as the jet liner dashed by.

"Don't know Babe, perhaps it has something to do with the time of day? We were here late in morning and mid-day, looks like most of the planes arrive and depart in the mornings and evenings."

I didn't really know, I was just grasping at straws looking for an explanation.

"Well I don't want to listen to that all night, I think we should go in the morning." Jan said.

Maiatla had her sailing orders so depart we did; however, the final decision was not made until we learned that the last flight to take off was at 1:00 a.m. and the first to arrive the following morning was at was 6:30 a.m. Aloha! Hanamaula Bay.

We were met with a stiff tradewind as we motored past the breakwater a little before 8:00 a.m. bound northward up the coast. This section of shoreline is low in profile for the first few miles inland then the mountains abruptly assault the sky. Known as the Coconut coast due to the great groves of nutty palms, this area has the highest population density of any around the Island but it didn't look overly busy. We could see many beach front houses and every few miles a hotel would crop up usually with a small boat marina cluttered with sports fishermen and trailerable boats. A two-meter wind-generated wave came with the tradewinds, forcing me to stay farther offshore than I would have liked; there were many small reefs that jutted out from the land, well offshore. If I strayed too close and I happened to lose track of exactly where we were, disaster could strike. I have a saying that I often recite in song which says: *"Give me open water every time, every time.... give me open water every time;*

the shore is not so friendly when her white teeth are showing…give me open water every time". A dumb song, but it serves the purpose to remind me to avoid the hard bits, both above and below the water!

Maiatla loved the beam-reach, scooting along at better than seven knots under main and headsail alone. The water beneath us was deep and blue, looking like perfect marlin or mahi-mahi country to me, so out went the fishing gear in hopes of catching dinner. I had already decide that we wouldn't stop again until reaching our next anchorage which would be Secret Beach, in the shadow of the Kilauea Lighthouse, some 20-odd miles and less than four hours away. While we were enjoying the ride, I began to flip through some of the brochures and pamphlets that we had acquired while driving around the island. One of which was a daily trivia sheet, similar to the type usually found in coffee shops to amuse patrons while they waited. I read the list aloud to Jan, which stated that laws were typically implemented because there was an ongoing problem with citizens behaving in a certain, unacceptable manner, actions that needed controlling:

In Hawaii, it is illegal to get a tattoo behind your ear or on your eyelid unless in the presence of a registered physician.

Coins are not allowed to be placed in one's ears.

In Maui County, Hawaii, building an atomic bomb is subject to a fine.

In Hawaii, it's illegal to kick a seeing-eye dog.

In Hawaii, it's a crime to use imitation milk in a milkshake without warning.

In Hawaii, feeding a shark is against the law.

In Hawaii, a person can legally take driftwood from a beach.

In Hawaii, it's a crime to own a mongoose.

In Hawaii, it's against the law to fish with dynamite, electric current or poison.

In Maui County, Hawaii, it's illegal to transport swill during the day within one mile of post offices in Paia, Kahului, Wailuku and Lahaina.

It used to be the written law in Hawaii that children had to obey all "lawful and moral" commands of their parents. But not anymore! Children don't have to obey their parents and it's legal. What a strange law to remove from the books.

And this is my favorite:

All residents may be fined as a result of not owning a boat.

I can think of many men who have a good reason now for moving to Hawaii. I can hear it now, "Hey honey, I just found out, it's against the law NOT to own a jet boat!"

Being an island nation, the above law makes sense, I think. However, considering how hard and costly the state was making boat ownership in Hawaii; I can only assume that this law would be broken in ever increasing numbers.

Kauapea, better known as Secret Beach is hard to miss with a landmark like Kilauea Lighthouse to signify your arrival. The towering cliffs are steep, harsh and forbidding. Along the summit is a guard rail where we could see hundreds of visitors peering over the edge at us.

"Wow, the view from up there must be spectacular," Jan marvelled as she brought the camera out.

"Yeah, I wish we could get some pictures of *Maiatla* sailing past, that would be cool," I added.

We rounded the little Island of Mokuaeae with its ring of breaking surf. I made a mental note to bring the dink out here for a little spearfishing expedition some time later. It was a little rough now but perhaps if it calmed down a little I could even get Jan out here to this magnificent 3 acre bird sanctuary. I retrieved the fishing gear, which had proven to be useless along this stretch, placing the rod back in its holder between the mizzen shrouds.

We dropped all the sails to motor into the bay, seeking the best spot to anchor. As the swell still wrapped into the bay, I carefully motored back towards the cliffs into the crotch of the point where the beach sand changes to red rock, with the Lighthouse just off to the left. It was the calmest water I could find and after setting the stern hook, we were both content as we, for the moment anyway, had the beach that ran for almost a mile all to ourselves. Secret Beach is well named as access is only gained after parking atop the great cliffs and climbing down one of several meandering trails that often pass through private lands, and I hear, whose owners sometimes objected to the intrusions.

"I'm going to launch *Fishkiller*. Do you want to go ashore, Jan?" I asked.

"No, I don't think so, I'm going to tidy up and then have a nap before making supper," she said.

We were content just to be here; it was a beautiful place with crystal water beneath us and an onshore breeze that kept the inside of the boat cool when the forward hatch was opened and the windsocks in place to snare the breeze. It was late afternoon and I was feeling rather lazy myself so after I helped to secure the boat, we settled down into the cockpit for a glass of wine.

"Well what do you think? Want to hang out here for a few days?" I asked Jan as she made herself comfortable in the corner of the cockpit by arranging a series of pillows.

"Looks fine, but I hope the swell doesn't get up. It wouldn't take much to get nasty in here."

She was right, it was calm enough now, but I have seen photos taken of this very beach during winter storms and waves can come crashing in with destructive force. One picture came to mind showing what must have been an eight-meter wave breaking precisely where we were now anchored. As we have always done in anchorages that may be tenuous, we kept *Maiatla* ready for sea, which meant keeping as much gear stowed as possible and the dinghy was brought aboard every night. The GPS was left running, with an escape route programmed in, just in case we had to leave in the pitch of night at a moment's notice.

I have been asked, what can possibly happen that would make us want to leave in the middle of the night? Anyone who has cruised long enough will have their own tales of hightailing it out of an anchorage in the middle of the night, and we most certainly have ours. However, the most common cause is weather. Once in Los Frailes, Mexico, we had gone to bed with flat calm waters and a few hours later, we had breaking waves washing over the bow as an unpredicted southerly gale developed. The arrival of, let's say, undesirables in the night, (Pirates - don't laugh, it happens!) may prompt you to haul anchor and ass and get the hell out of there.

THE TAHITI SYNDROME-HAWAIIAN STYLE

We have been fortunate not to have dragged our anchor or have our chain or rode part during the night, but others have. On a few occasions, one or more boats have either dragged or lost their ground tackle during the night; as they were anchored up-wind of us, we were forced to pull up our gear and get out of the way, in a hurry. Other things like medical issues may also compel you back to sea to seek a doctor in a distant port. Being able and prepared to vacate under the worst possible circumstances, to have an exit strategy, is not only part of being a good seamen, but it could save your boat and lives.

Our days at Secret Beach were blissful and one fine day melded into another, so much so, that I do not recall just how long we actually stayed. Three or four days or perhaps a week? Even my notes of this voyage succumbed to my general state of complacency, trailing off during this time as my cruise-timers had succeeded in overpowering me.

Each morning the spinner dolphins would arrive in our bay; after spending the night at sea feeding, they would rest at first, then frolic and play about the boat. We spent evenings in the cockpit, reading or just talking. Ever wary of the presence of indigenous wild life, I noticed that early in the mornings, as predictable as the arrival of the spinner dolphins several sets of female joggers, mostly topless, trotted down the beach, getting their morning exercise I presumed before their work. I would wave but other than giving some indignant looks, they never responded. I always kept the binoculars handy so we could get a better look at the native life whenever it happened to show itself, at least that is what I told Jan. We lounged, swam and collected seashells or disappeared down below for some one on one time.

We saw no other vessels, none that came into anchor or even passed by; we had the place pretty much to ourselves. As this was a day-use anchorage only, at night we refrained from using our anchoring light for fear of someone noticing that we had not left after dark, and report us. On the top of the wooded hills surrounding the bay, we could see the night lights of multi-million dollar homes and from what we noticed, most didn't appear to be lived in. The lights were on but nobody was home, or at least nobody of consequence was home. We had heard that Sylvester Stallone had a beachfront home in the vicinity and it was fun to think that Rocky Balboa himself could be staring down upon us and perhaps, just a little, envying us at that moment. We had a great time, but not all of our moments were spent in idle bliss as Janet would have at least one instant of panic.

We had taken the dinghy along the cliffs out to the point, directly below the lighthouse for a little snorkeling. I anchored *Fishkiller* in about three meters (10 feet) of water in a little indent in the cliff, out of most of the swell that was rebounding around the point. We donned our gear and rolled into the water and after taking Jan by the hand we commenced to swim along the rocky shore. This day the water was remarkably clear and the coral clinging to rocks was a little sparse, a condition I suspected had to do with the pounding that these cliff received during the winter storms. Nevertheless, the lack of coral did nothing to discourage the great schools of colorful fish, yellow angles and blue neons, pearl wrasses and red-barbed hawkfish all darted before us. The rocky shelf below us was flat with many holes, caves and tunnels for the fish to hid in and for us to explore. I had brought our underwater camera and strobe with us in hopes of getting a few good shots. Jan and I took turns snapping pictures and we even managed to get a nice shot of a school of keelfin needle fish hunting right at the surface as well as well as a curious moray eel whose lair we discovered next to a brilliantly red gorgonian coral.

We had worked our way right out to the point and could go no further without rounding the corner or heading offshore to Mokuaeae, the tiny Isle which lay a good 100 meters (330 feet) offshore across a deep and turbulent channel.

"Andy, it's getting a bit deep for me and the waves are bigger out here, I want to start heading back, I'm getting tired."

I looked at Jan then back at the dinghy, which was now close to half a mile away.

"OK, we can head back now, you OK? I can swim ahead and get the boat and bring it back if you like?"

"No, it's OK, just take it slow and I'll be fine," Jan said, she pondered for a moment, looking a bit concerned. "Hey Andy, I just thought of something, what if we see a shark? What do we do being way out here?"

I was surprised that she would have asked that question now, as we had already been in the water for a good two hours so what prompted her to think of sharks escaped me then; later, I would wonder if she had had a premonition.

"Ah, we don't have to worry too much about sharks," I said, with all seriousness. "Probably won't see any but if we do see a white or black-tip reef shark or a sand shark, just keep your face in the water and keep eye contact and just watch him and stay with me."

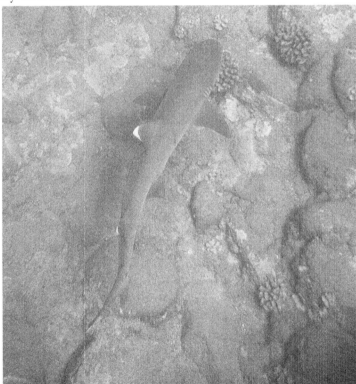

Figure 22.
The two meter white tip shark that swam directly below Jan at Secret Beach.

I could see Jan's eyes behind her mask and it was obvious that she was processing what I had just told her. Perhaps wondering if she should buy into what I was saying?

"They will be curious but they won't hurt us," I said. "But if we see a tiger shark or a Galapagos shark, don't panic, we will again keep an eye on them but we will either head back to the dinghy or the beach, whichever is closer, OK?"

Seeming satisfied with my response, Jan struck off in the direction leading back to *Fishkiller,* with me right behind her.

I had once heard that our very thoughts possess the power to attract or manifest the very things that we imagine by simply concentrating on them. I suspect this is what my lovely wife was doing. No sooner had she posed her shark question, when a two-meter white-tip shark passed directly beneath us and proceeded in the direction of our dinghy. I first saw the shark, then I saw Jan instantly tense up as she spied it also. Jan who was already floating on the surface snapped her head out of the water. I could see the near panic in her eyes as she first looked for me then for the dinghy then finally back underwater looking for our shark.

I think it's funny now about the way she looked. If she thought for just an instant she could walk on water, she would have given it a try.

"Hold on Babe, it's OK. It's just a reef shark; remember what I said? Put your face back in the water and just watch it, OK?"

I tried to reassure her by grabbing her hand and point off into the distance where I could still see the shark cruising along a drop off. She pulled me closer but I could see that she was calming down. But this only lasted a moment as our friendly shark suddenly decided to circle around, making a second pass at us, swimming not more than a meter or two (3-6 feet) below our dangling fins. This time Jan remained calm, but she was definitely vigilant as she clung to me. Fortunately, as the big fellow cruised by, I managed to snap a couple of pictures of him. He was beautiful as he moved with a poetic grace and later, much later, Jan also thought so.

We slowly worked our way back to the dinghy and by the time we crawled back in, Jan was exhausted and I wasn't very far behind. There was one more thing I wanted to do before we headed back.

"Hey Jan, do you mind staying in the dinghy while I swim out to that little Island and have a look? I want to see if I can find any lobster, OK?"

Jan looked over my shoulder to the distant Mokuaeae Rock; the waves were breaking big on the weather side, sending geysers into the air. The lee of the Island wasn't much better as the great waves surged around either side of the rocks to collide around the back, creating foam and spray.

"You're not going to take the dinghy out there with me in it!" she said, with a certain finality. "You can come back out later by yourself if you want but I'm not going!"

"Oh no Babe, I was thinking that I can move the boat closer to the point and anchor in calm water then I would swim over while you watch the dink, OK? I won't be long, just want to have a look while we are here."

Jan was a little reluctant but she agreed. I re-anchored over the spot where we had seen the shark and rolled out into the water. I dove the anchor to make sure it was solid before making my way offshore. From the dinghy, the tiny Mokuaeae Islet still looked a long way off, from the water it appeared even farther. As I left the shore, the bottom steadily dropped off until leveling out at about eight meters (25 feet). The bottom was flat and covered in a low-lying coral with colourful fish darting about, appearing much like the bottom at the Lahaina Yacht Club. I felt a little exposed floating about way out here and I couldn't help wondering if there were any tiger sharks about.

There wasn't much current in the channel, but as soon as I reached the island, I was caught up in a violent wave chop and surge that raced around the entire island. I dove down to get away from being slapped about on the surface, but even three meters down, the current sucked me along for several meters before reversing and dragging me back to where I had started. OK, it wasn't the best of diving conditions but the marine life was infinitely better than inshore and I was hopeful that I could find a couple of lobsters for dinner.

I moved closer in to the rocks but when I did, I found myself in danger of being slammed into the barnacle encrusted rocks, so I backed off to a safe distance. I swam around the Island as far as I could, but I was finally turned back by an ugly wave that pounded down onto of me, driving me not only deep underwater but dislodging my mask at the same time. I struggled blind for a moment, to get my fins back under me, to regain control of my tumbling body, and once I figured out which way was up, I bolted for the surface for a breath of air with my mask dangling from my neck. When I broke the surface I immediately drained my mask and slipped it back on but I was upset to discover that I had lost my snorkel when my ass was driven past my head by the breaking wave. As I bobbed on the surface of seething bubbles trying to get myself reoriented with the nearby land, I suddenly heard echoing in my head, harbourmaster's Al warning about the dangers of swimming around Kauai. "Well, I guessed I was done for now," I said aloud to myself. With that comment I quickly made my way back to Jan. The return trip was more difficult without a snorkel; I was forced to keep my head above water to breathe. To make matters worse, I couldn't keep a constant watch on the depths for any hungry sea creatures that might fin by. As I swam the last few meters back to the dinghy, I vowed to return to this tiny Island when the sea conditions were better.

Later that night while sitting out on deck under a cloudless sky, Jan relived her close shark encounter and I think she was pleased with herself and glad it happened, but she made it quite clear that she could do without another such encounter anytime soon. I wonder what she would have said if I told her that her next encounter with a big shark would be sooner than she hoped with infinitely more drama? Regretfully, we decided to move on the next day as it was predicted that the weather would deteriorate a little producing some cloud cover and possible rain over the next two days. So we set our sights on Hanalei Bay and a pier from my boyhood.

Chapter #25

The Wackiest Ship in the Army

The sea -- this truth must be confessed -- has no generosity. No display of manly qualities -- courage, hardihood, endurance, faithfulness -- has ever been known to touch it's irresponsible consciousness of power.

Joseph Conrad.

As predicted, the weather in the morning had turned a little snotty. The stiff wind came from a new compass heading and did so with authority, and felt comparatively cool to the skin. A light rain commenced to fall in the early hours of the morning, which we could hear pattering upon the deck. The rain, a reassuring sound that reminded me of home; the result of living-aboard for seven years in the inclement Pacific Northwest. The sound of the rain pounding the cabin top made it difficult, if only for psychological reasons, to get out of bed before 9:00 a.m. As I finally dragged myself on deck with tea in hand to actually look at the day, I received some measure of reassurance that the dismal conditions wouldn't last long as there was a bright patch of sky off in the distant west, bringing with it a promise of fairer conditions.

Sadly, in keeping with the black, scrappy cloud conditions that were now hovering above the shore and the creeping mist, reminiscent of the moors of Scotland, my topless morning joggers were nowhere to be seen. It was past the girls' usual jogging time and I was sure that I had not missed them as the rain had washed away their footprints from the previous days and there were no fresh ones this morning. Even the spinner dolphins had abandoned us; perhaps they were waiting on the sun to pierce the sea to signal that they should return. While watching the rain stipple the surface of the water, I mourned their absence, the girls and dolphins alike.

The wind had freshened, which brought with it a new swell that felt and sounded different, now slapping up against the hull, causing *Maiatla* to chaff and gnaw at the bit and bridle that was her stern tackle.

An hour after first crawling onto deck, Jan eased the throttle forward taking us back out to sea as I completed storing the bow and stern anchors. There wasn't a soul in sight anywhere along the shore of Secret Beach to wave goodbye to, not Rocky Balboa or the Bay Watch girls, but at least the spinners returned briefly for a few moments to play in our bow wave, for fun, and I like to think that it was their way of giving their blessing to our travels and to say good bye.

Maiatla, in the 25 knot winds on a beam reach made short work of the 12 kilometer (eight-mile) passage along the coast. Again, we stayed more than a mile offshore, respecting the rocky reefs that dominated the submarine landscape. I didn't bother setting the fishing gear as it was too short a run and for the most part, I thought it would be a total waste of effort. OK, I admit it! I'm not a fisherman!

The beautiful Kalihiwai Bay quickly appeared to our port, but despite the tranquil surroundings and fabulous beach, we decided to pass it by. It was only a few miles further along and I started to feel that we needed to get on with our circumnavigation, and besides, the thought of the woman who committed suicide here just a couple of weeks ago somehow cursed it and a dreary sadness now enveloped the place, for us, at least.

The rest of our passage was pleasant with the rain not entirely unwelcome as it not only gave *Maiatla* a much needed freshwater bath, it produced a set of cascading rainbows that straddled the interior mountains, producing shimmering bows of primary colours that escorted us all the way to Hanalei Bay.

Hanalei Bay is the largest and arguably the loveliest bay on the north shore of Kauai. The town of Hanalei is located at the mid-point of the bay. The main street, the Kuhio Highway parallels the shore a couple of long blocks up from the water. The main drag boasts a few restaurants, bars, surf and t-shirt shops, all of which seemed rather pricey despite their 1960s era facades. The best feature of this community is the nearly two miles of white sand beach, surrounded by mountains that have come to epitomize the image of the south sea isles. And it was the ragged peaks of the Na Pali coast that were featured in the 1957, classic movie, *South Pacific.* It was the lofty and ragged top of Kauai's Mount Makana that was portrayed as the fabled peaks of the exotic and forbidden Island of *Bali Hai.*

In the summer, the bay offers excellent mooring for sailboats which many of the locals take advantage of along with stand-up paddle boarding, swimming and snorkeling. However, during the winter, storms generate a large surf break here, making anchoring impossible but in exchange, transforming the bay into a surfers paradise. On the eastern point of the bay, a luxury resort commands the heights, but thankfully, Hanalei Bay Resort, which is actually located in Princeville, is the only large tourist complex in the area.

If you move inland, you will find the wetlands of Hanalei Bay that were once used to grow taro by ancient Hawaiians. However, by the 1860s, the new cash crop was rice, which was shipped to Honolulu to become the second largest export crop of the islands. The long concrete Hanalei Pier was built to help Hanalei farmers move their crops to market, and the covered pier's location, near the mouth of the

Hanalei River and Black Pot beach, has long been a favorite family gathering place for fishing, picnicking, swimming, and not to mention a rallying point for movie buffs as the pier has played a prominent role in many films. This is a fact that I was unaware of when we arrived in Hanalei Bay, but would quickly discover for myself.

Another reason I found this bay of interest was that it was the site of a famous shipwreck on which I was hoping to dive. On April 5, 1824, King Kamehameha II's royal yacht, *Pride of Hawaii*, sank near the mouth of the Waioli River, on the southwest corner of Hanalei Bay after it struck a shallow rock a 100 meters offshore. It was believed that at the time the captain and crew were all drunk. A large section of the ship's hull washed ashore in 1844 in a winter storm surge, but most of this historic wreck remains buried in silt in the bay. Between 1995 and 2000, archaeologists from the Smithsonian Institution's National Museum of American History excavated the wreck and recovered more than 1,200 artifacts. During this excavation, a 12 m (40-foot) section of the stern was discovered, surveyed then re-buried.

Our arrival at Hanalei Bay was rather anti-climactic; the wind died before we rounded the point, forcing Jan to fire up the old Perkins, and when we did finally motor around the bend, we found the bay congested with over 30 vessels, both sail and power, crammed into the eastern end of the enclave.

I said to Jan, "It's as if everyone said, let's get as close to that pier as physically possible." And from what we were seeing, they most assuredly did.

I asked Jan to throttled back the engine so I could assess the anchorage. What I found most interesting was that the bay wasn't cluttered with a collection of foreign mega yachts with helicopters and or shirtless socialites adorning their top decks, or even a gaggle of netherworld escapee cruisers with towels and underwear pinned to their lifelines; either of which I kind of expected, and even hoped for (at least in the case of the cruisers!). It was the fact that the bay was full of dammed locals that had me most intrigued. I say intrigued because I had no right to be upset, as it was their country after all, but you would think that they would save the best places for just the tourists, wouldn't you?

I brought *Maiatla* in as close to the beach and the central pier as possible, as it did appear to be the center of all the activity (OK, I'm not entirely immune to the netherworld mindset!).

Because of the numerous vessels swinging on hooks or moored to buoys cluttering up my bay, we were forced to anchor farther out than I preferred and in a location where the swell was more pronounced. There were tour catamarans, overflowing with snorkelers bound for the outer reefs. There were sports fishing boats fishing for anglers; great dugout canoes full of golden bronze skinned natives wielding ornately carved paddles, and black and red neoprene clad aquanauts clutching underwater cameras clambering aboard dive boats. There were yachts with Seadoos on the stern and sailing outriggers displaying wishbone rigs with tapa sails tacking between anchored sloops, ketches, schooners, yawls, stand-up paddle surfers, and boogie boarders. In addition, just to complete the mix, dozens of green sea turtles grazed and bobbed between all, creating living and very mobile aquatic speed bumps.

Almost inconceivably, all that comprised this veritable floating metropolis had achieved a state of equilibrium, finding a way to co-exist without fuss or fights. This was Hanalei Bay in the summer and I was proud to slip *Maiatla* into this cosmopolitan village upon the sea. After dropping our bow and stern hooks on the outermost fringe of this floating community, we launched *Fishkiller* and immediately headed for the pier in search of a place to land.

"Andy, do you know where the harbourmaster's office is, we should check in if we can find him." Jan said, as she peered over the bow at darting schools of tiny fish that fled before our dinghy.

"It's supposed to be over where the river comes into the bay, just over there to the left of that parking lot at the head of the dock," I said, while pointing towards the beach.

Because it was the weekend (I think), the beaches were busy with families building sand castles and the long pier was crowded with kids and adults alike fishing for whatever lived around the piles. There was a lineup of SUVs with trailers at the boat ramp and the parking lots were full to capacity. I managed to find an unattended strip of sand between a pair of ski boats where we beached the dink.

"Hey Jan, before we go to find the harbourmaster, I want to check out the pier, OK?

"OK, but why? It's just a dock and its looks very busy," Jan said.

"I'm not sure but it looks very familiar, I think I have seen this pier before," I said as we began to walk towards the road that led to the head of the pier.

"You've probably seen it in a travel ad or on a postcard or something." Jan offered.

She was probably right, but the closer we got, the more intense my feelings of recognition were, a sense of déjà vu swept over me.

We walked the entire length, meandering amongst what must have been all local people who sat in lawn chairs shaded by umbrellas with fishing rods dangling over the water. The end of the pier was the most coveted location as it was shaded by a tin roof and in the center, the adults set up tables and were cooking hotdogs and burgers on hibachis. The many young children yelled and squealed as they took turns leaping into the water, climbing back up on rusty ladders. The whole place had a block party feel and everyone seemed to know everyone else.

The harbour office was where Al said it would be but it was closed with no sign to say when or if it would reopen.

"So what do you want to do now?" Jan asked, as she moved under the tiny porch roof to get a break from the intense sun.

"Let's head into town and check it out, we'll just have to come back later, you wanna get a burger or see if we can find some fish and chips?" I said. "It's getting close to dinner time and I'm hungry!"

Kalypso's was an open air bar and restaurant that seemed to cater to the beach set as sandals and shorts were sufficient to meet the dress code, so we fit right in and it was as good a place as any to find something to eat. The waitress sat us next to a railing that separated our table from the street. Not the best table in the house but because it was packed, I thought us fortunate to get a seat. As Jan scanned the menu that our perky young waitress had left us, she gasped.

"Oh Andy, look at the prices! I hope you brought your wallet, I left mine on the boat."

"Nope, left my wallet behind as well but I grabbed some cash," I said as I searched to see if fish and chips was on the menu, but as I did, I suddenly realized why Jan was so concerned.

"Wow, the food is expensive here!" I said. "I only brought 40 dollars with me thinking that would surely be enough."

"What about taxes? What are they here?" Jan asked as she began doing some mental math.

Our waitress came and left twice before we had devised a food order that we hoped would not exceed our budget.

"Well, you know it may be a good thing that they put us next to the railing and the street as it will make it easy to make a quick escape if we can't pay the bill!" I said, only half joking.

"We'll be sure to give me a boost before you go over, I'm liable to get stuck," Jan added with a chuckle.

Figure 23. **Hanalei Bay pier surrounded by the mountains of Bali Hai.**

The food was fair but that may have been due to the anxiety we were both feeling as we dreaded the thought of the bill arriving. I had a one-piece fish and chips, Jan ordered a burger, no fries, we shared my fries and split a single glass of beer. Fortunately, our $39.40 tab saved us from bolting over the rail and becoming fugitives.

Next to the Kalypso's was a little strip mall complete with a grocery store, surf shop and high-end boutiques. It was a perfect time to let Jan browse as we were both utterly broke; I had left our probably disappointed waitress our last 60 cents as a tip. We got lost on our way back to the pier but after Jan had smelt every flower and orchid along our route and stopped ogling bunches of green bananas dangling from trees in peoples yards, we did manage to find a trail that cut between some cottages to finally dump us back on the beach.

We strolled hand and hand with our feet in the water, back to where we had left our dink, all the while trying to get a grip on the immensity of it all. I thought that if any place had Mana, or supernatural powers, it was Hanalei Bay. The whole spectacle and the interaction between the land, sea and the people was truly magical.

"Hey look!" Jan said while pointing. "It's a tour bus!"

We arrived back at the pier just in time to see 30-odd people disembark and form a semi-circle around what I presumed was their tour guide. I recognized the logo on the bus as one I had seen on a pamphlet that we had picked up back at Nawiliwili. The tour company specialized in taking people to locations around the Island where famous movies were shot. As the group moved onto the pier and out over the water, I was hoping that the guide would not notice that she had pick up one more tourist who was eager to hear what she had to say about this location.

After several minutes of raving about the movie *South Pacific* and pointing to a spot on the beach where the S.S. Minnow was once stranded, the guide said, "And this covered concrete dock was featured in the 1960 comedy, *The Wackiest Ship in the Army*, staring Jack Lemmon and Ricky Nelson."

That was it! That is where I had seen this pier before, as a child many, many years ago in one of my favorite movies. In the movie, the old schooner, which they were attempting to deliver for a top secret mission in the Solomon Islands came under enemy attack while tied to this very dock. I loved the movie; it was funny, had guns, war and fighting with no-one getting killed or dismembered and most of all, it had a beautiful old sailing schooner that I fantasized about sailing on. With my curiosity and déjà vu cured, we dragged *Fishkiller* off of the beach and headed home.

I made repeated trips to the habitually padlocked harbourmaster's office and even attempted to scout the parking lots in search of his vehicle with equally negative results. Well, we tried. I decided that if we couldn't find him, I would just wait for him to find me, which I suspected wouldn't be difficult as *Maiatla* stuck out with our great red and white Canadian flag clearly announcing our presence. At least he couldn't accuse us of attempting to hideout in the anchorage.

We fell into a lazy routine of domestic boat chores, snorkeling and beach walking and despite having to share it all with the masses, we utterly enjoyed our time there. We'd sit on deck, watch turtles, and say "Hi" and chit chat to the friendly kayakers and tourboat operators who motored or paddled by to say "Hello" and admire *Maiatla*, it was truly a life without discord or stress. We were happy. When we first arrived, I spotted what looked like a couple of foreign cruisers anchored in our midst, but the crew were never aboard when I went to visit and after just a couple of days, the boats vanished. I was mad at myself for not recording the vessels names so I could track them down later.

THE TAHITI SYNDROME-HAWAIIAN STYLE

One day after another late rising, I made an effort to locate the King's shipwreck which by all accounts was located just a few hundred meters off *Maiatla's* stern, but was unsuccessful, however I did discover another magnificent reef for exploring with an inquisitive green moray eel and a giant manta ray even banked in close to see what I was up too.

A blissful week passed with only one slight discord to mention. I had decided to take *Fishkiller* with its rather anemic 3.3 Mercury and motor across the width of the bay in an effort to find new reefs, rocks and shore to explore. My chart indicated a likely spot just over a mile away, around Makahoa Point at the eastern end of Lumahai Beach, a stretch of sand which was reported to be spectacular with no road access, only trails. Jan decided to have a lazy day and declined to accompany me, so I loaded up my gear and departed. *Fishkiller,* with the tiny Mercury may not be fast but it sure beat rowing everywhere. After half an hour I arrived at the point, skirted the rocks until finding a suitable spot to anchor, approximately fifty meters from the rocks and a good one hundred meters from the beach as I didn't trust moving in any closer. This stretch of the coast was fully exposed to the full force of the trades and the accompanying ocean swells that were now breaking large upon the rocks and beach.

After satisfying myself that I was securely anchored, I donned my gear and rolled out of the boat with spear in hand. I first headed for the rocks and worked my way along the shore. The water was clear but very turbulent making it a little treacherous when I drifted in a bit too close. Looking at the rough conditions, I was glad that Jan had not come along; she would never have gone into water this rough. Nevertheless, despite being pulled, pushed and sucked about barnacle-encrusted boulders, I had a blast poking in holes, caves and chasing fish with my Hawaiian sling. A couple of hours passed before I became tired and returned to the dink with a nice little hawkfish for the barbeque.

I sat in the bouncing dink, popped the top off a beer and just sat recovering from my recent exertion. While tipping the can, I began admiring the long crescent shaped beach before me. Lumahai Beach was as advertised, and what I liked about it was that it was mostly deserted as only a handful of couples (one obviously gay couple) were visible. After finishing my beer, I decided to swim ashore for a better look, but that would be more difficult than it sounded. The waves were breaking in the three-meter (10 foot) range and from the way the beach sand was undercut, creating a steep drop off, it was obvious that there were serious currents working along this shore.

Never deterred, I placed my fins on my feet, mask over my face and jumped back in. I managed to time my beach assault, catching a convenient wave and body surfed most of the way in. As I attempted to struggle out of the water up the steep sand embankment, I learned that I was correct about the current as it was so strong that it took my feet out from under me every time I attempted to stand. After staggering about for a few seconds, I realized that I had to come up with a different plan. As if under enemy fire, I belly crawled out of the surf until finally, I was safely ashore.

I hid my gear in the tree line and began hiking down the beach where I could see a small river or stream cutting through the sand, draining into the ocean. The beach was not very wide, as the jungle with leaning coconut palms challenged the shore. This must be one of those beaches that Al had warned me about with its wicked currents and a propensity of launching inexperienced swimmers off towards Japan. It was beautiful but I could well imagine that it could be deadly for the unwary. As I enjoyed my stroll, casting off the chill of my hours in the water, I had no idea that the guardian spirits, the Mana of this place wasn't about to let me stroll the beach and leave again totally unscathed.

I was only gone for an hour or so but as I wandered back towards my dinghy I began to get an uneasy feeling, I could now see *Fishkiller* off in the distance and something was terribly wrong. I bolted the rest of the way back, only stopping after reaching the spot where I had clambered out. I couldn't help myself but I cursed out loud as I stared at my dink. She was right where I had left her but either the tide had gone out or a new set of waves was coming in, but whatever caused it, *Fishkiller* was now bobbing on the inside of the three meter breaking waves and each comber washed directly over her. Moreover, what was worst of all, she had capsized and all my gear, fuel tank, cooler and oars were flotsam tumbling through the surf headed for shore.

In a near panic, I grabbed my snorkeling gear from the bush, dressed in and dove into the surf. The first thing I had to do was to rescue my oars and little gas can, before the strong current swept them down the coast. I had to save my oars since I could see the leg and propeller of my Mercury sticking straight up into the air which meant the engine was now under water and in all likelihood, it was flooded (pun intended) and wouldn't start. I reached my dink as another wave broke, burying us both in a deluge of water and foam. How I managed to keep a grip on two oars and the gas can, I do not know and thankfully, there now appeared to be a lull between the big waves giving me a few moments to try and salvage my boat. I shoved the oars and can under the overturned boat to free my hands, I then crawled on top, grabbed the rope that I dangle over the side to secure my goodie bag and spear too, and thankfully they were still there.

Holding the rope, I stood up and leaned back. I flew backwards and the dink flipped back over, just as the next wave broke, filling the dink with water up the gunnels. Again, I grabbed my gear before it floated away, tossing it inside. Seizing the anchor line, I dove down, snatched the anchor and swam like a madman headed for open water. Several more waves broke, jerking me backwards and threatening to cast us both up on the beach. I battled to stay on the surface, clutching the three-kilo (seven-pound) anchor while struggling to tow my dink beyond the pounding surf. For a time, I thought I was going to lose the struggle but eventually, I found *Fishkiller* and myself on the seaward side of the breakers and miracle of all miracles, my oars had stayed put. However, the gas can had jumped ship again and was making a beeline for the shore. After re-anchoring the dink in ten meters (30 feet) of water, I chased down my fuel can and I even managed to retrieve my cooler with a couple of beer still intact. The ham sandwich I had packed was not so fortunate as they were a little soggy and over seasoned with salt.

By the time I made my way back out to *Fishkiller,* I was exhausted but I couldn't take time to rest. I set the oars into the locks, just in case the anchor started to drag. Then using my cooler, I bailed out all the water. Now that I was safely afloat and able to maneuver, I turned my attention to the little Mercury but not before tossing the sandwich and cracking open a beer. I was not hopeful that it would start but I gave the cord a several quick pulls anyway. Nope, no go. I looked back towards *Maiatla* that appeared as a tiny speck in the distance and for the first time since finding my transportation capsized, I realized that my home was up wind and current from here and the thought of having to row all the way back nauseated me. What was worse was that I didn't bring enough beer! I was also kicking myself for not bringing the hand held VHF radio as I usually do, but I neglected to grab it as I left, so I was on my own.

Now inspired more than ever, I began working on the engine. I stripped the cowling off, and thankfully, I had taped a small tool kit to the inside for just such an emergency. I pulled the spark plug, cleaned the carburetor, and did my best to dry off all the electronics. After it was reassembled I attempted to start the engine but with no success. I suspected that somewhere water was creating an electrical short preventing the engine from firing. I made a vow to carry a can of WD 40 next time to chase water out of the electrical system. I pulled the starter cord until my arms ached.

Figure 24. The 1000 meter tall cliffs of the Napali Coast.

I looked up at the sky to notice that it would be dark in less than half an hour; Jan would be starting to get worried. She too would be cursing me after she found the handheld VHF still sitting in its charger. Well there was little else to do other than start rowing, but before I did, a thought occurred to me. Taking my little gas can, I poured gas overtop of the engine and over the wiring. I felt a little guilty about the oil slick that began spreading about the dink, but I was desperate. I thought that if WD 40 can displace water, perhaps gas can also. After giving the motor a good dousing, I pulled up the anchor and began rowing, thinking it best to give the fuel some time to chase the water and to evaporate before attempting to start the engine.

Thirty minutes had passed and I had made little progress in my effort to get back home. I estimated that at this rate, it was going to take me another two or three hours, that is if I could keep up the pace. I was already exhausted before my shipwreck; now I was nearly dead and the beer was all gone. I paused long enough to give the starter a pull all the while getting ready to leap into the sea if the engine decided to erupt into flames.

The first few pulls were fruitless, but after half a dozen pulls, the little Mercury finally sputtered for a few seconds. I was elated and felt like a man on death row, minutes away from the chair hearing through the wall that the governor had just called. A reprieve was close at hand. I pulled the engine cord and again it sputtered, then died. Each time, the sputtering lasted just a bit longer. It was now completely dark, but I kept pulling at the engine until the little Mercury finally coughed for the last time and roared to life. Well, maybe not roared exactly, but at least it was whining like a weed whacker!

"I was getting ready to call somebody," Jan yelled through cupped hands as I motored to the stern and tied off.

"Why didn't you take the radio?" she asked, sounding more concerned than mad.

"Sorry, just forgot and I had a little engine trouble. But I did get a fish for dinner." I said, with a big grin as I held up the goodie bag containing the hawkfish.

The next day I tore the little Mercury down, cleaned, and reassembled her. She ran just fine after that, never giving me a moment of grief, or at least none I didn't deserve.

Chapter #26

Category Four Hurricanes Even Teach Whales to Pray!

It is better to meet danger than to wait for it. He that is on a lee shore, and foresees a hurricane, stands out to sea and encounters a storm to avoid a shipwreck.
— *Charles Caleb Colton*

I sat wistfully at the ham radio, flipping through the stations looking for something of interest while I sipped my morning cup of tea. Jan was still in bed in our great aft cabin in a restless slumber as it was still before 7:00 a.m. We had been at anchor at Hanalei Bay for the better part of a week and loving every moment. I was thinking, as I blew the steam from my mug, how difficult it would be to leave here; we had been seriously infected with oceanic languidity. I was ignorant as to what kind of biting or sucking bug could possibly spread such an affliction here, on Kauai; but in Mexico, where this disease of indolence is also prevalent, I think it may be carried by that little worm in the bottom of a tequila bottle.

It would be a test of sheer will to sail off in search of someplace better, if there was such a thing. However, if any destination had a chance of uprooting us, it would the Na Pali Coast. Still, I felt it would take an act of God to make me want to haul anchor to sail around the next bend, to abandon this place of serenity, but an act of God was precisely what was going to shake us loose.

Most of the early-morning radio shows, which I came across on the ham radio were comprised of typical netherworld chatter. The announcers were either talking about raising orchids, children, land development or squabbling over island politics. After several minutes of listening to this tripe, I gave up surfing the commercial radio bands and switched to the high seas weather forecast on the upper sideband. In my state of bliss, I had been rather remiss in checking on the weather; it was easy to get complacent when the weather stations seemed to play the same forecast each and every day. It reminded me of the comedy movie, *Groundhog Day*, except with the sun and wind as feature characters.

The computer generated monotone voice was clear, my ears perked up when it stated that a tropical depression was moving westward out of the Gulf of Panama and was expected to deepen as it migrated towards the Hawaiian Islands. I jotted down the coordinates of the potential hurricane and pulled up the chart of Eastern Pacific Basin on my computer, sliding the mouse around to locate the coordinates, placing an electronic mark upon the chart.

Tropical Depression *Flossie* was the sixth named storm to develop in the Eastern Pacific, east of 140°W, in the 2007 storm season. One of the drawbacks to cruising the Hawaiian Islands in the summer months, May through October, is that it is the Eastern Pacific's hurricane season. Typically, tropical depressions are born either in the Gulf of Panama or have migrated overland from the Caribbean after being gestated in the Western Atlantic. As in the case of *Flossie*, they can originate off the coast of Africa and derive enough strength out of the tropical seas to circle one-third of the globe before dissipating in the colder waters north of Hawaii.

I wasn't overly concerned with this storm; the wind speeds were still below 60 knots (70 miles per hour) and she was well over 1600 miles east of the Big Island of Hawaii. Normally, storms in this region, west of the Mexican mainland, due to the spinning action of the earth re-curve or "hook" to the northwest, dying soon after encountering the cooler waters above 20 degrees north latitude. In all likelihood *Flossie* wouldn't come close to us but just in case, I began searching for a spot to hole up if, *Flossie* decided to make a run for Kauai.

As I looked at the island with the perspective of hiding from a severe storm, it occurred to me that Kauai was a poor place to be during a real blow; there are only two good locations that offer reasonable protection from cyclonic storms when wind directions are constantly changing as the storm passes. Port Allen, situated on the south shore has a substantial breakwater and good holding in the harbor; however, it offers no protection from the winds. After seeing the conditions of the docks at the state facility there, tying to a dilapidated dock during a hurricane was unthinkable and more than likely the docks would probably bust loose and charge around the bay tearing up everything in their path. It could be like anchoring your boat in the middle of a giant wood chipper.

In 2003, I returned to La Paz, Mexico right after Hurricane Marty struck, which sank or damaged over 80 vessels;. most of the boats were lost when the docks at Marina de La Paz decided to float away with all of its charges still attached. The now free-floating island comprised of docks, cruisers and yachts crashed against the nearby concrete promenade. The three-meter waves then began to grind the boats to pieces with the powerless owners watching from shore. I was there to help our friends Travis and Emily of *Mystery Tramp* take their boat back to the States. They were most fortunate as the *Tramp* was on the hard at another marina and aside from a little scorching from a lightning strike, the *Mystery Tramp* survived Marty unscathed.

Nawiliwili is the only true hurricane hole (well protected anchorage) on Kauai, it has a large breakwater, good holding and is surrounded by steep mountains to break the winds. It also has the Huleia River with its adjacent mangroves at the mouth; during storms, many locals take their smaller boats as far up river as possible then tie a spider web of lines between the trees securing their vessels in the center of the narrow channel. It is there that they can confidently ride out most anything that can strike. Going up river would not be an option for us, but the bay would still offer a lot of protection.

I heard Jan come to life in the aft cabin, I grabbed the cup of tea that I had prepared and went aft.

"Morning Babe, another beautiful day out there," I said as I handed her the mug and slid back into bed next to her.

"So what were you doing on the radio?" She asked while rising up on her elbow before testing her tea for temperature.

"Just checking on the weather, it sounds like we have a tropical depression to the southeast of us that could hit Hawaii in five or six days." I said while remaining as casual sounding as possible.

"How strong are the winds?" she asked as she peered out the aft windows, searching the sky for any signs of what might come. "What's the chance of it hitting us?"

"Winds are now in the 60 knot range. They aren't sure if it will build or even if it will reach us, but even if it dies before getting here, we could get some stronger winds and big waves for a few days," I said.

I could see Jan mulling over what I had just said while sipping on her tea.

"So what's the plan then?" she asked, looking and sounding no more concerned than a suburban housewife who had just learned that snow was predicted for later in the week.

"Well, I think we need to get moving. Nawiliwili is our best bet to ride it out if this tropical depression turns nasty." I offered.

"So you want to turn back for the harbour now?" She asked.

"No, I think we have some time. We can get back in a long day from any part of the island, so let's carry on to the Na Pali Coast and hang out there for a couple of days and watch this storm. See what it does, OK?"

"What if it picks up speed and we can't get back to Nawiliwili in time? Go to Port Allen?" Jan asked while sounding just slightly more concerned.

"Well, if we get caught, there is no way I would go to Port Allen, it would be a death trap during a serious hurricane. I think our best option would be to sail like madmen to the southwest, drop down below the storm's path and wait it out; it may be a bit rough but it's better to be at sea then to be trapped in a place like Port Allen."

"How far would we have to go to get below it?"

"Maybe 500 miles, maybe 800, depends if it curves to the north as it should do."

"That's a long way to go and remember we will have to come back."

"Yeah, I know, but I always wanted to see Tahiti," I said with a big grin.

We made a plan, of sorts. We would finish our tea in bed. I would make breakfast, and we would get ready to get underway and when ready, weigh anchor and head out. But first I would give Jan one of my "come hither" looks and try to put the moves on her; after all, we were anchored beneath the romantic, emerald hills of Bali Hai, which should have improved my chances immensely.

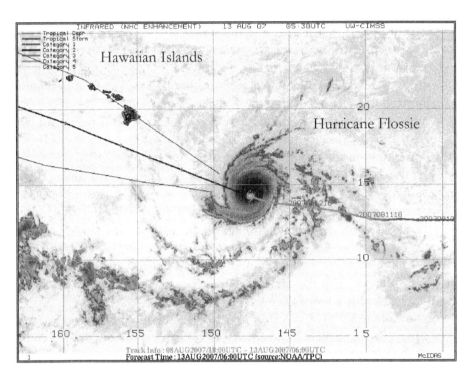

Figure 25.　Hurricane Flossie developed into a category 4 hurricane on August 13 2007. The immense storm generated winds in excess of 130 miles per hour (113 knots). The potentially lethal storm had her sights set on the Hawaiian Islands and more importantly, on *Maiatla* and her crew.

Chapter #27

The Great Na Pali Coast Rescue.

Heroes take journeys, confront dragons, and discover the treasure of their true selves.
Carol Pearson.

We left Hanalei Bay without fanfare or running into the elusive harbourmaster to report in, so thinking about checking out when the time came became moot.

The winds began to build as we cleared the land until reaching the outer bay where a full 30 knots of wind was waiting to greet us. The tradewinds were again stronger than normal but I didn't believe that it had anything to do with Flossie. I tucked a single reef into the mainsail, set the pole for the headsail, and unfurled the genoa to expose its full girth. *Maiatla's* speed surged to seven knots as we cleared Kolokolo Point; running for open water with our next planned stop being the legendary Na Pali Coast, a land centuries behind the one we had just departed.

The farther west we sailed, the more dramatic the coast became as the jagged mountains capped with fluffy nimbus halos, seemed to migrate ever closer to the shore as if to greet us.

Haena Point, with its crescent shaped Kee Beach and enclosed lagoon, marks the end of the paved road and the start of the foot trail, which is the only land access beyond this point. We shaped our course more to the south, following the shore while making sure to keep off of the broad shallow reefs. A small clearing became visible up on the hillside just above the beach where we could see several people peering to seaward.

The cut in the trees doesn't look like much today, but it was once a busy place with two great temples and many alters with powerful Mana, according to the Ancient Hawaiians. It was reported to be one of the most important archeological sites in all the islands as it was here that the Na po'e hula lived (hula people). Legend tells that this was the very birthplace of the Hula dance (the people of Molokai would dispute this assertion) and that students came from all of the Hawaiian to dedicate themselves to learning the art of recounting history though the most seductive and beguiling of all dances.

Along the trail that leads from the parking lot to the Kaulu Paoa Heiau, lie several honing stones along the shoreline. Once used to sharpen adze blades, these stones can be recognize by their deep straight grooves. Because adze-makers needed to keep their sharpening surface wet, they usually worked close to the sea or a river. When we had driven here in the car, we did not see the stones, but it was suggested to us that the tide was in and they were hidden by the water. According to one tradition, a graduation rite for a haumana hula (student) required them to swim from this point of land to the outer reef, while in the channel, lurked a shark who would devour anyone who had not lived up to her/his obligations as a student. From the look of the waves now breaking around the lagoons channel, even for those who had been studious in their studies, and without a hungry shark, swimming the channel in rough seas would be a serious trial in its own right.

Along the shore just past where the trail turns uphill, lies a big boulder appearing like a piece of black Swiss cheese, named Kilioe. The stone Kilioe contains many small holes in which Hawaiians used to deposit their newborns' umbilical cords in the hope of securing long life and divine protection for their children. After the trail turns farther uphill, it passes Kaulu Paoa. From its remains it's obvious that its construction was intricate and had been completed with great forethought, it clearly must have been an important center of worship. The temple's physical prominence may have also made it a navigational marker for those who fished or traveled this coast by canoe.

Finally, just a little further up the mountain lies the hula platform called Ke Ahu a Laka (the altar of Laka, the hula goddess). Presumably, a halau hula (temporary structure used for hula instruction) would have stood on or near this spot. In it, a group of dancers would spend their term of study, secluded with their kumu hula (teacher). Such training, it was said, demanded the highest degree of physical and mental discipline, for hula was no mere entertainment in those times as it was a vessel for their very essence as a people. Like most advanced cultures, the Hawaiians evolved ways of passing on their history, cultural values, scientific theories, and other forms of knowledge and the hula dance was the most vital of forms to the Ancient Hawaiians. The hula's importance to the preservation of Hawaiian society was such that the Ancients demanded absolute dedication of those who would learn the dance. No worldly distractions or diversions could interrupt the training period, least of all distractions of the flesh. When their studies were completed, the dancers demolished their halau and staged a public performance to display their newly acquired skills.

From the deck of *Maiatla,* it was hard to imagine what this site would have looked like hundreds of years ago; much of the vegetation and trees that now cover the area, are not indigenous, so it would have looked much different back when the sacrificial pyres were burning. Nevertheless, it is possible to make some educated guesses as to what life was like. As the honing stones and remains of taro patches near the modern parking lots indicate, people were doing much more than just coming here to worship, sacrifice and to learn how to hula. They were enveloped in their own primitive version of the netherworld. I wonder how many of them looked off at the sea that never seemed to end and dreamed of paddling off into the sunset?

I had expected the wind to diminish as we bore off to the south, but it didn't. The strong tradewinds not only held their strength but they built two to three meter (six to ten feet) breaking seas that paralleled the shore. We were able to stay on our downwind run as we made our turn southward.

"Why are the waves so much bigger on this side, Andy? I thought we would be sailing into the lee of the mountains?" Jan asked, as *Maiatla* picked up her stern to surf down the face of a rather steep wave.

"Not sure Babe, the wind seems to be getting sucked around the corner, might have something to do with the high cliffs here. As for the waves, we could have a contrary current doing battle with the wind, which would explain these steep waves," I offered.

I didn't really know, I was just speculating. I had been expecting different conditions as well, and I began to fear that our Na Pali adventure may very well be a bust. Whatever the reason for the current winds and sea state, it was obvious that we were in for a rough ride; we were not only going to have a tough time getting in close enough to shore to get a good look, but finding a place to anchor out of the wind and waves may prove to be impossible.

We shot along while staying out about a mile from shore. I set the fishing gear up in hopes that this new territory may be a bit more generous when it came to giving up a fish or two. Jan grabbed the camera and began snapping pictures of a sublime coast that must be seen to be believed. No picture would ever do it justice.

"Wow! Look at those cliffs, they go straight up, and look at that waterfall, its amazing!" Jan said, with more than a little awe.

It was a spectacular waterfall by all accounts, but only a trickle of its former self. We had learned that there used to be many great waterfalls along this coast. After all, on Mount Waialeale the wettest spot on earth is located. But, sadly as water was needed for irrigation down in the eastern valleys, the headwaters of almost all of the great waterfalls were diverted for the cane, taro and cattle. As we progressed along, the remnants of many of the waterfalls could still be seen as the water leached out many of the rocks' minerals leaving bleached stains to show where the cascading water once fell. The coast was basically a series of deep valleys separated by massive knife-edged ridges. Some of the valleys, where they met the shore, had fine sand beaches, others dropped 20 or more meters (60 feet) straight into the sea. In Cook's time, all of the isolated valleys supported communities, each surrounded by its own nearly impregnable fortress.

We had sailed for only a couple of miles but it quickly became obvious that we were not going to be able to get ashore to explore along here; conditions were much too rough. Perhaps farther long would be better. Even Auto was have a hard time keeping a straight course, forcing me to steer by hand. Jan was still taking pictures from inside the cockpit when she suddenly peered ahead and began pointing to something.

"Andy, there is something in the water over there, looks like a fin or something," she said.

I turned Auto back on, so I could leave the helm for a moment to have a look. I snatched up the binoculars and braced myself in the companionway while scanning the seas ahead.

"Oh man Jan! That's not a fin, it's a paddle! I think I see two people in the water!"

"Two people in the water?" She repeated. "What are they doing way out here?"

"Don't know Babe, drowning I think. I guess we better slow the boat down and ask them if they want a ride. Let the headsail sheet go, I'll furl it."

By the time we got within hailing distance, I could see a man and women, perhaps in early thirties clinging to a partially sunken kayak. It was the man's paddle Jan had seen as he waved it in the air, and as if she still wasn't sure that we had seen her, the woman was still frantically waving her arm in the air in obvious desperation. The wind was still blowing hard and the waves as steep as ever with breaking crests and I wasn't entirely sure how to get them aboard.

Checking the water depth, I thought how fortunate it was that it was shallow enough to drop the anchor. It was only 40 meters (130 feet) deep here, a mile farther down the coast the bottom drops off to over several hundred meters (more than 1000 feet) making anchoring impossible.

Maiatla passed them on our port side, at no more 10 meters (33 feet) distance. I needed to talk to them, so I had to get within yelling distance. With Jan taking the helm I quickly left the cockpit to stand on the foredeck. From the tears streaming down the young women's face, I knew I didn't have to ask them if they wanted rescuing.

Leaning over the bow pulpit I cupped my hands and yelled across the stiff wind that I knew would try to snatch my words away, "I'm going to turn into the wind and drop our anchor! Do not swim to the boat until I instruct you to! OK?"

They both waved an acknowledgement. I just hoped they really understood. If they approached before I was ready, I could suck them through the prop, or crush them beneath *Maiatla's* heaving bow.

"So what are we going to do, Andy? What do you want me to do?" Jan was tense, but ready.

I told Jan to start the engine as I ran everything through my head one more time to make sure I knew what we were going to do.

"I'll take the helm as I need you to keep an eye on them. I need you to keep track of them because I can't see them in these waves from the helm. I'll handle the engine and the mainsail. We will motor back past them, you can take the wheel when I go forward to drop the hook. Try and keep our head into the wind as long as possible as we drift back down to them. Once it's safe I'll put the boarding ladder over the side and then get them to swim over. OK?"

I made my turn to point our nose into the wind. The mainsail and boom began to flog madly so I sheeted it in tight; we now had 35 plus knots (40 miles per hour) of apparent wind and three meter (10 foot)waves to drive *Maiatla* into. I reached behind me a second time to give the mainsheet some slack so the mainsail couldn't fill with wind as we drifted back.

As we motored back past the be-draggled couple, the women began to swim towards us, but her companion stopped her, I was glad that at least one of them was keeping a cool head. At what I hoped was the right distance, I put the engine in neutral, ran forward to the bow, dropping to my knees next to the anchor windlass. The bow plunged deep into the waves; thankfully, none broke aboard *Maiatla*. Satisfied that we had lost all forward motion, I released the windlass brake and the big CQR anchor dropped from the rollers, hitting the water with a splash. The chain raced out so fast that it resembled the business-end of a chainsaw. I watched the chain, waiting to see the tye-wrap markers, indicating that 100 meters (330 feet) of chain had paid out, then I locked the windlass brake. As *Maiatla* drifted backwards, she started to turn broadside to the waves. Jan struggled to keep us pointed into the wind but without the trust from the engine it was a losing battle. The boat began to roll, and I then feared we would take a green one over the side. Suddenly, through the sole of my sneaker that I had placed upon the chain, I felt the rode strain as it dragged over the bottom; from the grinding sounds it was emanating, I deduced we were over a hard rocky or coral bottom. We still had considerable backward momentum and the bow began to swing back into the waves. I watched the chain shake as we continued to drag chain, then anchor over the bottom. I looked back at the couple treading water and I was afraid that we would drag right past them, but just as they came abeam, the anchor grabbed with such force that our bow dipped low in the water and a big wave came dangerously close to washing over the bow.

We were holding fast, secured to the seabed, for now at least.

I ran aft, grabbed the boarding ladder and set it over the side. Taking a line that I had on deck, I tossed it over to the couple, who proceeded to secure it to their stricken craft. So far, the plan had gone well, if only for the sake of sheer dumb luck. As I pulled them over to *Maiatla*, I realized just how lucky we were; the current was very strong and if I had misjudged any part of this rescue, the couple would have been swept away, leaving us to chase them down the coast and try it all over again.

We hauled the whimpering women aboard first, then the man and then finally a very water-logged kayak loaded with supplies and camping gear. Aside from suffering from mild hypothermia and being scared half out of their wits, they were fine and more than a bit grateful for the rescue. I was eager to get their story, but we needed to get back underway which would prove to be no small feat in these conditions and to confirm what my foot had told me, a large coral rock came up pinched between the anchor flukes.

Finally back underway, I had time to talk to our new guests. Tom and Beverly were a married couple from Waimea Bay who had planned a four day kayaking trip down the Na Pali Coast with some friends. They departed the same morning as us but their friends had left the day before, so they were trying to catch up. They were over half a mile from shore when their boat started to take on water through a previous patch that had let go; the boat quickly flooded leaving them to tread water. It was their saving grace that we came along when we did as the strong current was taking them farther offshore, well beyond anyone from shore seeing them and beyond any route that a charter boat would have taken. In all likelihood, they would have perished after being swept out to sea or worse, they could have attracted the attention of a passing tiger shark. Either way, their prospects were not good.

Their group was planning on meeting at Kalalau Beach, another two miles or so down the coast, where they were spending the night. After giving them a caulking gun, and other materials to repair their boat and receiving hugs and a contact information in return, we anchored *Maiatla* just beyond the surf line. Using *Fisherkiller*, I ferried them and their battered boat ashore. After the couple found their friends camped up in the bush, I called Jan on the radio to see how she was doing.

"You OK out there, Hon?" From the beach, I could see our home bucking and reeling about as if suffering from an epileptic fit. Two sets of three meter plus (10 foot) waves separated us. Looking back at *Maiatla*, I realized that it was nearly a miracle that we were able to land without getting swamped.

"Yes, I'm OK, but I have the engine running, just in case the anchor starts to drag," She sounded a little nervous but I was sure she could handle herself and the boat.

"Well, if you do drag, it will be along the shore and not into the breaking waves," I said.

"Well thanks! That's comforting to know!" She was being sarcastic so I knew she was OK for now.

"Hey Babe, mind if I take a few minutes to walk around the corner to have a look at that cave? Hate to leave without seeing it," I asked.

There was a long pause which betrayed her apprehension. Finally she replied, "Well, OK. But don't be too long, I don't like being out here by myself!"

I hated leaving her, but someone had to take care of the boat and I was here now. Might as well play tourist even if it was only for a short while. I walked along the surf to a rocky point about half a mile away; on the way, I spotted several more campers who were set up to live in a small cave. I wished I had time to stop and talk, but there was a monster cave around the corner that was quite famous.

I was forced to wade in waist deep water to access the adjoining Honopu Beach with its accompanying valley. At first sight, it took my breath away! Stunning and mysterious, the valley is accessible only by swimming out to a ledge and climbing a dangerous 25 meter (80 foot) sea cliff and crossing the narrow ridge into Honopu Valley proper. The remoteness of the valley has inspired many rumors and legends. Until the mid-19th century, pre-Hawaiian people of uncertain origins flourished in this valley, but then disappeared, which is why it's sometimes referred to as the Valley of the Lost Tribe. It is also rumored that this valley was the last home of the fabled Menehune: Hawaii's "little people", the architects of many of the oldest structures in the islands.

Legends notwithstanding, it is known that the beach and surrounding cliffs were once used as burial sites for the chiefs who lived along the coast. Their bones were carried by hand and placed hundreds of feet up the cliffs. Warriors would volunteer to climb these cliffs, placing the bones of their beloved chiefs into a suitable cave. When they were satisfied the bones were secure, the warrior would jump to his death, thus securing the location's secret. The Hawaiians believed that their chiefs were the direct descendants of gods and that the "mana" or life force of the chiefs was so strong that, if found by the wrong people, it could be used against the tribe. We were told that when walking along the cliffs or on the sand dunes, bones can be seen after being exposed by the elements.

What I found most interesting was not the prospect of stumbling onto a cache of old bones, but walking through the giant cave that I had seen in so many movies. This cave and beach had been featured in several movies, including the 70s version of *King Kong* with Jessica Lang, the third *Jurassic Park*, *Six Days Seven Nights*, and *Raiders of the Lost Ark* with Harrison Ford and sometime later, *Pirates of the Caribbean: On Stranger Tides*.

In truth, the cave is just a great stone archway large enough to pass a typical cruise ship through. I walked over a large rubble pile, sections of collapsed arch to a large sand dune sporadically covered with scrub bush. The top of the dune provided a spectacular view of a tiny crescent shaped beach being pounded by tumbling surf. To my left, the ramparts that protected Honopu valley ran with a cascading waterfall that exploded into a shallow pool fit for lounging during the hot afternoon. Despite the perspiration trickling down my forehead, I didn't have time to dive in. I felt dwarfed by the immensity of the arch and positively minuscule compared to the towering cliffs. After unsuccessfully finding any signs of King Kong's foot prints, I ran back down the beach to *Fishkiller* and my nervously waiting wife.

Figure 26.

Tom and Beverly, a few days after their rescue. They are happy that their Kayak is still afloat and the patch is holding.

Back aboard, Jan gave me a hug in thanks for my safe return, but my little excursion hadn't come without a price; somewhere along the way, I dropped our handheld radio. I guess the ghosts of Honopu Beach wanted a sacrifice and my brand new VHF was it.

We proceeded to get *Maiatla* back underway. We had already covered 10 of the approximately 20-odd miles of the Na Pali Coast; at our present rate of travel, we would see the entire coast in another hour and a half.

"It doesn't look good for finding an anchorage, Babe. At this rate, we may have to go all the way to Port Allen to find a place to stop," I said. It was disappointing, but one of the realities of cruising. Jan took up one of our many guide books and after flipping through a few pages, she checked the chart that I had up on the computer.

"Well, you know, there are a few shallow indents up past that headland there. Perhaps the wind and waves will be less there," she said, hopefully.

I hoped that she was right. We had come a long way to see the Na Pali Coast; to have it all flash by within a few hours and not being able to stop, made me feel just a bit sick. Or perhaps it was just the ugly motion of the boat! We carried on sailing and picture taking until we rounded the headland at Makaha Point. It was as if the gods had heard us! As soon as we turned the corner (so to speak), the waves vanished and the wind dropped to a gentle breeze after switching to our nose. We were elated. I navigated *Maiatla* in as close to the beach as I dared in search of a sandy bottom on which to anchor.

By 4:00 p.m. we were safely anchored, bow and stern, a 100 meters (330 feet) from our own private beach surrounded by what looked like mile-high cliffs. This was the Na Pali Coast that we had been dreaming of, grand and remote; the only thing that could possible spoil it was Flossie.

Once settled, I dropped below to check on the weather while Jan commenced to tidying up the cockpit. The news from the radio wasn't good. I went back topside to fill Jan in.

"Well Dear, its official! Flossie is now a category two hurricane and getting stronger and the bitch is coming our way!"

From the speed at which Flossie had grown in the last twelve hours and the fact that she was still headed for the warmer waters of Hawaii, the National Hurricane Center was predicting that it would continue to grow; they were anticipating that it would shift north but there was still a chance we could get hit. The only good news was that she had not picked up any speed and was still over 2000 kilometers (1300 miles) away. There was a lot of ocean between Flossie and us and I was hoping to keep it that way.

"So what do you want to do now?" Jan asked with great concern.

"We stay here tonight and check on her in the morning. If we need to we will make a run for Nawiliwili, OK?".

We spent a nervous evening listening to news of hurricane Flossie as she exploded that night into a category 4 hurricane with sustained winds of 220 km/h (140 mph). If a storm of that strength were to hit the islands head on, the carnage would be unimaginable and I was starting to doubt the security of Nawiliwili. With an eye to running to sea, and unbeknownst to Jan I began plotting my escape route to the southwest while trying to think of a way to get her ashore and into a hotel far inland.

The morning broke as clear and as beautiful as ever. I checked on Flossie, which seemed to have slowed a little during the night but had lost none of its strength. I then made us a breakfast of French toast and bacon and we ate sitting in the cockpit then sipped our morning tea as we waited for the sun to broach the escarpment behind the boat. I was surprised to see a layer of dew that had collected on the deck in the early hours of the morning. The air was obviously moist but the earth behind us looked so dry and parched, in complete contrast to the northern stretch of the Na Pali Coast.

"So how about taking the dink around the point for some snorkeling, hey Babe?"

"Sure but aren't you worried about the storm?" Jan replied.

"It's not moving very fast so I think we have time; it will still take four days or so to get to us, if it's coming at all," I added, downplaying the danger.

We spent the afternoon diving along several reefs and I managed to grab a couple of spiny lobster for the BBQ. By the time we arrived back at the boat, the sun was ready to set and the best news was that Hurricane Flossie had run headlong into her kryptonite in the form of a cold wind shear that sucked the life out of her while she was still 1000 miles out. Born from a wave off the coast of Africa on July 21, Flossie migrated across the Caribbean and the Panama Peninsula; by August 10, she was declared a hurricane. By August 11, she had mutated into a category four storm of monstrous proportions, but by the 16th, Flossie's remnants brushed by the Big Island with hardly a whimper. Hawaii, by a fluke of nature, dodged a bullet and thankfully, so had we. The winds were disorganized over the following few days but tucked close into the Na Pali, we hardly noticed.

Jan and I spent the next few days, snorkeling the reefs, exploring up the coast with the help of *Fishkiller* and laying naked on deck or on our private beach. We had seen boats off in the distance but none that paid us any attention. One day we awoke to the sound of distant explosions. After heading topside, we watched as several warships, cruising just a few miles to the west, fired their big guns at some distant targets.

Our third day at anchor, we had some visitors; Tom and Beverly and their friends paddled by. They stopped in briefly to say hello and to thank us again for saving them. It was late in the day and they couldn't stay, but they did invite us to a BBQ planned for the following weekend in Waimea if we could make it. It wasn't likely, but we appreciated the invite nonetheless.

Nights on the Na Pali Coast were magical! As the sun set on the hills behind us, they shone gold; they were the last mountains to see the sun each and every day in the islands. At night, we could hear the braying of feral goats that lived high up in the hills.

On our last day, I went shore alone and climbed up the mountain as high as I dared. From my lofty perch, I took a series of photos that encompassed the full length of the nearby Barking Sands and the southern portions of the rugged Na Pali Coast. In addition, off in the distance, the volcanic isle of Niihau sat mute and forbidding. We were loving every moment of our time here and I was thankful that Jan and I could share it together, but I still had twinges of guilt for not permitting

Melissa to come back. She was missing all this and I was truly starting to believe that I had made a mistake. Regardless, we would spend one more night here before moving on. Where to I wasn't quite sure at that moment, but the urge to venture further west was strong.

Chapter #28

The Forbidden Island of Niihau

I am tormented with an everlasting itch for things remote, I love to sail forbidden seas, and land on barbarous coasts.

Herman Melville

From *Maiatla's* anchorage at the base of the great cliffs of the Napali Coast, Niihau could been seen off in the distance, hovering above the sea as if the island owned no terrestrial roots; a mere charcoal smudge on a pale blue horizon that would, from time to time, melt-in with the distant clouds, vanishing as if sucked up, into the sky, only to reappear un-expectedly between whipping mares' tails. Even from our vantage point, the island appeared enchanted and wildly hostile. Niihau was known as the Forbidden Island and if this moniker wasn't enough to entice me to cross the sea between it and us, the sight of her now would have been enough.

"We aren't supposed to go there are we? Don't you need special permission to go to that Island?" Jan asked, as we sat in the cockpit eating our morning toast while sipping on cups of Red Rose.

The morning sun was still hiding behind the towering cliffs and would be for some time. The shade cast by the mountains was cool; the deck was still glistening with the morning's dew.

"We have been lucky so far and haven't been harassed by the authorities for any of the illegal anchoring that we have been doing," Jan continued. "Might going there force them into saying something to us. Couldn't we get in a lot of trouble if we go there without permission?"

"That's what I heard, but that charter boat guy I met in Port Allen last week said that they sometimes take dive charters out to the little Island of Lehua, off the tip of Niihau and they didn't need permission for that. He said they have a submerged mooring buoy in the lee of the island that they tie up too. He said we can use it to stay overnight there."

Jan has all ways been the prudent voice in our duet, the cautious one, and I understood her concern, but this Island had been caught in a time warp and I wanted to see what all the fuss was about.

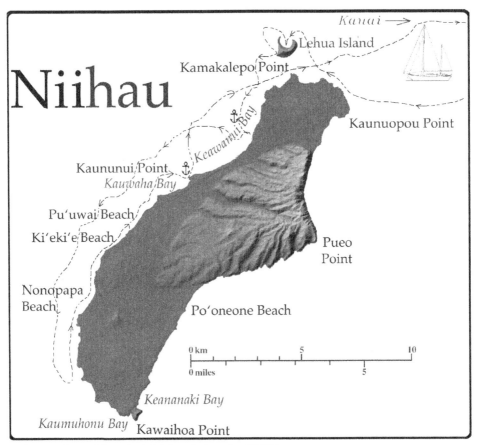

Figure 27. **The forbidden island of Niihau.**

"I was just thinking that we can go out there, sail around Niihau and have a look, then spend a couple of nights at Lehua before coming back. Could be some good diving on that little crater, it looks just like Molokini except without all the tourists. So what do you say, Babe? Want to go? I think we should, we have come this far and we can see what most never will!"

I could see that Jan was reluctant, but after a little more verbal prodding, she relented. By 10:00 a.m. I had retrieved the stern and bow ground tackle and we were motoring out of Kauai's wind shadow and crossing the boisterous 27 kilometer (17 mile) Kaulakahi channel to our next destination. This stretch of sea not only separates Niihau physically from the rest of the island chain by miles, but also by 100 years in human cultural evolution and progress.

The tradewinds were still blowing strong and we had *Maiatla's* sails set for a run with the headsail poled out to starboard. It felt good to be back under sail and headed somewhere new. I was excited about the crossing but as I looked behind us at the two to three meter (6 to 10 feet) white caps that had filled in once we cleared the protective shore, I started to wonder if I would regret the decision to make this crossing.

We were due back on Kauai in eight days to pick up Maui Mike and Kara. This would necessitate our beating back, up-wind, into these strong winds and big seas; it would be a hard slog to windward, and we would have little choice in the matter. The only other option would be to put the boat on a comfortable heading and make a couple of long tacks which would probably take us 80 kilometers (50 miles) or more offshore of Kauai; turning what should be a four-hour crossing into an overnighter. Not the best use of our time, but infinitely more comfortable and ultimately easier on us and the boat, but I wouldn't have to make this decision for at least a couple of days.

Niihau is the seventh largest of the inhabited Hawaiian Islands, having an area of 115 square kilometers (70 square miles) encompassing some specular sand beaches and all just a short 17nm southwest of Kauai. Niihau has a declining population of around 130 souls who claim to possess mostly Hawaiian blood and speak Hawaiian as a primary language with English as a backup. Most of the population is living in a pair of rural villages located on the southwestern or west-central side of the island, with the remainder scattered about the relatively flat land covered in scrub bush. Some islanders support themselves largely by subsistence fishing and farming. Others depend on welfare, but all lead a rural, low-tech life, much as their ancestors did.

Niihau has no telephone service or automobiles. Horses are the main form of transportation with bicycles coming in as a strong second. There are no power lines; solar power provides all electricity and water comes from rainwater catchment. There is no hotel or general store on the island, but a weekly barge delivers groceries from Kauai. Residents are permitted radios and televisions, although poor reception effectively limits the latter to watching VHS tapes and DVDs. In the past, the residents were not permitted newspapers, and most books were banned but these restrictions have since been lifted as well.

Niihau was purchased in 1864 from the Kingdom of Hawaii and the Island has been under private ownership ever since. The Island is generally off-limits to all but relatives of the Island's owners: the Robinson family, U.S. Navy and government officials personnel and invited guests. All these restriction caused Niihau to be given the nickname "The Forbidden Isle". Being an arid island, Niihau was barren of trees for centuries and as reported by Captain Cook in 1778, the Island was treeless but after falling into private hands, new owners planted 10,000 trees per year for many years. The forestation project fundamentally changed the climate of the Island with increased rainfall as an added benefit.

Beginning in 1987, a limited number of supervised activity tours and hunting safaris have been opened to some well-heeled or connected tourists as many exotic species such as eland and aoudad are abundant, along with oryxes, wild boars and feral sheep were introduced for just that purpose. Despite the loosening of the rules in this regard, many restrictions are still enforced in an effort to preserve what remains of the original Hawaiian language and culture.

I found it interesting that this little island has an unusual claim to fame because the Islanders took what was reported to be the first Japanese prisoner of war within hours of the start of the Second World War. The Niihau Incident, as it was dubbed started when a Japanese fighter pilot named Airman First Class Shigenori Nishikaichi, crash-landed on the island as he attempted to return to his aircraft carrier after the attack on Pearl Harbour. The locals captured him, confiscating his papers and belongings, but the would-be Japanese war ace escaped and after salvaging a machine-gun from his downed air craft, a Mitsubishi A6M2 type 0, or what is better known as a Zero, Nishikaichi enlisted the aid of a pair of Japanese Americans, a married couple and terrorized the relatively defenseless and isolated islanders. For the better part of a week, a drama fit for the movies ended when the islanders devised a trap which resulted in the death of the pilot. As for his Japanese collaborators, the husband committed suicide and the wife was sentenced to jail for their trouble.

On closer inspection, Niihau proved my first observations of her to be wrong; she did possess terrestrial roots in the form of a shallow reef that reached out to greet us as we approached its northernmost point of land. This part of the island had not been visible from Kauai because the land was low and down below the horizon. From a distance, the island had appeared much smaller than it really was.

The crescent-shape of Niihau's closest neighbor, Lehua, came into view as we worked *Maiatla* around the perimeter of the island. A mere kilometer (.75 mile) of water separates the two islands with a shallow, boulder-strewn reef just below the surface that later, made for spectacular snorkeling. Lehua, is barren and uninhabited with a land mass of approximately 300 acres and is designated as a State Seabird Sanctuary. The tiny island rises like a fortress to 215 m (704 feet) above sea level and is part of the extinct Niihau volcano, located at the south end of the island.

The water around Lehua became rougher as we rounded its northernmost limit; the ocean swells rebounded off the cliffs to create a crisscross pattern of wave action which caused *Maiatla* to wobble and roll sporadically. I was hoping to anchor and snorkel in the crater, as we had done on Molokini, but the waves that were pounding in made this impossible. We handed (furled) all the sails and motored *Maiatla* into the crater, to snap some pictures and to see if we could spot any wildlife on the towering cliffs. However, we were out of luck, aside from a few birds hovering about and the odd, scraggly shrubs. The brown crumbling rock seemed devoid of life, without even a lazy seal lounging about or a sunning gecko.

We traced the shore until reaching the far side, where a great split in the island appeared. The narrow gash passed straight through the island with the sea freely flowing through it. At the top a natural stone causeway bridged the gap. The "keyhole", as it is locally known, looked high enough for us to pass under, even with *Maiatla's* tall spars, but the white water surging through killed any thoughts of attempting it. The west side proved to be somewhat calmer as we slowly motored along. The brown rock, streaked with white bird droppings, rose straight up from the sea and every so often, the ceilings of submerged tunnels or lava tubes could be seen as the passing swells dropped the water level along the cliff face.

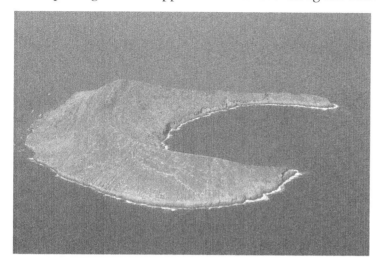

Figure 28.

The island bird sanctuary Lehua.

We found the location where the charter boat guy had said there was a mooring buoy, in an indent in the island where a large sea cave was visible.

Jan took the helm and throttled down as I donned my snorkeling gear, stripped off my shorts and jumped. The water was warm, but deep, dark and cloudy. I could not see the bottom that our depth sounder said was just 30 meters (100 feet) below. I swam to within 20 meters (60 feet) of the cliffs, where the float, three meters (10 feet) below the surface, should have been - but it wasn't. I paralleled the shore for some distance one way, then the other without luck. The wall of the island was surprisingly devoid of marine life and coral, most likely the result of Kona storms (seasonal cyclones) sweeping this side of the island clean. I was about to head over to one of the sea caves for a peek, but I suddenly felt rather exposed and vulnerable as inexplicably my senses were on high alert. As I hovered on the surface, I spun around, half expecting to see some sea creature sneaking up behind me, but as I turned, I saw nothing; the creature was either very quick or just beyond my vision. The visibility was hazy, because of all the tiny bubbles whipping about in the rebounding waves, which un-nerved me all the more

Maybe I was having a flashback of my snorkel around the back end of Molokini when that big shark came in! Or perhaps I was actually being watched from the deep by a creature I could not see. Whatever it was, I was done swimming. I signaled Jan and swam back into deep water where the bottom first dropped to 100, then 300 meters (330 to 1000 feet). I swam out to meet the boat, all the while carefully watching the empty black water below me. A sense of relief filled me as I quickly scooted up the boarding ladder.

"Sorry Babe, can't find the buoy. Either I misunderstood where he said it was, or it has since been carried away. Either way, we aren't staying here for the night. It's too deep to anchor properly and rather rough anyway."

"So where are we going to go for the night? It will be dark by the time we get back to Kauai!" Jan said.

As I looked past our bow, I pointed. "There! We can tuck into that big indent in Niihau by that beach and anchor for the night. If anyone says anything, I'll tell them we were exhausted and needed to rest or that we were having engine troubles, they won't turn away sailors in distress," I said.

Jan drove as I pulled up the charts and pick an approach to the beach over the reef. As we closed on the shore I scanned the several miles of sand dunes for signs of a welcoming committee, but none was forthcoming, or so I thought.

The water shoaled to 10 meters (30 feet), and a flat coral bed with its various shades of whites and blues became visible. Quite the change from the forbidding shores of nearby Lehua. Spooked by *Maiatla's* shadow, colorful fish darted between the boulders or hid under ledges. I didn't notice him at first, and I have no idea when he had spotted us, but if I had taken a moment to look over my shoulder I would have seen that we were being followed by one of the fellows that own this stretch of otherwise uninhabited beach. We came within 100 meters (330 feet) of the shore and found a large sandy patch. Jan throttled down as I went forward to drop the hook, but before I could, our "tail" pulled up alongside, startling Jan in the process.

"Hey Andy! We have company! Look at this!" She called, excitedly.

I turned to look at our unexpected host. He was at least two meters long (seven feet), was brown, almost black with big brown eyes, long whiskers and nostrils that flared when he breathed. The monk seal was alone and apparently, he followed us in to check us out!

"Ah, he's cute! I'll get my camera for a picture," Jan said as she darted below.

I launched the hook, letting 50 meters (160 feet) of chain rattle out before snubbing up the chain and locking the windlass in place. If all the noise and commotion upset our visitor, he gave no indication of it; he continued to float alongside, apparently amused by our activities.

Jan returned to the deck and started to take pictures while I backed the boat down to set the ground tackle. Satisfied we were fast, I shut the engine down.

"Look at him, he's beautiful, and he's not the least bit afraid." Jan suggested from behind the view finder. "What do you think he would do if we got in the water with him?" Think he would stay?"

The animal was just a few meters away and it was intent on watching us.

"Don't know but there is only one way to find out!" I said, as I grabbed my mask and leapt overboard.

When I had cleared the water from my mask, I was surprised to see the seal, three meters away, bobbing up and down on the surface, just as I was. He or she didn't appear the least bit concerned about sharing his aquatic turf with me; we both just bobbed while staring at each other for several minutes.

"Hey! You don't have any shorts on! You better hope he doesn't think you're dangling some bait! You still have some tender, white bits you know - that might attract him!" Jan said while chucking to herself.

"Yeah thanks!" I said. "Don't worry, I'll watch myself!"

I reached out and began to swim slowly towards the seal in an effort to touch him, but our friend was not that trusting; he did a slow back paddle, keeping an eye on me while staying an arm's length out of reach. I swam faster… and so did he.

Before long, I was frantically finning after him and he would playfully dart around, forcing me to display my relative awkwardness in the water. After half an hour, I was tired so I retreated to the boarding ladder with my new friend right behind me. We would spend the better part of a week here and every day around 9:00 a.m. the monk seal would appear as if he were coming for breakfast. He would hang about for a bit. Some days, Jan and I would swim with him and when we did, he stayed until we tired and retreated to the boat, then he would vanish for the day to leave us in our solitude.

Figure 29.

Our friendly Monk Seal that came for a visit every morning.

Marine biologists have long assumed that monk seals mostly fed close to shore, in the shallow reefs teaming with fish. However, using electronic sensors and cameras attached to the monk seals' backs, biologists were surprised to discover that these strong and agile swimmers actually bypass shallow reefs to spend weeks at a time in the open ocean, ranging as far as 65 kilometers (40 miles) from shore and diving at astonishing depths of up to 500 meters, (1650 feet) where not even sunlight penetrates.

Hunting in these deep, dark cold, waters, the Hawaiian monk seals use their snouts and heads to overturn rocks weighing up to ten kilos (22 pounds) on the ocean bottom, flushing out various fish, eels, and octopus on which they feed. Another advantage the monk seal has at these depths is that deep waters are shark free. Although adult monk seals are agile enough to evade shark attacks, the deep water reduces the threat of attack. It's the same trick used by green sea turtles who also have learned to dive to great depths and sleep, as they slowly float back to the surface. After these long and solitary hunting forays in the open ocean, the Hawaiian monk seal returns to the warm, sunny beaches of Niihau and Kauai to rest. Exhausted, they often sleep for days in the sand just above the surf, soaking up the sun.

As I scanned the beach for signs of life I couldn't help but wonder what life was like here. Living on this parched strip of land like the ancient Hawaiians, choosing to live their lives like in the days of old, struggling to survive in these modern times on what must be a fragile island that has come close to being blown away as man had decimated its delicate ecosystem.

A sailing boat on the high seas likewise may seem fragile and vulnerable, but like an island, it is complete in itself, self-contained and self-sufficient. It has to be because of the surrounding water. A boat is a movable island and just to see her seize the wind, canting to the invisible forces, projects an image of power, freedom and mystery. A singly isolated kingdom with her captain as king or queen, unquestioned and unchallenged and fully in command. Sailing off is to have the whole world to yourself, where you can do as you please, making your own rules while fulfilling your own private vision or fantasy. I suspect that in many ways, living on an island, like this island of Niihau is like living on a boat, equally freeing and imprisoning all at the same time.

Keawanui Bay was the quintessential tropical anchorage. A beach devoid of human footprints ran for 2.5 kilometers (1.5 miles) in either direction with white dunes rolling up to greet the keave forest, 50 meters (165 feet) back from the gentle surf. The curvature of the island shielded us from the constant ocean swell, leaving our home to drift about on a millpond-like sea, and I was happy not to have to set the dreaded stern hook. During our weeklong stay, we saw, at a distance, four people.

The evening of our first night, Jan and I were having a glass of wine in the cockpit waiting for the sun to set when we noticed an open jeep sitting atop of a nearby sand dune. There were three men in it, holding rifles and they were watching us. I was a little nervous; we were definitely within shooting range. We don't normally carry firearms aboard, so we had none on this voyage, so returning fire if fired upon, was not an option. Nervously, I watched them through my binoculars, but to my relief, after a few minutes they waved and drove off, never to be seen again.

"What do you think they were doing with guns way out here?" Jan asked.

"I guess they were hunting something. Hunting what, I don't know. And I don't really care, just as long it's not cruisers!"

We settled back down to our wine and to watch the last of the day fade, As we did, the answer to Jan's question strolled down the beach.

"Oh look, Andy! There's a big dog on the beach!" Jan said, pointing towards shore.

"That is a strange looking dog, its front end looks awful heavy," Jan noted.

I took up the binoculars for a closer look.

"Well, that's because that ain't no dog! I said, excitedly. "That's a wild boar and a damn big one at that! I can see its tusks from here!"

The boar was huge and must have weighed over 200 kilograms (440 pounds) and old and smart enough to wait until dusk to come out into the open. We watched as the boar rooted his way along the beach, passing the spot where the hunters had stopped, an hour before.

The only other person we saw during our time on the island was a lone fisherman, a rustic looking fellow who materialized out of the bush a couple of days after our arrival. Jan and I were snorkeling in the buff at a point midway along the island in a tide pool created by the reef. Our fisherman was riding a rather large horse along the shore and every 50 meters (160 feet) or so he would stop, cast a net into the water, retrieve the net full of tiny fish and move on. We were bobbing on the surface nearby as he passed, waving as he went. Jan remarked that he resembled a Gaucho , a Mexican cowboy, and if he resented our presence or offended by our state of undress, he neglected to tell us.

That same morning we awoke to find a rather precocious Brown Booby perched upon the pulpit. The huge seabird permitted me to creep ever closer until he was an arm's length away, allowing me to take several pictures before flying off.

The reef along this stretch of coast was fun to explore as it was made up of layers of old lava flows covered in coral. The bottom was mostly flat, but there were trenches two to three meters (6 to 10 feet) deep that led from shore out to deep water. Between the trenches there were many "potholes", one to ten meters (3 to 30 feet) in diameter and if you dove down into them you would often find that there were connected to adjacent potholes by underwater tunnels. The entire seabed was honeycombed with tunnels and we soon learned that this was where the really big fish hung out. Jan freaked out the first time she saw me dive down and disappear into one of the potholes; she didn't see me pop out of another hole, ten meters behind her. She was already anxious because I had not re-emerged, so when I swam up from behind her and grabbed her arm….. Well I caught shit, for scaring her first by disappearing, then for grabbing her unexpectedly.

Janet had truly learned to love snorkeling, and this was a perfect spot for a novice; it was only one to three meters (3 to 10 feet) deep over much of the reef. When she tired, we would resort to "sledding". Sledding is great fun and easy to do. I would take our flat bosom's chair and secure it to a long line, the swimmer with mask and snorkel would hang onto the seat, holding it flat in front of them and use it like a wing to dive or sore from side to side as the dinghy sped along. I would tow Jan along behind the dink, so she could effortlessly cruise the undersea gardens, releasing her grip and diving down when something of interest caught her eye.

Janet received another fright later in the week and again it was entirely my fault (or so she informed me). We had spent the better part of the day snorkeling and we were both starting to get tired so we agreed to move the dinghy to a new spot for one more swim before heading back to *Maiatla*, laying at anchor, within sight, a good mile away.

After finding an interesting little rock pinnacle, we prepared to enter the water. I donned my mask, fins and grabbed the speargun that I had brought along for the first time.

"What are you going to do with that?" Jan asked immediately, sounding rather concerned.

"Thought I would get a fish for dinner! Been seeing some big amberjacks, you know those big silver, bluish-looking fish that have been hanging around."

"Well, if you are going to be dragging dead fish around, you can go without me!"

Jan was adamant; she did not want to be around when there was blood in the water. Go figure!

"Don't worry, I'll just take the gun along and just before we are ready to get out, I will shoot a fish! OK?".

Jan was not entirely convinced that this was a good idea, but she reluctantly slipped over the side anyway.

It was another beautiful spot with lots of grottoes, coral and colorful fish and after almost an hour Jan indicated that she wanted to return to the dinghy, so we began our swim back. We were just a few meters short of the dinghy when I spotted a large, orange goatfish and it was a perfect BBQ size. I halted Jan and pointed to the fish while giving the cocked pistol and shooting sign. She looked at me, the speargun, then the fish, and then nodded her head. I loaded the gun and fired. It was a good hit but the fish commenced to thrash violently. I grabbed the line and began to retrieve my spear. I could see Jan's wide eyes as she watched the struggling fish. I grabbed the meter (3 foot) long spear and was about to pull the goatfish off, when there was a sliver streak and the spear was suddenly jerked out of my hand! The two-meter (6 to 7 feet)long blacktip reef shark shot right past Jan's face and took my goatfish! I may have pissed, but Janet was gone! I surfaced to see her making a mad dash for the nearby dinghy. As I bobbed there, watching her tear up the water with arms flailing, I knew I was in for it. I cursed aloud, then cursed the shark.

I dove back down to retrieve my spear and gun which I had dropped during all the excitement; both were lying on the bottom and thankfully, the hungry shark was nowhere in sight; but a school of amberjacks were! I quickly reloaded my gun and gave chase. They were quick and I was not, so after several minutes, I gave up and headed back to the dink and to what I knew would be an upset Jan, but apparently I didn't know just how upset.

I made two mistakes that day, the first was obvious: Never, ever shoot fish with your wife at your side. In addition, if you are dumb enough to do so, and you do encounter a shark attack, go back to the dinghy right away! It seems that she may be so upset that she is unable to get back in without your help and thinking that you have been eaten as you had not returned.

All in all, the shark attack notwithstanding, we had a glorious week anchored at Niihau and we were happy that we didn't have to fight off the local cannibals or explain our presence to the big kahunas. We swam, snorkelled and explored, played with seals and photographed big turtles and even bigger boobies. (The winged variety!)

We drank good red wine and dined on fresh fish (Jan never went spearfishing with me again!) and in the evenings, we would cuddle in the cockpit, watch the sunset, read and make love on the deck. Well mostly cuddle and read anyway! It was grand but it was time to go. We would have to pull anchor, find our clothes which we hadn't seen in days and set sail for Nawiliwili Harbour, back on Kauai to fetch our crew for *Maiatla's* return voyage to Canada.

Chapter #29

Wine, Stogies and Fire, A Tribute to the Old Man.

There is nothing quite so good as burial at sea. It is simple, tidy, and not very incriminating.
Alfred Hitchcock.

With the hot wind scorching our cheeks, the Forbidden Island quickly vanished in our wake as we drove closed-hauled to windward with Kauai once again on our port bow. I thought it strange that you could visit a place, love it, and never set a foot ashore; such was our time at Niihau.

We hadn't even cleared the land, when the first of the large swells began to chastise us and in doing so, we discovered all the gear and books that we had neglected to store properly after idling a week at anchor. Upon hearing a series of bangs and crashes, Jan disappeared below to begin stowing the stragglers. I decided to see if I could tempt a fish into dining on a rubber squid.

Maiatla was sailing well with our number two headsail, a double-reefed mainsail, and a full mizzen sail. For up-wind work, a mizzen sail is critical on a ketch; it allows the boat to point higher in the wind.

The sea was pale blue today and every now and then, a coconut drifted by, some with fronds commencing to sprout, others that were olive green and fresh. A result, I assumed, of hurricane Flossie blowing them to sea from some island upwind of us.

We were bound for Port Allen, a short 50 kilometers (30 miles) from our last anchorage, where we planned to spend a couple of days before make a run to Nawiliwili to pick up our crew who were soon due to arrive. By noon, we were sailing off of Waimea Bay; here, my luck changed and we landed a nice tuna. He struck my line fast, and as soon as I had him alongside, Jan took over the rod as I dispatched him with the spear gun, dragging him along behind the boat until he bled out. No fish seems to have as much blood as a tuna. Five litres (10 pints) of blood in a four liter body.

As the afternoon wore on, the wind shifted more to the north, forming an offshore breeze, allowing us to remain close-hauled while hugging the shore on flatter seas. The south coast of Kauai is amazing; the shore is quite low but the land ever-so-slowly gains elevation until a mile or two inland, the land shoots up vertically, dramatically forming the southern shoulder of the Na Pali mountain range; green, fluted and serrated.

"Andy, according to the guidebook, there is a little sheltered bay just after Waimea that we might be able to get into through a cut in the reef," Jan said, as she reclined on the cockpit bench next to me, taking in the sun that shone through the partially open dodger.

"Can I have a look at that?" I asked, while taking the book from her. What looked like nothing more than an indent in the coast was actually a tiny bay, protected by a barrier reef and at the eastern most end, a natural gap in the reef beckoned to me.

Figure 30.

The tuna caught after leaving Niihau breaking my run of bad luck with fishing.

"You know, we might be able to get in there if we are careful, it's calm enough now with this offshore wind," I said. "Let's give it a try!"

Pakala Bay is one of the jewels we discovered. The shore was essentially deserted because there was no easy road access despite being situated between the community of Waimea and Pakala Village located out on the point.

As I brought us in closer, I could see the westerly swell breaking on the outer reef and the calm waters behind it. Off to the far right, was a flat section of water that betrayed the presence of the submerged channel that was to be our path to the inner, shore side of the reef. The place looked perfect for what I had in mind. Ever since we arrived in the islands, I had been looking for just such a piece of Oceania to fulfill a request my younger brother, Greg had made of me just before we departed from home. This would be the perfect place!

It was easy to negotiate the channel as it was wide and with the sun shining over our shoulders, the dark green of the reef stood out, in stark contrast to the white sand bottom of the pass. As soon as we found the calm of the inner lagoon, I set the hook in 10 meters (30 feet) of crystalline water just beyond the ruins of a tiny quay that must have had difficulty staying above water on a high tide. Surprisingly, it was so calm that a stern hook was not even necessary, which just delighted me; ah, but the Admiral not so much, as she still thought that I should set one, you know - just in case. After I promised to set the stern hook if conditions changed, Jan relented to my pleas.

As it was getting late, we just settled in. Jan began to rustle up some supper while I dragged the cooler to the foredeck to clean my long overdue fish. Jan cooked pasta and sauce which I devoured but Jan focused on the raw tuna dipped liberally in wasabi sauce. After dinner, we retired to the cockpit to watch the sunset. In addition to the usual evening spectacle, the floor show commenced!

We had anchored directly in the center of the cut in the reef with two meter (6 foot) waves breaking on the shallows, just twenty meters (65 feet) away, on both sides of the boat. The knot of teenage boys on surfboards were pleased to show off for us as they took turns surfing right past *Maiatla*, waving and gesturing as they went. The boys performed as long as the daylight lasted and only quit when it became too dark to make out the beach a scant 100 meters (330 feet) away.

We rose very late the next morning, for no particular reason. We packed a shore bag taking the camera, water, a few snacks, and a package my brother Greg had given me. We landed *Fishkiller* next to the old stone quay and set about exploring. The beach was isolated from the road by several acres of private lands which is what limited the public access. On the south end of the beach was the little community of Pakala which looked more like a collection of retirement homes and aside from a few old people wandering about, two young children and a stray dog, there was little life. However, of more interest to us was the half- mile of deserted sand beach with reaching palms and bushes crowding the water's edge; a little piece of Polynesian heaven that arched to the northwest. It was here I would carry out my brother's request.

It was early afternoon by the time we had found a sandy spot beneath a coconut palm next to the water. I scrounged up some dry bush, leaves, and set about making a little fire. As I squatted next to the growing fire, Jan dug into the dry-bag and pulled out a bottle of red wine, a baggie containing a single cigar (White Owl Brand) and a sealed jar, which she placed in the sand beside me..

It had been almost eight years since my father had passed away, despite his demise he had accompanied me on every journey we had undertaken in *Maiatla*. When he passed, he was cremated and each of his four children took some of the ashes along with a few bottles of his home-brew red wine, and in Greg's case, a box of the Old Man's cigars, which he would later smoke on very special occasions. At the commencement of this voyage, Greg had given me his last bottle of our Dad's wine, his share of our father's ashes and the last cigar along with a request to find a nice beach, on which to sprinkle the old man's ashes, smoke the cigar and drink the wine.

Neither Jan nor I said much as I twisted the lid off of the jar and sprinkled the ashes along the beach. That done, I pulled the cork from the bottle and filled a pair of fine long stemmed wine glasses (OK acrylic! They survive longer on a boat!). I do not smoke and as the old stogie was as dried out as King Tut's pecker, I ceremoniously place it in the fire. We took up our glasses, toasted my father, and then drank. Well I drank, Jan instantly spit her sip back out.

"Ah God, that is awful!" she stammered, choking. "Give me the bottle of water out of the bag will ya, I need to rinse my mouth out."

OK, the wine had gone bad but out of respect for my old man, I did my best to make an attempt to drink the bottle.

Figure 31.

My father's beach on Kauai.

We sat together, talking little, watching the smoldering stogies turn into ashes. The power that smells have to evoke vivid memories, is well understood, so I was not surprised that the aroma of the Old White Owl enticed, from deep within my vault, comforting memories of my father.

Over the next hour, while Jan went about hunting for seashells, I took delicate sips and cringed.

As is usually the case, the second and third glasses of normally biting booze goes down a little smoother than the first, but not in this case. By the time Jan returned, half the bottle was gone and I was saddened that I couldn't stomach any more. Chugging a liter of Buckley's Cough syrup would have been more pleasurable!

"So, you ready to head back to the boat yet or are you really going to stay here and try to finish that?" she asked, looking none too patient.

"Yea I'm done; the wine's a bit too rough, even for me," I replied.

Thinking that I would be able to douse the fire and get rid of the remaining wine at the same time, I poured the bottle on the fire. The resulting explosion of blue flames scared the crap out of me! Apparently, some wine turns to vinegar, others mutate into pure alcohol which would explain my staggering down the beach and subsequent force 12 headache later that evening. As my mission was now complete, we up-anchored not so early the next morning, and carried on to our next stop.

Chapter #30

Kona Coffee and Wahiawa; the Bay That Bleeds.

Avoiding danger is no safer in the long run than outright exposure. Life is either a daring adventure or nothing.-Helen Keller

The morning winds were light, so much so that we had to motor for the first hour, making our run up to Port Allen, by all accounts uneventful, if you didn't include that one single moment of utter terror.

Auto was driving and Jan was down below messing about with something domestic in nature. I was in a very happy place sitting in my helm seat, feet up on the bench sipping my morning tea while admiring the finer homes along this particular part of the shore. We were perhaps half a mile from land, in deep water and according to the chart, well clear of all obstacles. Every once in a while I would glance at the chart plotter and *Maiatla's* position on it, the depth sounder, and the radar in search of anything that may be creeping up on us, or for anything amiss. I had just completed my visual rounds and was quite sure that all was well, when suddenly, as I glanced over the side… I could see the sea-bottom right next to the boat! My heart dropped into my stomach as I feared that we were about to run hard aground; and at seven knots it would be very hard indeed!

In a panic, my tea flew as I grabbed the throttle and gear shift, throwing the engine into full reverse! *Maiatla's* prop tore up the water! The roar of the cavitation echoed through the boat bring Jan topside in an instant.

"What's the matter Andy?" she called, eyes wide. "Better grab something and hang on, I think we are about to run onto a reef!" I shouted back at her.

Jan braced herself in the companionway as I stood at the helm holding my breath, fighting off the urge to turn the boat seaward while impatiently waiting for

Maiatla to come to a full stop. *Maiatla* began to turn to starboard as the prop-walk tried to slew our stern around; I stopped her by counter-steering, keeping us on a straight course. Seconds passed as we slowed, until coming to a complete standstill amidst a radiating ring of foam and bubbles caused but the churning propeller. I again began to breathe.

"Sorry Babe! But we just ran over a shallow spot, I didn't want to hit bottom," I finally said, as beads of sweat trickled down my forehead.

From my place at the helm, I could still see the bottom, and not wanting to head the wrong way, I left my seat to have a look. I stepped out on deck and stared down into the perfectly clear water all the way to the bottom, but it now looked a lot deeper than I had first thought. I glanced back at the depth sounder and it said that the water was over 25 meters (80 feet) deep, but that couldn't be right! Again, I stared down, into the sea, first beside us then behind at our frothy wake. It took me several minutes and some back tracking to convince myself that there never was a shallow spot, but the incredibly clear water had created an optical illusion that caused the bottom to appear as if it was just below the surface. Upon realizing this, Jan laughed then made some derogatory remark about my senility, before heading back below to whatever she was doing before I put the emergency brakes on. I think it took half an hour for my heart rate to return to normal.

When coastal cruising, running aground is always a danger and if you sail long enough, you will strike bottom at one time or another. Running aground can be caused by complacency, simply not paying attention or you may just have the wrong information. While cruising Mexico, it wasn't unusual to find islands and reefs up to two miles off as plotted on the charts. In the Sea of Cortez, we often anchored for the night and the computerized chart showed us parked in the desert or even in a town square a mile inland. I have only struck bottom once with *Maiatla*, in La Paz harbour, the cause of which was shifting channel markers (my story and I'm sticking to it!). Thankfully there was no damage and we got off with the combined help of sail and engine power after plowing a trench through the soft mud bank. I also struck bottom three times with our previous boat, our old Columbia 36'. Fortunately, the first two times were on muddy bottoms, resulting in no damage and we were back off in a short while. However, the third time we struck bottom with the Columbia, we were not so fortunate.

Back in 1983, my father and I were doing a bit of winter sailing. The conditions were blustery with a bit of snow whipping about. We were headed for Jedediah Island out in the middle of the Strait of Georgia, in British Columbia. A friend had told us of a tiny anchorage at the head of a deep cut that ran into the island. There were many deep cuts that looked like possible anchorages. My father was standing lookout on the bow, staring straight down looking for rocks; I watched the depth sounder while bringing the boat in at a speed best described as a crawl. We were about 80 meters (250 feet) from shore with the sounder reading 30 meters (100 feet) of water, but getting shallow slowly. I had just called forward to tell my dad to keep a sharp lookout and when I glanced back at the sounder, it was reading 3 METERS! Before I could even react, my dad yelled back, "Rocks!"

Apparently, I had missed the bay my friend had described and turned into the wrong one - my first mistake.

I quickly threw the engine into full reverse and this is when I made my second mistake - I turned to starboard. The boat swung 90 degrees but we struck solid rock before completing the turn, not with the strongest part of the boat, the bow, but with the fragile spade rudder. The tiller was jerked from my hand as the rock pinned the rudder all the way over. I could hear cracking fiberglass as the boat healed onto the rocks - the worst sound to hear on a fiberglass boat, a sickening, bowel loosening sound.

Thankfully, the offshore wind carried us back offshore, off the rock; once in deeper water, I dropped the anchor to inspect the damage. The rudder took the brunt of the impact, it would swing to starboard, but when I tried turning to port, it got stuck along the centerline of the boat. We were a long way from home and any possibility of a tow; we had to fix the damage ourselves. I dug the mask and snorkel out of the lazerette and dressed only in a t-shirt and jockey shorts, slipped over the side into water that was hovering just above freezing. I found our rudder shaft bent to starboard by 20 degrees and backward by another 10 degrees. The backward bend that prevented the rudder from turning from port to starboard. Over the next hour, using a hacksaw, while freezing to death, I methodically cut away the upper portion of the rudder blade to regain steerage. I don't think my core temperature returned to normal until 9 hours later, when I got back home and sat in front of a roaring fire clutching a stiff rum. I learned my lesson that day, to take the collision "head-on" to protect the boat's soft underbelly. If Captain Smith had done likewise and had taken the iceberg on the nose, perhaps the Titanic would have survived!

Historically known as Eleele Landing, Port Allen Harbor is located on the southern shores of Kauai, about 28 kilometers (18 miles) west-southwest of Nawiliwili. Located on the shores of Hanapepe Bay, Port Allen Harbor is near the town of Eleele, with a population of about two thousand, and Hanapepe, home to over 2100 people and one of a handful of towns in Hawaii that was not created by the establishment of sugar plantations. The port acquired its modern name in the early 1900s when the Kauai Railway, a narrow gauge railroad, connected Eleele Landing with Koloa and Kalaheo on Kauai's south coast. At that time, the railway changed the name to Port Allen Harbor in honor of Samuel Allen. Allen had provided much of the funding to improve and expand Port Allen Harbor of which he personally received a great benefit.

As Kauai's second commercial harbor, the port's principal function is the shipping, receiving and storage of liquid bulk cargoes, mainly petroleum products and liquid fertilizers in nine storage tanks at the rear of the pier. The harbour is also extensively used for the mooring of excursion, charter, and military vessels. It was here that the charter boat captain had given me the lowdown on sailing to Niihau. The United States' Pacific Missile Range Facility and Naval Undersea Warfare Engineering Station also maintain a large warehouse here full of who knows what. And as seen on our road trip, the Port Allen Small Boat Harbor is located some 122 meters (400 feet) north of the Port Allen Harbor Pier. The Small Boat Harbor reports having six moorings with 34 berths and a two-lane launch ramp and a loading dock. The harbor office and public restrooms are located here, all of which we found in typically deplorable condition.

By the time we were within eight kilometers (five miles) of the Port Allen breakwater, the wind was gusting to well over 30 knots; the force seven winds kicked up a nasty chop and smashed us right on the nose. With the engine alone, we weren't gaining much ground and to make matters worse, we were getting pummelled and were forced to close the hatches because spray was constantly exploding over the boat. To ease our suffering, we hoisted some sail and made a series of long tacks offshore, up to 30 kilometers (20 miles), just to make headway against the wind, waves and strong west-setting current. It was almost dark by the time we slipped in behind the rubble wall and found a spot to anchor between the State's small vessel docks and the light aircraft airport. The holding was good which proved fortunate as the wind howled all night and most of the next day. Port Allen was definitely not a place to be during a tropical storm. Even in these conditions, waves were exploding against the rubble wall and from the looks of it, it wouldn't take much of a storm surge to overwhelm the sea wall.

We landed by dink in the morning to check out the facilities. The harbor master was friendly but not the least bit interested in checking us in or collecting an anchoring fee, which suited us just fine. He did give us permission to bring *Maiatla* alongside their concrete loading dock to take on water and to leave her there while we went into town to shop for groceries. It had been almost two weeks since seeing the inside of a store, so many of our supplies were running low. My rum cache desperately need restocking!

The loading dock and boat launch were busy for most of the day as sports fishermen, both charter and private boats alike were constantly coming and going. And of course, there were the ubiquitous chickens getting under foot and making a nuisances of themselves as they had staked a claim to the grassy park and parking lots. In fact, there were chickens and territorial roosters everywhere, perhaps more here than anywhere else we had seen on the island.

It was apparent that having a vessel like *Maiatla* alongside was a rarity, as we became quite an attraction. Feeling something like celebrities of sorts, Jan and I fielded a steady barrage of typical questions as we gave the boat a freshwater bath. Many people asked us where was our crew? However, when I informed them that we didn't have one, that we were sailing with just the two of us, they were very surprised and I guess impressed that we could handle such a large boat all by ourselves. After our boat chores and provisioning were completed, we took a stroll along the shore, east of the harbour. We found a "No Trespassing" sign, next to an unauthorized trail that cut thought the tank farm. On the far side of the tank farm, we could see the ocean, after a little coaxing, Jan and I ventured forth.

We found the shore quite rocky, and it dropped off abruptly down to the water; a sheer cliff of three or more meters (10 plus feet). The tide was out, exposing many tide pools perfect for exploring. It was obvious that this site had been a commercial center for a very long time as scattered in the rocks and pools were countless bit of old machinery, engine blocks, vehicle frames and other unrecognizable congealed masses of rusting iron. I had also noticed when scanning the harbour chart that somewhere out there, just beyond the breakers were a pair of shipwrecks, and I suspected that some of this debris could be accounted for by their presence, but I doubt that they were responsible for all.

Here, as it was in many other places of the world, the ocean was used as a garbage dump and everything of no value was often cast into the sea. I thought it would be a great place to dive, as you never know what you may find; trash from the past can be today's treasure. Years ago while diving near an old light house on the remote Patos Island in the American San Juans, I found the lightkeeper's old dump site which included miles of old fire hoses and water lines, an air compressor and rusty tin cans buried in the sand. However, what really got me excited was the old Coke and Seven-up bottles that I discovered. Made in Anacortes, Washington in 1932, these little treasures of Americana were lying on the bottom for over half a century just waiting for me to swim along! Unfortunately, along the shore at Port Allen, the waves were pounding in with such force, that diving close to the rocks could prove suicidal; a calmer day was needed for attempting such an adventure.

We spent the rest of the afternoon hiking a trail along the deserted shore, exploring tide-pools, blow holes and sea caves. Just inland of us, the earth was rusty red, rich volcanic soil which was planted with some sort of crop, a low green bush in tidy rows that neither Jan nor I recognized. Whatever plants they were, the fields stretched for miles and way off in the distance stood a mysterious little factory with its tall, single brick smoke stack. The plant looked deserted as not a wisp of smoke could be seen from the stack nor could we see any movement on the grounds. The old red brick plant looked intriguing but it was a much farther walk than I was prepared to make this day.

We felt like we had hiked for miles along the twisting shoreline, but in reality we were just over half a mile from the tank farm with the town just beyond. As we rounded another bend, the shore cut far inland creating a beautiful little bay with a black sand beach at the head. A small stream emerged from a clump of trees and bush, to trickling over the sands, to mingle with the calm waters. Despite having huge breaking waves on either side of the mouth of the bay, the inner waters of Wahiawa Bay were pond-quiet. I was surprised to find that the place was utterly deserted! This bay wasn't even mentioned as a possible anchorage in harbour master Al's, list of designated anchorages; but in all likelihood, it fell into the 72-hour category.

"Ah Jan! Look at that, isn't this nice?

Jan moved closer to the shore to snap some pictures.

"It's beautiful but why isn't it mentioned in the cruising guidebook? I wonder if its private property and you aren't allowed to anchor here? Do you think we can get in here?" she asked, as she studied the white-water surging around the entrance.

"If its deep enough I don't see why not. I'll check the chart when we get back to the boat and if it is, I think we should move over here tomorrow and stay a couple of days. What do you think?" I asked.

"I think you better check with the harbor master and ask if its OK. I don't want us to get into trouble," she said.

"Well he didn't seem to care one way or the other about us being in the harbor so why would he care if we come here? I think we should just move, you know what they say, it's easier to beg forgiveness than to ask for permission," I offered with a big grin.

"Who says that?" she asked, smiling.

I just shrugged my shoulders, "Don't know, but it sounds appropriate, don't you think?"

By noon the following day, after a few nervous moments cutting between the breaking waves and the rocky horns of the cove, we were peacefully anchored in Wahiawa Bay. At first, I was a bit concerned as the inner part of the bay was quite shallow, *Maiatla* had less than a half a meter (1.5 feet) under her keel at low tide. I donned my snorkeling gear to investigate the bottom. Due to the flow of fresh, muddy stream water, the visibility under the boat was very poor, less than a meter and the water was very dark. As I swam checking the water depth and looking for rocks that could bite *Maitala's* ass, more than once I turned to look behind me, fearful that I was being followed by a hungry shark, lurking in the reddish murk. I spent an hour swimming about, covering most of the center then perimeter of the tiny bay. I returned to the boat satisfied that I had seen all that I needed to.

"So what's it like down there? See anything interesting?" Jan asked as she came topside carrying a towel for me.

I moved forward to the mainmast to stand beneath the black sun shower bag and started the flow of very hot water. We keep the camping shower bag on deck to warm in the sun and we used it to rinse off the salt from our skin and bathing suits (if we wore any); this is how we avoid taking unwanted salt down below after a swim.

"The visibility sucks which is too bad really as there are some incredible coral formations around the mouth of the bay and I found several great boulders of yellow brain coral over there," I said, as I pointed off into the distance.

"Great! But what about under the boat? We going to be OK here? It's really shallow."

I understood Jan's concerned but it wasn't going to be an issue.

"No, it's not going to be a problem," I said as I took the towel from her and began to dry off. "The bottom is really soft, I could stick my arm straight down into the mud and I still couldn't feel a hard bottom. I did a circle around the boat to make sure nothing was sticking up, found nothing. We will be fine," I offered, with all confidence.

We spent the next couple of days relaxing and getting the boat ready for going back offshore which included a repair to wind generator. The day of our arrival at Wahiawa Bay, I looked up into the rigging and was shocked to see the wind generator, canted like a palm tree in a hurricane! The wind generator is mounted on a one-meter (3 foot) long aluminum pole, bolted to the top of the mizzen mast. One of the two half- inch bolts securing it, had sheared off, allowing the generator to pivot on the remaining bolt. Jan hoisted me up the mast using the genoa winch so I could make the necessary repairs to the wind generator. While I was up there, I inspected the rest of the rig and serviced the three connections located in the antenna I use for my Ham radio. Clean connections assured better transmission and reception, a condition most desirable considering we were about to venture off across thousands of miles of open ocean. From the top of the mast, besides having a spectacular view of the surrounding area, I noticed something quite striking. As *Maiatla* spun about her mooring, her keel came so close to the bottom that it she stirred up the bright red mud, leaving a crimson trail that the outgoing tide captured and took seaward. It looked as if we were a knife cutting into the very flesh of the earth, causing it to gush blood.

Figure 32. Jan and *Maiatla* at the Bay that Bleeds.

Our second morning was as tranquil as expected but I awoke to an odd smell that was very pungent but not unpleasant. The aroma of freshly brewed coffee filled our great cabin and as Jan was still by my side and sound asleep, I knew she was not responsible, in fact, I wasn't entirely sure we even had the makings for coffee aboard. I'm not a coffee drinker. I will swill a cup if that's all that's available, but I certainly wouldn't go out of my way for a coffee. After several minutes of sucking it in, I had to go find the source of the great aroma.

I crawled out of bed and headed topside, fully expecting to see another vessel anchored right beside us with its coffeemaker percolating away. I didn't bother putting on shorts as I believed that if anyone were to anchor so close as to be able to see enough of me naked to get offended, then they were anchored too dammed close anyway. It's amazing how the mere sight of a white arse can compel a ship to weigh anchor in the most deplorable conditions, leaving you in peace.

As I stepped into the cockpit I scanned the bay, I was both surprised and pleased that we were still alone, but where was that smell coming from? I went back down below to make tea and breakfast for Jan and I. The strong aroma persisted all day, but by the next morning, the smell was gone. I would later mention the coffee smell to Al when we arrived back at Nawiliwili, he had the solution to our mystery. It would seem that the great fields we had seen were part of a Kona coffee bean plantation and that little factory we saw off in the distance was where they roasted the beans on each and every Friday!

Wahiawa proved to be a jewel and we were very happy to be here; Jan and I were still wallowing in the luxury of being alone and indulging ourselves in each other. We were basking in pure contentment. Some years later while at work, I would remember this feeling as it would be triggered by an unusual conversation.

As a Quality Control Manager, I was at work one day in our field office up in the Oil Sands; things were rather slow and our entire crew was on standby, waiting for the boilermakers to complete their tasks before we could start ours. For the better part of two weeks, we waited, so I took the opportunity to do a little writing. At the time, I was left alone with one of our general foremen who was likewise trying to entertain himself by watching movies on his laptop. It was when he paused his movie to make popcorn that he turned to me.

"So Andy, you still working on that book?" He asked, pointing to my laptop. "When you went out earlier, I read what you had up on the screen and I saw a typo where you were talking about Kara and the birds."

I think most people would have been upset at having someone trespass upon their thoughts while they were still formulating and organizing them. Seeing their scattered or ill-conceived ramblings of the mind before they have achieved any sort of cohesiveness, or reason. I am perhaps as insecure as any writer when it comes to showing my work to others, especially when it's not finished, but this was different; I felt surprised and in a minor way even flattered that he would even show an interest in what I was doing! Besides, I had no one but myself to blame for leaving my computer open for anyone to see, and I guess Andrew's curiosity got the better of him

Andrew was a typical construction bricklayer who worked his way up to supervision through sweat and toil. He started his working life a grunt for the railroads but switched to refractory in his late 20s. He wasn't as coarse around the edges as some and somewhat less abrasive than most construction folk and he bore an air of confidence which his men seemed to like. He was a bit of an enigma to me despite having known him for over four years. We had been on many project together but we were usually on opposite shifts so our contact had always been limited. We truly didn't know anything of each other. At best we could be described as colleges or acquaintances, but certainly not friends as there was no substance between us. This was not necessarily how I wanted it, it was just the way it was. While Andrew snatched his bag of popcorn from the microwave, I thanked him for noticing my error then took a moment to engage in some small talk in an effort to get to know him better and to perhaps eliminate some of the awkward silence that filled the room.

"So Andrew, what are your aspiration for the future? Have any dreams? Goals? Desire to travel?

It was little more in-depth than just small talk but it seemed like a good place to start. He paused from shaking his bag to look at me, I think he was surprised at my question. He smiled as he seemingly pondered. I was expecting a sarcastic blow- me-off remark but it wasn't forthcoming. Instead, I received a remarkably sincere and poignant response.

"You know Andy, I have been asked that a lot, mainly by my girlfriend who I have been with for over seven years and her mother, and you know, I will tell you what I told her. I'm very happy doing what I'm doing. There isn't really another place I want to be and I told her that I don't want kids and if she does she better leave me now."

It was an extraordinarily honest and profound answer full of conviction.

"People have been telling me that I should do other things but I don't want to. I go back to Germany once in a while for a holiday. I work, play the stock market and that's it. I'm happy."

He spent the next few minutes filling me in on some of his life. I don't know if he knew what he was doing but he was gushing details and sentiment. It was as if no-one had ever really cared to ask before. Why he felt safe telling me, I don't know but I'm sure I should have felt honored that he had.

Most people in society would find Andrew's stance rather narrow minded, lacking vision or even downright selfish, but if they did I believe that they would be missing something as they really couldn't have been listen to what Andrew was saying. Aside from the reality that society, the netherworld doesn't have the right to judge this man, I maintain that it doesn't matter what anyone else thinks. He wasn't causing harm so let him be.

I sat back into my chair to mull over what he had just said. As I watched him rip open the steaming bag I realized that he had in his possession something that I always wanted, (not the popcorn although it did smell good). I have grasped it and held it for fleeting moments in my life but it always seemed to wiggle free from my fingers.

"Well you know Andrew, I wouldn't let what other people think you should do get you down, after all it's your life and you are the one who has to live it. As long as you're honest with your girlfriend about who you are and what you want out of life that's all you can do. She will have to decide to do what she thinks is right for her. But you know Andrew, whatever else you do in this life, you have already got what most people wish they had. You have already achieved what all want and most will never get."

I paused for effect and to see if he was actually listening or even cared to hear what I had to say.

He gave a nervous laugh, "Oh yea, what is that? What have I got that everyone else wants?"

I leaned forward again, "One of the hardest things to achieve in this world is personal contentment, and if you have it, be grateful and don't apologize for it as you are way ahead of most of the rest of us."

If he took to this heart I do not know. He went back to his chair to restart his movie and to finish his popcorn. I watched him for a few moments, it might have been imagined on my part, but he looked to be more at peace with himself, perhaps from having someone, even if it was a veritable stranger to vindicate him and his feelings, to validate his thoughts, to validate him. I corrected my spelling error and went back to writing.

We hiked into town one day just for exercise and an ice-cream. When we cut back inland to take a shortcut we discovered an old Japanese cemetery dating back to the last century. It was a lonely looking place with crumbling and toppled tomb stones, and when photographed against the backdrop of the ocean and setting sun, it made for some eerie pictures.

Three days was all we could give this idyllic spot as Kara was due to arrive the day after next, so with some regret we went on one last long run for Nawiliwili. I think our reluctance to leave Wahniawa may have been partially due to being enchanted by the bay, but I believe that it was more rooted in the realization that our solitary time together was about to come to an end. We would now have to share each other and our time with others. We would have to consider and cater to others and even wear cloths when we really didn't want to. The winds were still brisk when we departed but they continued to blow from the beach making for a great sail along what would prove to be a beautiful and sparsely populated seventeen miles of coast.

Chapter #31

The Crew Arrives & Around We Go----- Again

I have found out that there ain't no surer way to find out whether you like people or hate them than to travel with them. - Mark Twain

Back at anchor in Nawiliwili Harbour, we made ready for Kara and Mike's arrival. We cleaned their respective cabins and discussed what we would do with them for the week before Jan flew home and we sailed from this harbour for the last time. I checked back in with harbourmaster Al who immediately began to admonish me for not checking in when we were anchored at Hanalei Bay. He never mentioned Port Allen.

I explained that I had tried, but couldn't. Big Al wasn't truly mad; in fact, I think he had trouble not smiling while scolding me. He went on to ask how we were liking the island and of course I told him that there was nothing not to like. I began to describe where we had gone, but I didn't have to, as he already knew where we had anchored and for how long. Seemingly, all the charter boats that we kept seeing around the island constantly kept him posted as to our whereabouts, so Big Brother Al was definitely watching. We had been caught, breaking most if not all the rules set down by the State, but instead giving us a fine, he just asked us what our plans were for the next week.

"We have two crew flying in tomorrow, so we will be taking a few days to do a quick sail around the island just to show them a few of the best places, then we will come back here, re-provision and head back north around the first of September," I said, to Big Al.

"OK, but don't forget that you need to check out with Customs and

Immigration before you leave for good. You need to sign off your cruising permit.

"Sure thing Al, not a problem," I said, feeling relieved that this government official wasn't so anal about the regulations.

After getting the number for a local fuel delivery service that Al recommended, we left the office and placed a call on my cell to the fuel depot. The man on the other end of the line was very sympathetic to my needs and he agreed to sell me fuel down on the dock without me having to have an eco-permit. He would be delivering fuel to a couple of sports fishermen next week and he said he could slip me some, but there was a catch, I had to take at least one hundred gallons to make it worth his while.

"Can you take that much?" the disembodied voice asked.

Hearing this, my gut dropped. Totally empty, I only carry 600 liters (150 gallons) of fuel, and we filled up less than a month ago when we departed Honolulu so I was pretty sure that we couldn't handle that much, maybe 50 gallons in a pinch. Not wanting to be either dishonest with him as he was doing me a favor, or depart on a long sea voyage without full tanks, I was forced to make a decision. I could lie to him or I could rent a car and use a couple of jerry cans to ferry diesel down to the boat 10 gallons at a time. Neither option was particularly appealing but in the end, my back won out.

"Yeah, no problem. I'll be able to take at least that much, you know it's a long way back to Canada," I replied with as much sincerity as I could muster. My thinking was that if I could only handle fifty gallons of so, what was he going to do? Suck it back out of the boat?

Still, gratefully, here was another person willing to flaunt the rules. From a cruiser's standpoint, Kauai was the most tightly wound when it came to regulations but they seemed to be to less than enthusiastic about enforcing them. Perhaps it had something to do with the remoteness of this island from the others in the chain, coupled with its frontier attitudes. Not that I was complaining, it was just an observation.

Kara and Mike arrived without a hitch. Kara settled back into her old cabin on the port side, with Mike taking the V-berth. Kara had seen Mike at a distance back on Maui when she was getting ready to fly home, but they had never really met. It was only now upon arriving aboard *Maiatla* that they would have an opportunity to size each other up and to get to know one another. Despite Samantha and Kara's initial agreement to "share Mike for the summer", much had changed. Mike and Sam were calling each other on the phone regularly and making plans to spend some time together once Mike arrived in Canada. He was even talking of staying for a while and perhaps getting a job.

This did not bode well for me as I was starting to fear what my brother would do when I showed up with what could very likely be his future son-in-law! It didn't take long for the two to settle in, or for Jan and I to notice that from the very instant Kara and Mike met, there existed a strange tension between them. An aura of electric energy filled the gap between them with an alternating current whose rapidly switching polarity was grossly out of sync-twin poles attracting and repelling at the same time. There was the usual sexual tension that can exist between young people thrust into intimate quarters, but there was something more brewing between these two. What it was, we did not know, but this tension would quickly develop to what I would later describe as a sibling type rivalry, with incestuous overtones. Whatever it was, it would create for some very odd moments, not just over the next few days, but throughout the ensuing voyage.

We wasted no time in getting underway. There was much Jan and I wanted to show them, but so little time, so we made a fast passage back to Secret Beach to commune with the spinners, stroll the wide sand beach, and snorkel the cliff below the lighthouse. The water was a little calmer this time around so I felt comfortable cutting in close to Kilauea Lighthouse to show it off. We anchored *Maiatla* in the exact same spot as before and it was much easier this time as I had crew to take the stern anchor out and set the hook, swinging our bow into the gentle swell.

To Jan's delight, Mike took over much of the cooking, giving him an opportunity to show off his culinary skills by creating a dazzling array of exquisite dishes which usually included fish, rice and coconut. I remarked to Jan that if Mike kept this up all the way back to Canada, that I would be arriving 20 pounds heavier. I was delighted to see my old friends - the topless joggers the next morning and for the first time, they waved back.

Figure 33.

Kauuapea Beach (Secret Beach) with the little Island of Mokuaeae to the left where Maui Mike and I hunted for bugs.

I had fully expected Mike and Kara to bond enough to want to do things together, to entertain themselves, because I wasn't really in the mood to entertain anyone. The past month of bliss had spoiled me, so I was still in a selfish mood. After the spinner dolphins arrived in the morning, Kara went ashore alone to hike up the beach, so I suggested to Mike that we head to the point to do a little bug (lobster) hunting. Mike readily agreed, so while Jan hung back to read, with spears and goodie bags in hand we headed off in the dink and anchored in the spot where Jan and I had encountered the shark just three weeks previous.

The underwater scenery was as sparse as I remembered it, so I suggested to Mike that we swim out to the island to hunt for bugs. The tiny Island of Mokuaeae, the one that rebuffed me last time I was here, was now waiting for me, beckoning with near perfect conditions. I think Mike felt a little intimidated by the long swim through open water to get to the island, but not wanting to be left behind, he braved it, following me out across the channel. Mike's anxiety wasn't entirely unfounded as you never know what deep water pelagics you could encounter in the ocean's wilderness. I have always found that hanging out in deep, open-water has always made me feel a little like a worm dangling from a fishhook! Looking a lot like a seal lazing on the surface, humans appear palatable when in fact we truly aren't, more often than not, a shark will usually spit a human out after only a sampling. An interesting tid-bit, but not in the least bit comforting, and more than just a bit disturbing on many levels!

The waves were pounding the beach with some force; nowhere near as badly as last time, so the water in the lee (sheltered side) of the island was calmer today, although a strong surge still raced around the corners of the island, pushing us about. Choosing our location, we split up and began to search the deep holes and crevices. After locating several lime-green moray eels and an octopus, I finally found my first bug, a nice half kilo (1 pound) spiny lobster. Finding the bugs is only the beginning; next, you have to get them out of the hole. Easier said than done! Often you can just reach in with a gloved hand and grab them. They have no claws, so there is no risk of being pinched, but spiny lobster live up to their name, so care must be taken not to get stuck by one of the many long and potentially painful spines lining their backs. Sometimes a poke with the spear will also suffice, but I hated spearing them, I preferred to keep them alive as long as possible. Besides, having a goody-bag hanging from your belt full of wounded and bleeding critters may just attract something else that you would rather not see!

When we were in Mexico, I learned a trick for catching lobster; it works well if the sea is calm and I can stay still enough to pull it off. As a lobster's eye-sight is poor; they touch things with their antenna to help them determine what is food (prey) and what is foe (predator). The trick is to wear two different colored gloves, one white, the other black; after locating a suitable victim hiding deep in a hole, I would slowly wave my white gloved hand in front of his lair. Curious, the bug would often come out of its hole, trying to touch the waving white glove. Meanwhile, my black hand is ever-so-slowly moving in for the snatch! If his antennas touch either glove, the lobster will flee with lighting speed! The "glove trick" works well but it takes calm conditions and good breath control if snorkeling.

We worked around the little island until the breaking waves turned us back. After a couple of hours we had succeeding in capturing three bugs apiece and I corralled a giant Kona crab hiding in a hole,. The crab had great black spots the size of quarters and it was delicious. Just as we were getting ready to leave, I looked down into a deep grotto where something bright yellow caught my eye. As I hovered on the surface, I couldn't believe it, but there it was! I was sure the depth was at my extreme limit, so I took several deep breaths in preparation for one last plunge into depths. Like a porpoise I dove, finning hard, straight down, until I was forced to clear my ears, grabbing my nose and blowing hard, all the while still descending in a spiral. Just when I had decided that I had gone deep enough, I reached out, snatching up my lost snorkel as I shot back to the surface. Mike outdid himself in preparing the lobster and crab. The four of us dined like King Neptune and drank wine while talking well into the night.

Hanalei Bay was next on our list of stops, but this too would prove to be a short one. The bay was as busy as last time and the harbourmaster, as scarce as ever. I could see that Big Al would be giving me hell again in a few days for not reporting in, yet again. I regaled Kara and Mike with stories of our previous visit here and showed them my famous pier, where the wreck of the SS Minnow sat, after which we explored the town. It was surprising that even though we had only been on Kauai for a short time, it was already feeling familiar, not quite like home, but at this rate it wasn't going to take much longer before I would be mahaloing everyone, living in sandals and board shorts, smoking pot while flashing shaka signs at my brahs - a de-evolution of sorts, but not an entirely unpleasant one. The Tahiti Syndrome with all its viral agents was now infecting my very marrow and in turn, destroying, my netherworld genes, along with my desire to return to any kind of real civilisation never mind work. Life, our lives were definitely good in Hawaii and I knew I was going to miss it when we finally had to leave this place.

After a dinner of barbequed steaks, we all sat in the cockpit watching the beach-goers retreat to their cars after a hard day of sun and surf, I suggested to Kara and Mike that perhaps they should leave the old folks and go ashore to check out a bar or a club, just to see what the young people were doing in town. The pair looked at each other for a moment. It was Kara who spoke first.

"No, I don't think so. I would rather just hang out on the boat tonight, I'm tired," she said.

Mike quickly concurred, reciting similar excuses. I may have been wrong but I sensed that if Kara were willing, Mike would have gone. I pushed them to reconsider, but both were now adamant, they didn't want to go. I may have tried a bit too hard to motivate them as I suddenly felt Jan, who was sitting next to me, squeeze my forearm. I know that signal; it meant shut up, think about what you are saying or let's go home! From the glare she was now giving, I knew what she wanted me to do, so I let it drop. Perhaps my desire to get these two together went beyond just wanting them to have a good time or desiring a happy ship for this voyage, maybe my motives were more self-serving, having something to do with making amends to my brother Steve, Samantha's father.

Chapter #32

A Haunted Village and A Celestial Extravaganza.

The ocean has always been a salve to my soul...the best thing for a cut or abrasion was to go swimming in salt water. Later down the road of life, I made the discovery that salt water was also good for the mental abrasions one inevitably acquires on land.- Jimmy Buffett

Reluctantly, after a couple of days at Hanalei Bay, we were off again, headed around the corner to the Napali Coast but this time the conditions were much more conducive to site seeing. I brought *Maiatla* in close to hug the shore and thankfully, we weren't required to perform any more rescues. The Napali was as spectacular as ever and all were suitably impressed. Since our last trip down this shore, I found in our guide book another spot that we could anchor if the wind conditions were tame and I believed today qualified, so we would give the old village site of Nu`alolo Kai a try.

Nu`alolo Kai is an ancient Hawaiian fishing village located approximately eight miles (13 kilometers) from the northern end of start of the Na Pali Coast, a truly remote village only accessible by boat. This small land area is backed by sheer cliffs and was useful to Hawaiians because of its protected reefs. The area contains a collection of cultural and archaeological sites, which are still being unearthed today giving historians a better insight into ancient life. Archaeological evidence suggests that the Nu'alolo village has been continuously occupied for over 800 years, from the 12th through the 20th centuries. Some of the structures at Nu'alolo Kai are among the most impressive along the Na Pali.

Being one of the first sites in Hawaii to have been studied extensively by archeologists, surveys of Nu`alolo Kai reveal remnants of structures of impressive complexity and sophistication. The old village site is situated in a deep bowl cut into the towering cliffs guarding it from invasion from land. It is likewise protected from the wrath of the sea as it is nestled behind an extensive and prolific reef system. Now designated as a historical site, the Parks' Board has placed submerged buoys around the reef for visiting boats who have obtained a special permit to visit the site. Where you get the permits I didn't know, so we didn't have one, but I thought we would stop and give it a try and if anyone asked, we would just play dumb tourist. We were back to that it's easier asking for forgiveness thing again.

Our sail down the coast was much more tranquil this time. The wind was still blowing along the shore so under full sail we ran along wing and wing in a hot breeze that was thick with jungle smells. By the time we reached the site, most of the visiting charter boats had already departed for the day giving us our pick of mooring sites. Mike dove over the side to first find then secure us to a buoy hidden below the surface. Once secured, *Maiatla* aligned herself with the wind but in doing so, she put us broadside to the remnants of the swell that overpowered the reef, causing us to take on an uncomfortable roll.

"Hey Mike can you swim inshore and see if you can find another mooring over there that we can tie our stern too?"

Anchoring was forbidden here so a stern hook was out of the question.

"Yea no problem Andy I'll have a look," Mike replied as he took off towards shore.

Luckily another buoy was in the right position so I tossed Mike a line which he passed through the eye of the float, then returned the end of the line to the boat. I secured one end to a stern cleat then ran the other to a cockpit winch and with ease, I slowly cranked the line tight until we were comfortable lying nose into the seas. There were a couple of small charter inflatable boats on nearby moorings and a boat beached ashore with several people milling about with cameras. Nearby, looking important, were a couple of men who appeared to be their guides. If anyone thought that we didn't belong, they didn't say anything and no one approached us asking to see our permit, so I thought us safe for at least for now. We settled in for the night. Going ashore would have to wait till morning.

It was now August the 28th, 2007 and as it turned out, our arrival here, though purely by accident, at this point in time could not have been better planed as we were in a perfect location to witness the full eclipse of the moon which would occur directly overhead that evening. If the skies remained clear, we would be able to see the full moon disappear into the shadow of the Earth for about 90 minutes. The radio announcer on a Kauai radio station reported, "The moon will start to go into the shadow of the Earth at 10:51 tonight and be fully eclipsed by 11:52 p.m. It will start to emerge from the shadow at 1:22 a.m. and be out of the partial eclipse stage at 2:24 a.m."

Moored in the shadow of the thirteen-hundred meter high Napali cliffs, we would be shielded from all city and shore lights, perfect for viewing.

After dinner we sat on deck in the cockpit cooled by the evening breeze. As the day's light faded and the shadows crept down the mountains like a silent spectre, poised to smother the deserted village, a faint ethereal cry echoed off the cliffs to drift out to us over the water.

"What was that?" Kara demanded as she turned, staring off into the twilight that cloaked the shore.

What was what?' Jan asked, "I didn't hear anything."

Kara turned back, "No I heard what sounded like someone crying or calling from shore, but I can't see anything, it's too dark!" she said.

"I heard it too Jan", I said as I took another sip of wine. "It sounded like a ghost to me, one of those night marchers we have read about and he sounded ticked off to me. Maybe he's mad because we are here uninvited," I offered with a big grin.

I hadn't really heard anything but I couldn't help myself, I had to screw with them.

"Shush there it is again!" Kara said excitedly as she gazed intently back at the hidden shore. All aboard heard it this time, including me and I must admit that the sound did send a chill up my spine and just for a second, I wondered if I might not have been too far off the mark with my ghost theory. Everyone suddenly fell silent, waiting to see if we would hear it again, but we didn't have to wait long as moments later, our night marcher called out to us, but this time with more authority.

"BAAAAA!" it was plain as day and it echoed though the canyons.

"That's a goat," Jan called out as she began to laugh.

After the sun had sun set the goats upon the mountain began to call to one another in the dark and for most of the night we were entertained to a chorus of what must have been a dozen or more nannies braying and bleating back and forth. At one point Kara claimed to have even heard a goat fall from the mountain. What such a thing would sound like evaded me, but she was adamant about being sure of what she heard. By 9:00 p.m., it was black as any night could be, so I opened the top of the dodger so we could gaze up into the sky where we were treated to a little meteor shower accented by the odd satellite and the international space station as it passed overhead, the overture for tonight's pending moon dance. Nothing beats cuddling with a loved one at anchor in a secluded bay and wishing on falling stars.

It was just after 10:00 p.m. that we noticed a glow emanating from behind the cliffs and over the next several minutes, we all watched in silent awe as the full moon ascended the upper reaches of the Napali. The brilliant moon rose, flooding the mountains, valleys and ocean with a mellow radiance, bathing the deserted village in a ghostly light; it was an eerie but spectacular sight. No sooner had the moon appeared that we noticed that it was starting to change, evolving into a reddish-orange orb, the eclipse had begun. Over the following hours, we talked while gazing at a moon that darkened into an eerie copper color until finally disappearing altogether, only to reappear a little over an hour later, replaying the whole process but in reverse until the blazing moon once again commanded the sky. It was truly a magical night on the Napali.

The morning was as beautiful as they come and it was especially so as I gazed upon an ancient vision as old as time itself and thankfully, no humans or their trappings were in sight to spoil the view. A gentle swell rolled easily over the reef as it was now high tide, permitting tiny wavelets to break upon the rocky shore creating a rhythmic whooshing sound that echoed up the cliffs. In a wide cleft in the rocks high above the village, a lone whist of delicate mist rose up the face only to evaporate the instant it left the shadows, to be killed by the first rays of the morning sun that broached the mountain top. We would enjoy the quiet moment while it lasted, because by ten o'clock, the first of the charter boats would arrive. To beat the rush, we were ashore by eight.

We landed at a man-made clearing amongst a cluster of watermelon-sized black rocks and hauled *Fishkiller* beyond the high tide line. We hadn't seen any lights ashore the previous night, so I was reasonably sure that there wasn't a resident park ranger, but that wasn't to say that one wouldn't show up in a boat anytime soon and if that were the case, we had better make our rounds while we still had a free run of the place. It was early and the sun was still behind the mountains, but with the sweat already trickling down between my shoulder blades, it was obviously going to be a hot and humid day.. Kara led the way along a trail that took us to the northern reaches of the village where the sheer cliffs met the sea.

"I want to see if I can find those goats we heard last night!" Kara said with great excitement, as she dashed ahead onto a trail leading from the beach, up to the rock wall. I think she was just looking for an excuse to try a little rock-climbing. She was obviously excited; she had never before seen anything like this place before.

It was easy to image the people who used to live here. There were criss-crossing trails curbed on either side with black volcanic rocks. Plotlines, not unlike modern subdivisions were similarly laid out by rocks marking the boundaries of each of the ancient households; the footings of hales (homes), were still visible complete with pathways leading up to their puka komo (doorways). The village was shielded from the sun and wind by the ubiquitous coconut palm, candlenut trees and great banyan trees. Jan walked over to a strange looking tree with broad leaves, bearing a pear-sized fruit that looked like it was covered in warts.

"Hey Mike, what kind of tree is this? Are these edible?" Jan asked, as she plucked one of the greenish-yellow fruit from a low hanging branch, giving it a cautious sniff.

Mike followed Jan up the trail to see what she was looking at.

"I can't remember the name of the tree but it was used by the old Hawaiians for medical purposes, you can eat it, but it don't taste too good and if you break it open, it smells like shit!" he said.

We would later learn that the tree was actually the Noni, which was probably the native Hawaiian's most important medicinal fruiting plant, although most of the medicinal applications are from other parts of the tree, not the fruit itself. It is a common naturalized tree on all of the major islands, identified by its large, glossy green leaves, and warty, white/green fruits that have a very strong and disagreeable odor, as Mike had described so elegantly.

Kara never did find any live goats, but she did manage to locate a rather pitiful soul that had apparently lost its footing on the high cliffs, only to tumble to its death. If it was the creature Kara had heard last night, we will never know, but the pulped remains did appear disgustingly fresh.

There we no signs or plaques describing what we were seeing. It was a little difficult to tell one pile of rocks from another, but we did find what must have been the remains of a hale or house of a person of great importance, or perhaps it was a Heiau, a place of worship; it was grand and located on the most prime realestate at the loftiest part of the village.

"Hey, I wonder if this was where they made human sacrifices, it looks like a good place to disembowel or behead someone, what do you guys think? I asked.

"Oh, that's creepy!" Kara replied.

"Hey Mike! Lay down on the flat alter-like rock and see how it feels, maybe you will be able to sense other victims as you lay there," I said, ghoulishly.

Mike's reply to my suggestion was immediate and short, containing only two words and most assuredly, anatomically impossible for me to do to myself!

On the far southern end of the village was a trickling waterfall that most likely provided the village with all its fresh water. There was every indication that the flow had been much greater in the past, so I had to believe that much of the headwaters of this stream had been diverted for irrigation as most other streams have been. I waded into the shallow pool and had a drink. As we made our way back to the landing, we encountered several dozen people accompanied by their guides on their way to the waterfall, but none paid us any mind other than greeting us with a "good morning".

On the way back to the boat, next to the trail, we found a large spike sticking out of the ground with hundreds of broken coconuts covering the ground. Mike decided to show us how to open and drink the milk from a nut, Hawaiian style. After selecting an appropriate green nut, he clutched it between his hands and brought it down upon the spike. Again and again he brought it down on the spike but without the desired results. Looking a little flustered, Mike attacked the resistant nut with a vengeance. I must commend him for his effort but if we were dying of thirst, we would have been dead. Despite all his frantic effort, we never did get to drink that nut which goes to prove that just because you live in Italy, doesn't mean you know how to make pizza. It wasn't until sometime later that day that Mike finally succeeded in cracking another nut, it proved to be delicious but those of our crew who over indulged themselves came down with a bad case of diarrhea.

As we walked along under the cover of the dense canopy, holding hands, I said to Jan, "You know, if any place in Hawaii is haunted it should be here. We should come ashore tonight and look for night marchers, what do you think, Babe?"

Jan just gave me her, "do you think I'm stupid?", look before answering.

"Hey, if you want to go ghost hunting you can do it without me! As long as I have the boat and your insurance policy, you can hunt whatever you like!" she said, while chuckling.

"You chicken!" I said.

Back aboard *Maiatla,* we all decided to spend the afternoon snorkeling along the outer reef. The girls wanted to look at the pretty fish and Mike and I were eager to go bug hunting. We had survived our excursion ashore without encountering any resistance from the locals or officialdom, but that was about to change.

Jan, Mike, and Kara had already loaded themselves into the dinghy and were waiting on me as I was the last to slip below to change into my swim suit and pull on my shorty wetsuit. I was in my cabin and had just stripped off to change when I heard small boat motor alongside. Our cabin port was open so I heard it all.

"Hey, Man! You have to move your boat! You can't be anchored in here on the reef! You're going to fuck it up!"

The voice was loud and very angry.

It was Mike's voice I heard next.

"We aren't anchored, we are tied to the mooring, both bow and stern so we aren't damaging the reef," Mike said.

With that, I thought the debate would be over, but I was wrong.

"Well, you can't be tied to two buoys at the same time, cut one loose!" The agitated fellow shot back.

Again, Mike responded, "I can't, not without the permission of the captain."

Mike's reply obviously pissed off this guy even more!

"Why are you tied to two buoys anyway?" he shot back.

This guy was now yelling.

"We did it to keep the bow into the waves," Mike said.

"Well, if your captain knew what the hell he was doing, he wouldn't have to do that!" the unidentified man shouted.

Despite being naked, I was about to head topside to confront this guy but I realized that Mike was holding his own and unless the confrontation turned violent, I decided to stay out of it. I had a high-powered squirt-gun loaded with ammonia and water in the cockpit and if it really got ugly, I would just shoot the guy in the face. By the time I got dressed and topside, our visitor had left, leaving my crew looking rather flustered, Jan included, who began to tell me of the encounter, but I halted her in mid-sentence.

"Yes, I heard the whole thing and don't worry, he's just probably mad because he wants one of our buoys, in close to the beach, instead of being stuck out where he is. So don't worry about him, let's go snorkeling!"

The reef was as good as expected and we even managed to dredge up a couple of lobster for dinner and thankfully, we had no further contact with angry locals or permit demanding rangers. We succeeded in flaunting the regulations once again, but I was secretly hoping that Big Al wouldn't hear about this.

Time was running short so we departed the next day bound for the little anchorage along the Polihale shore that Jan and I had discovered at the extreme southern end of the Na Pali, at the head of the Barking Sands. Again, Mike ran out the stern hook and once settled, Mike and I took the dink around the corner for some more bug hunting. Kara opted out for this trip, and Jan decided she wanted a quiet day.

Despite Mike's obvious eccentricities that made a habit of rubbing raw nerves until they bled profusely, I truly enjoyed his company on these foraging trips. It wasn't unusual for me to literally spend hours in the water alone while covering miles of shoreline, and it was nice having someone along that could not only keep up, but someone that I didn't have to look after as he could take care of himself. The reefs of the Na Pali were grand but as we soon discovered, a little short on bugs for the taking. In Mexico I could have up to a dozen lobster bagged in less than an hour, but here, after the better part of the day poking and burrowing into holes, Mike and I were lucky to come back with three or four decent sized bugs. Nevertheless, we had a blast.

September was fast approaching which meant the winter storms weren't far away. We needed to get north before all hell broke loose in the North Pacific. We spent two glorious days and it was with great sadness that early one morning we hauled anchor to make a mad dash for our last anchorage before returning to Nawiliwili, in preparation for heading home.

Our final stop would be the place that I would always remember whenever I smelled a fresh brewed cup of coffee, Wahiawa Bay, just east of Port Allen. The tiny bay, our place of bleeding sands, sprawling fields of Kona coffee, Asian cemeteries, and roving gangs of wild cocks that sounded the alarm at the first hint of sunrise. I had to stand on deck alongside Mike and Kara as they admired Wahiawa Bay; it struck me as it had the first time, leaving me almost speechless - a rare occasion!

Our first morning at anchor we all rose late despite the best efforts of the cocks that were concealed on the nearby shore. It was brunch and tea in the cockpit and as we devoured Jan's pancakes, we discussed what to do for the balance of the day.

"I need to mail some post cards home; they are for my sisters and Mum," Kara said. "How far is it into town from here?"

I pointed off into the distance. "It's about half a mile that way, there is a trail that cuts through the old Japanese cemetery, but you can also take the shore path, it's twice as long but a really interesting walk," I added.

"I think I will do that then," Kara replied. "I'll mail my letters and maybe get some ice-cream, I've been having a craving."

"That sounds like a good idea, mind if I come along?" Mike asked of Kara.

"Sure, should be fun to explore here."

Mike turned back to Jan and me; "Did you hear those roosters this morning? Can't believe that they can make that much noise," he said.

"Yeah, they are pretty bad, if I lived here I think I would get a gun and thin them out a little and have a big barbeque!" I said.

"Don't imagine they would taste all that good," Jan added. "Wouldn't they be tough?"

Mike waded into the debate, "They might be OK for a stir fry or stewing, I can bring one back and we can give it a try, what do you think?"

"Yeah, sure Mike, bring back a couple, we'll roast one, and dice the other!" I was serious - there was a lot of free food just wandering about, and I'm sure nobody would miss a couple of the pesky birds!

Kara laughed, "What are you going to do? Hit it over the head with a stick? I can just see Mike running after a chickening swinging a bat, should be hilarious!"

"Yeah, why not? If I can get close enough I can kill it with a stick!" Mike shot back sounding none to confident.

I think Kara had just thrown down the gauntlet, and I was going to help Mike pick it up and accept the challenge

"You don't have to kill it with a stick, I have something that will do the trick," I said. With that, I jumped down below to root around the games cupboard in the main salon. When I returned topside, I handed Mike a high powered slingshot and a big bag of glass marbles.

"Here, this belong to Thomas, but it will kill your birds if you get close enough."

There! Now Mike had no excuse not to give it a try, and just to up the ante a little, I said, "You know Mike, Kara is an old squirrel hunter from back home, she takes them out of the trees with a throwing knife, so maybe I should be giving this to her?"

And of course, Kara was going to make sure he manned up by throwing in one last dig.

"Mike couldn't hit anything with that; he would have to get them in the head!" she said, laughing and with that remark and from the look on Mike's face, I knew then that "the game" was on.

By noon, Kara and Mike had loaded themselves into the dinghy with murder in their hearts, armed with a slingshot, a bag of marbles, a shopping list from Jan and directions from me to get cash from the ATM so I could buy fuel later. The pair set off for town. Let the chickens beware!

I was happy to see Mike and Kara leaving together as over the last few days they seemed to be getting on each other's nerves more with each passing day. Mike, from the first day that he met her, started taunting Kara as you would a meddling younger sister. I don't know if he was doing on purpose, but it was as if he was constantly trying to goad her into a confrontation. He never seemed to miss an opportunity to hurl a biting comment her way when the opportunity presented itself and unfortunately, living in such tight quarters afforded many opportunities. Still, more often than not, Kara resisted by taking the high moral road, refusing to take the bait, refusing to buy into his game. Nevertheless, occasionally Mike would score a direct hit and the war of the sexes would break out in the form of verbal jousting that at times, resulted in one of them being wrestled to the floor. As the pair were pretty evenly matched, it was usually a coin toss as to who would have to say "Uncle" (Mike was stronger but Kara had a better technique!).

By late afternoon, our hunting and foraging party had still not returned. I went on deck to scan the fields to see if I could see any sign of them, but the pair was nowhere to be seen. However, I wasn't worried, if one had killed the other, the victor would have returned triumphantly by now and if they had gotten arrested for shooting birds in front of the post office, I'm sure I would have received a call from the bail bondsmen by now. I was just about to head back down below when I noticed something wrong with the dinghy at the beach. I called to Jan, who was in the galley preparing dinner to pass me the binoculars.

"What's the matter? Do you see something?" She asked as she could tell by the tone of my voice that something was amiss. I took the glasses from her as she came topside to stand beside me.

I looked shoreward to study *Fishkiller*.

"It's the dinghy, the tide has come back in and it's now floating free," I said.

"What? Well, didn't they tie it to a tree?" Jan asked, with some alarm.

"Don't look like it, because here it comes," I answered.

Over the next several minutes we watched the offshore breeze blow *Fishkiller* our way and if we didn't intercept it, it's present trajectory would take it out to sea and or precious dink and outboard motor would never to be seen again, not by us anyway.

I called Mike on the VHF hoping he would answer the handheld radio, but I got no reply. I scanned the fields again in hopes that the wayward pair were nearby so they could swim after the dink, but no luck - they were still nowhere to be seen.

"Ah shit!" I said, "I better get my fins on and go after it."

I handed Jan the binoculars and went aft to my deck box to retrieve my fins.

"You better hurry Andy," Jan called after me, "the dinghy is picking up speed!"

I looked up to see that the dink had closed the distance between us and the beach by half, and at its present rate of speed it would cruise right by us in a matter of a minute or so. I wasted no time in donning my fins and leaping from the stern but by the time I surfaced, *Fishkiller* had already passed us and being powered by strong gusts of wind, she was making for the open ocean as if possessed. I swam as fast as I could, but it almost wasn't enough. By the time I caught up to the dink, we were over 100 meters (330 feet) outside the bay bouncing in three meters (10 foot) swells.

When I got back to *Maiatla*, I was furious! If Jan and I had been napping at the time, we would have lost our second dinghy on this trip, an expensive and downright embarrassing situation.

"I wonder why didn't they use the painter to tie it to a tree?" Jan asked again, when I finally climbed back aboard.

"You would think Mike would have known better," she added.

"Yes you would think so, I will have to give them both shit when they finally get back."

As I sat impatiently in the cockpit drying out after my marathon swim, a thought occurred to me that I might be able to throw a bit of a scare into Mike and Kara. Taking the dinghy, I moved it to the far side of the boat so when they returned they wouldn't be able to see it from shore, then I went below to wait.

About an hour later, I was laying quietly on my bed reading when I heard Mike calling on the radio. I just continued to lay there.

"Aren't you going to answer that?" Jan asked as she lay next to me flipping through the pages of a magazine.

"Nope, he didn't answer my radio call so I'm not going to answer his, just want him to sweat it out a little," I said.

Jan smiled. "You're nasty, but I love you anyway."

Mike repeated his radio calls for several minutes, each time his voice sounded more agitated until he finally gave up on the radio. In the distance, I could now hear voices calling out our boat name. I waited several more minutes before going topside where I saw Mike and Kara standing on the beach waving their arms. As I waved back, Mike called though cupped hands, "Do you have the dinghy out there?"

I made a gesture as if I wasn't sure what he meant, and then I yelled back, "No! Don't you have it?"

Even from 50 meters away I could see a wave of anxiety overcome both of them as they began to look all around as if perhaps they had just missed seeing the little boat, and moments later they appeared to be arguing over something. I would later learn that this discussion involved a great big, "I told you so", from Kara as she had apparently suggested to Mike when they landed that they should tie the dink down, but Mike insisted that it wasn't necessary. They had dragged it high enough up the beach.

"How long are you going to let them stew before you go get them?" Jan asked with a big grin.

"Oh, just a little while longer," I said as I put my arm around her, making myself comfortable.

Finally back on board, the pair apologized profusely. I couldn't stay mad for long as Mike was doing a good job of beating himself up over losing the dink. Taking pity on him I decided to change the subject.

"So where are the chickens? Shoot any?" I asked. I didn't see him toting any bags with feathers sticking out, so I already knew the answer but I had to ask.

The moment I mentioned the chickens, Kara started to laugh. She may have found it funny but from the disgusted look on Mike's face, it was obvious that he didn't find it amusing at all.

"It was funny as hell!" Kara began. "After I mailed my letters and I got your money from the cash machine, Mike bought us a couple of big cans of Hawaiian beer at the store for our walk back but it tasted nasty and I had trouble drinking mine."

I reached across the cockpit to give Mike a poke.

"Hey, what are you doing feeding alcohol to a minor? Isn't the drinking age in Hawaii 21?" I said. I didn't really care, I just wanted to bust his chops a little.

"Hey man, she wanted it," he said with a big grin, "so I bought her one! No harm done!"

Kara said again, "Yeah, but I couldn't finish it, so anyway we came back by cutting through the tank farm and some industrial area and that is when Mike started shooting marbles at chickens and it was so funny. There was a herd of chickens running about and he was chasing them and shooting but he couldn't hit a single one!"

Kara now had herself so worked up and laughing so hard that she looked as though she was going to cry. Mike decided it was his turn to tell the story so he interrupted her, "Hey it wasn't my fault! You were supposed to head them off so I could shoot, but you didn't!"

Kara snapped back, "I wasn't going to get in front of you with a loaded sling shot, you crazy?"

Again Kara burst out laughing and Jan and I couldn't help laughing at the image Kara was aptly painting. It was obvious Mike didn't like where this story was going.

"It was that damned slingshot, it didn't shoot straight and when I finally did have a good shot, one of the bands broke, it was crap!" Mike said with all seriousness.

Mike wasn't quite so upset now and even he started to see the humor in it, at least until he suddenly remembered how Kara had failed him at the moment of truth, as it were.

Mike pointed his finger accusing finger at Kara and said with all urgency, "We would have a chicken for dinner if you had not let that one go that I had corned by the fence. I almost had him!"

Kara leaned back into the cockpit seat, taking a moment to compose herself, "Well Mike, shooting them is one thing but beating it death is another, besides I didn't want to eat that old bird anyway," she finally admitted.

So perhaps she had sabotaged his efforts after all. If she had, it wouldn't be the last time during the long voyage.

Kara turned back to Jan and I as she was now done with Mike. We were still having a good chuckle about this so I couldn't resist taking one last shot.

"See Mike, I told you that you should have let Kara do the shooting!"

Perhaps feeling like he couldn't win, Mike just clammed up and asked me if I wanted a beer. As it was a rhetorical question he just dropped below to pull a pair of cans out of the fridge.

"Hey why didn't you answer the radio when we called," Kara asked.

Mike handed me my beer.

"Oh Jan and I were fooling around and didn't want to be bothered."

Jan's elbow was sharp and her meaning unmistakable.

"Oh don't listen to him Kara," Jan said while grinning like a school girl, "he's just joking."

Kara laughed, "See Mike I told you, I was right!"

"You were right about what?" I just had to ask.

"Well we were almost back and I told Mike that we should call on the radio to warn you we were almost there as you guys might be naked on deck or doing stuff, but Mike said not to call."

"See Mike I told you!"

"We weren't naked or doing anything! Jan shot back as again I felt the wrath of her elbow.

"Now see what you started you dolt!"

We departed the following morning without further incidents and nothing more was said about the fleeing dink or our chickenless state. The wind was light that morning so I decided to motor as close to shore as possible, playing tourist as we went. The first three miles of coast was remarkably rugged as the black lava rises straight out of the sea, up to thirty meters in places before levelling out, turning into red and rich agricultural lands with miles of coffee beans and pineapples. It was a beautiful, but there was nowhere safe to land or anchor until we rounded Kalanipuao Rock, the rock being the only navigational hazard offshore that was of concern to us, but fortunately, it was well marked with a large red bell buoy to warn of the drying reef.

Beyond Kalanipuao Rock, the residential homes began to appear, getting denser until four miles later we passed the community of Poipu, a well-developed tourist town with many rental condos, hotels and all the amenities for land based visitors, but for us cruisers it didn't look so attractive. There were few decent anchorages but most were too exposed and what marinas there were, focused on small trailer mounted vessels as opposed to ocean going yachts, so we sailed on. As the day wore on the wind filled in so we were able make a fast upwind passage along the coast and our final seven miles, we sailed past undoubtedly the most beautiful uninhabited and least accessible beaches on the entire island.

    Nevertheless, we couldn't stop as we had run out of time. It was already 4 pm and it would be dark by 6 pm and we needed to be at the dock in the morning to rendezvous with our fuel delivery guy. Kara and Mike's free Hawaiian cruise was now over and from here on, they would have to work for a living.

Chapter #33

Homeward Bound.

A smooth sea never made a skilled mariner.
                          -English Proverb

We were back at anchor at Nawiliwili and if harbourmaster Al disapproved of our antics as we went around the island this time, he said nothing as we checked back in and for that I was grateful. Our last couple of days before our departure north found the crew busy provisioning and making the boat ready for our next great assault of the expansive Pacific. To make provisioning and boat chores easier, we moved *Maiatla* from the anchorage to the concrete wharf where the charter fishing boats loaded passengers and unloaded marlin caught just from offshore.

Mike duct taped closed the chain locker hawse pipes to prevent water from entering whenever we took a wave over the bow. Our slog north could very well be a wet one. He would later regret not doing a better job of taping them closed, although he would ultimately take advantage of having a soggy berth. The dinghy was deflated, rolled up and stored on deck next to the starboard shrouds along with the gas jerry cans with the emergency jugs of fresh water on the port side. At the base of our companionway stairs is a hatch which leads down into what we call the "Pit" which is over a meter tall and wide and two meters long. I always joked that the pit was big enough to smuggle six illegal aliens. The Mercury outboard was placed deep within the "pit", along with our Rubbermaid tubs full of dry goods and diving gear.

Kara and Mike spent the better part of two days re-stitching the batten pockets into the disgraceful mizzen sail. Mike had a good idea to double up the sailcloth in order to strengthen the pockets. It was a good plan but the multiple layers of tough new sailcloth made it very difficult to palm the sail needle through the material. It was Mike's idea, and he took it upon himself to take charge of the job. As I watched the pair slave away in the cockpit with Mike criticizing Kara's every stitch, I was sure blood would flow before they were done. I was betting on Kara as I envisioned Mike stumbling below with a thumb-length, three-sided sail needle stuck between his eyes! Despite developing painful sores on their fingers and palms, the job came off well but I can say that if I had not had crew to do the work, the mizzen would have just received multiple layers of duct tape to keep the battens in place. Plans for a new sail were already in the works, we just needed to get home first.

We took on water and had fuel delivered to the dock, surprisingly just under 375 liters (100 gallons) more than what I was expecting and what was more astonishing - it was at a reasonable cost. Big Al came through again. At the end of this voyage I calculated that the total fuel bill for the full four month voyage was under $800.00. *Maiatla's* venerable old Perkins burns a meager one U.S. gallon per hour at six knots, with full tanks we could motor over 1100 nautical miles. Respectable to say the least, but as sailors we rely heavily on the generosity of the winds and our engines are mere encumbrances, unless we needed them, then the iron Jenny rules!

Figure 34.

Mike and Kara repair the mizzen sail just before departure.

I rented a car to help with our re-provisioning and to take Jan to the airport when the time came. After returning from a jaunt into town with the car, Mike came down below with something he bought and naturally, as captain I needed to know what he was bringing aboard (might need to break out a shot glass). When I asked him what it was, he unwrapped it and held it out to me cradled in both hands as if it was a great prize or an offering to the Gods.

He handed me what looked like a glass beer stein with a flattened egg-beater in the bottom and a lid on the top.

"What is this?" I asked, while thinking that the shot glass may still be involved.

Obviously pleased with his purchase he announced, "It's a French Press, it's used for making coffee!"

I held the press up and examined it, "This glass looks awfully thin, its liable to break easily don't you think?" I said, as I opened it up to examine the guts.

"It's supposed to be like that, it won't break!" Mike assured me.

"You do know we don't carry any glass items on this boat because it does get rough out there and things tend to go flying, you do know that don't you?" I asked, perhaps coming across a bit more sarcastic then I wanted. We were barefoot more often than not so having something aboard that could explode into a billion razor sharp shards didn't seem to be a good idea to me.

"Don't worry Andy, it won't break, I'll take care of it."

I spun the odd looking apparatus in my hands in an effort to gauge its seaworthiness.

"Well OK, but I have 20 bucks that says it won't make it back to Canada alive." Mike laughed. "You're on!"

On our second to last night in the islands, Jan and I found a rather upscale waterfront restaurant where we sat at a romantic table overlooking the harbour with a warm breeze that rustled the slanting palms and plastic leis dangling from the rafters. Holding hands by the light of a tiki torch we reminisced about the two fabulous months that we just had together. The time seemed to have flown by. It appeared that the island's gods had reneged on their promise as Maui time suddenly seemed to have failed us, our time was all but gone. The spell was broken and our cruising genie retired to the lamp.

During the trying previous years, the ties that had securely bound us had been stressed to almost a breaking point; illness and financial worries had exacted their toll. Jan and I had desperately needed this voyage, the solitude and a chance to revel in one another once again and reconnect, physically as well as metaphysically. Being gilded in a tropical moonlight, making unhurried love on the deck of a boat as it gently sways to the warm breeze in the lee of a deserted tropical isle can do that for you. (Jan will want me to take this part out! She would just say, "That never happened!"). This voyage was a fitting end to a rather difficult chapter in our lives. Our landfall on Maui signaled a fresh start for all of us. Jan and I knew it, although Melissa would not see it for several years to come, changing her for the better all the same.

As Jan watched a gentle swell roll in to crash upon the groomed beach, she turned to me and smiled.

"Thanks for being crazy and working so hard to get us all here. It's been wonderful but I just hate to have to leave you and fly home. Wish I could sail back with you guys; you may need an extra hand. Are you going to be alright with just the three of you?"

"Well Babe, I like to think of myself as being eccentric, not crazy, there is a difference you know. It may be a fine distinction between the two but I think an important one! I couldn't help but smile. And I wish you could come too, Babe, but Melissa needs you home and it could be rough slog back and you don't need that. We'll be fine. Mike is very experienced and Kara is broken in - foolish for coming back maybe, but I'm glad she's here. It will be fun." I could sense that Jan was truly concerned, so I did my best to make light of it all.

In my effort to eek out every possible day in Hawaii, we pushed our departure date back until my weather window resembled more of a "slit". September is a great month for sailing the temperate waters of Hawaii, but we were bound to chase the pole star, heading north and by the time we arrived off the Pacific Northwest, October, the start of the storm season would be greeting us.

Jan suddenly laughed as a thought crossed her mind, "Do you think you can coop those two up for three weeks without them killing each other?

Mike and Kara's rivalry was still intensifying by the day and had reached a point where we were sure they would come to blows and by all account, Kara seemed to be getting the worst of it. Mike rarely missed an opportunity to thrust with a cutting remark whenever Kara left herself open. They reminded me of a pair of siblings squabbling over petty issues in the backseat of a car. I felt like I might have to reach around and give them both a good clout just to settle them down. I was naively hopeful that once the routine of the voyage took hold and they were separated into their own watches, peace would reign again on *Maiatla*. However in reality, it was more likely that the war of the watches and the sexual tension between them would escalate.

"Those two are driving me crazy. You're going to have fun on your trip back. I was talking to Kara," Jan said, "and I told her that if Mike didn't quit bugging her that she had my permission to throw him overboard!"

"Well if she does, it better be on her watch when I'm asleep, if I don't see him go, I won't have to testify! He can be just another sailor who was lost at sea while taking a whiz over the side!" I said, joking.

After dinner, Jan and I walked the surf line with our shoes in hands and talked about what we would do next and where we would go aboard *Maiatla*. This trip wasn't even over yet and here we were excitedly planning our next.

Neither of us wanted this night, nor this trip to end, but Melissa was about ready to start school and Jan needed to be with her. With the harbour lights dancing off the water and reflecting through the stern windows of our great cabin, we slipped into bed and made love for the last time in the islands.

In the morning with tears in her eyes, I put Jan on a plane that would get her home in just six hours with dinner service, glasses of chardonnay and a choice of chicken or steak. By contrast, our journey would last 23 long days, see us drain the wine locker of my home brew and eat tuna for virtually every meal.

By the evening of September 2nd, all was ready and *Maiatla* was again fit for sea duty. As the shadows slid down the hillsides and dusk carpeted the harbour landscape, the crew dispersed for one last night on the town. Mike and Kara decided to walk together along the waterfront and stroll through the touristy boutiques and cafes for a final time. I retired to the quiet of the empty boat and my SSB radio. With a glass of wine at my elbow I dutifully downloaded the latest weather faxes and plotted our course around the island, intent on picking up the cleaner winds of the northeast trades on the far side of Kauai.

I contacted the Pacific Seafarer's Net and informed them of my sail plans and that's when I learned that we were not the only cruisers headed north, there were two other cruising boats headed that way also. An Endeavor 43', *Blue Streak,* had departed two days earlier from Lahaina bound for Seattle with a crew of three; the owner and two crew he picked up in Maui. The *Blue Streak* had done as we had and spent the summer cruising the islands. Mike would later inform me that while he was still on Maui, he had heard that *Blue Streak* was trying to find crew and having a difficult time of it. It wasn't because there wasn't anyone who wanted to make the voyage, but it was the terms that the captain was setting and his dogmatic manner that dissuaded most would-be voyagers.

Apparently, he wanted the prospective crew to not only pay for a share of the food and fuel but to cover the cost of any damage that the vessel might sustain along the way. I had not met the skipper but I was already developing a dislike for the man. *Blue Streak* was also reporting to the Net on a daily basis so I would be able track him and I planned do my best to overtake him. Being a mid-displacement boat, he had the edge over *Maiatla* in speed as well as a two-day head start (seemed fair to me!), but I felt that with careful course plotting and taking advantage of the weather along the route, playing the wind shifts while getting a push from swirling currents. I believed I could take him on tactics. I had no doubt that he would be watching our progress as well, and I suspected that he also knew that you can't put two sailboats on the same ocean and not have a yacht race. Ours would cover the better part 2600 miles.

The sailing vessel *Takaroa II,* a 9-meter New Zealand registered yacht, was owned by a British Columbia couple Chris Malchow, 31, and Courtenay Steele, 27. They had bought the yacht in New Zealand the previous June, and were returning to Canada on what they said was "an adventure of a lifetime". However, by all accounts that had been printed in a local newspaper, their voyage so far had been a trying one, including close encounters with freighters, gales and a freak wave that climbed aboard and broke the boom, washing Chris overboard in the process. Fortunately, it was his harness that saved him this time. The *Takaroa II* was planning on departing Hilo on September the 8th, a full five days behind us, rather late I thought for a safe passage home in a greatly smaller and potentially slower boat. I would have loved to contact them and remained in touch during the voyage as we would be sharing the very same water, but that was not to be. They would be leaving Hilo without a long range radio - sea water had destroyed theirs near Tahiti, an unfortunate circumstance that many would later come to regret.

The dark had scarcely taken hold, when I was surprised to hear the crew returning after a very short absence. Getting an early night, I thought. Despite having some similar misgivings about leaving Hawaii, they both were as eager as I was to get underway. Glancing at the chart upon the galley table, you wouldn't have to be Captain Cook to see that Tahiti was less than half the distance to Vancouver and over much more hospitable seas. I was starting to have serious misgivings about the northerly heading that I had chosen!

At sunup, just beyond the Nawiliwili breakwater, we were met with a rising swell and 15 knots of tradewinds from the east-northeast. After securing the dock lines and fenders for the long trip home, Mike and Kara quickly hoisted the mainsail and no sooner had the sail filled with air, I sheeted her in, swelling her belly. Before I had even cleated the mainsheet, there was a great "bang". Momentarily confused, I watched as the great sail begin to flog violently with the mainsheet block whipping around, dementedly, at the end of the main boom, threating to smash any skull that foolishly got too close.

"Mike! Drop and furl the mainsail on to the boom, we just lost the mainsheet traveler!" I called out, spinning the wheel to bring the boat back into the wind while ducking the thrashing block that was only inches from the back of my neck. Mike and Kara quickly wrestled the big sail down and secured it as I desperately tried to subdue the flailing block to prevent it from taking a gouge out of the deck or my head.

"What the hell happened? Sounded like a gunshot!" Mike demanded excitedly as he entered the cockpit.

"Looks like the bolts securing the traveler to the deck sheared off, the main block just slid off the track."

Mike turned to Kara who had just appeared beside him, with an exaggerated groan he declared, "Wellllll, that can't be good! That's a bad omen you know."

That was the first time I heard that annoying little phrase I would grow to hate over the duration of this voyage! Already feeling frustrated, I couldn't help but shoot back, "Don't start that bad omen crap! Shit happens! Stuff breaks! all we need to do is deal with it as it comes up so let's leave all that superstitious bad omen crap alone! Here, steer and keep us off the rocks while I have a go at fixing this."

I jumped out of the helm seat to examine the damage, letting Mike take the wheel. It was obvious that the traveler track was shot, it was in three pieces and it wasn't going to be put back together, it had to be replaced.

Mike groaned again as he looked at the shattered track that I was holding, he said, "Guess we will have to turn around and fix it. I don't think you can get the parts on Kauai, you will have to have them flown from Oahu, that is, if they have parts there. If not, I can have my buddy on Maui have a look as well. Should be able to find something to work."

From Mikes comment, I suspected that finding a proper replacement track in Hawaii would be a problem. *Maiatla's* track was outdated and obviously fatigued as the old bronze track had cracked like a ceramic tile. I had no doubt that Mike was a master at improvising and was capable of devising a solution out of whatever junk his friend could dig up from whatever boneyard he knew of, but I was not prepared to delay our departure, not even one single day. The season was already getting late for heading into the North Pacific, turning back to make repairs which could take days or a week or more, was not an option.

"Mike, lay the boat off-the-wind and we will pop the headsail and hoist the mizzen, let's get under sail first, before worrying about fixing the mainsail track. "I said. Orders followed; with sails set, *Maiatla* quickly settled down on a heading paralleling the shore at about three miles distance. Despite her shortened sail-plan, she scudded along at 4 knots while spitting sea-spume to leeward. (Spume is a type of foam created by the agitation of seawater)

I was reasonably sure I could jury-rig something; I already had a plan fermenting. I secured a half inch line, into the deadeyes that were bolted through the deck at the terminus of each end of the old traveler, drawing it up as tight as I possibly could. I used a second line and shackle to secure the mainsheet block at the first line's midpoint. With fingers crossed we hoisted the full main and I sheeted her home. *Maiatla* took on a new attitude and surged up to eight knots, nosing with authority into the growing swell.

I plucked the rod-tight lines like guitar strings as I declared triumphantly, "It ain't pretty but I think that will do it! We will just have to check it daily to make sure it's not chafing through anywhere."

With the first crisis of the voyage under control we all began to relax and enjoy the nice sail along Kauai's eastern shore. As we passed the abandoned harbour at Hanamaulu Bay, the winds were brisk and the swell long - a perfect sail.

"Hey Mike! Jump down below and kill the engine blower, will ya please?" Without hesitation, he slipped below and flicked the appropriate switch as I coiled the bitter-end of the mainsheet. I was just about to comment about how well the boat was sailing when we heard Mike's curse from below.

"Ah, Andy! You better get down here now, we are taking on water!" Mike called.

Kara and I gave each other puzzled looks before rushing below.

"What the hell are you talking about?" I demanded, but before Mike could answer I saw several inches of water sloshing about the lower cabin sole. It instantly occurred to me that if we had water above the floor, that below that, the 18 inches between the floor and the hull must be full of water as well. A lot of water!

From behind me, I heard that phrase for the second time in less than two hours.

"Well, that can't be good!" Mike's apparent fatalism would surface every time anything went wrong, a condition that would grind away on me throughout the voyage.

I didn't have time to respond to Mike's comment. Frantically, I lifted a floorboard expecting the worst, but what I found baffled me. Aside from the water that drained down the now open hole, the space was dry. The water was just sitting on top of the floor, but where was it coming from?

I pulled the drawers out of the cupboards on the port side, where I found water running down the wall. A quick check of the bookshelf below the stainless steel porthole revealed water. But this shelf was above *Maiatla's* waterline, so how could that be? As I pondered the problem, the culprit suddenly materialized as *Maiatla* commenced a heavy roll to port. As we charged over each swell, our leeward rail would momentarily become awash, the porthole would likewise be submerged, and with each dipping, water shot into the boat from the improperly dogged porthole. Another crisis adverted, just a bit of water to mop up after synching down the bolts.

The voyage had barely begun and I was already fearful that the gremlins that plagued us on our outward passage to the islands were back and already working overtime in an effort to scuttle us. However, as luck would have it, the flooding would be the last of our trials for a while.

The center of the North Pacific High was stationed well north of us, by 1000 miles. The center of the high which was almost 300 miles in width and 1000 miles long, contained light and variable winds, possibly doldrums with their none existent winds which could frustrate our passage. Sailing around the western end of the high in order to stay in the steadier winds was not an option as that would mean sailing halfway to Japan. We would just have to suck it up and sail straight through the center of the high and take whatever winds lay in wait for us.

With the gremlins satiated for the time being, our passage north became one of ease and blissful routine. We comfortably slipped into our 4-hour watches and *Maiatla* settled down onto a starboard tack under full sail, clipping happily along at six knots with 15-18 knots of warm tradewinds on the starboard beam. These near perfect sailing conditions would last the better part of two weeks. The crew had little to do other than some minor sail trimming as Auto kept our nose pointed due north. The radar was kept off during the daylight hours as visibility was exceptionally clear all the way to the horizon. On our night watches the radar was routinely set to turn itself on every 15 minutes to sweep the horizon for shipping. During the first leg of our voyage, nothing appeared on the screen and the alarms remained silent. Our days consisted of monitoring basically benign weather reports, reporting to the net and lying about in the sun and fishing, lots of fishing.

Mike in particular had the fishing bug - if the rods weren't out when he came on watch, he would set them -day and night we were dragging hooches. We landed a couple of large dorado, but it was tuna that constituted the bulk of our catch. Mike would take great satisfaction in dispatching the flailing fish with the spear gun before bringing it aboard or if small enough, it was killed on deck with a squirt of rubbing alcohol to the gills before being expertly filleted and packed for our freezer. Mike would usually save the choice pieces for that day's dinner. As a trained chef, he delighted us with his culinary skills and neither Kara nor I were fools it just took a little fawning over his dishes and he was more than ready to take on most of the cooking!

On most evenings, after an often delightful dinner taken in the cockpit, Kara would clean up as I reported to the Seafarer's Net while Mike took the helm. One of *Maiatla's* eccentricities was that whenever I hit the transmit button on the high-powered Ham set, Auto would have a brain-fart and turn hard to starboard. The electromagnetic interference of the radio played havoc with Auto's fluxgate compass a condition I tried hard to resolve, but finally I had to admit defeat and allow *Maiatla* her idiosyncrasy.

By the start of my watch at 2000 hours, it was movie time. I would set my laptop up on the companionway hatch and plug into the boats cockpit speakers for the surround sound effect. With the boat boldly charging through the night, we would devour popcorn, drink wine and watch movies well into the night. While taking an intermission between flicks, we would often wander onto the deck to admire a night sky that displayed a brilliance that we felt sure was designed just for us. Passing satellites and shooting stars were the only indications that the heavens were in constant motion. We watched intently as the waxing moon grew in brilliance with each successive night, until it's full body seized command of the night and illumined the seas surrounding us.

Just north of Kauai, the bioluminescence filled in and on the nights when the moon had not yet broached the horizon, *Maiatla's* wake produced a dazzling light show. Dolphins came and went at all hours and the odd seabird would roost on our deck for the night, taking to the wing when the sunrise was a hint of colour on the eastern horizon. A morning tour of the deck usually produced a few flying fish, found lying stiff in the scuppers. We could not have asked for a better passage and it appeared that the battle of the sexes had been sedated by our blissful sailing conditions. Mike and Kara appeared to have formed an informal truce. In fact, they seemed to be displaying an unusual tolerance for one another and signs of coupling were becoming evident. I decided that whatever was going on was better than that relentless bickering that defined their earlier relationship. The ship was happy and that is all that really mattered.

The only disheartening thing occurred within the first 10 days out of Kauai. During the net we listened to *Blue Streak's* daily reports. Apparently, he was blowing us away! He reported speeds of 8 to 10 knots with daily runs in excess of 180 to 200 miles compared to *Maiatla's* 130 to 140 miles. I couldn't believe that a late 1980s Endeavor 43' was that much faster than us in similar wind conditions, but apparently it was. I had been plotting his daily positions on the chart and a pattern was starting to emerge that looked rather suspicious - *Blue streak* would have to be watched a little closer.

Takaroa II departed from Hilo on schedule and would be incommunicado until they made landfall in three to four weeks. They, like us, had near perfect sailing conditions for leaving the enchanted islands.

Chapter #34

A Close Encounter

To travel hopefully is a better thing than to arrive.

Robert Louis Stevenson

The morning of our 12th day at sea found us sailing at four knots on a port tack with 8 to 10 knots of wind out of the northwest. The sky was clear and the sea calm as I peered out of the galley window at the long swell drifting out of the west. It was a beautiful day and I felt energized and decided to treat Kara and myself to a breakfast of bacon and pancakes. Mike was still up forward in the V-berth sleeping after his night watch. While the bacon was sizzling on top of the gimbled stove that swayed to the rhythm of the sea, I placed a mug on the corner of the stove and poured a cup of hot chocolate. Once stirred, I went topside. Kara was sitting comfortably in the helm chair with her legs crossed resting on the cockpit bench; with glazed eyes she stared off into the barren horizon beyond the bow.

"Here Kara, breakfast will be ready in a few minutes, hope you are hungry?" I said, as I passed her the steaming cup.

"Thanks Andy, I'm starved! Smells good," she offered, wrapping both hands about the mug, sipping the hot brew.

As I stood in the companionway looking aft at Kara, I spied over her shoulder a small freighter motoring up behind us. It was moving fast and traveling in roughly the same direction as us and it appeared that it would pass us nicely at about half a mile to windward. I heard Kara make a slight course correction prior to my coming topside and I naturally assumed that she had done it in response to the freighter's sighting. All looked good and there was no need for concern, but I had a standing rule that I was to be notified of all ships sighted, day or night and I was a bit annoyed that Kara had not called me. I dropped back down below to grab my tea and then hopped back topside to perch in the companionway with the binoculars to watch the tiny ship pass.

"So, when did you see him?" I asked.

Giving me a puzzled look, she paused before inquiring.

"When did I see who?" she questioned.

"Him!" I said, pointing to the ship that was about to overtake us a few hundred meters to port. She turned to look where I was pointing.

"Oh shit! I didn't see him, where did he come from?" she said, with a surprised look.

I was rather upset that she had not noticed the ship that was probably visible for at least 25 minutes as it came over the horizon. It was a clear day, the radar and alarms were off so we were relying on the human eye to watch for danger. Kara knew I was upset so I didn't flog her for missing the ship. I just informed her that she needed to do a better job of standing watch. When Mike later came on deck, I informed him what had transpired and reiterated to both of them that even though this was the first ship sighting in almost two weeks, we must be careful not to be complacent and let our guards down. We were approaching the shipping lanes from Asia to California and would most likely be seeing more traffic over the next few days. Satisfied that my warning would be taken to heart, I left it at that.

The following day was a carbon copy of the previous, but this time it was Mike who was nestled in the helm seat on watch. I was at the galley stove pouring a cup of tea when I just happen to peer out of the galley window. To my horror, I saw a container ship only a hundred meters away with a bone in its teeth about to overtake us! I shot topside.

"Mike did you see him?" Mike turned and seeing the ship cursed aloud.

The ship would miss us but not by much. Considering the closeness of the encounter, I doubted the ship saw us. It looked as if I could toss a beer bottle from my deck to his. Within a few minutes, we were staring at his stern and getting buffeted by his wake. I was extremely upset and I called Kara out of her cabin.

"OK, guys, that's twice in two days we had a ship sneak up on us and I've got to tell you that I, for one, <u>do</u> <u>not</u> want to **die** out here! So we all need to keep a better watch. Do you both understand? "I demanded in my best captain's voice while trying to sound authoritative but not angry.

Kara and Mike were visibly shaken, and looking a bit sheepish while remaining silent. They knew that there was no defence for what they had allowed to occur. Mike started to say something but after seeing the look on my face, he thought better of it. After admonishing the crew I couldn't help but wonder how many other narrow escapes we had had and not been aware of and I couldn't help likewise wonder if it had happened to me on my watch. Could have I missed a ship as well? We all needed to be more vigilant especially now as we were crossing busy shipping lanes and the traffic would get thicker as we closed on the coast.

Our mystery ship wasn't even out of sight before a second vessel breached the horizon, then another, and another. Surprisingly, over the next two days, there was almost always a ship or two in sight. There was a steady parade of vessels of all sizes following some invisible highway. I felt like a tortoise on the L.A. Freeway during rush hour. I would joke about how the ubiquitous sea-kayakers at home were mere speed bumps for *Maiatla*. The tables had now turned and we were the speed bump out here, a rather insignificant one at that. I called all the sighted vessels on the radio to make sure that they knew we were there and when necessary, they graciously altered course to go around us. Not one of them asked me to get out of their way; I appreciated their courtesy and professionalism. However, we would learn in a few days that not all mariners sailing this North Pacific were so accommodating. But our present situation reminded me of another time, years before. Some 300 miles off the coast of Mexico, in the wee hours of the morning I sited a ship in the distance. A quick check of the variable bearing lines on the radar indicated that he would miss us by a mile or so. Fortunately, I continued to track him and noticed right away that the vessel had unexpectedly changed course and would run us over if we didn't do something, and quick! I grabbed the VHF microphone and put out a frantic call while attempting to tack the boat at the same time. As *Maiatla* started to come about, I dropped the microphone to sheet the headsail back in. I turned back to see where the ship was and I was surprised to see the ocean around the freighter lit up; every deck light and spotlight onboard had come to life. Above the sound of wind and waves I could hear a great engine rubble and through the water, amplified by *Maiatla's* hull and echoing through the boat, the sound of a caviatating propeller in full reverse tearing up the water.. Thankfully, within a few minutes, the great ship had come to a complete stop.

Maiatla, on her new heading quickly gained speed and I had just finished engaging Auto when an anxious voice came over the VHF. The voice had a thick, Asian accent and it announced his vessel name and position.

Snatching up my hand held radio, I responded. "This is the sailing vessel *Maiatla*. I'm the boat that is quarter mile off your starboard bow, do you see me, sir?"

The voice shot straight back. "Stand by Captain."

A few seconds later a calmer sounding voice returned, "I see you, hold your course and I will go around you!"

I acknowledged his instructions and thanked him. I thought it strange that the ship had come to a complete stop but after giving it some thought, I could imagine that the deck watch of that ship was probably half asleep, but after hearing a call on the short range radio they perhaps feared that they were about to run down another vessel and initiated an emergency stop in hopes of avoiding a collision. Their reaction time was amazing and much appreciated on my part. After that, I always made it a habit of contacting all vessels sighted, if nothing else, just to say hello. Most were curious about where we were coming from and to where we were headed. After our latest encounters with shipping, I could not help but think of *Takaroa*, who was somewhere behind us, destined to cross this same busy shipping lane without the benefit of a radio.

For the next two days the winds stayed light, around eight knots and we had a hard time breaking 100 miles in 24 hours. But, later on the net after reporting our position and condition, I heard *Blue Streak* report similar light air conditions, but proudly announce that he had logged 238 miles in the previous 24 hours!

"Bullshit!" I called out to no one in particular. "That's Bullshit! The bastard's got to be motoring! Or lying, or both! There is no way he averaged 10 knots of speed in 8 knots of wind!"

Mike heard me ranting and came down from the cockpit to see what had me all worked up. I grabbed his arm and dragged him down into the seat next to me to look at the chart displayed on my laptop.

"Look at this Mike! This guy has been logging between 50 and 80 miles per day more than us, since we left Hawaii! He had a two day head start! With his reported speeds, he should be at least seven days ahead of us, but he is not, he is only 4 days ahead! We have been sailing roughly the same course the whole time, so this does not make sense!"

Mike studied the chart showing *Blue Streak*'s position, as logged since leaving the islands and ours.

"Well maybe he is reporting miles sailed through the water, not between point to point as you usually do? Or he's had some strong head currents, that would push him back, wouldn't it?"

Mike's reasoning made some sense, *Blue Streak* could be sailing fast but not necessarily in the direction he wanted to go; perhaps tacking frequently, adding miles to his course but not necessarily towards his destination. Still it didn't feel right. If he had a head current, then so should we! And we did not!

"Maybe Mike, but look at today's log, he said he made 238 miles in the last 24 hours, in these light winds! He must be motoring! There is no other way he can be doing that!" A thought suddenly struck me. "You know what? I bet he's been motor-sailing most of the way, which would explain how he seems to be pointing higher into the winds than we are and clocking off all these miles. Wouldn't it?"

Mike quickly agreed but considering the excited condition I had worked myself into over this matter, perhaps he thought it best to just agree with me! It's always safer to agree with the captain; it's better than risking pissing him off and having to walk home! *Blue Streak* was an enigma and despite my best efforts to figure it out, it would remain so.

The pitifully light and variable winds that I had feared, never materialized. Instead, the wind steadily built as an Aleutian weather front suddenly overpowered the Pacific high which quickly retreated to the south, causing it's doldrum-like center to pass us by. 1200 miles out from the coast of Vancouver Island, the weather suddenly changed. During the night, the northeast wind quickly filled in, arriving with a vengeance, the temperature plummeted from the mid-20s to 10 degrees Celsius. After almost two weeks of perfect sailing conditions, we were now reefed down heavily and beating hard into gale force winds that quickly formed boisterous six-meter waves with breaking hook-shaped crests. By dawn's early light, the wind was so strong that it seemed to possess shape and substance, delivering a cold "slap-in-the-face", causing you to brace yourself against the nearest shroud. There was no doubt that our halcyon days, the balmy nights with movie and popcorn binges in the cockpit, were over.

On our 16th day at sea, I was off watch in the mid-afternoon, cocooned in a thick comforter in my berth when the first wisps of smoke drifted past my nostrils. Next to sinking, fire is the most dreaded threat that a mariner can face at sea. Bounding from my berth, my nose quickly led me to the cupboard next to the engine room which contained a single electronic panel - the brainbox of our Auto-helm 6000. My stomach dropped as I spied the little grey box smoking like an ant under a magnifying glass. It appeared that the tumbling seas had tossed our slumbering gremlins out of their comfy beds and they were now pissed and up to no good! After killing the power, I carefully popped the cover off the unit. Any hope of repair instantly vanished as I exposed Auto's smoldering brain. Auto had suffered a stroke of apocalyptic proportions and was now hopelessly beyond salvage.

"Where's that burning smell coming from?" Mike demanded to know, as he burst into my cabin in search of the source of the smoke.

Kara who was on watch and reading at the time, had to take the helm as *Maiatla* inexplicably fell off the wind, bringing the big seas onto our beam; instinctively, Kara rounded her back up into the wind and sea while trying to re-engage Auto.

"It's Auto! He's fried!" I said to Mike, as I pointed into the open cupboard.

It had been a while, but there it was again - that groan followed by, "Ohhhh, that can't be good!"

Hearing Mike's lamenting dirge was like having someone behind me poking a needle into the back of my brain. But instead of screaming, I removed the mattress from my bed and began to root around in the dark recess next to the rudder post.

"What are you doing? Mike queried.

"I have replacement parts for the autopilot. I'll just wire up the spare controller. Give me an hour and Auto will be back on duty. Do you want to tell Kara what's going on and could you stay with her? She's not used to driving in these rough conditions? If we aren't careful, we could broach in these seas." I said.

Mike vanished topside as I found the pocket that contained the spare autopilot. We had purchased the spare many years ago, for just such an emergency and while still feeling proud of myself for having the forethought to anticipate such trouble, I pulled the slimy vacuumed packed bags out of the hole. As the bag slipped from my fingers I began to get an uneasy feeling about what I would find inside. I stripped the outer plastic which was no longer vacuumed sealed to revealed the box that contained the new electronic brain. I opened the a second bag wrapped tightly around my electronics and peeled away the soggy box to reveal a grey brain box that was oozing green slim from holes that were intended for the wire leads. I cursed out loud. I spent most of the day trying in vain to clean electronic components and cannibalizing the old unit in an effort to bring the brain back to life, but to no avail, my little Frankenstein sat lifeless on the table before me - Auto was dead and there was no resurrection forthcoming. After a quick and un-ceremonial burial at sea, I informed the crew that from now on, all watches would entail hand steering *Maiatla*. We were still 1000 miles out from Vancouver Island and due to the rough conditions, driving the boat - continuously palming the wheel back and forth - would be very tiring, so I split the watches up. For the remainder of the voyage, we would stand two-hour watches. Reading and napping on watch were now a thing of the past.

As we worked our way north, the conditions continued to deteriorate as the wind brought a cold and intermittent driving rain. Despite the ugly conditions, everyone was still in remarkably good spirits but that was about to change for one of us. Kara and Mike's rivalry had taken on a new form and instead of being right in each other's faces, their bickering banter had gone underground and they were much more subtle when it came to attacking one another - a tactic Kara was much more skilled at than Mike.

It had been an ugly and wet night when Kara came on watch, finding Mike wet and shivering behind the wheel. After spending many years in the tropics, Mike was very susceptible to the cold, soggy air and he was obviously suffering for it now. Kara took the helm and Mike disappeared down below to get into some dry clothes. I came on deck to inspect the sail trim and rig. *Maiatla* was working hard to windward so I decided to furl a little more of the headsail. As I eased the sail's sheet and pulled on the furling line, the snatch block that attached the sheet to the jib's clew suddenly popped open! Free to do as the wind demanded, the sail started to whip so violently the whole boat shook like a sopping wet dog caught in a down pour. I was afraid that the expensive sail would just tear itself apart in the strong winds. I had to furl the big sail, re-attach the controlling sheet and get it back under control but that wouldn't be easy, not in these conditions.

As the sail cracked like a bullwhip, I quickly leaned down into the open companion hatch and yelled, "Mike, come back on deck! The sheet has come off the headsail and I need help."

Mike appeared on deck dressed in what I would later learn was his last set of dry clothes. He had packed lightly and the thought of the weather turning cold never occurred to him. Living in Hawaii for so long, he didn't have much in the way of warm clothes to begin with. Perhaps that's the price you pay when you live in a place that seldom requires a person to put on long pants.

"We need to go on deck and lower the headsail to re-attach the sheets. I'll handle the halyard; you pull the sail down just far enough to clip the sheet back on the clew, OK ? Kara, bring the nose of the boat off the wind until she flattens out a little, but don't head down too far, she'll start to roll like a bitch in these seas if you do."

"Ok Andy," Kara acknowledged.

Being seated behind the helm when the sail cut loose she was all ready to drive as we required. Even though it wasn't raining for the moment, I put a foul weather jacket on, mainly to protect me from the biting wind.

"Hey Mike, you may want to get a jacket?" I said.

Mike peered forward for a moment before declining.

"It's not that bad out there and it will only take a minute."

I led the way on the windward side but stopped at the mainmast, hanging on tight as the boat canted heavily to starboard with each large wave that rolled beneath us. Crouching low to cling to the lifelines, Mike passed me to make his way up to the bow pulpit, once wedged between the forestay and the lifelines, he signaled that he was ready. Still crouching to keep from getting knocked off of the foredeck by the whipping sail, Mike pulled the sail down as I slackened the halyard. *Maiatla* was still charging on like a whipped horse despite Kara bring the head of the boat off the wind a little, but at least we were no-longer taking any water over the bow, for the moment anyway. It only took Mike a few minutes to snap the block back into place and wave to me to hoist away. Kara left the helm long enough to sheet the sail back in so it could fill and draw and with a "snap" filled full of wind, we felt the boat accelerate. I gave Mike the thumbs-up to indicate a job well done.

I have always loved going up onto the pulpit in rough conditions, leaning over the bow to watch the prow cut through the water. To see firsthand and up close *Maiatla* with a great bone in her teeth. Out on the bowsprit, the motion of the boat is exaggerated, not unlike being in a rollercoaster and it can be fun bouncing up and down as the boat drives over the waves. Obviously, Mike thought so too.

Instead of coming back to the cockpit, he stood upright on the bowsprit while clinging to the headsail foil and port life-line. He braced himself as he took the full force of the gale right on the chin. It was easy to see from the grin on his face, that he loved it. After a few minutes, Mike decided that he had pushed his luck with the weather far enough; he turned aft and began working his way back to the cockpit. I was about to do the same when *Maiatla* suddenly turned 30 degrees hard to port, rounding up into the wind and waves! Before I could call a warning to Mike, *Maiatla's* port bow smashed into a great wave; a column of water shot first straight up into the air a good 3 meters (10 feet) then cascaded back down onto Mike like a waterfall, soaking him to the skin. I was fortunate and only received a light shower. Mike, resembling the proverbial drowned rat cursed all the way back to the cockpit and when I entered the dodger, Kara had a mischievous cheek-splitting grin on her face. A sopping and moaning Mike pulled himself back inside the cockpit and then began to yell at Kara.

"You did that on purpose! This is my last set of clothes and there is no way to dry them, what am I to do now?" He was furious!

I couldn't help but laugh which did nothing to help matters. Kara eventually loaned Mike some dry cloths which smoothed things over a little but when I suggested that Kara could give him a pair of dry panties, he stomped off, refusing to take my bait.

Despite repeated denials that she had done it intentionally, Mike refused to believe her. I wasn't sure either way, but I did notice that the timing of *Maiatla's* turn into that particular wave was perfect! I also noticed that Kara had a smile on her face for hours afterward and to steal a line from a country song, there was a little devil behind those angel eyes!

Once everyone settled down, I went back on deck to takes some pictures. I stood on top of the propane box located beside the mizzen mast raising my head a full 4 meters (13 feet) above the sea. While standing on the box with *Maiatla* in the trough between waves, I was forced to look upwards to see the crest of the waves as they charged towards us. The waves appeared tall but quite thin. As the waves approached, I could see the setting sun through the wave tops. If there were fish present, I'm sure I could have seen them swimming about above my head! Conservatively, I estimated the wave height to be pushing seven meters (23 feet) with the odd monster wave, that I had difficulty taking my eyes off of. But the crew and *Maiatla* seemed to be taking the weather and waves all in stride.

Later that night the wind backed to the west, putting us onto a dead-run with 35 knots of apparent wind coming over the stern. *Maiatla* was sailing well with the mainsail swung all the way out to port and secured to the rail by a four-to-one block set. The full number 2 headsail was poled-out to starboard. The result was that the two sails spread out in front of the boat, catching the wind, like a pair of giant wings. A perfect wing-and-wing sail. *Maiatla* loved running off the wind like this, as she was so well balanced that she would practically sail herself, which made it easy on the helmsmen to steer. We were still almost 900 miles from land, but tearing off the miles fast as *Maiatla* would periodically catch the perfect wave just right, surfing down the surface of the wave, "pegging" the knot-meter at 10 knots. It was exhilarating but potentially dangerous as it was easy to lose control of the boat surfing at these speeds as the boat may suddenly roll hard to one side and turn sharply exposing the beam to the breaking seas, causing a roll over, or a " Death Roll".

During my watch in the pitch of the night, a large breaking wave unexpectedly slammed into *Maiatla's* port stern-quarter causing me to momentarily lose control. *Maiatla's* nose rounded up into the wind; I fought the helm in a vain attempt to keep the boat on course and from broaching in the big seas.

Maiatla rolled sharply to windward and slid sideways down into the deep trough of a wave. All I could do was hang on to the helm seat and wait for the next breaking wave to slam into us and possibly roll us over, but before that could happen, the vanged-out mainsail back-winded with such a force, that the tackle securing it exploded. The mainsail boom, now free, crossed the boat with incredible speed, barely clearing the dodger and slamming into the starboard shroud with such force that the heavy spruce mainboom split with a lightning bolt crack! The impact felt horrendous and shook the entire rig so violently that I believed that the 20 meter mast (60 feet) was about to come down around my ears! It was one of those "bowel loosening" moments that we all dread.

Maiatla was now dead in the water and refused to answer to the helm despite my having the wheel hard over in an effort to turn her back down wind. For several seconds I hunkered down in my chair with my arms over my head, fully expecting to be clobbered by the main or mizzen mast or decapitated by one of the wire shrouds as it parts under the incredible strain. While I was preparing for the "roof to cave in", the headsail suddenly refilled with air and began to point the bow of the boat back downwind. Feeling *Maiatla* to begin to recover, gain speed and begin her turn, I encouraged her. "Come on baby you can do it! Please before we get swamped! "

Painfully slow at first, *Maiatla* started to turn, but turning downwind she was! Someone must have taken pity on us or our gremlins blinked, because the next breaking wave that could sink us never came.

The whole experience, which seemed like an eternity to me, probably transpired in less than two minutes and aside from the green light emitted by the

GPS, it all occurred in utter darkness. By the time I had *Maiatla* straightened out and sailing again, Kara had hit the spreader lights and both her and Mike were on deck wondering what the hell had happened.

"Kara! Take the helm while Mike and I go forward, start the engine in case you need to use it to keep us sailing straight, OK?"

When I reached the mainmast, I was sick to see a horizontal split that started at the mast, from the gooseneck extending almost a third of the boom's length. However, there was no time to mourn; we quickly dropped and furled the mainsail. I checked the rig for additional damage but didn't see anything of concern. I thanked the Kaohsiung Shipyard for building such a strong boat.

Once we tidied up the deck, we slipped back into the cockpit.

"Andy, the motor won't start! I've been trying and she won't go," Kara said.

F***king gremlins, I thought. I was exhausted and emotionally drained but it was over, for now at least.

"Don't worry about it Kara, I'll have a look at it in the morning, everything is under control now."

Mike gave me a hand hoisting the mizzen sail and we set it opposite to the polled-out headsail, vanging it tightly to the rail. We killed the spreader lights and carried on into the night.

In the morning, there were a couple of chores to take care of. First, I attempted to start the engine, but it was no use, I changed fuel filters, bled lines and tapped the fuel injector pump with a hammer and the engine still failed to start. So, I got a bigger hammer and the bugger still refused to start! I would later learn that the fuel injector pump had packed it in, likely caused by dirty Hawaiian fuel.

Despite the squally conditions, we had been making good time along our rhumb-line, but the wind began to clock to the northwest, forcing us to change to a more easterly course. We were now headed directly for Grays Harbour in Washington State. If we stayed on this tack, we would miss the mouth of the Juan De Fuca by 169 kilometers (100 miles)! I didn't want to have to beat up the coast of Washington in foul weather, so I initiated a series of tacks that would work us up wind and to the north while we were still far offshore. On our new headings, at times we found ourselves sailing away from the coast, adding many more miles to our already long voyage. The frequent tacks and staying hard-on-the-wind while hand steering was grueling on the crew.

"What does everyone want for lunch?" Mike called up the companionway as I steered with Kara lounging on the cockpit bench next to me. She wore her harness and had the tether wrapped around the genoa winch to keep her from rolling off the bench. Kara was ambivalent about lunch so I made a command decision.

"Kraft dinner and hot dogs!" I shouted back.

Mike popped his head out of the companionway.

"You sure? I have some tuna from the fish I caught last night, I could do a rice stir-fry with fish?"

"No fish! Just the macaroni and hot dogs will be fine, thanks Mike!"

Perhaps feeling a bit slighted, Mike dutifully slipped back down to prepare lunch. He had not been gone long when the boat suddenly lurched to starboard in reaction to a small but freakish wave. As we rolled back upright, we heard a teeth jarring crash and the shattering of glass from down below. Kara bolted to the companionway to see what broke and to see if Mike was alight.

"You OK, Mike?" Kara demanded to know.

Mikes response was slow but positive.

"I'm fine but I have a mess to clean up," he said, sounding rather sullen.

It sounded like the dish drainer full of drying dishes and cutlery had hit the floor! All our dishes were unbreakable Corelleware (yeah, right!) and plastic Timmy's coffee mugs, so the sound of breaking glass was a bit of a mystery.

I yelled passed Kara, "What broke, Mike?"

Again, Mike was slow to respond but when he did, he sounded worse than before, "My French Press!"

I did a little happy dance behind the helm,

"That will cost you twenty bucks Mike!" I yelled back.

In truth, I had started to get worried about that French press… we were nearing home and that damned little press was proving to be more of a survivor than I had anticipated. But no more!

Kara and I turned back to our idle chatter, she was telling me how she would like to buy her own boat when she got back and start cruising.

"I want to go to Mexico!" She said longingly, as her gaze drifted off to a place far away.

"Good idea, you know it will never be easier to do than now, before husband, kids, mortgages and careers and vested pension plans!"

At eighteen, Kara literally had her whole life ahead of her and unlike many at her age, she seemed to understand the possibilities that were almost limitless - her "old soul" perhaps giving her an edge over her peers. But that said, I still believed she would struggle to find real meaning in her life just as the rest of us old farts have done.

"That's one of the regrets that Jan I both have, is that we didn't start earlier, we had the boat and means before kids, but we always thought that there would be a better time, we would be better prepared and have more money, which we thought meant more freedom, but that is not always true. That's not what happens- life just gets more complicated making it harder to get away."

Most cruisers that we have met over the years have said the same things; they should have started sooner - sailed away before they got too old and could no longer climb that volcano to gaze over the entire island that they had sailed so far to see! Or to even be capable of helping a tiny village build their first one-room schoolhouse in a third-world country, when the rest of the world is oblivious to its very existence. I thought of something the author of *Walden's Pond* had written, where H. D. Thoreau observed, "the man with the fewest possessions is the freest".

Likewise, a 1960's beatnik poet turned musician said, "When you got nothing, you got nothing to lose." Bob Dylan and Thoreau were over a century apart, but shared similar ideologies when it came to the concept of freedom and life's meaning. On quiet evenings watches, Kara and I would discuss things like the meaning of life but in truth, I was perhaps more ignorant than her as I believe she was able to draw wisdom from that old soul of hers.

I would later explore this subject more and it both scared and surprised me when I asked myself, what the meaning of life was. Just asking the question, one is assuming that there *is* a meaning to life in the first place - but we just don't know what it is. Eventually I realized that it was just too general a question. Asking, "what is the meaning of life," we are inquiring on behalf of everyone and all life that exists in the universe - and to answer that question would require god-like omnipresence and infinite knowledge which is clearly beyond the scope of mortal man or this cruiser. When we ask the question, we are more likely to be asking for ourselves - "what is the meaning of *my* life?", a less cumbersome question, but still incredibly complex and deeply personal. And when we ask this question of ourselves, it is usually because we are trying to get our bearings in the world; seeking advice to help us set a course that will allow us to navigate through a time of uncertainty or strife in our lives - the illness of a child, for example.

In order to get a handle just who we are, we must to ask ourselves, is there a God and do we have a soul? Does life in general have value; does *my* life have intrinsic value? All these questions are extremely relevant and go into determining who we are and what our place is in the world. If you were to ask these question from an atheistic point of view, I think you would find that the answer is rather a negative one. The view that the world is strictly a physical phenomenon created by sheer happenstance of cosmic dust and radiation leaves no room in the universe for real meaning - as though we are nothing more than freaks of nature, just a glutinous mass in motion. Even if we feel personally fulfilled and happy with our lives, it still would have no ultimate meaning in the cosmos. If we indeed rose up, out of the primordial ooze, born out of the fermenting excrement of the heavens to first crawl then walk upon this earth without the guidance or help of a superior being, then there cannot be any meaning or purpose to life. From this atheistic platform, you can see that whether civility or anarchy rein, it's irrelevant as in the end nothing truly matters, which renders the question, is there any meaning or purpose to my life, rather moot.

The whole atheistic, naturalist or secular point of view is hard to swallow as the whole idea of nothing having any value or meaning is just so unpalatable. We are generally rational beings and when we don't understand it drives us crazy. If there is any saving grace in all of this it's that the atheistic or naturalist theories are just that; theories, as there is no real way of proving we evolved from a single cell ameba to rule the earth. We can't prove that there was nothing in the beginning, we can't prove a negative, but even if we fool ourselves into thinking that we can, the universe just doesn't care.

When I thought about all of the above, I couldn't help but get a bit depressed; but what is the alternative to nothingness? The flip-side, is the version which the theists (the God people) tell us and that is they believe that God created the universes for a certain purpose and that the creator in turn brought about our existence within the cosmos for a distinct purpose as well. What that meaning and purpose is they are a little vague but we are assured there is one. We are told that there are objective values rooted in the very nature of God and just by living by these values we not only receive a purpose and meaning for our lives we give meaning to the universe as a whole. An empowering concept to say the least.

All of the above is heady stuff for a dumb agnostic sailor who just wants to know what the hell he is doing way out in the middle of the ocean. After much contemplation and soul searching between distant islands and goblets of wine, I have come to believe that my purpose in life is a lot less lofty than helping the universe define and validate itself; and if God needs me to fulfill his plan, then I'll do what I can, but for now, just to keep my head from exploding, I'll focus on my purpose as I see it. Do I think life has a meaning and a purpose? The answer is yes, that is if you give it meaning; but the scope of our ability to give it meaning is extremely narrow as it is solely limited by our understanding and to the sphere of individuals that we touch with the positive values that we embrace. Love, honor, commitment to the betterment of myself and family are just such values. I believe that to find purpose and value and meaning in life you don't need to venture off on a religious pilgrimage, to scale the Tibetan Alps to confer with the Dali Lama or to breach the walls of the Vatican for an audiences with the Pope as all you need to do is embrace you family and friends to find your purpose in life to give meaning to your life. If you are loved, then you have intrinsic value and what more than that do you need? It may not be all eternal, but we won't know that until we reach the end. Or will we?

Kara seemed to be drinking in all that I was saying about following your dreams and finding yourself and place in the world, and I hoped that she would follow through and chase her dreams, whatever they were. I was also pleased that she had received some inspiration from the way Jan and I had chosen to live. I just prayed that whatever she ultimately did, that we wouldn't be the ones her family would blame!

"You know Kara, We wish we starting cruising long ago, but excuses not to go were too easy to find."

The reality is that doing nothing is immensely easier than doing something. Jan once found a quote by a very wise man that I believe is as relevant today as in his own time:

"*Twenty years from now, you will be more disappointed by the things you didn't do than by the ones you did. So throw off the bowlines. Sail away from the safe harbor. Catch the trade wind in your sails. Explore. Dream. Discover.*" - Mark Twain

Kara was lying quietly contemplating what I had just said, or perhaps I was just flattering myself to think she was taking to heart any of my utterances. She appeared to be processing my words when suddenly she remembered that she was hungry and turned to look at the closed companion hatch.

"What's taking Mike with lunch? It's been a while and I'm starved!" Kara said.

I checked my watch and indeed it had been over an hour since we had placed our food order with our resident chef.

"Here Kara, take the helm while I go check on lunch and get myself a beer."

As I pushed the companion hatch back, a billowing cloud of steam burst up into my face. I jumped down below to find Mike frantically stirring a great pot that was boiling its guts out on the stove.

"Hey Mike, what's going on? Where's our lunch? The crew is getting ugly from starvation!"

Mike, looking rather sheepish turned to me with either sweat or condensation dripping from his brow, "Well, I think I screwed up the Kraft dinner. Guess I should have read the instructions on the box first!" he said.

"What do you mean you screwed it up? You can't wreck KD, everyone knows how to make it! What did you do?" I asked, incredulous.

"Well I brought the water to a boil and put the macaroni in, along with the powered cheese packet, didn't realize I did it till it was too late!"

"OK, it's screwed, so what are you doing now?"

"Well I've been trying to render it down by boiling it, to thicken it up!"

I peered into the steaming pot and dipped the big ladle into the bubbling cheddar-colored brew. I started to laugh at the sight of it; it was a runny, murky mess, gruel-like and full of noodles that they were in the process of being puréed into mush by Mike's desperate stirring.

"Hey Mike, just dump this seagull shit and start over, we have lots of KD," I said.

"Oh no! I can save it, it just needs to boil down some more!"

Mike was in earnest and obviously on a mission to save the KD and perhaps his reputation as a chef as well.

"No Mike, I know you hate to waste food, but just dump it over the side and feed the fish!"

That was one of the things we noticed about Mike, he hoarded leftovers while scheming to find ways to incorporate them into our next meal. He got upset with me one day for tossing a two day old pancake overboard!

"I was going to have that for lunch!" he indignantly informed me when he discovered what I had done.

The captain won the debate and a new box of Kraft Dinner was broken open.

Chapter #35

Twilight Visitors

When men come to like a sea-life, they are not fit to live on land.
-Samuel Johnson

Four hundred and fifty miles out from our landfall at Victoria B.C, the wind slipped back down to the 30 knot range and mercifully decided to back to the west, putting us onto a dead run. The waves had settled some, dwindling to a less intimidating three to four meters (10 to 13 feet) with a long, comfortable period between them. We were running with a full number two headsail, poled-out and a reef-less mizzen driving us through a cold drizzling rain. The conditions were squally and wet but preferable to that of the previous four ugly days. With the engine useless for charging our large battery bank, the wind generator took over and in the gale force wind had no problem producing enough power to run all of *Maiatla's* electrical systems, including the deep-freeze that Mike kept working overtime, freezing all the fish that he felt compelled to hook and slaughter in numbers that I believed would surely attract the attention of Greenpeace. Gales be damned, Mike had to fish, and it was a good thing that a fishing licence is not required on the high seas!

By 4:00 a.m. Mike was due to relieve me at the helm. *Maiatla*, balanced, was easy to steer and would run straight for some time before requiring a minor caress of the helm to keep her on course. The ability to track well is one advantage of a full or modified keel boat, but you pay for this with poor handling while tacking during light air or motoring backwards. In these conditions this night, for the most part, I was enjoying the sail. It had been an uneventful night and I had spent most of my watch listening to my MP3 player and the salty tunes of the Sons of Maxwell.

As programmed, the radar screen lit up on time to scan the horizon, but instead of making half a dozen sweeps before shutting down, the air was filled with the high-pitched chirp of the perimeter alarm. I tilted the screen to have a better look. There, off in the upper corner of the radar screen, a tiny enigmatic smudge betrayed the presence of a ship. I was a little surprised, as we had not seen another vessel after leaving the shipping lanes a couple of days ago.

I ran a variable bearing line on the smudge and began tracking the speck, that could well have been mistaken for an island if not for the target's apparent movements. The vessel was a full 25 kilometers (15 miles) away, which first suggested that this was a big ship as a ship of average height and length wouldn't show up on the radar until it was within 20 kilometers (12 miles) or so, of us so to be visible to our radar at 25 kilometers, it must have been a monster of a ship. However, what kind of ship, I could not ascertain from the radar. It appeared to be alone, so it was unlikely that it was another aircraft carrier. Perhaps a container ship with steel boxes piled high on the deck or an auto transport that hauled cars from the Orient; they are both very tall vessels. For several minutes I peered through the rain-streaked dodger windows in the direction the radar had indicated. As soon as I saw the first hint of a glow on the horizon, I realized what type of vessel it was. The cruise ship, looking like the Parliament House on Christmas Eve, lit up the ink-black night. My tracking of the ship indicated that it was travelling fast, in excess of 25 knots was my best estimate, and we were on a collision course. I had little concern, as she was still many miles away. I reached for the VHF microphone and put out a call to the cruise-liner. The English speaking deck officer responded right away. He informed me that she was one of the "Holland American line", which ship exactly I missed, but she was the Rotterdam or Zaandam or something 'dam, and they were bound from Honolulu to Seattle. The name of the vessel would prove appropriate as I didn't know it then, but I would soon be damning their very presence on my ocean this night!

"Good evening, Sir," I replied. "This is the 53-foot sailing vessel *Maiatla*, I'm approximately eight miles off of your port bow traveling due east at seven knots. We appear to be on a collision course, do you see me?"

"Stand by, *Maiatla*."

At her present speed, the "dam" ship would run me over in less than 20 minutes if neither of us took evasive action! To make *Maiatla* more visible, I left the helm to turn on the spreader lights and running lights. To conserve power, we usually run only with a 360-degree white light at the masthead, only switching on the running lights when a vessel is encountered. I quickly jumped back into the helm seat to wait for a response. A few moments later, I received my reply.

"*Maiatla*, this is the ----dam, we have you on radar and a visual on you, you will need to alter course, do you copy?"

"What the hell!? I'm a sailing vessel! And should have the right of way! Doesn't this Damn asshole know that?"

Here I was again, talking to myself. I must have been stressed! I snatched up the microphone.

"Holland American liner, this is the *Maiatla*, I'm a ketch under sail and engineless, altering course significantly is difficult, can you please jog around me?"

Their response was immediate and final.

"*Maiatla*, we will not be altering course, you will have to alter to stay clear, good evening Captain."

Well, that was it; I was told and dismissed all in one breath! The belligerent ship was now looming large off to starboard, so I had no choice or time to debate the rules of the road with this moron. Cursing the asshole on that bridge who was probably laughing to himself over this, I left the dodger and dropped the mizzen, flaking it loosely around the boom. I thought that if I could slow us down enough he would just pass in front of me. I slipped back inside out of the rain to the helm to wait to see if this tactic would be enough. With the mizzen gone, we slowed, but it quickly became obvious that it was not enough. While still cursing, I furled up part of the headsail then slipped back to my chair, and checked the radar. *Maiatla* slowed even more, until we were only moving at two knots, not much more than a crawl, just enough to maintain good steerage in seas that seemed to be mounting in the increasing apparent wind.

I watched nervously as the massive ship cut across my bow at less than 150 meters (500 feet), the vessel was so long that I was forced to further alter course to starboard to cut behind the liner's stern. The poled-out headsail violently flogged as it began to backfill with wind; I continued to turn to starboard to clear the liner's tail, which now towered above us like a ten-story apartment block. Eerily, the pots on the stove began to vibrate and resonate as the thrum of the great ship's engines reverberated up through *Maiatla's* hull. It was the middle of the night and the ship's decks were deserted, I couldn't see a single soul onboard. Not a late night stroller taking air after leaving the casino, nor a galley steward wishing he was somewhere else as he peered longingly out a porthole. Perhaps that was a good thing because I would have probably raised a fist and shouted obscenities at anyone that I had seen. *Maiatla* had been engaged in a game of "Chicken" with a bully at sea, but discretion and survival came before my ego. Thankfully, the arrogant liner vanished as quickly as it had come.

After crossing the liner's foaming wake, I reset *Maiatla's* sails and got her back underway, grateful to have the sea all to ourselves once again. I dropped back down below and quietly, so as not to disturb her, reached into Kara's cabin to kill the spreader lights. Despite all the commotion on deck and the liners' engine noise, no one stirred. I glanced at my watch to see that it was almost 5:00 a.m. and past the time Mike was supposed to relieve me. I wasn't upset; I wouldn't have gone to bed with the liner nearby anyway, it was better to let Mike have the extra hour of rest. I went forward to the V-berth to roust Mike, but when I opened the door, his bunk was empty! Heading aft, I went to the head in search of him, but he wasn't there either! After a quick check of my cabin, I still could not locate Mike! I started to feel anxious, did he actually come topside to relieve me to find me on deck handing sails only to fall over unnoticed? There was nowhere else he could be! The boat was not that big that I would have missed him. Starting to feel sick to my stomach, I rushed back to Kara's room to roust her to help me look for Mike and, if the worst had happened, to turn the boat around.

I burst into Kara's dark cabin and hit the light. I was startled to find both Mike and Kara spooning in the bunk built for one, obviously sound asleep, cocooned in a comforter!

The berth in Kara's cabin is just over two meters long (six feet) and I can stretch out comfortably, but it is a good sea berth, and therefore, very narrow to keep you from getting thrown about in big seas. When I lay on this bunk, my shoulders reach from side-to-side, so I was very surprised to find both of them wedged into the small space behind the lee cloth. I was also taken aback by how they appeared to have reconciled their differences!

I shook Mike's shoulder.

"Your watch, need you topside." I said and left the room.

A groggy and dishevelled Mike appeared some minutes later to flop onto the cockpit seat next to me. I waited in silence to see what he would say; he offered nothing in explanation as to how he found his way into Kara's bed. I knew they were both adults and he really didn't need to provide one. Finally, after several minutes of silence, I broke down.

"S-o-o-o, Mike, don't like your room, or what?" I said while fighting to conceal a smirk.

Mike shifted a little and smiled at me.

"No it's not that, the hawse pipes to the chain locker are leaking and the foot of my bed is getting wet and I was cold so I crawled in with Kara to get warm, that's it."

"And Kara didn't bitch about you getting in with her?" I asked, perhaps sounding a bit skeptical.

"She did at first, but I told her I was cold and I needed her dry bed, if she wanted to stay she could, then I got in!"

Mike seemed to ignore the fact that my berth was empty at the time, warm and dry and there was the settee in the main salon that is also a good, dry sea berth. However, I can certainly understand how Kara's bed would have been more appealing for Mike under the circumstances!

Apparently, unbeknownst to me, the two had temporarily formed an uneasy truce. Perhaps out of necessity, what with being at sea for so long and the lack of any other possible bedfellows to choose from. But whatever or whoever initiated this truce escaped me; however, that didn't matter, I just found this new development rather amusing considering their tumultuous history. It was nice to see, but it also put me in a bit of a dilemma. I believed that Mike was dating my niece, Samantha; what if anything, should I tell her about this? Was there even anything to tell?

However, tonight in my general state of ignorance, I was a bit concerned, but I was too tired and needed to find my berth, I would just ignore the situation for now and cross that bridge when I came to it.

The closer we came to the coast, the better the weather conditions became. The wind continued to blow from the west but eased even more and we were happy to see a break in the clouds for the first time in a week, revealing patches of washed-out blue. On the evening cruiser's net, I heard *Blue Streak* make his final report, he was a little over 800 kilometers (500 miles) ahead of us and was about to arrive in Victoria. We had gained ground on him during the last week but I suspected that was only because he was running low on fuel and had stopped motor-sailing. Not being able to catch *Blue Streak* frustrated me. Nevertheless, in the end, I would have to let it go and be happy that he made it home safely even if it was ahead of us.

I also heard a health and welfare announcement on the net concerning a Japanese yacht with a single handler on board that was also bound for Vancouver from Yokohama. Seemingly, radio contact was lost with him a week previous, about the time of our first gale. The net was asking all shipping in the area to keep a lookout for him and report any contact. I plotted his projected course and estimated that he should be in our area if he was still sailing. I made a note to watch for him. As expected, there was no news of *Takaroa II*. Being a much smaller vessel, she had little chance of catching us due to *Maiatla's* longer waterline and our big head start. More than likely, she would be encountering the leading edge of the gale that had battered us last week.

Takaroa II would be battened and reefed-down heavily, taking the stiff north easterlies and big waves on the nose, as she approached the busy shipping lanes. A bad combination of circumstances that would make the tiny boat all but invisible to the radars of the commercial vessels. *Takaroa II* would appear as a single white speck amongst the sea clutter (indistinct scattered returns from a radar pulse) on the radar scope. If the officer of the deck set the gain on the radar too high, a small vessel like *Takaroa II*, may not even show at all.

It would be some months after our arrival home before we would finally hear of the disappearance of *Takaroa II*. Despite the US Coast Guards best efforts the little boat was first listed as overdue, then declared lost at sea with all hands.

Figure 35.
Lost At Sea-The Crew of Takaroa II departed from Hilo Hawaii just days behind *Maiatla* but they would not arrive in British Columbia as planned.

A tragic end for a brave couple who dared to try and live out their dreams. I choked up when I first heard of their loss and I dearly felt for their families.

It was turning into a beautiful evening with clearing skies to the west and we watched as the sun began to set. Kara went down below to turn the masthead light on for the night and to see if Mike wanted a hand making dinner. Another tuna dish as he landed two great fish this day. His fishing endeavors were relentless. I on the other hand had long tired of reeling and gutting and left the rod tending and cleaning to Mike. By the time we arrived home, the freezer was full and it would take almost two years before Jan and I barbequed the last of Mike's catches.

I was content watching the day fade when I heard a little thud and flutter coming from the aft deck. I turned to see a small bird, the first winged critter spotted for weeks. I called to Kara to tell her about our little visitor, and just as I did, another bird dropped to the foredeck with a sickening thud, then another on the cabin top. In the matter of a minute or so, a couple dozen black, scruffy-looking birds crash landed and began scurrying about as if trying to find someplace to hide!

"Where are they coming from?" Kara demanded to know.

"I don't believe, I've ever seen this type of bird before, it's probably a flock of shore birds that were blown offshore," I offered, speculating as I didn't really have a clue but as captain I was expected to know these things.

"They are probably exhausted and need a place to land. I've had birds hit the sails at night and fall to the deck, but never a flock that tried to land before!"

The three of us watched intently as several more birds flew in low to attempt a landing, as if we were an aircraft carrier. Mike and I were shocked, and Kara was horrified as some birds overshot the landing zone only to bounce off masts, grab-rails and winches only to tumble over the rail, falling into the sea to be swept away. It was a surreal sight and not unlike the game Angry Birds only with real feathers flying about. The lucky ones that managed to put the brakes on and come to a stop while still on board were wandering on the deck, jumping up onto the slippery cap-rail (wood trim running all around the perimeter of the deck) only to find themselves tumbling over the side as well. Frantic to save the birds, Kara grabbed the plastic Rubbermaid laundry hamper, dumped the dirty cloths, and attempted to collect as many of the scrambling birds as possible.

It would have been comical if the consequences didn't appear so dire for the tiny birds.

"Come help me Mike!" She demanded.

For several minutes, the pair chased birds around the deck. The birds flapped and ran and dodged, doing their best to avoid capture - and to Kara's horror, most preferred the turbulent deep to imprisonment and without hesitation they jumped, as if mindless lemmings, into the sea! It was pandemonium on the deck as my crew chased the little creatures that ran, and then jumped about, finally hurdling overboard; surprisingly, none took back to the wing. What resembled an old fashion chicken-catching party raged across *Maiatla's* deck! And all the while, new birds flocked in, crash-landing on the boom and cabin-top, and tumbling into the scuppers. The new arrivals who survived the landing, joined the fray, getting chased around the deck until finally doing their own kamikazes into the sea! For almost ten minutes it was chaos on deck and funny as hell, what with Kara pleading for Mike to help all the while calling to the frighten birds not to jump and crying out in pity when they did.

As soon as the last of the light had gone, the incoming birds stopped arriving. Sadly, for all their effort, my crew only managed to capture and save 8 birds out of the 40 or so that settled on our decks and god knows how many over shot the boat and went straight into the drink.

Kara brought the hamper full of birds back to the cockpit. "What should I do with them now? Where can I put them?" she asked.

I peered into the basket at the tiny birds that now refused to move, just black balls of feathers huddling together, panting heavily in silence. A pitiful site and I could tell by her drawn expression it troubled Kara deeply.

"Just put the basket on the aft deck, give them a chance to rest and in the morning you can let them go," I said.

But won't they still be lost, they won't be able to find the shore, we are still a long way out, aren't we?" Kara asked.

"About 300 miles, but rested up they should be able to make it and I'm sure they have some kind of homing mechanism so they can find land again."

I offered. I could see that Kara was very troubled so I added, "You may be able to keep them till we get closer to shore, that may help." I personally believed that the birds had little or no chance of surviving this far out, but I wasn't about to tell Kara that.

With renewed hope for her newly adopted flock, she took the laundry hamper full of scared and exhausted birds to the aft deck and placed a towel overtop, for shelter.

Over the next several hours, Kara offered the bird's bread and water, but none took to it. In the morning when she went aft to check on her charges, she was shocked to find all but one dead.

Her voice on the verge of cracking, she asked, "Why did they die?"

"Perhaps they were too exhausted and beyond recovery when they got here," I offered. "Or maybe being confined and scared killed them; not sure, but you tried your best, unfortunately it didn't work."

"What should I do with them now?" she asked as she reached into the hamper to see if she could jostle the birds back to life.

"Well, toss the dead ones over the side; give them a burial at sea," I said.

"But what do I do with the live one? It will probably die too if I keep it!" Kara was clutching the last remaining living bird in her cupped hands as she stroked the bird with her thumbs, the tiny head swiveled, responding to Kara's gentle touch.

"You'll just have to let it go! Toss it high into the air and hope it has the strength to fly away," I said.

Kara didn't like my idea but realized that there wasn't an alternative. Cautiously she went to the rail, whispered something to the bird, and tossed it high into the air. The tiny feather-ball rose into the sky, and then began to fall back, towards the water; but before hitting the surface, the bird stretched out its wings to soar away from the boat, while just clearing the wave-tops. It darted from side-to-side for several seconds before climbing high up into the air. We watched as the bird seemed to revel in its freedom; it swooped down only to climb back up again, an action he performed several times.

"He made it!" Kara excitedly exclaimed as she turned to give Mike a big grin.

However, as Kara turned, I saw over her shoulder our little friend suddenly shudder as if hit by a load of buckshot and take a nosedive into a wave top. It did not come back up. Thankfully, Kara missed the crash; I did not have the heart to tell her.

Subsequently, I did some research into our little feathered visitors and what I found was both fascinating and puzzling at the same time. I was surprised to learn that they weren't shore birds at all, but were actually a species of Storm Petrel; a pelagic bird that spends most of its life at sea only going to shore to nest for brief periods.

Figure 36. Kara with her single surviving visitor preparing to let it fly away.

It's no wonder they preferred jumping ship to being taken prisoner but why they attempted to land on us was still a mystery. Apparently species of Petrels are believed extinct, most are endangered and little is known about them. The word petrel came from the word peter-the birds that appears to walk on water. The more specific 'storm petrel' or 'stormy petrel' is a reference to their habit of hiding in the lee of ships during storms. Early sailors named these birds "Mother Carey's Chickens" because they were thought to warn of oncoming storms; this name is based on a corrupted form of Mater Cara, a name for the Blessed Virgin Mary. Breton folklore is not so kind to the little birds which holds that storm petrels are the spirits of sea-captains who mistreated their crews, and now are doomed to spend eternity flying over the sea. It is also said that they are the souls of drowned sailors. A sailing superstition holds that the appearance of a storm petrel foretells the approach of bad weather. If this is so, considering what we had been beating into the past days, I would say that they little bastards were running a bit late.

Chapter #36

Juan de Fuca Gales

Avoid destructive thinking. Improper negative thoughts sink people. A ship can sail around the world many, many times, but just let enough water get into the ship and it will sink. Just so with the human mind. Let enough negative thoughts or improper thoughts get into the human mind and the person sinks just like a ship.

Alfred A. Montapert - The Supreme Philosophy of Man: The Laws of Life

The weather continued to improve over the next three days which was a godsend as we approached the notorious west coast, the "Graveyard of the Pacific". We started to encounter an assortment of ships that were headed either into or out of the Strait of Juan de Fuca; thankfully my crew had learned their lesson concerning keeping a good watch and all encounters between them were benign ones.

The sea was taking a rest, letting the wind and waves lay down enough for us to almost call the conditions pleasant. Kara was steering while I lounged in the cockpit when suddenly Mike began to howl. He was fishing on the aft deck when something struck his line.

"Andy grab the spear gun I've caught a huge sea snake!"

Mike had fished his way across the pacific and he managed to catch so many fish that I no longer gave a crap anymore when the rod began to jump and line sped out, but his assertion that he caught a snake and need the gun got my attention. I left the cockpit, snatching up my spear gun as I passed the fishing rod holder (spear gun holder) strung between the mizzen shrouds and joined Mike. As I watched the action, I was a little surprised that the heavy fishing rod was nearly bent in two as Mike, with great effort reeled the monster in.

"You know Mike we don't have sea snakes up here so I don't know what you've got there, but I'm pretty sure it's not a snake," I said, perhaps sounding a little condescending.

I was about to make another snide remark when I caught site of what looked like a tan bulbous head and a long slender body that ended in a pointed tail that whipped the surface. Mike continued to reel and pull forcing the creature to slither alongside the boat. With my gun in hand I peered over the side to size it up the three meter long monster before shooting it.

I patted Mike on his shoulder as I turned to walk away.

"Good catch Mike but just as I though, bull kelp!" I said with a great smile. "You shouldn't have any trouble cleaning that one buddy." I couldn't help having a little fun at his expense.

Mike, who was first an urbanite from the eastern states, then a beachcomber from the tropics, may never have seen bull kelp, the long whip-like plant with its bulbous head (mermaid's bladder) so perhaps his confusing was understandable. In the northern hemisphere, the kelp beds along the Pacific coast are the most extensive and elaborate submarine forests in the world. The giant kelp is only one species of marine algae found along the Pacific coast of North America and grows in the cool waters from Alaska all the way down to Baja, California. Although it begins life as a microscopic spore on the ocean floor, after anchoring its self to a rocky seabed, this species may grow to lengths of sixty meters (200 ft.) with its upper fronds forming a dense canopy at the surface. The free-floating kelp that Mike had hooked was a good indication that that land was not far.

Onehundred miles out and a day away from sighting land, the winds were now a steady westerly at 10 knots and were predicted to hold for the next few days. However, as always, they were to build back to 35 knots or more as we approached the strait. The Strait of Juan de Fuca is 150 kilometers (90 miles) long, 25 kilometers wide (15 miles) and lies between the 47th and 48th north parallels of latitude with the U.S and Canadian border running directly up the middle. It was first discovered in 1592 by the Greek pilot Juan de Fuca, whose real name was Apostolos Valerianos, and who was sent north by the viceroy of Mexico on a voyage of discovery. The strait is bordered by the majestic Vancouver Island Mountains to the north and the Olympic Mountain Range of Washington State to the south; these great mountain ranges typically funnel the air inward towards inland waters of the Straits of Georgia, producing gale force winds in this region, a condition I was thankful for since we were engineless. Having an abundance of wind to maneuver and drive us up one of the busiest shipping lanes on the west coast was preferable to wallowing about like a lethargic sea lion. I must have said this aloud, because our devious little gremlins heard me; forever scheming, rather than tear my boat to pieces right beneath my feet, they decided to employ a subtler and more cunning tactic .

With the dawn break of our last day at sea, we found ourselves totally becalmed on an ocean that resembled an undulating mirror. The gremlins had struck! We were within 40 miles of the coast; the mountains would have been clearly visible if not for the proverbial pea-soup fog that draped equally heavy over the boat and our spirits. For most of the day, *Maiatla* had little or no steerage as the headsail and mizzen slatted back and forth to the rhythm of the deep, groundswell that originated several thousand miles to the west. On several occasions during the day, we found ourselves pointed back towards Japan, with no ability to turn ourselves, aimlessly drifting, at the mercy of the tide and currents. Our normally trailing green hoochie ineffectually dangled pendulum-like, directly below the boat in the clear cold water.

As if to tease us, the marine weather station was still forecasting gales for our area; as usual, they could not have been more wrong. The final insult came with the discovery that those little gremlin bastards had broached my spirit locker – they drank my entire stash of red wine! The beer had mysteriously vanished the week before, so we were now officially a dry boat. The type of dry boat that in previous centuries could have spawned a mutiny when the crew no longer received their grog rations. No wonder the little gremlin beggars were so quiet, they were all probably prostrate in the bilge sleeping it off! We were left utterly spiritless and moral was beginning to suffer. We drifted throughout the day, becalmed and out of control, just as depicted in the *Rime of the Ancient Mariner*:

Day after day, day after day,
We stuck, nor breath nor motion;
As idle as a painted ship
Upon a painted ocean.

Water, water, every where,
And all the boards did shrink;
Water, water, every where,
Nor any drop to drink.
     -*Samuel Taylor Coleridge, 1798*

I made a mental note that 40 liters of homebrew wine was insufficient for a four month voyage. We kept our wine in four liter plastic bladders which were stored in convenient lockers about the boat. While contemplating our new dilemma, I suddenly recalled something that I had read long ago. Back in 1966, before Sir Francis Chichester attempt to sail solo around the world aboard his yacht *Gipsy Moth IV*. He was seen loading supplies in Plymouth and it was observed that a rather large quantity of gin and a hand-pump Whitbread beer system was taken aboard. Considering that the beer people were sponsoring his voyage it is understandable why he would sail several kegs aboard. When questioned about this Sir Francis's reply was "Any damn fool can navigate the world sober. It takes a really good sailor to do it drunk". If you were to read Chinchester's book of his record breaking voyage you would see that his statement was anything but a hollow boast as he was forever finding an excuse to either celebrate or commiserate with a drink, which was easy to do as he had a spigot and hose next to his gimbaled chair that lead to a pressurized beer keg.

Chinchester's success while DUI notwithstanding, I do not want to suggest in any way that we operated *Maiatla* in a similar condition. On the contrary, a bulk of our spirits were consumed by the crew while at anchor or limited to a couple of glasses of wine or beer for the evening meal or during a late night movie. Life on the high seas was dangerous enough without adding drinking and driving to the mix. Francis Chichester was knighted by the Queen with Sir Francis Drake's own sword, and I could not help to wonder if Chichester was sober for the ceremony?

Kara's young ears heard it first; off in the distance, but the sound of a large bow cutting through the water was unmistakable. I had been tracking the ship for a while on radar and she would pass very close. I called the vessel to inform him of my location and predicament. He didn't sound very sympathetic but altered his course anyway to give us a wide berth. Throughout the day many ships passed by, none of which we saw. Feeling a little nervous, I decided to contact Tofino Vessel Traffic Services, to inform them of my position and engineless condition. VTS Tofino was quick to locate us on their radar and to inform all commercial traffic of our condition and intention of sailing up the strait engineless. I was then able to relax somewhat, knowing that VTS was now watching out for us.

By the afternoon, the wind had slowly developed into a light breeze from the east, so we were able to sail again, managing to work our way shoreward until we were within a couple of miles of Cape Flattery Lighthouse, on the American side, in Washington State. Disappointingly, the fog held and the predicted westerly gales never materialized. The wind never blows when you want it, and when it does blow, it's always from the wrong direction! With the minimal steerage provided by the light winds, I was able to avoid the center part of the commercial shipping lanes. However, entering and sailing upwind into the mouth of the comparatively narrow Strait of Juan de Fuca, was going to be tougher; I would have to tack back-and-forth numerous times across the Strait, from the American to the Canadian side, against the easterly winds - while dodging ships! If you could imagine having to cross a busy freeway half a dozen times while peddling a child's tricycle, you may be able to begin to understand our dilemma.

Vessels of all sizes and nationalities entering and leaving the Strait continually passed close by - very close, but at least I didn't have to worry about contacting each one as VTS was doing that for me. By sunset, we were only a couple of miles offshore of the Canadian side of the Strait when Mike came on deck.

"So, what does everyone want for dinner? I can do some tuna steaks with rice, sound OK?" he asked as he looked at Kara and myself expectantly.

After three weeks of eating fish almost daily, I had had enough, hell I was down right sick of fish and I guess my response was a bit shorter than it probably should have been.

"No fish, Mike! No tuna steaks! No fish shish-kabobs or tuna stir-fries or dorado casseroles! Dig into the back of the freezer and grab a couple of beef steaks and boil some potatoes and mash them!" I said. I may have sounded indignant but I wanted to make myself clear to Mike.

"But...But ", Mike stammered, "I still have tuna in the fridge that we should eat, I can't put it in the freezer now… it will spoil if I don't use it!" he continued with genuine concern. "How about I take the fish and…….?"

"Don't argue with me Mike! I shot back, raising my voice. I want a steak! Bloody red meat! Fried grilled or shredded but I'm going to eat meat tonight… even if I have to butcher the cook and barbeque him… do you understand me!? Meat I want meat!" I said.

For a moment I though Mike was going to continue to argue with me but I suspect that the glare in my eyes changed his mind.

As we drifted along, it was glorious as we dined on steak for the first time since leaving Kauai, with a cook who was uncharacteristically withdrawn.

A little after 10:00 p.m. the wind died completely. We drifted until the onshore current set us toward the shoreline that was part of Vancouver Island's infamous West Coast Shipwreck Trail.

Built in 1907, the West Coast Trail stretches for 80 kilometers along a treacherous section of southern Vancouver Island's west coast that is densely wooded and part of Vancouver's Island great rain forest. Part of the Pacific Rim national park and a popular hiking trail today, but it was originally built between Port Renfrew and Bamfield to assist in the rescue of shipwreck victims.

We were only a few miles from Port San Juan, a semi-protected bay but it was a port only in name as there was nothing to be had or no help to get the engine fixed coming from there. Victoria was our best bet, it was easy to get into, good docking facilities, and I could leave the boat there until the engine was repaired.

Unbeknownst to our darling daughter Melissa, Jan and I had discussed it and decided that we were not going back to our home town of Mission and our old lives there. We had already arranged for a dock at Townsite Marina in Nanaimo, about an hour's drive up the coast from Victoria. So by all accounts, we were almost home. Our decision to move had been a difficult one and not taken lightly. For Melissa, age sixteen, it meant a new high school and friends and a new "island life" for all of us. I was dreading telling Melissa, an act that may well have all the repercussions of taunting a tornado when you reside in a trailer park, but we believed it would be best for us all in the long run.

"Andy, I can hear breaking waves over there!" Kara said, pointing off to port. Kara had her head outside the dodger – listening - as we knew the shore was near.

I had been watching the depth sounder and the bottom had been slowly creeping up until there was less than 30 meters (100 feet) of water below us.

"Mike, go forward and drop the anchor, we will wait for the wind to fill back in," I said.

The chain rattled out and we came to a stop. I called VTS to inform them that we were now at anchor, waiting for the wind. They, in turn, informed me that they had us on radar and that we were safely out of the traffic lanes and we were to call them every hour to report our status. It was nice to be able to relax and not to have to work the boat for a while. We planned to take turns keeping watch but we just started to settle down for the night when I felt a gust of wind on the nape of my neck. Within 20 minutes, I reported to the VTS that we were back underway and sailing at five knots up the east shore of the Strait, bound for Victoria.

After the fog cleared, it was a beautiful night; a brilliant, waxing moon illuminated both shores of the strait and 15 knots of wind graciously did our bidding and clocked back to the west. With the mainsail still out of commission, I decided to break one of my offshore rules by flying our asymmetrical spinnaker at night. On a dark night, it's virtually impossible to see the approach of severe weather; getting caught with the big sail up in a sudden squall, could prove disastrous for the sail as well as the boat. It's a good way to lose a mast!

Everyone was full of anticipation as the lights of B.C.'s Capital City of Victoria came into view off the bow. None of us wanted to go below to sleep, so we all sat in the cockpit most of the night, talking about the voyage that we were on the cusp of completing; after 20 days at sea, we were in sight of our destination and despite our reluctance to leave paradise, it still felt good to be back. The briny scent of the shore, the fragrance of the woods and our home was now thick in the air, enveloping us like a comforting cloak.

By mid-morning we were preparing to round the mussel encrusted and kelp fringed Race Rocks, a popular diving spot and ecological reserve and more important to us at the moment – the last point of land before our landfall at Victoria. Once around Race Rocks, we would be able to alter our course to the north and sail the last 10 miles into the harbour of Victoria. The tide was flooding, giving us a boost as we cut close to shore. The whitewater raged around the Race rocks, creating gyrating whirlpools powerful enough to capture small boats and floating debris. Great flocks of Glaucous-winged Gulls cried from their rocky perches and grunts and snorts betrayed the presence of indignant-looking sea lions, lazing on the black rocks. Once clear of the hazards, we jibed the spinnaker on a port tack, bringing the boat onto a broad reach. *Maiatla* was like a packhorse that crested the last hill to finally see its barn - she bolted forward, giving us one last thrilling ride before our journey's end. Once settled down on our new course, I contacted the VTS and thanked them for all their help. I no sooner ended my call, when the Victoria harbourmaster radioed us.

"*Maiatla*, this is the Victoria Harbour Authority, we have been monitoring your transit up the strait and under no circumstances will you sail into the harbor, is that understood? You will have to be towed in, the harbor is too congested for you to be maneuvering about under sail!"

To say I was stunned that they forbid me from sailing in would have been an understatement, and to be towed into the dock after the completion of a 7000 mile voyage would be insulting to me and a disgrace for *Maiatla* - I couldn't do it! Several times over the years, for one reason or another, I have been forced to return to the dock under sail-power alone. It can be a little nerve-wracking in a congested harbour, but I have never had a problem doing so and I had no qualms about doing it here. Victoria Harbour is sufficiently wide for maneuvering under sail, and the Government Docks where the Customs Office was located, is easily accessible. I didn't believe it to be a problem. I also had considered inflating the dinghy and mounting the outboard; the dink could act as a little tugboat to help maneuver us about if necessary. Mike and Kara were ready to pump it up. The harbourmaster was waiting for a reply.

My first thought was to just ignore him and head in anyway, but the thought of being met by the harbour police and a possible fine shook that notion out of my head. My next alternative was to alter course and find another, more friendly port, but the look of my tired crew prompted me to pick up the VHF Microphone.

"Victoria Harbourmaster this is the sailing vessel *Maiatla*, I wish to enter, what provisions can you make for a tow?"

"None, you will have to contact the Sea Tow people and make arrangements with them, I will give you their cell phone number".

I reluctantly took down the number, but before I could even go to look for my phone, another strange voice boomed over the radio.

"Sailing vessel *Maiatla*, this is Sea Tow, I have been monitoring your situation and we are prepared to come out and get you, but we will need your credit card number when we arrive. Do you copy?"

I know Sea Tow fulfills a needed function, they are the CAA on the water and have been credited with saving countless boats and possibly lives, but I couldn't help but viewing them as vultures, patiently waiting for my body to stop convulsing before swooping down to pick me clean! Reluctantly, I asked about the charge for his services. I must have had a massive brain fart that affected my hearing, because I had to ask him to repeat himself - twice!

"To hell with that! No way I'm paying that, that is piracy!" I said aloud, to no one in particular, I was just talking to myself again. After calming myself a little, I squeezed the Microphone.

"Ah, Sea Tow, this is *Maiatla*, I will not be requiring your service today, I will be carrying on to Nanaimo, have a good day!" And, "kiss my ass," followed, but I had already released the key on the microphone!

Mike and Kara, who were on deck admiring the scenery heard every word and were visibly disappointed by my decision to add another 60 miles to our journey, but the wind was in our favor and the weather had turned warm and sunny; however, our pleasant sail was about to change.

Chapter #37

Becalmed Again

There is no unhappiness like the misery of sighting land (and work) again after a cheerful, careless voyage. - Mark Twain

The Capital City of Victoria - after snubbing us - quickly fell far behind as the wind held, giving us an exhilarating run past the Discovery Islands. But as we jibed the spinnaker to start heading north, up Haro Strait, the wind suddenly died, leaving us utterly becalmed. The giant red sail hung limp and useless, so the chute(spinnaker) was dropped and the headsail unfurled, but even the headsail did little good. It was now late afternoon on a beautifully warm day, an "August in the Pacific Northwest", kind of day. A picture postcard kind of day and that's how *Maiatla* looked, like a picture…. as nothing was moving. We took advantage of the lull in the wind to examine the boom with an eye to making a repair. If the winds were going to be light - fickle and generally uncooperative - we were going to need the big mainsail to work our way up the coast, which meant performing a little surgery on the shattered boom. Over two meters of boom drooped down resembling gaping jaws.

With Mike's help, I cut one of Janet's good wooden cutting boards into strips, forming a splint (I would get hell for butchering the board). Taking two 8" C-clamps, I squeezed the two parts of the boom back together. I placed the splints on either side of the boom, along the crack, and wound a ¼" poly-line repeatedly around the boom, as tightly as possible for the full length of the splint, leaving the clamps in place. It was ugly, but we thought it worthy of *MacGyver* - and it worked! With a single reef in the sail, we hoisted the main. Nevertheless, with all the sail "out" that we could possibly carry aloft, we still were at a standstill and utterly stagnant; unless the wind filled in soon, it would prove to be a long, frustrating and a dangerous night drifting on the tides, again in the middle of the busy shipping lanes. We were so close to home, yet so powerless to complete the voyage.

I could now empathize with the sailors of old who manned the tall ships - sans engine. I was getting frustrated all over again, feeling beaten and bedraggled. After the sun set, a light breeze filled in from the east, allowing us some steerage and more importantly, we were able to hold our own against the retreating tide.

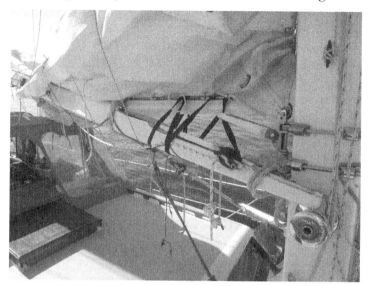

Figure 37.

The broken Main Boom after *Maiatla's* near broaching.

We spent the night trimming sails and hugging shore in an effort to eek out as much speed as possible while hiding from currents and using back-eddies behind points of land to make incremental gains. I was too excited to sleep properly and I believe Kara and Mike were the same as our watch system of two hours on two off quickly fell by the wayside; we ate and catnapped when convenient, mainly on deck.

Figure 38.

Main Boom after repairs using rope, clamps and Jan's cutting board.

With the sunrise, the wind once again retreated leaving us to wallow on a slick shimmering sea, but at least we had gained some ground during the night, almost 10 miles; not a lot but they were 10 miles in the right direction. It was a minor miracle of sorts, but we managed to round our last major headland during the night: East

Point, with its wicked currents up to 7 knots with boiling rips over Rosenfeld Rock and Tumbo Reef. It was now a straight-go of 49 miles around the Gulf Islands and into Nanaimo, but first we would have to get moving again.

By 9:00 a.m. we were off of Saturna Island, only three miles from East Point with 45 miles left to go. The wind was still refusing to make a show; to make matters worse, the tide was due to change and if we didn't get clear of Tumbo Reef, we would get sucked back out the strait, around East Point or, if the current was wrong - onto the rocks. I couldn't let either happen. Kara was still down below sleeping, but Mike stayed up after I relieved him of his watch; he was fitfully napping in the cockpit next to me, lazing about in the warm morning sun like cat sunning himself. I think this was the first morning in over a week when he hadn't complained about being cold after his watch. I gave him a little nudge on his shoulder.

"Hey Mike, lets blow up the dink, mount the motor and strap it alongside and fire it up, we need to get going!" I said.

The little, very little 3.3 horsepower Mercury was called to task one last time for this voyage but running flat out, she only managed to get *Maiatla* up to one full knot. Using the tiny outboard engine to deploy a stern hook or push *Maiatla* into a dock was one thing, but driving a 20 ton boat almost 50 miles, at times against the tide, was quite another. In truth, I thought we would burn it out long before reaching Nanaimo, but as long as we kept feeding her fuel, she kept us moving and with the help of the incoming tide, we actually didn't do too badly.

By late afternoon, we had covered some miles, almost four and the crew once again felt like the journey was nearing an end; Mike and Kara were almost jubilant and they resumed their taunting of one another in earnest. After a lull in hostilities that started the night Mike and Kara shared a berth, the truce was now over. Repairers were again drawn and the dueling was about to renew at a feverish pace.

By all accounts, it was a beautiful day, especially considering it was almost October. It was hot on the windless water and we were all sorry the liquor and beer lockers had been cleaned out; a cold one would have been appreciated at this moment!

As if the gods yielded to our yearnings, Mike, who was doing a bit of cleaning-up after making lunch, found a single can of cold beer way back in the fridge. Now instead of doing the smart, but unscrupulous thing by hiding in his cabin and guzzling the 10 ounces of nectar, he decide to wave it in front of Kara's face and announce that he, and he alone was going to drink the very last beer!

The fight was on! Before I knew it, my crew was wrestling around the galley, fighting for possession of the coveted last Budweiser. Like they were children, I shouted down below for them to quit it - but it was too late! The last thing I saw before the "Crash" was the pair shooting by the companion hatch; Mike had a squealing Kara in a tight headlock!

I left the helm to see what damage my crew had caused and when I jumped below, I found the handle of the oven, snapped in two and my crew still wrestling on the floor! Mike must have really wanted that beer because I think he was actually winning at this point.

"OK, you two! Knock it off! Split the damned beer, OK?" I said.

Not exactly worthy of King Solomon, but it worked. When I returned to the cockpit to resume basking in the balmy weather, I realized that I should have confiscated the Bud and drank in front of them - just to teach them a lesson of course! As it turned out, the fight over the last beer was actually quite fortuitous.

Later that day, talking to Jan on the cell, I was recounting the brawl that ensued with the discovery of the last beer and that we were a totally dry boat and had been so for some time.

Sounding surprised she said, "I know you didn't have a lot of beer aboard when you left, but you couldn't have drunk all that red wine. Could you?"

"I guess we must have, Babe; I pulled the last bag out from under the settee over two weeks ago and it didn't last long with the three of us having a glass or two every night".

"Did you get the bag of wine out from under the floor in your closet?" She asked.

"Closet? My Closet?" I repeated. "Wait a minute, I'll be right back!"

While clutching the phone I shot down below, flung open my closet door, tossed a pair of shoes and a duffle bag aside and lifted the plywood floor to stare into the cubby hole, and there, to my joy, was four-liters of my Nanaimo home brew. Oh, yeah!

"Hey Babe, did I tell you "I love you" today?"

I settled down, back in my captain's chair and with the riotous crew now under control, I had a few moments to reflect on how incredible the past four months had been. In hindsight, the memory seemed to be so fleeting as if just a dream, but it wasn't a dream, this was actually our lives, Jan and mine and despite all its hardships, it was grand.

Whenever I have the opportunity to meet some of my readers, they often declare that I'm living their dreams, that I'm living the good life. They look at what I have (*Maiatla*) and what I am doing with my life and for lack of a better word, they covet it. They want what the life Jan and I have. Doing what we have done has taken great personal sacrifice as everything comes with a price. Separation from shore-side friends and family; especially now, with two wonderful grandkids, it's particularly hard. Still, the life we live is worth the pain and it's also well within the means of anyone living within our western society.

Nevertheless, to live the life of a cruiser takes hard choices and commitment; I tell people that the hardest part about becoming a cruiser is making the decision to actually do it. Once the decision is made, and a plan formulated, a date set, the rest comes relatively easy. Living the good life isn't just sailing off; it starts with an inner circle of family and extends to friends and co-workers. The good life involves freedom, love, work, pleasure, challenge, friendship, creativity and a sense of community, even if it's a community of cruisers sharing a potluck in the far flung Tuamotus. Living the good life - living the dream, has nothing to do with possessions or even vices, they can either enhance or hinder; they are not what makes us happy. The greatest obstacles to living the good life - to being happy, are not external things such as possessions, but internal vices such as resentment, bitterness, envy, malice, greed and prejudice. These are the things that can keep us from being happy, to keep us from living the good life. The best life is meaningful and creative, open to adventure that brings opportunity to learn, laugh, love and bringing joy to the others in our lives. A good life is one that aspires to the highest possibilities and morality. I have found no better place to achieve this then on the deck of *Maiatla,* surrounded by my family, friends, and the sea.

It took just over 32 hours to cover the remaining (24 miles) to Entrance Island at the top of the Gulf Islands and it was here just after dark, the wind filled in, allowing us to give our courageous little mercury outboard a rest.

I was grateful for the wind and grateful that we were able to arrive home with our dignity intact as we sailed the final eight kilometers (5 miles) of our Hawaiian Voyage, straight past Gallows Point and directly into the bosom of Nanaimo Harbour.

I placed a call to my buddy, Mark Taylor, and he motored out with the manager of Townsite Marina where I had arranged to take a slip, we were less than a hundred meters from our new home. As *Maiatla* ghosted along, I dreaded what was coming next and that was telling Melissa that Nanaimo was going to be our new and permanent base, our new home. It was going to be tough, but we believed it would be the best thing for her- and a fresh start for all of us. Kara and Mike dropped all the sails while Mark, in his dink, nudged us the few final yards into our slip.

Hurray, we made it!......

Ah crap!.....We're back!

Epilogue

You can choose to set your sails to voyage to the destination of your choice, or you can let the winds and tides of fate take you where they may; both actions are the result of choices, but the latter is rarely as satisfying in the end.

Andrew W. Gunson.   S.V. Maiatla.

We had been home many months before I began to commit this voyage to paper but as I did, for the first time since landing in Nanaimo, I began to analyze all the various stages and events that would ultimately be encompassed in this text. As I sat at my computer desk on *Maiatla* safely secured to our dock in Nanaimo, British Columbia, I couldn't help but smile. Many of my negative preconceived notions about this voyage were shattered as completely as Mike's delicate French Press upon *Maiatla's* teak sole.

Cruising to the Hawaiian Islands had not been my first choice as a sailing destination. Despite the oppressive governmental regulations; bullying Coast Guard; obnoxious harbourmasters; decrepit harbour docks and the state's opposition to people having fun in boats, it was a grand voyage. A voyage that I enjoyed immensely - more than I ever thought I would. I wouldn't hesitate to do it again as either a stepping-stone to other far-flung isles or as a destination in itself. The weather was nearly perfect while in the islands and we found the citizens of Hawaii, (both native and transplants) friendly and extremely eager to help when the opportunity presented itself and for this, I wish to thank all that we encountered.

After the publication of my first book *The Voyage of the Maiatla with the Naked Canadian*, readers began asking what became of the people that were so crucial to that story. We have been fortunate that we have kept in touch with many of our cruising friends so it's a pleasure to pass on what we know. In anticipation of being asked to update my readers about the fates of the crew from this voyage, I thought an update might be appropriate here. A full five years post-voyage, much has happened:

My Sister Jackie and her husband Jim apparently failed to learn their lesson on this voyage and purchased their own 45-foot ketch; they have spent the last five years living aboard and cruising the west coast. They are now retired and planning their own great adventure and are heading south. Our father would be proud.

Kara returned home to find employment at the Department of Corrections; she is now married and has a beautiful son of her own. Despite making noises about buying a boat of her own and cruising, the netherworld quietly slipped into her subconscious to erase all her ambitions of sailing off. (Or at least gagged them!) We stay in touch and she has informed me that she is searching for a day-sailor for summer weekends. She admits that her child, husband and career have her firmly anchored well inland, but she still has plans to travel and perhaps cruise again......... when she retires.

Maui Mike's relationship with my niece Samantha held together for a year, but despite Sam making a trip back to Maui to spend Christmas with Mike (that's when they ran aground on Molokai), their long distance love affair quickly faded. Mike continued to live and work as a charter boat skipper on Maui, eventually finding the true love of his life in a lovely and intelligent lady by the name of Kelly; together they were hired as skipper and crew aboard a private yacht, sailing the Caribbean. Unfortunately this job didn't last long; the pair quit due to unwanted sexual advances made by the vessel's male owner. It's interesting to note that the advances were directed towards Mike and not his bodacious girlfriend! Go figure! While spending a couple of months at my home in Nanaimo, B.C., working on *Maiatla*, Mike and Kelly received another job offer. I was fortunate enough to be invited along on Mike's yacht delivery from Tahiti to Mexico. Maui Mike, Kelly and I shared another outrageous adventure bringing a luxury motor launch through Melville's Marquesas and back across the equator during the 2010 hurricane season. Mike and Kelly returned to work in Maui and were married in the spring of 2012; just before tying the knot, they purchased a 40 foot sloop-rigged sailboat and after a refit, left Hawaii in September 2012 for San Francisco and ultimately bound for Central America and beyond.

After arriving back in Canada, Jan and I decided to call Nanaimo home for a while. Despite Melissa's vehement protests and pleas to return to Mission and her old school and friends, we enrolled her in a new school, vowing to stay put long enough for her to graduate which would take another three years. So, we settled in as liveaboards at a downtown marina. We did not cruise in 2008; I spent a few months in Qatar, in the Middle East, working on contract at the Ras Laffan Oil Refinery attempting to pad the cruising kitty. 2009 found us chasing migrating whales off the west coast as we undertook a circumnavigation of Vancouver Island over the summer months. In 2010, we purchased a little bit of property with an old house on it, with the intent of building our retirement home, a place to return to when we are done cruising. Our motivation to buy land at this time was not fueled by the dire need to set down roots or as sailors say, "Swallow the anchor". Our need was for a place to live while *Maiatla* was hauled out of the water to spend four months in a covered storage, undergoing a major refit at a local shipyard; for the first time in ten years we moved ashore.... temporarily.

Melissa grew up to be the beautiful and smart lady I always knew she would .

With her health issues well under control, to my delight and in time for the boat's refit, she landed a job at the West Marine store in Nanaimo - where dad received a serious discount. Melissa went on to graduate from high school then the Vancouver Island University where she studied Business and Legal Administration-finishing at the top of her class. After completing her practicum at a prestigious law firm in Victoria, B.C. she was hired on full time and moved away from home.

Now in the fall of 2012, Jan and I are effectively empty-nesters and with *Maiatla* freshly groomed, we prepared to sail back down the coast, bound for Mexico then on to Costa Rica where we will get re-acquainted with another cruising friend, Travis of *Mystery Tramp,* before making up our minds which direction to point *Maiatla's* bow. We might even hook up with Mike and Kelly in Central America! It will be a coin toss whether we brave the marine congestion of Panama Canal's infamous locks which would take us into the Caribbean or to head west across the South Pacific, to Australia and beyond. There is also a third possibility, which I have not yet mentioned to Jan, and that is to continue sailing south to Columbia, Peru and Chile, and around the Horn, the southernmost tip of South America, to Brazil. The thought of rounding Cape Horn scares Jan, so I will just not mention this option for now; the longer I keep it a secret the better her peace of mind and my peace.

With the start of our next, long awaited voyage, a new chapter of our married life will commence, and if the past thirty years are any indication, I anticipate the next thirty to be just as wonderful and adventurous!

Figure 39. S.V Maiatla line drawings

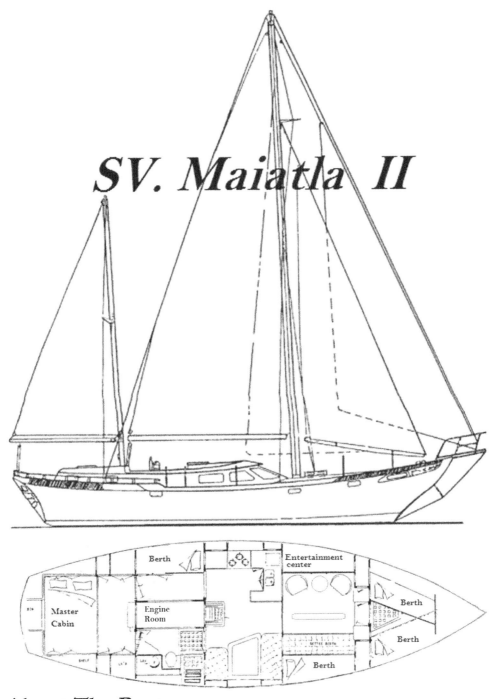

About The Boat.

SV *Maiatla* II is a Voyager 44 designed by Hardin International and built by the Kaohsiung Shipyard of Taiwan in 1980. Her name was derived from a West coast native dialect which means "Friend". The Hardin sailboats were sold until 1982 through a U.S. Distributor, East-West Yachts of Marina Del Rey, California. The first production Hardin 45's came with very large salon windows, which in hindsight proved to be a liability offshore in big seas. Redesigned, the boats transformed into the Hardin Voyager '44 which came with a slightly lower profile and much smaller windows, creating lines that are more pleasing and a fine, offshore cruiser--- that *Maiatla* would prove herself to be.

Maiatla is 45-feet on the deck and 52-feet overall (54 by my harbour manager's tape measure!); she has a beam of 13-feet-4-inches and a water-line of 32-feet-3-inches. She has a fully modified keel with a cutaway forefoot and a draft of 6 feet. *Maiatla* is a three-cabin model with a large V-berth forward in the bow and a great master cabin with a queen-size bed aft and a single berth in a tiny privet cabin on the port side next to the engine room. The master cabin is accessible from both sides of the vessel: through the head on the starboard side or through port side cabin. The galley is amidships port, with a large salon table to starboard. The main salon is forward and sunken with a sofa on the starboard with a pilot berth above against the hull. Opposite the sofa is a diesel heater flanked by a pair of upholstered armchairs and a bookshelf/entertainment center above.

Shortly after taking possession of *Maiatla,* I began the first of a long list of modifications and upgrades, a chore that spanned many years as *Maiatla* evolved from a family cruising boat to one destined to be occupied by empty nesters. The galley boasts a top-loading, 4 cubic foot fridge with a laminated oak butcher-block lid adjacent to the gimballed, three-burner propane stove.

On deck, *Maiatla* is equipped with a Furlex roller-reefing system to manage the big headsail. On the foredeck, a 18 to 24-foot telescoping whisker pole is stored and ready for use to improve *Maiatla's* stability on downwind runs when sailing wing-and-wing with the mainsail. And of course the item no sailor ever hopes use - a Viking, 4-man offshore life raft mounted just behind the cockpit, over the aft cabin. The boat has a 45-pound CQR anchor along with 350 feet of 1/2-inch chain and a Lofrans power windlass. Our secondary anchor consists of 350 feet of one-inch gold-braid anchor rode and shackled it to 40 feet of 1/2-inch chain and swivel topped off with a 65-pound CQR to complete what I call my "Hail Mary" rig, better known as hurricane ground tackle. Later, the 65-pound CQR found its way onto my main anchor rode and became part of our everyday tackle and we never had the misfortune to drag, even in the foulest of weather. On the aft deck, I have a spare 35-pound Danforth with 40 feet of chain attached to 200 feet of ½-inch, three-strand nylon rode.

Maiatla's electronics consist of a Raytheon Pathfinder 24-mile radar with the display in the cockpit next to the helm and Simrad apparent wind, speed and depth instruments. For long distance communication and for downloading weather faxes, satellite photos, and high-seas weather reports, there is a HAM/SSB high frequency radio; an ICOM 700 pro and a 130 automatic tuner, with fourteen meters of backstay for an antenna. This system has given exceptional service over the years.

My laptop computer, interfaced with GPS is equipped with Nobeltec charting software; our primary navigation system with electronic charts for over half the world. But in case of disaster, we carry a complete set of full size paper charts, most purchased form a Bellingham chart reproducer.

Our passive electrical system consists of a 100-watt Siemens solar panel mounted on the dinghy davits, and a pair of 45-watt panels. These smaller panels are mounted on the lifelines, port and starboard, aft of the cockpit. As if all that solar energy is not enough, the 800-watt Air Marine wind generator at the top of the mizzenmast nicely tops up the 750 amp-hour battery bank. Just to ensure we have ample power for all of our electrical devices whenever the sun does not shine or the wind will not blow, we carry a 1000-watt gas generator for good measure. As it turned out, the generator came in very handy over the years.

Maiatla is equipped with hydraulic steering and a Raymarine Automatic Pilot. This has proven itself a dependable system. The heart of *Maiatla's* luxury systems is the Village Marine "Little Wonder"; a 200 US gallon-per-day watermaker neatly installed in the engine room. The boat is equipped with a pressure water system with a Bosch, hot-water-on-demand system. *Maiatla* has two, 75-gallon water tanks. with 150 gallons of onboard water and the watermaker to keep them topped up, water has never been a problem.

Maiatla's propulsion system consists of a very fuel efficient, 68-horsepower Perkins diesel engine. With 150 gallons of diesel in the main tanks and a 30-gallon reserve tank primarily used for the diesel heater, we had almost 1300 miles of cruising range under power---as long as we kept her at six knots and didn't use the cabin heater!

In the many years we have owned her, *Maiatla* has proven herself time after time, to be a capable offshore boat, equipped in a manner that not only provides us with a comfortable and safe home, but affords her crew the self-sufficiency that we cherish so much as we sail about the world.

Glossary of *Hawaiian* Terms

- **Alii**: a Hawaiian chief, Hawaiian royalty.
- **Aloha**: love, affection, kindness. Also means both greetings and farewell.
- **Aumakua**: family or personal gods, deified ancestors who might assume the shape of, for example, a shark, owl, dog, hawk, plant, or cloud.
- **Hale**: a house.
- **Haole**: white person. Formerly any foreigner.
- **Heiau**: an ancient Hawaiian temple.
- **Hula**: the dance of Hawaii.
- **Imu**: underground oven.
- **Iwi**: bone.
- **Ka**: the definite article.
- **Kahuna**: a priest, doctor, or other trained person of old Hawaii, endowed with special professional skills that often included the gift of prophecy or other supernatural powers.
- **Kai**: the sea, saltwater.
- **Kalo**: the taro plant from whose root poi is made.
- **Kanaka**: originally a man or humanity in general, it is now used to denote a male Hawaiian or part-Hawaiian.
- **Kane**: a man, a husband.
- **Kapa**: also called tapa, a cloth made of beaten bark.
- **Kapu**: taboo, keep out, prohibited, sacred.
- **Keiki**: a child.
- **Lanai**: a porch, balcony or deck.
- **Lani**: heaven, the sky.
- **Lei**: a garland of flowers.
- **Lokahi**: unity, agreement, harmony.
- **Luau**: Hawaiian feast. In the past the word for feast was paina.
- **Mahalo**: thank you. Mahalo nui loa: thank you very much.
- **Mana**: the spiritual power that the Hawaiians believed to inhabit all things and creatures.
- **Wahine**: a female, a woman, a wife.
- **Wai**: fresh water, as opposed to saltwater, which is kai.
- **Wikiwiki**: to hurry, hurry up.

Figure 40. The Author.

About the Author

The author is a storyteller with the heart of an adventurer; he has the ability to infect others with his zeal for life and his love of the sea. Andrew Gunson grew up in and around boats on the Great Lakes and always dreamed of following the paths of such intrepid sailors as Joshua Slocum, and Eric and Susan Hiscock. A Canadian National sailing champion at fourteen, he raced aboard some of the fastest yachts then afloat, competing against the very best at the world championship level. At the age of eighteen, he moved to Canada's west coast and discovered a completely new world of sailing. Leaving the hi-tech racing yachts behind, he began to follow his dream of becoming a "cruiser." Together with his father, he purchased his first cruising sailboat, a Columbia 36', and never looked back.

Although a fourth generation mason, Andrew's adventurous spirit led him to attend the College of Oceaneering in Wilmington, California. By age twenty-one, he was a commercial bell diver working on oil-drilling ships in the Beaufort Sea. He eventually became a co-pilot in the submersible program aboard a Norwegian drill ship and worked beneath the frigid waters of the Davis Strait, off the coast of Labrador. Before his thirtieth birthday, he retired from commercial diving to focus on raising his young family. With his wife Janet, they purchased and operated a convenience store in Vernon, BC. After selling the business, Andrew obtained his securities license and became a personal financial analyst and small business tax consultant.

Andrew's love affair with the sea endured. He continued to dream, just waiting for his own chance to sail off. After a series of life-altering events, that included a brush with a deadly skin cancer, a pair of automobile accidents that almost claimed Andrew's life and being accidentally shot while bear hunting, the couple decided it time to stop dreaming. The Gunson's started planning their escape before it was too late. Hence the saga of the sailing vessel *Maiatla II* and the *Naked Canadian* began.

The Gunson's preceding voyaging inspired the author to write, *The Voyage of the Maiatla with the Naked Canadian, One Family's Mexican Odyssey*, followed by the second book of the series, *The Tahiti Syndrome, Hawaiian Style*.